D0083648

CATCHING SERIAL KILLERS

Learning from past
serial murder investigations

Earl James, J.D., Ph.D.
First Lieutenant (Retired)
Michigan State Police

International Forensic Services, Inc.
Lansing, Michigan
United States of America

Publisher's Cataloging-in-Publication Data

James, Earl, 1931 -

    Catching serial killers: learning from past serial murder investigations / by Earl James.
        p.   cm.
    ISBN 0-9629714-0-5 (h.c.)
    ISBN 0-9629714-1-3 (pbk.)
    1. Serial Murders. 2. Murder Investigations. 3. Murder—case studies. I. Title.

HV6530.J36   1991
364.1'—dc20   91-72098

Manufactured in the United States of America

THIS BOOK IS DEDICATED TO MY WIFE, BETTY, AND TO THE GIRLS AND WOMEN WHOSE LIVES HAVE BEEN PREMA-TURELY ENDED BY SERIAL KILLERS.

Earl James 1991

FOREWORD

During my forty years of association with men and women in both law enforcement and the military, I have met many interesting people. What made many of these people interesting to me was their commitment to their chosen careers. Those individuals who continue to stand out in my thoughts as having a higher degree of success have the common thread of loyalty. Loyalty to the organization to which they belong and loyalty to their associates. Often it was and is a dedication.

A second common factor in the make up of these interesting people is their great devotion to family, to God and to their country. Always in perspective; this devotion was, and is manifest in their honesty; integrity and spirit of caring for family, for associates and for those who follow in their respective fields of endeavor.

Needless to say, I place Earl James among those interesting people I have been associated with over many years. Several years back I was seeking an individual to form an internal investigations function within the Michigan Department of State Police. Recognizing there was an inherent fear of such a unit and the thought prevailed that it was not needed, I knew my selection of the person to head the organization was extremely important. I looked for a person who was a good investigator with exceptional interviewing skills and writing ability. Most important was the necessity to appoint an officer with an excellent reputation for fairness and integrity. I selected Earl James for the assignment, and I was not disappointed by his performance nor were his peers or subordinates.

In the recent past, Earl has directed his efforts to continued education and to the publication you are about to review. He has spent countless hours researching the material available as well as interviewing many respected investigators all in an effort to enhance his knowledge in preparation for this publication.

Catching Serial Killers represents an indepth review of the cases the author studied and contains observations Earl James has contributed as a result of his experience and those of many other investigators he has consulted. In many respects this material becomes a working manual for the trained investigator faced with circumstances which identify with what may be a serial murder.

Many of us who have retired from active law enforcement often look back to both reminisce and to question what we have left for those who follow in our path. I must believe that Earl James has done his best in this work to provide information which shares his investigative expertise and the fruits of his research of a subject which became a very significant part of his Michigan State Police career, that involving the Ann Arbor, Michigan, murders of young women in the mid and late sixties.

Colonel (retired) George L. Halverson, Director
Michigan Department of State Police

PREFACE

The primary purpose of this book is to help the criminal investigator who is working on a serial murder case. It is meant to show him/her the methods which have yielded positive results in the past. By examining these previous successful cases, we can best determine the course(s) of action that would most likely result in the apprehension of a serial murderer in the future. There are no ten easy steps to arresting a serial killer, but there are certain things that can be done to increase the probability of his capture.

The book will also try to point out some of the errors made in previous investigations so we can learn from them and try to avoid making the same mistakes again.

Another purpose of this book is to present the full story of the series of murders that became known as the "Michigan Murders", "The Ann Arbor Murders", and "The Michigan Coed Murders."

Those murders terrorized the communities of Ann Arbor and Ypsilanti, Michigan for a two year period between 1967 and 1969. During that time, women were asked to travel in pairs at night and to check in and out of their dormitories. An escort service was established for them. The people wanted the murders stopped. They were frustrated that the police were not able to arrest the perpetrator. They wanted the Federal Bureau of Investigation called in to help catch the killer. By Governor's Proclamation, the Michigan State Police was put in charge of the investigations to coordinate the efforts of the several police departments involved.

When John Norman Collins was arrested and charged with murder, Major Dan Myre, the Michigan State Police Chief of Detectives, assigned me the task of going through literally thousands of pieces of information and making decisions on the material that would be used in the prosecution of Collins. Myre assigned two very capable detectives to help me with that task. They were detective Gordon Hurley, now deceased, and detective Harold Janiszewski. I will be forever grateful for their help. Without their aid it would have been an almost impossible task.

Collins was convicted and sentenced to life in prison, but was Collins really guilty? For the first time ever I'm going to reveal some information the police have been holding back just in case Collins ever did decide to take a polygraph (lie detector) test. I'll also confide in you some other information that the police were holding in reserve for over twenty years in the event that

Collins was given a new trial and this time —decide to take the witness stand. For example Collins has said he never slapped a girl in high school. But what about beating a beautiful young college coed into submission with his forearm and then raping her—does that count?

I'll relate to you the full story of the two Michigan backup cases and the California case that could have sent Collins to the gas chamber if he were convicted. You be the judge on whether he killed a girl there.

Also included in the book are several other cases where the information has been acquired from the literature and from investigators whom I interviewed both here and in Europe. I did not make a detailed written analysis of each case that I studied, but I did record the information and it can be found in the tables at the end of the book.

Some serial murder cases were not considered for inclusion in the book because the perpetrator was not caught. One such case was the Zodiac serial murderer who was active in California. Two police officers actually questioned him briefly after he killed a cab driver, but the dispatcher told the officers that the murderer was black—when in fact he was white—and Zodiac escaped. Other cases were not considered because the primary targets were boys or young men. Finally some serial murder cases weren't included because the perpetrators were women. Most often this involved elderly patients in nursing homes or people who were killed to collect their life insurance.

At the end of each chapter, I have included my observations and some-times—where there is more than one opinion on how something should be handled—I have included that viewpoint too. This critique is not meant to be criticism of those down in the arena doing battle. I know there is no such thing as a perfect criminal investigation. The reason for this is quite simple. Since all criminal investigations are conducted by human beings, and since all human beings make mistakes—there will obviously be errors in criminal investigations. My primary goal is to hold such errors to an absolute minimum and try not to repeat such mistakes. And whenever possible we should learn from the errors of others. Some people might ask,"Who is this guy? Why does he think he has the right to critique anyone? Who does he think he is anyway?" All of these are fair questions.

While I do not profess to know everything there is to know about the phenomenon of serial murder, I have devoted over forty years of my life to the study of, and the battle against crime. During those struggles, I have been cussed at, shoved, punched, kicked, had my clothes ripped, a couple watches destroyed, confronted criminals armed with knives, guns, or both, have had to jump out of the way when they tried to run me down with a car, and on two occasions—shed my blood. Of the total time, eight of those years were devoted to the problem of sex related multiple murders.

When I was eighteen years old, I began my career in the criminal justice field as a United States Marine Military Policeman on a Naval Base. Subsequent to that, I have served as a city patrolman in Sturgis, Michigan, as a private with the Washington, D.C. Metropolitan Police Department and with the Michigan State Police for over twenty-three years. During that time, I had many diverse and interesting assignments. I have worked as a trooper in both the Upper and Lower Peninsulas, as a detective and detective sergeant for eight years in the Detroit metropolitan area, and in the Michigan State Police Crime Laboratory as a laboratory specialist. I was the Chief Polygraph Examiner of the Michigan State Police sixteen man Polygraph Unit. Later, I founded the Internal Affairs Section , and for a time, was also the Employee Relations Officer. Then I was promoted to First Lieutenant (now Inspector) as assistant division commander of the Emergency Services Division.

After leaving the Michigan State Police, I continued to serve as a consultant to the Director of the Forensic Laboratories, taught in the Michigan State Police Polygraph School, wrote a computer assisted polygraph evaluation program, and served as the Internship Training Supervisor for Bruce K. Havens, J.D., Esquire, who was, at that time, a deputy sheriff with the Ingham County (Michigan) Sheriff's Department.

I have also served for eight years on the State of Michigan's Board of Forensic Polygraph Examiners. For four of those years, I was the vice-chairman , and for four years the chairman.

I've taught courses in Homicide Investigation at Madonna University, in Livonia, Michigan, and Police Supervision and Police Organization and Management courses at Lansing Community College in Lansing, Michigan.

I've been a guest lecturer on Criminal Investigation at Michigan State University, on Polygraph at the Cooley Law School and the Windsor University Law School in Canada. I have also taught Eye Witness Identification in Criminal Cases, Nonverbal Behavioral Clues in Detecting Deception, Polygraph, Latent Prints, Field Note Taking and Report Writing, Crime Scene Investigation, and Statements and Confessions to Michigan State Police Detectives and other police officers. I have also given lectures in

German at their Police Training Academy at Selm, Germany, and at the Federal German Police Leadership Academy located at Munster-Hilltrup. I have also participated in seminars to help future top ranking German Police Officers learn English. And this spring, (1991) I team taught "Serial Murders in Michigan" with Supervisory Special Agent John Campbell at the FBI Seminar on Violent Crime in Ann Arbor, Michigan.

While studying these past investigations, we should be aware of a factor that makes the evaluation of the detective's actions extremely difficult. This is particularly true regarding the errors they have made. The reason for this is that in some instances, when one is not present during an actual event, and one is not in possession of all the facts surrounding the incident which has occurred, it is an exceedingly arduous task to second guess those officers who were actually there and were privy to all the information which led up to the manner in which a particular incident was handled. What complicated matters even more, was sometimes additional information was received after the fact, of which the original officers were not cognizant, but those passing judgement acted as though they were aware of the information. Nevertheless, we must study these past cases and glean from them whatever knowledge that is possible to obtain. The caveat I would add, however, is to bear in mind that the critique was based upon the best information that was available. It is possible that the information was misleading, incomplete, or inaccurate. If that has occurred, I would appreciate hearing from those officers and others who were actually involved in the past investigations so any errors can be corrected.

It was pointed out by two different reviewers that I did not spend enough time writing about all the things the police did right during the various investigations and dwelt on the things they did wrong. Obviously, the police did many more things properly than they did wrong or they never would have been able to convict the killer(s). I did not spend much time on what the police did correctly. A defense attorney will not devote time praising the police for their outstanding investigation that led to the arrest of his/her client. Rather the defense will attack what the police did that was wrong or what they neglected to do. That is one reason why I spent so much time writing about police errors.

This is not a book on how to conduct a murder investigation. There are numerous excellent books on this subject that have already been published such as Lieutenant Commander (ret.) Geberth's book entitled, Practical Homicide Investigation. Rather this book is a supplement to those books because frequently the serial murderer is a unique criminal type of person who is extremely difficult to apprehend. And with the exception of Geberth's book, many of the standard books contain little information about dealing with serial killers

ACKNOWLEDGEMENTS

The author would like to acknowledge the assistance of all those people who helped contribute to make this book possible. There are so many it is impossible to name them all, but there are some persons who deserve special recognition.

I would especially like to thank my wife, Betty Brueck James, LL.B., B.S.N., M.A., Miss Virginia Mc Phail, B.S.N., M.S.N., and Mrs. Patricia Campbell, R.N., M.S.N., Ph.D. Candidate from Wayne State University for reviewing the manuscript and offering changes and suggestions.

I would like to acknowledge the assistance given to me by all levels of police, both here and abroad. Without their help, this study would not have been possible.

I would also like to express my sincere gratitude and appreciation to Sidney Moormeister Ph.D. of Columbia Pacific University for her suggestions, for her many letters and telephone calls, for recording and sending me a video tape regarding serial murderers, and for proof reading the manuscript.

I would like to thank, former Prosecutor, now Circuit Court Judge G. Michael Hocking, for the materials and time he contributed regarding the Miller Case, Prosecutor William Delhey, Esquire, for the opportunity of assisting him during the trial of John Norman Collins, Colonel George L. Halverson, Michigan State Police (retired), Detective Lieutenant John Fiedler, Michigan State Police (retired), Sergeant Mark James, B.S., M.S. of the Indiana State Police, and Patrol Officer Diana James-Downes, R.N., of the Tampa Police Department for reviewing the manuscript and making suggestions. In addition, I would like to thank Mary J. LePiors, the Michigan State Police Librarian, for the materials she furnished to me.

I would also like to acknowledge the style used as "borrowed" from Field Marshal Erwin Rommel's book, *Attacks*, and a debt of gratitude to those authors from whom I have quoted in this book.

Finally, I would especially like to acknowledge the conscientious work done by Miss Annette Rudick, a teacher at Faith Lutheran School in Hialeah Florida, and Mrs. James Waddell of St. Louis Missouri, for typing and retyping the manuscript.

In the collection of information regarding the serial murder of girls and women, it is anticipated that some information might have been missed, misinterpreted, or misplaced in this book. The readers who chance upon such errors are respectfully requested to contribute corrections or advice for future research and publication.

For legal reasons, to prevent embarrassment, and to enable the writer to present the true facts to the best of his ability, some names have been changed. The names given are totally fictitious and any resemblance to persons now living or dead are purely coincidental.

Earl W. K. James
International Forensic Services, Inc.
Post Office Box 80242
Lansing, MI 48908

TABLE OF CONTENTS

LIST OF TABLES

TABLE OF APPENDICES

CHAPTER I

CONTEXT OF THE PROBLEM

During the year 1989, there were about 21,500 murders in the United States. Of those murders—2,546 remain unsolved. Thus, only about sixty-eight percent of the cases have been brought to a successful conclusion in the nation, and the problem is getting worse instead of better. In 1990, there were 23,600 murders in the United States, an increase of ten percent. (FBI Crime Reports -Release Date April 28, 1991)

There are essentially two main groups of murderers who are committing these crimes. Supervisory Special Agent Roger L. Depue who headed up the National Center for the Analysis of Violent Crime has categorized these criminals as the "most" and the "best".

Murderers who are in the "most" group tend to be from the lower socioeconomic strata of our society. They tend to be black because they are in that group. They are mainly in the eighteen to twenty-four year old age group. They tend to be below average in intelligence and the vast majority of the murderers are men. In fact, about seventy percent are males.

Because we are aware that this age group is responsible for most of the murders, all one must do to predict when the next rash of murders will occur is to simply determine when a large number of that particular age group will peak again. These high crime peaks have occurred in the past in 1875-1880, 1930-1935, and 1963 to the present time. But we are expected to have another peak around the turn of the century as the aforementioned age group moves into that period when most of the crimes are committed.

On the other hand, there are those criminals that Depue has described as the "best". "This," he said, "is where the organized serial killer is at." Their intelligence level is average to bright. Their crimes for the most part are well planned. They tend to become better criminals with practice because they tend to critique their "work" as they strive for perfection. And for the most part, they are Caucasian.

By their own admission, eighty-one percent of them are window peekers. In addition, the serial murderer tends to assess a situation differently than a normal person.

For example, if he were to see a woman walking to her car in a parking lot, he would tend to evaluate whether she would be a vulnerable crime victim. He would note whether there was anyone else around to help her, whether the tight dress she was wearing would make it difficult for her to run away. If for some reason there was something extraordinary about the woman, the serial murderer would probably become preoccupied with his fantasies regarding her.

Whereas in fifty-four percent of the murder cases, the victims were killed by either a friend or an acquaintance (1989 FBI Crime Reports, p.12), in serial murder cases more often than not—the victim was a complete stranger. Also, in 1989 only twelve percent of those arrested for murder were women. Women for the most part were involved in only a very small percentage of serial murders. In some cases, they have actually helped a male by assisting him in acquiring victims. They have also been involved in murders for profit, and murders for psychological reasons. But the fact remains, ninety percent of the women killed were murdered by men. Cases where women were involved in sexual related homicides were very rare. The arrest of Aileen Carol Wuornos in Florida for the alleged murder of Richard Mallory near Daytona Beach in December 1989 was exceptional. She is suspected of killing seven men over a thirteen month period of time. Wuornos posed as a hitchhiker. She offered the men sex in exchange for money. She would apparently kill the man if he failed to pay her or became too aggressive.

It has been said that one reason we have a near epidemic of murders in the nation today is that children were encouraged to "act out" hostilities and externalize restraint to a degree that someone else is always responsible for one's failures.

Doctor Donald T. Lune of Stanford University has said that the young adults today have been raised differently in many instances than young people in former generations. There has been more affluence, permissiveness, greater expectations (by the young adult), and therefore greater frustrations.(if his expectations are not met.) In addition to this, there probably has been no other time in our history when a substantial amount of the training a child received was from someone other than the parents of the child. It is probably too early to determine what impact, if any, this will have on the child's values in later life and upon the subsequent crime rate statistics.

CHAPTER II

What are the problems dealing with a serial murder case? The author has already mentioned a few of these. Namely, when the police are dealing with this type of killer whom the Federal Bureau of Investigation's Behavioral Science Unit has classified as an "organized serial murderer", the suspect would tend to be above average in intelligence, his crimes would be well planned, he would strive for perfection and would, therefore, tend to leave very few clues.

In addition, there are other problems that are inherent in serial murder cases. First, there is the problem of definition between what constitutes a "serial murder" case and how does it differ from a "mass murder" case? Then there are problems associated with family or personal loss, community loss and terror when a serial murderer is at large —killing victims, whenever and wherever, he can find them.

There are also problems which these murders create within the law enforcement community. There are ethical problems, communication problems—both intradepartmental and interdepartmental. There is also the law enforcement problem of taking proactive measures to educate potential victims about the *modus operandi* of serial murderers in an effort to reduce these types of killings.

Most important of all, is the apprehension of the serial murderer. This problem includes many facets including the organization of a task force, how tips should be dealt with, investigation, surveillance and undercover operations, the arrest of the murderer, the recovery of incriminating evidence, the interrogation of the killer and the conducting of photo show ups, and preparing the case for trial. All of the above are extremely important and a good deal of them must be handled in close cooperation between the police, the prosecuting attorney, the crime laboratory, and the medical examiner's office.

Further, there is the police problem and involvement during the trial itself which means insuring that evidence is present for the trial, sometimes assisting in jury selection, helping to insure the arrested person is not murdered before the jury has an opportunity to pass judgement, the handling of evidence throughout the appeal process, the storing of evidence after it has been returned from the courts, and also the storing of other evidence from other serial murder cases where the defendant was not charged and brought to trial on those cases. Also there sometimes may be evidence from crimes of breaking and entering or vehicle theft where weapons, vehicles, or other items may have been subsequently used in one or more serial murders. The police must make proper disposition of these items.

Finally, there is the problem of returning personal possessions owned by the victims to their relatives and giving them an opportunity of telling the police their feelings about how the police handled the case and perhaps clearing up some misunderstanding they might have regarding the investigation and the reasons why certain things were--or were not done. The latter might be termed a problem of police public relations.

Recently some states have passed Victim's Rights Acts which mandate that the criminal justice system do certain things to insure that victims and their relatives have a voice in the criminal justice process. Generally, these acts were passed in response to the perception by the public that the accused in a criminal case had a great many rights, but little consideration was being given to the victim and her relatives.

For example, under the Michigan Crime Victims Rights Act, a few of the things victims are entitled to are:

To be notified by the Police Agency of emergency and medical services.

To be notified of the number of the police department to contact to determine if the defendant has been released from custody.

To be notified of the address and telephone number of the Prosecuting Attorney who can be contacted to obtain information about victim's rights.

To receive an explanation of procedures to follow if threatened or intimidated by the defendant.

To be provided with a waiting area separate from the defendant, the defendant's relatives, and defense witnesses.

To have property promptly returned which was taken during the investigation except as otherwise provided for by law.

To receive notice should the defendant escape from custody while awaiting trial.

CHAPTER III

THE SCOPE OF THE BOOK

The scope of this book is limited to the problem of the apprehension and conviction of the serial murderers of girls/women usually for sexual reasons.

The book also discusses the collateral matters previously mentioned in chapter II, and it also deals with errors made during the course of investigations and offers suggestions on how to prevent such errors in the future. These are located at the end of the various case analyses under the heading, "Observations." To help differentiate these remarks from the case studies they are set in a different type.

The methodology that was used in this study was inductive rather than deductive. Over twenty different serial murder cases where women/girls were the primary targets were analyzed. Graphic information is included in the book which visually demonstrates significant information very quickly. However, there is a *caveat* regarding this information. It reflects the things we know about the serial murderer, but there may be items that are not checked because we simply do not know about these things.

There is also another *caveat* and that is that the knowledge contained in this book is by no means complete. Twenty years ago we knew little about serial murderers. We can expect as time passes and we gather more knowledge about them, and as forensic science becomes even more effective through the analysis of DNA found in blood, seminal fluid and hair, the law enforcement community will be more successful in apprehending serial murderers. Obviously the more we know about them, the more successful the law enforcement community will be in dealing with them.

The efficacy of the application of modern technology to crime fighting in the United States will, to a large degree, depend upon whether civil libertarians are capable of blocking the use of these new crime fighting tools. To be effective, what will be required is to have a blood sample from every person convicted of a sexually related offense including window peeking. The DNA fingerprint would then be placed into a central data bank for use at a subsequent time if and when DNA evidence was found at the scene of a serial murder or on the suspect. At this time, however, there are still some technical matters to be solved, but the scientists are working on these problems. DNA fingerprinting and AFIS (A fingerprint identification system where a computer reviews the records) should play a significant role in criminal investigation during the 1990's .

This book does not concern itself with the causes of why a person becomes a serial murderer, nor does it consider any possible cures for a serial murderer once he has been caught. It also does not address problems better left to experts in penal institutions.

It does not consider those cases where the serial murderer picks men or boys for his primary targets. The reason for this is that those perpetrators may or may not have many of the same attributes as killers who have attacked females.

Also not included in this study—at least to any meaningful extent—are serial murder cases such as those committed by the "Zodiac" and the "Green River Killer" simply because they are unsolved.

Only cases which were solved were used in this study. It was this writer's opinion that if we looked back at the many serial murder cases that have been investigated during this century—both here and abroad— and analyzed them carefully, we would be able to arrive at some meaningful conclusions which would help the law enforcement community in future cases by making it possible for them to take a given set of facts—extrapolate—and then make decisions on the best possible methods of apprehending a serial murderer. In short, the best way to catch a serial killer is to use what has worked before to apprehend him.

It is not being suggested that only one method be employed. To the contrary—it is specifically encouraged that several different means be utilized at exactly the same time.

And the law enforcement community should be totally aware of what has yielded the most favorable results in past cases and where mistakes have repeatedly been made.

CHAPTER IV

THE CASE STUDY OF JOHN NORMAN COLLINS

BRIEF HISTORY OF THE MURDER OF MONA F.

On the evening of July 9, 1967, Mona returned to apartment number fourteen at 413 Washtenaw Avenue in Ypsilanti, Michigan. Mona shared this apartment with another young woman, Naomi Dahlberg, with whom she also worked part time at Eastern Michigan University's Field Service office. It was hot in the apartment. So, after quickly changing clothes, Mona told Naomi she was going out for a walk. This was about 8:30 p.m. When she left the apartment, she was wearing an orange sun dress with large white polka dots and plastic sandals that appeared like straw. (18.)

Her father thought this was unusual because she ordinarily did not take walks. On rare occasions she did, however, go for walks with her cousin, Melissa Brim. These walks were usually not more than a half mile and then she would return. She would tire quickly. (26.)

At about 8:45 p.m. an Eastern Michigan University Campus policeman who knew Mona F., saw her walking on Cross Street. A few minutes before 9:00 p.m., a man sitting on the front porch of his Hamilton Street home saw Mona F. walking alone toward Washtenaw Avenue. It appeared that she was returning to her apartment on the next corner.

Just after Mona F. had passed his house, he saw a light blue or grey late model car come down the street traveling in the same direction as Mona F. was walking. The driver, a young man, slowed down and spoke to Mona through the open window on the passenger's side. Mona looked at him, shook her head and kept walking. The driver then sped off, turned right at the next corner and a minute later the driver came back by the house. He had only driven around the block.

This time he drove past Mona into a private driveway where he blocked the sidewalk with his car and made it easy for Mona to just open the door and get in his car. Mona simply walked around the car. The driver then backed the car out of the driveway and with tires squealing drove away again. That was the last time Mona F. was seen alive by someone friendly toward her. (54)(48.7-8)

At about 9:00 a.m. the following morning, Mona's roommate called Mona's parents. Naomi told Sylvia, Mona's sister, that Mona had not come home from her walk, nor had she appeared for work at the Field Service Office. Sylvia then advised her mother, and her mother immediately traveled to her daughter's apartment. She entered the apartment using an extra key Mona had given to her.

She observed Mona's car parked in the apartment parking lot. She checked her daughter's clothing, purse, and dirty clothing in the apartment. Mrs. Foust fre-

7

quently washed her daughter's dirty clothes. She noted a small quantity of blood in her daughter's dirty panties and concluded that her daughter was just finishing her menstrual period. After again checking with her daughter's roommate where she was working, and obtaining confirmation that Mona still had not come into work, she called her husband to tell him. Mr. Foust, the head of an engineering department for a manufacturing plant, told his wife to report their daughter's disappearance first via telephone to the Ypsilanti police to be followed by a personal appearance at their police station.

In a city where a college or university is located, police do not generally take a report from the parents of a missing nineteen year old coed very seriously until at least a twenty-four hour period of time has elapsed, unless there is something that clearly indicates there may have been some foul play involved in her disappearance. A police report is generally taken, but not much beyond that. If the woman is still missing then, the information is entered into the computer's data base and sent to other departments. The reason for the delay in actively investigating Mona's disappearance was because in a college or university town many parents report their daughters missing.

Some parents have a difficult time accepting the fact that their little girl has grown up. In some instances, the police have been forced to change this delayed reporting policy due to pressure from feminist groups who want immediate action, but due to severe restrictions in police resources most departments still adhere to this practice. In Mona's case, the Ypsilanti police put the matter of her disappearance on the "back burner" for forty-eight hours.

On July 12, 1967, Detective Lieutenant Vern Howard began the investigation into Mona's disappearance. He immediately had Michigan State Police Laboratory Scientists examine the car Mona had been driving to obtain all latent prints. He obtained books, papers, and other material from which her latent fingerprints might be obtained which might help in identifying her if she were later found dead. Subsequent to this—her parents, friends, relatives, and possible suspects were interviewed by him. All efforts to find her failed. It appeared that she had disappeared off the face of the earth until about a month later. (40)

Then on the afternoon of August 7, 1967, two youths were working in a corn field near the site where a farm house and outbuildings once stood in Superior Township of Washtenaw County. This site was located along Geddes Road and would tend to become very significant in the crimes that would occur during the next two years. It was located about a half mile west of LaForge Road and just a few miles north of the city of Ypsilanti. One lad was putting gas in the tractor while the other was making a spark plug adjustment when they heard a car door slam. Curiosity got the best of them and they decided to investigate. As they walked through heavy overgrowth toward the old farm site, they heard the car door slam again and then the sound of the auto driving away. They never saw it, however.

As the lads reached a clearing, they smelled what they believed was some kind of dead animal. Following their noses down a path about one hundred feet east of the U-shaped drive, they came to a trash pile which was originally made by the inhabitants of the abandoned farm site. There on top of the pile they saw the skeletal remains of what appeared to be a human body. They went to the Ypsilanti Post of the Michigan State Police and reported it at 2:30 p.m. (54)

Two veteran Michigan State Police detectives immediately went to the scene and examined the remains. They were in such a state of decomposition that, from a cursory examination, one could not determine the sex of the body. The detectives radioed for the Medical Examiner to come to the scene, alerted the county prosecutor's office, and also requested that the area departments be contacted for information on any missing persons. Within a short time, colleagues from the Ypsilanti Police, the Eastern Michigan University Police and the Washtenaw County Sheriff's Department were at the scene along with Chief Assistant Prosecutor Booker T. Williams and a Washtenaw County Medical Examiner. (54)

The following day an autopsy was conducted by Dr. Bertram Noldon, a British Pathologist who was working at the University of Michigan hospital in Ann Arbor. He determined that the victim was a young woman about twenty years of age. She had sustained about thirty deep lacerations in the chest and abdomen. At least twenty of the wounds had been inflicted by a sharp instrument. Her feet had been severed at both ankle joints, the right hand was severed above the wrist, the left thumb and parts of the remaining fingers of the left hand were also missing. It was unknown whether this severing was the result of animal activity or cutting by her murderer. It did appear, however, that the bones of the legs had been smashed above the ankles. There were indications that the victim had also been beaten.

A comparison was made between the chart from the corpse and Mona's known dental records obtained from her dentist by Detective Lieutenant Howard. The comparison appeared positive. At the same time the autopsy was being conducted, a more thorough search of the scene was being conducted by Detective Sergeant Ron Schoonmaker and two other detectives. They found all the victim's clothing under what appeared to be a large square wooden frame with cardboard over it.

THE VICTIM

The victim of this murder was nineteen-year-old Mona F. She resided in apartment number fourteen at 413 Washtenaw Avenue in Ypsilanti. She was born on December 4, 1947, at Beyer Memorial Hospital in Ypsilanti, Michigan. She was a white female, five feet one inch tall, one hundred and five pounds, with brown hair and green eyes. She was a sophomore at Eastern Michigan University in Ypsilanti. She also worked part time there in the Field Services Office. She wore horned rimmed glasses.

Mona had a Michigan operators license and drove a six year old car which belonged to her father. (26)

9

Mona had natural talent in the musical area and had taught herself how to play several musical instruments. These instruments were the guitar, piano, drums, and the organ.

Mona was Roman Catholic. The evening before she was murdered she played the organ during Mass at St. Joseph's Roman Catholic Church in Whitaker, Michigan. On the day she disappeared, she attended early Mass before going to work at the Eastern Michigan University Field Services office.

Mona was above average in intelligence. Her I.Q. was 123. She had been attending the university on a scholarship. One of the conditions for the scholarship was that she reside on the E.M.U. Campus. The reason she moved into Ypsilanti in June 1967, was to comply with that requirement. According to Lincoln High School records, she was a member of the National Honor Society.

Mona was in good physical condition, but she lacked stamina. She had hurt her back in a judo course she had been taking at Wayne High School. She had begun that course on April 17, 1967. She completed only half the course.

On May 5, 1967, about three months before she was murdered, Mona contacted a doctor at the Women's Hospital in Ann Arbor. This is part of the University of Michigan Hospital. She told the doctor she thought she was pregnant.

She wanted an abortion. She told the doctor on the night of April 18, 1967, she gave a fellow student a ride to Willis, Michigan. She said she stopped the car to let him out in this little village, and he had raped her.

The doctor's initial examination was negative, and he recommended a pregnancy test. It was his personal opinion, however, that she was pregnant at that time. The doctor said Mona was extremely frightened — almost out of her mind. (43) A female classmate recalled the night of April 18, 1967. She said after class Mona left alone. There was no one in the car with her. Thus she contradicted Mona's story.

Mona's roommate said that on the day Mona disappeared, she did change her panties before she went for the walk. Naomi, Mona's roommate, said that Mona was having her period. The life guard at Half-Moon Lake where Mona visited after working at the University that Sunday said Mona waded in the water, but did not go swimming.

It was the confidential opinion of Mona's doctor that she was not having a period but Mona was "spotting from a post abortion operation." He did not perform the abortion. This information regarding Mona having a period would become meaningful as time went on.

A close girl friend said that Mona did not have a steady boyfriend. She had dated a Mexican male whose name was not known.

Mona had many hobbies. She liked to read and was reading, "Death of a President" before she died. She was an expert seamstress and made her own clothing. She also like to knit and paint.

Mona, while a very kind person, was not very physically attractive. In fact, she tried to help some boys by cooking for them at least 30 times, but they considered her somewhat of a nuisance. One of them said that the mistake they had made was being nice to her when she first came to their apartment. Basically she was a homebody who did not wish to offend anyone. She was obviously quite a lonely woman. This was probably exacerbated because her roommate had an intimate relationship with a young man, and Mona's sister, who was a year younger than she, was an exceptionally beautiful young woman who never lacked for male companionship. (43.1-8)

METHOD OF OPERATION

The victim was picked up while she was out for a walk. She may have gotten into the perpetrator's vehicle willingly as all indications were that she was quite lonely.

It is not known where the initial attack occurred. Her dress was ripped in the front from the top nearly all the way to the bottom. One of the straps to her bra was ripped apart, and the top of her panties was torn. Her clothing indicated that the assailant removed the victim's clothing rather than the victim herself. It is not known whether she was conscious when this happened. At some point in time, Mona was beaten severely. She was then stabbed repeatedly. Her body was then thrown on a trash pile that had been made by residents who had lived on this farm many years previously. All of the victim's clothing, except one of her shoes were hidden under the cardboard, as previously mentioned.

A significant item that was missing was an Expo 67 Canadian Silver dollar which Mona wore around her neck.

VEHICLE INVOLVED

The suspected vehicle involved was a late model blue grey, or blue-grey full sized car. It was believed by a witness that this vehicle may have been a Chevrolet, however, there was no degree of certainty about that.

Since the location where Mona's body was found was about four or five miles north of the city of Ypsilanti, where Mona was last observed alive, it can be reasonably assumed that a vehicle was used to transport her body there.

INVESTIGATION

The preliminary crime scene search was conducted by detectives and other police officers. The photographs of the scene were also taken by them. The Crime Laboratory personnel were not requested to process the scene.

A subsequent and more thorough search of the crime scene was conducted under the supervision of Detective Sergeant Ron Schoonmaker. During that search, the victim's clothing was found.

State Police Detectives from other posts were sent to the Ypsilanti Post to assist in handling the investigation. As part of an orientation to the case, a third, very extensive search was made of the location where the victim's body was found. A .32 caliber S & W cartridge case was found near the location where the girl's clothing had been hidden. It is not known whether this had any nexus to the crime itself.

An officer also contacted Mona's mother to obtain known samples of her hair in the event a suspect developed and suspected samples of hair were found in his car or apartment. Known samples of head hair were obtained from a hair brush that only she used and samples of pubic hair were obtained from her ski pants. These were submitted to the Michigan State Police Crime Laboratory at Plymouth to be kept on file in the event they were later needed for identification.

A police detail attended Mona's funeral to identify any possible suspect who might appear. No one was observed attending the funeral who was driving a blue or grey late model Chevrolet. A young man had appeared at the funeral home and asked to take a picture of Mona's body. He did not have a camera. The person at the funeral home was not able to provide any description of him.

EVIDENCE

There was no evidence discovered with which officers could work during this investigation.

SUSPECTS

The driver of the gray vehicle that was observed trying to pick Mona up was the prime suspect in this case. No physical description of him was available since the witness who saw him really did not get a good look at him.

REMARKS

Within a short time, all investigative leads were exhausted and officers returned to their home areas. No thorough investigation was done into the victim's life at that time.

OBSERVATIONS

It was observed that the detectives in this case, particularly the first senior (in time in grade) detective chose not to involve the crime laboratory specialists because in his judgement there was nothing more they could do because the body was so badly decomposed.

The detective was criticized by some of his peers for this decision. One of the functions of laboratory specialists at a crime scene is to conduct a thorough search of the scene where the body is found for evidence or anything that may even possibly be connected with the crime. Frequently, at the time a body is discovered it might be difficult to determine whether a certain item is relevant or is not. Whenever this occurs such doubts should be resolved in favor of the possibility that it might be of value later during the investigation.

Whether the laboratory scientists would have found the victim's clothing that first day is a matter of speculation. After all they're human beings too and on rare occasions have been known to overlook significant items of evidence, but these circumstances are rare. And whether the senior detective acted properly by not calling the crime laboratory personnel to the scene is still a matter of debate.

I would submit, however, that in most instances evidence technicians or laboratory specialists should handle the scene investigation because for the most part they are better trained to handle such matters, they are better equipped for it, and by being present and involved at the scene they may be better prepared to analyze the evidence, both that which is found at the scene and those items of evidence which may turn up later through investigation. This also includes the intangible factor of laboratory scientists doing a very thorough job in their work when they have a personal feeling for what the case involves.

In this case, note that the victim went for the evening walk *carrying only the keys to her apartment*. Note also that her mother, her roommate's boyfriend, and her roommate also had keys to the victim's apartment.

Two years later when a suspect was arrested on another murder, many items of stolen property and a large number of keys were confiscated both from the suspect's apartment, and from the incinerator in the apartment where the suspect lived. His attorneys fought vigorously to prevent anything found in the incinerator from being used as evidence against the defendant. An affidavit admitted into evidence taken from the owner of the apartment, stated in substance that the defendant did not have any right to be in that portion of the building where the incinerator was located. No meaningful evidence was found there.

The problem was that the locks on the door of Mona's apartment had been changed during the two years, and no one had kept the extra key they had to the apartment nor the locks, so laboratory scientists had nothing with which to make a comparison to determine whether one of the keys the suspect had in his possession, or that was found in the incinerator matched the key to Mona's apartment. The keys Mona took with her have never been identified.

It is suggested in future cases where the victim is carrying keys which are not recovered that the police obtain at least duplicate keys to be used for later comparison purposes. These would be valuable in assisting in the identification of the victim, if they are found at the scene where the body is discovered, or would be damaging evidence against a suspect should they be found in his possession. For the same reason, should the apartment owner or tenant decide to change the aparment door lock, the police should ask for the old lock to assist in later identification.

During the investigation of Mona's death, Michigan State Police Detectives and Ypsilanti City Police Detectives worked together in teams. From this author's observations, he has never seen a better team effort. In fact, this may have been due to the abundance of serious crime in the area. There certainly was no shortage of good police work to be done, and these officers had, from time to time, worked together on other serious criminal activity.

In addition, in the City of Ypsilanti across from the Michigan State Police Post was the Bomber Restaurant, so named due to the large number of bombers manufactured in the Ypsilanti area during the Second World War. In the back portion of this restaurant was a large round table. There was no reserved sign on the table, but every one in the community knew that this table was reserved for the police officers, retired police officers and their guests. Before, during, and after the murder of Mona—officers from, not only the state police and Ypsilanti, but from all area departments would gather for a cup of coffee, eat lunch, or supper and discuss the various cases on which they were working, and they would receive input and suggestions from their colleagues.

While the author never kept data on the number of serious felony cases solved by such meetings, he can report that it was indeed a significant number which quite probably exceeded the number of cases ever solved in the police station or squad room. During these meetings theories of cases were discussed, bits and pieces of information were exchanged, as well as the names of possible suspects.

When officers leave these little informal meetings after a cup of coffee, they are much better prepared to deal with some of the cases they are investigating than previously.

The reality is, whether police administrators in a metropolitan area like it or not, that police detectives working in that area are like little departments within departments. These detectives from various departments know that, if one is to do a good job and really be an effective detective, he cannot accomplish much by himself. He must rely upon his colleagues working in other departments and must cooperate closely with them. This means that there must be a high degree of trust, and every good detective knows that there is no quicker way to destroy such trust than to be a glory grabber.

When one encounters a "glory grabber", this information is put out to others and eventually the "glory grabber" will learn that his behavior has only hurt himself, and his effectiveness as a detective will become over time, very limited. For example, one instance involving "glory grabbing" in the author's personal experience occurred when detectives from several different jurisdictions were working on a series of armed robberies. Some of these detectives met at a restaurant and discussed their respective cases. From this meeting a good suspect was developed. The suspect was arrested and confessed. He named an accomplice living in another jurisdiction.

As officers were surrounding this suspect's house to arrest him—a detective from one of the jurisdictions also working on several of the robberies these suspects had also committed was contacted by telephone and invited to take part in the apprehension. This detective showed his gratitude and appreciation by calling the suspect at his house which the police were in the process of surrounding, and telling him to quickly get out of the house and drive to his office and surrender himself to him as he was about to be arrested. In this instance, not only was such glory grabbing tactics utterly stupid, it could have resulted in brother officers being killed or wounded should the robber have decided to shoot it out with the police. Luckily he was arrested without the death or injury of another officer. Needless to say the information that officer received from that time on was severely limited.

One of the least understood aspects of "glory grabbing", or lack of cooperation between officers, or by whatever name we wish to call it, is that it does not just occur between police departments, nor is it in any way unique to them. It also exists within departments where we observe police officers withholding information from their fellow officers—or trying to take credit for a "collar" they don't deserve. Furthermore, it is not in any way even unique to police work. Who has not heard of those in corporate life who try to claim credit for ideas or work of another? Isn't it common knowledge of how one reporter tries to beat his colleague to a "scoop"?

As one who has enjoyed the close working relationship and camaraderie of literally hundreds of outstanding detectives, the author can relate the difference between being an inner member of this "club" and being outside it.

When a new detective begins to work in a metropolitan area if he seeks information over the phone from another detective in a different organization, he will quickly be told to send a teletype. Within a year or two—after he is accepted into the club—the other detectives will now, not only provide any information they have available, but if one needs assistance on an investigation, will drop whatever they are doing to help. It is understood clearly that this is a two-way street. Should they later need your help, they have trust in you and know that you will reciprocate. It is sometimes difficult for police administrators to understand this relationship between "club" members.

One administrator for whom this writer worked, could not understand why a few minutes earlier the writer was too involved to make a check on a breaking and entering complaint, and yet could stop to take time to help another detective from another department. He thought top priority should be always given to the work in one's "own department." Nor could he understand why a detective from another department would not trust him with information to be passed on to this writer. The simple fact of the matter was the administrator was not in the trusted group. He was not in the "club." A detective who is in the "club" in a metropolitan area can generally accomplish over the telephone in a couple hours, work that would require several days by conventional methods. And it requires time before one is accepted into the "club."

To become accepted one must join the key organization to which most "club" members already belong. In the Detroit Metropolitan Area, for example, it is the Wayne County Detectives Association. In that particular organization one will also find Circuit Court Judges, and Prosecuting Attorneys and their assistants. Then one must work hard to build the trust that is required. If you have come to the conclusion that what the "club" really consists of are a large number of detectives who over a period of time build up close interpersonal relationships—you are absolutely correct, for that is exactly what it is.

These relationships cross departmental organizations, in fact, they have nothing to do with the department in which a certain detective is a member. For example, in the author's experience, he related some confidential information to a federal agent concerning a hijacking operation within the United States and Canada.

The agent wanted the name of the source of the information. This was provided on the agent's word that the informant would not be contacted and that any request for further information be obtained through the author. Within hours, the author received a telephone call from the informant who was furious that he had been contacted by the agent. He promised that he would never again provide information, and he never did. Later the agent called and wanted the name of another informant, but the author would not give it to him.

At the same time, the author worked very closely with another federal agent on a bank robbery where $44,000 was obtained, and confidential information flowed both ways due to the complete trust and the fact that there was a good professional rapport between us.

The reason that the author is writing so extensively about this matter is because the news media, and some others, tend to be critical of the cooperation between police departments when serial murders involve more than one jurisdiction. The point the author would like to make is that when this does occur, and it does happen, it is not so much a lack of cooperation between "departments", as it is a lack of a good working relationships between the men and women who make up those departments.

It is important for anyone working on serial murder cases to know that a team effort is required by everyone involved to bring the case to a successful conclusion. This includes not only the police, but the prosecutors' staff, the medical examiner and his staff, the laboratory scientists, the witnesses, and the relatives of the victim.

Too often the grieving relatives of the victim are totally uninformed about what the police are doing to apprehend the murderer. While, for the most part, Mona's parents were kept advised, it is obvious that many police departments are falling short in this area. It results in frustration for these relatives, and the police are sometimes shocked

16

when the relatives of a serial murder victim "go public" and are critical of law enforcement efforts after police have really been working hard to solve the crime. So it is important that contact with the victim's relatives is continually maintained. This is especially true when a young woman is involved, but really it pertains to all murder investigations.

Regarding obtaining a complete physical description of the victim at the time she disappears, this also applies to earrings and other forms of jewelry. In the instant case, two years later, after the police had seized many different items in the suspect's possession, the defendant through his attorney filed a court order for the return of certain items which were not found to be stolen. There were literally hundreds of these items which were being returned to the defendant.

One of these items was a Canadian silver dollar. The defendant, who was in jail, denied that he had this in his possession and would not accept its return. Originally the police had found it on the top of Collins' dresser in his apartment.

Mona's sister, Sylvia, was called to the Crime Center, which was set up to deal exclusively with the serial murders. Sylvia said that Mona had a Canadian silver dollar which she wore around her neck on a chain. She said she was with Mona when the latter purchased it just a short time before she was murdered while attending Expo 67 in Canada. If this was not Mona's is it was indeed ironic that he should reject this from the hundreds of items which were returned to his mother. Unfortunately this coin had no known identifying characteristics and, therefore, neither laboratory scientists or investigators could positively state that it was Mona's silver dollar.

The reader will undoubtedly have noticed that it was not until *after* her body was found that investigators sought to obtain known samples of her head and pubic hair. One does not know whether these items will be necessary later, but it is suggested that if there is even the possibility that the missing girl has been the victim of foul play, investigators should immediately take steps, not only to procure her books, papers, and anything from which her fingerprints can be obtained, but also hair samples, copies of dental records, eye glasses prescriptions, and anything else which might be beneficial for her later identification or to be used for comparison purposes with samples found on the defendant's clothing, in his car, or dwelling.

Dr. Marx, a psychiatrist at the State of Michigan Hospital outside of Ypsilanti was contacted by the author during the early stages of the investigation of Mona's death. Dr. Marx was shown photographs of the scene where Mona's body was found. The purpose behind this was to obtain the input from this outstanding professional.

After viewing the pictures, Marx said that it was no accident that her body had been thrown on an old trash pile. This was the murderer's way of expressing his view that this is where she belonged. "In fact," he said "the murderer probably thinks all women belong on a trash pile."

Events that occurred during the two year period subsequent to Dr. Marx's comments proved him to be remarkably perceptive and left little room for disagreement.

17

CHAPTER V

BRIEF HISTORY OF THE MURDER OF JEAN S.
(AKA "Jill Hersch" in Michigan Murders)

On the evening of June 30, 1968, the victim returned to Ypsilanti from her home in Plymouth, Michigan, with her parents. Upon their arrival they stopped at Haab's Restaurant and ate dinner. This was at about 7:45 p.m. They finished eating and left the restaurant sometime between 8:45 p.m. and 9:15 p.m. and returned Jean to her apartment, number two at 703 Emmet Street in Ypsilanti. (43.9) Her roommate put the time of her arrival at about 9:30 p.m. The roommate, Sandy, told Jean that her boyfriend, Drew, had called for her sometime between 7:00 p.m. and 9:00 p.m.

Upon learning this, Jean immediately called Drew at the Mental Health Research Center at the University of Michigan in Ann Arbor where he had been working since he had deserted from the United States Army. She told him she wanted to come over and see him. They made an agreement that if she arrived in Ann Arbor, about eight miles west of where she was at that time, before midnight she was to go to Chelsea's apartment. Chelsea was a mutual friend. If she arrived after midnight, she was to come to the laboratory. Jean then made preparations to go to Ann Arbor. (43.14)

Jean called the local bus station and was told there were two more buses leaving that evening for Ann Arbor. The next bus would be leaving at 10:30 p.m. This would be followed by another bus ten minutes later.

She related this information to her roommate. She called Drew again and told him the same thing and advised him that she was enroute to Ann Arbor. Sandy was concerned for her safety and told her she would accompany her to the bus stop which was located near the Eastern Michigan University Student Union Building. This was about a five minute walk from the girl's apartment. (43.10)

The young women arrived at the bus stop at about 10:30 p.m. Shortly after that a bus bound for Ann Arbor passed by without stopping. It was fully loaded with passengers. Jean and Sandy continued to wait until about 11:15 p.m., when Sandy said she was going to return to their apartment and call the bus station to determine whether there would be any further buses going to Ann Arbor that evening. Sandy returned to their apartment and called the station, but there was no answer, so she returned to the bus stop at approximately 11:20 p.m.

About two minutes later a red car with a black top, which Sandy thought was a General Motors product, possible even a convertible, containing three white males drove past them and stopped. The man on the passenger's side of the front seat got out of the car. He was wearing a green tee shirt with the darker letters "E.M.U." on it. He yelled back to the young woman, "Do you want a ride?" Jean ran up to the car and asked them if they were going all the way to Ann Arbor. Sandy heard one of

18

them say, "Yah,—all the way." Jean then, yelled back to her roommate, Sandy, who was standing some distance away, that she would call her from Ann Arbor. (43.10)

Two witnesses, one of whom was Sandy, stated that the car did not move out into the main traffic lane of Washtenaw Avenue going to Ann Arbor, but rather made a right turn on the drive going alongside the McKinney Student Union Building, through the parking lot to Forrest Street, then made another right turn and disappeared. It was as though at that point in time, the driver had no intention of going to Ann Arbor.

A short time later, Elliot and his girlfriend, Daphne, were with a mutual friend named Duke. Duke was a United States Marine who was home on leave before going overseas to Vietnam. They were enroute to the Casa-Nova Restaurant at 11 W. Michigan Avenue in Ypsilanti to pick up another girl named Deidre who worked there. Then they were going on a double date. At 11:23 p.m. as they passed the intersection of Emmet Street and College Place, both Elliot and Daphne said they observed John Norman Collins, the man who was later arrested and convicted of another murder in the series, on the south side of Emmet Street. This was the corner of the street where the apartment was located where John Collins lived. Collins was with Jean. They were in the process of crossing the street, and were walking toward the apartment where the victim resided just across the street. As they passed, Elliot and Daphne waved at John Collins and Jean, and they waved back.

Elliot knew both of these people well because he worked with Jean, the victim, in the McKinney Student Union Building, and he was a fraternity brother of John Collins in the Theta Chi Fraternity. Daphne also knew them both, but not as well as her boyfriend. Both Elliot and Daphne were absolutely positive in their identification of both parties. (45.)

Drew called Sandy after midnight on July 1, 1968, and advised her that Jean had not reached Ann Arbor. He asked her to contact the Ypsilanti Police Department, which she did at 1:47 a.m. on that date. (43.14)

Five days later, on July 5, 1968, a construction worker working on the outskirts of Ann Arbor with several other workers smelled a strange odor. They found a body, later identified as Jean, along Glacier Way Road about one hundred and fifty yards west of Earhart Road. (55.) (Official police reports)

VICTIM

The murdered victim was Jean. She was a Caucasian female who was five-feet-five inches tall and weighed ninety-eight pounds. She had long brown hair and very large hazel eyes. She had blood type B. She was twenty years old when she was killed. She was born in Theda Clark Hospital in Neenah, Wisconsin, on December 14, 1947. (43.9)

When she was murdered, she was living in apartment number two at 703 Emmet Street in Ypsilanti, Michigan. She had only lived there for twenty-five days before she was murdered. She was last observed alive on June 30, 1968, between 11:30 p.m. and 12:00 midnight while in the process of crossing the street near where she lived. (43.)

Jean's parents resided in Plymouth, Michigan. At the time of her death, her mother suffered from a serious heart condition. Her father was a communications expert, a former radio announcer, and was managing a large sporting goods store in the Detroit Metropolitan area.

Jean had attended grade school in Kirkwood, Missouri, and the Public High School in Plymouth, Michigan, from which she graduated. Some teachers indicated that she was a friendly student who was well liked by her classmates, but she was difficult to get to know well. Other teachers described her as a slow learner who was a day dreamer. Since Jean had an I.Q. of 119, the poor performance of the victim was probably the result of a lack of motivation rather than any inherent deficiency in her mental capabilities. When she graduated from high school she ranked 189th in a class of 400, so she was in the upper half of her class. She was interested in art and that was her major at the university. (43.9)

Jean was a very impulsive girl. She had the tendency of doing what she wanted to do—when she wanted to do it with little regard for the consequences. This tendency manifested itself when she skipped several classes as well as university examinations even though she knew this was going to cause problems for her. This impulsive tendency showed itself again on the night she disappeared when she climbed into a car with 3 young men. In her defense it appeared that much of her irrational behavior could be attributed to her love for her boyfriend. It appeared that he was the most important thing in her life, not her studies, and she was willing to take considerable risks to be with him.

Jean enrolled at Eastern Michigan University in the fall of 1967. Her goal was to become an art teacher for little children. She loved little children and enjoyed working with them. In early November 1967, she began working at the McKinney Student Union Building at Eastern Michigan University. This was where she met and worked with Elliot who was one of her last friends to see her alive.

Jean smoked about a package of Old Gold filter cigarettes per day, but she never smoked in the presence of her parents. She did drink an occasional beer, and she drank white wine with her boyfriend. She had experimented with marijuana. She would never use drugs or drink any alcoholic beverages when she was doing art work as she didn't want these drugs interfering with her creative abilities.

The night she disappeared she was wearing a dark blue Crazy Horse brand mini-skirt, which was in fashion at that time, a pair of size 8M sandals, and she was carrying a red burlap handbag which was never recovered.

Jean was having an intimate relationship with Drew which began while she was in high school. They were very close. They did their laundry together, shopped together and studied together. Although she had been taking birth control tablets to avoid pregnancy, she did not care whether she became pregnant or not because she wanted to have Drew's baby. She often told other boys she was engaged to be married or was already married.

Drew, Jean's boyfriend, had deserted from the United States Army, after Jean had sent him the money to fly back to Michigan. Drew could not adopt to military life, and Jean was lonesome. (43.14) He had reluctantly enlisted into the Army after he was arrested for breaking and entering and was given the choice—enlist in the Army or go to prison. He chose the former, and the State of Michigan dropped the charges. Did he commit the crime to avoid military service? Since the Army was reluctant to accept one convicted of a felony, this was one of several means used by some young men to avoid service in the undeclared war in Vietnam.

Jean did not believe in God, rather she believed in evolution and the inherent goodness of man. She thought that any person who lacked this inherent quality of goodness was sick. She was not, however, a trusting person. In fact, she was wary of other people, and her boyfriend was amazed by her uncanny ability to evaluate people very quickly.

She was enroute to spend the night with Drew when she was picked up by the three young men.

WEATHER CONDITIONS

The weather conditions on July 1, 1968, reached a high of eighty degrees with an average temperature of seventy-four degrees. From the time Jean disappeared, up until July 5th, when her body was found, there was no precipitation in the Ann Arbor-Ypsilanti area. On June 5, 1968, however, there had been a trace of rain at 9:45 a.m. which lasted until 10:05 a.m. The remainder of the rain on that date occurred after 3:53 p.m., when there was heavy rain with hail.(43.7)

INVESTIGATION

Witnesses who found Jean's body were interviewed and statements were taken from them by Ann Arbor Police Officers. The police also made photographs of the scene and took appropriate measurements to record her exact location.

An autopsy was performed on Jean by Forensic Pathologist Robert Hendrix, M.D. of the University of Michigan. Detective Sergeant Caudel identified the body as being the same as the one found at Glacier Way. The body had twenty-five puncture and stab wounds in it. There were three stab wounds in the back and twenty-two wounds in the front of her. The left carotid artery was severed. The spinal bone in

21

the back of the neck was cut by the force of the blow. There were two cuts into the spinal bone. The right lung was stabbed through from a blow to the back. The liver was punctured from a blow placed in the midsection from the front. There was a stab wound at the base of the left ear traveling upwards into the top of Jean's head which fractured her skull. There were other wounds, but these were the most serious. There were also abrasions to the victim's left elbow.

In Dr. Hendrix's opinion, the cause of Jean's death was the result of receiving the above mentioned stab wounds. He was of the opinion that the weapon which caused the fatal wounds was probably a knife which had a blade about four inches long and one inch wide.

During the autopsy, Dr. Hendrix found partially digested pieces of meat, potatoes, and a green leafy material in Jean's stomach. From the digestive condition of this food, it was estimated by him that the victim was either dead or in great fear of death approximately three to four hours after she ate her last meal. This would put the time of her death between 12:00 midnight and 1:00 a.m. on July 1, 1968, or within about thirty minutes to an hour and a half after she was picked up at the bus stop.

Tests conducted on the vaginal swabs indicated the presence of acid phosphatase frequently found in seminal fluid. Jean had blood type B.

Personnel from the Michigan State Police Crime Laboratory were called to Ann Arbor on July 6, 1968, and were present at the autopsy.

Additional photographs were also taken of Jean at Schroder's Funeral Home in Plymouth. Finger and palm prints of the victim were also obtained. Crime laboratory personnel processed the victims personal property.

When the victim was found, her head, neck and a small portion of her upper torso were in a highly decomposed state, as though this portion of her body had been exposed to extreme heat. The lower portion of her body, however, was very well preserved, as though her body had been placed in a cool northern trout stream until just before she was found.

Jean was identified by Dr. Samuel Kolp, D.D.S., after making a comparison of Jean's dental records obtained from Dr. Evans, who was Jean's personal dentist.

She was also identified from an Avon cream lotion bottle found in her room. Jean's right middle finger matched the print found on the bottle of lotion from Jean's dresser in her apartment.

WITNESSES INTERVIEWED

Acting on a tip alleging that two Eastern Michigan University Students had seen John and Jean together, investigators located and interviewed the students in mid-August 1968.

One of these students, Elliot, told investigators initially that he did not want to get John Collins in any trouble. He said he had talked with Collins about being with Jean the night of June 30, 1968, and John had told him he did not even know that particular girl. Elliot was vague about the time too, which he thought was around 9:30 p.m. when he saw Jean with a young man who he initially thought was Collins. He left investigators with the impression that he probably had erred in his identification of Collins as the young man with whom Jean was crossing the street. (48.42)

Daphne, Elliot's girlfriend, was also interviewed. She said she also was unsure about the time when she last saw Jean. She put the time between 11:15 p.m. and 11:30 p.m. on the evening of June 30, 1968, as they were enroute to pick up Deidre. (48.43)

A year later, after John was arrested and charged on another murder, Daphne told another investigator that about two days after Jean's body was found she and Elliot discussed seeing Jean and John together the night Jean had disappeared. Daphne said Elliot told her he did not want to tell the police that he had seen them together because he knew Collins was stealing motorcycles, and he didn't want to get a fraternity brother in trouble.

A year later, again after John Collins' arrest, a different detective reinterviewed Elliot. Elliot was then a commissioned officer in the United States Army stationed at Fort Knox, Kentucky. Elliot said that on the night of June 30, 1968, he had seen John and Jean walking across College Place on the south side of Emmet Street. The time was between 11:30 p.m. and 12:00 midnight. They were enroute to pick up Deidre at the Casa-Nova Restaurant in Ypsilanti. Elliot was definite on his identification of both persons, and he indicated that there was no possibility that he was making an error in identifying either person.

Elliot said he talked with John after Jean's body was found. John denied knowing Jean and said he had been home in Warren, Michigan, (sic) that particular weekend. (49.)

Jewel of Ypsilanti, Michigan, was also interviewed by detectives. Jewel worked in the Alumni Office with Collins during the time period when Jean disappeared and after her body was found. She said John talked incessantly about how Jean's body was found and how badly it had been cut up. John said he had learned about Jean's condition from his uncle who was a corporal in the Michigan State Police assigned to the Ypsilanti Post. This was very disturbing to her! She contacted a doctor who prescribed tranquilizers for her. She reported Collins' actions to her supervisor, who in turn, called the Eastern Michigan University Police.

She related the above information to the same investigators who interviewed Elliot and Daphne. She said she was interviewed during the last part of July or the first part of August 1968. She said, "Later the investigators came to the office looking for John, but he was not there."

Then, after John had been interviewed by the investigators, but before the people at the office were aware of it, she heard someone in the office tell John that the police were there looking for him. John told them that was probably because the night Jean disappeared he had a date with her, but did not keep it. (45.24)

Sally, the wife of the state police corporal was also interviewed by detectives. She stated on July 6, 1968, the day after Jean's body was found, she had made a telephone call to her nephew, John. She asked him if he was acquainted with or knew Jean. John told her he did not know Jean.(43.71)

The state police corporal was interviewed. The author asked him about conversations he had with his nephew regarding the murder of Jean. He indicated that one evening John was at his home in Ypsilanti for dinner, and John asked him if he knew anything about Jean's murder. The corporal told him the only thing he knew about it was what he had read in the papers. This was the truth because the Michigan State Police was not actively involved in the investigation of her death at that time. (43.69)

Arnie, John's friend, who had a room in the same house as John, was interviewed by the author. He stated that on the night of June 30, 1968, he was with John and another man when Jean got into their car by the Student Union Building.

They returned to their apartment on Emmet Street. John said he would take Jean to Ann Arbor in his car, an old gray DeSota. John was gone about two and a half hours. When he returned, he appeared angry. Arnie asked John if he "got any." John told him, "No, just a little tit." He then asked John why it had taken him so long. John indicated that he had tried, in substance, to seduce her, but she had run away. He had caught her and had tried to put her back in the car, but she had gotten away from him again. Arnie said John had Jean's red purse which he said she had left in the car. John leafed through her wallet and had told Arnie, "The bitch lied to me and told me she was married."

Arnie said John had asked him not to mention anything to the police about picking this girl up. Arnie said John had given him a hunting knife on July 29, 1969, and told him to hide it so the police couldn't find it. Subsequent to Collins' arrest, Arnie gave the knife to the police who had the forensic pathologists examine it. Dr. Hendrix said it could have been the weapon that caused the victim's fatal wounds.

Arnie said he knew that the girl whom they had picked up at the bus stop was Jean. His identification was based upon pictures that he had observed of her. He was shown a photo array by detectives of several girls. Arnie easily picked out the victim. (16.)

Witness Duke, the United States Marine, was interviewed by detectives on November 10, 1969. He said the night of June 30, 1968, was the last night of his leave before he had to return to the Marine Base at Camp Pendleton, California. He was with

Elliot and Daphne in Daphne's apartment in Ypsilanti. He was dating Deidre, who was working at the Casa-Nova Restaurant. They waited for her call so they could go get her, as she did not have any transportation. At about 11:30 p.m., they received the telephone call from Deidre to come and get her. The three of them set out together to pick up Deidre so they could go on their double date. Duke was driving.

He recalled Elliot and Daphne seeing and waving at a couple they knew who were walking across the street at the intersection of College Place and Emmet Street. Duke had to reduce his speed so they could cross in front of the car (in the headlights). Duke remembered that the girl had long brown hair. These were the only people Duke observed on the street. Since that time, from the night of June 30, 1968 until November 10, 1969, he had not discussed this with either Elliot or Daphne. (45.37A)

SUSPECT

John Collins became a suspect in Jean's murder after the tip was received by the police that Collins was talking about how badly the victim had been cut up with female co-workers in such graphic detail that it caused one of them to seek medical help. In addition another tip was received which indicated that it was rumored that two university students had seen Collins and Jean together the night she vanished.

Collins was interrogated by two investigators. John told them that he was not even in Ypsilanti that weekend. "You can check with my mother on that because I spent the entire weekend at my mother's home in Centerline," he said. "I did not return to Ypsilanti until well after midnight— Monday morning." Also, they could check with his friend who lived across the hall from him. He stopped in and they talked for awhile after he returned from Centerline. As they were leaving, John said to them, "I sure hope you catch that guy!" One of the investigators thought that was rather a strange remark, especially in the light of the case facts which indicated that Jean had gotten into a car with three young men. Why didn't Collins say, "I sure hope you catch THOSE GUYS?" (48.43-44)

The investigators checked with John's uncle by marriage who was a command officer in the Michigan State Police. John was held in very high regard by him. In fact he had attempted to get him to enlist in the state police, but John told his uncle that he was interested in becoming a teacher.

Several other police officers knew Collins. John would from time to time visit with other officers at the special, large round table at the Bomber Restaurant in Ypsilanti. He was well liked by all the other officers. In addition, John would go motorcycle riding with one of the sergeants from the Eastern Michigan University Police Department. John was an expert motorcycle rider.

Probably due to John Collins' demeanor, his clean cut appearance, the high degree of trust and respect the police, who were acquainted with him, had for him, and the convincing manner in which he talked, all resulted in Collins all but being totally eliminated as a suspect in Jean's murder. It would be over a year later and six more women would die—five in Michigan and one in California—before he would become a suspect again.

METHOD OF OPERATION

The perpetrator was with two other friends when they observed a young woman who was not able to obtain a bus to her destination for a meeting with her fiance. The perpetrator told her that the others were not going to Ann Arbor (the victim's destination), but he was. The victim got into the car and they returned to the area where both the perpetrator and victim lived—less than five minutes away from the bus stop.

They got into the perpetrator's car. It appeared that he then took the victim to a remote area—probably within sixty miles of the Ann Arbor-Ypsilanti area where he raped her. He probably told her he was going to kill her. He was motivated to do this out of self preservation. She tried to flee. He chased after her with his knife and stabbed her in the back. As she fell down, he ran past her. He then stopped, turned around, and stabbed her behind the left ear driving the knife deep into her brain and skull as she was lying face down on the ground. His knees would have been near her shoulders. He then rolled her over and stabbed her repeatedly in the chest to make sure she was dead.

He then hid the body in a small stream until the night of July 4, 1968, when he became upset that the police had not recovered Jean's body. This disappointed him because there was no publicity, and he was not getting credit for what he had done. He then thought he would keep his word and take her body into Ann Arbor. During the early morning hours of Friday, July 5, 1968, probably shortly before day break, John transported Jean's body into Ann Arbor and put it a short distance from Glacier Way. He left her lying on her back and pulled a few clumps grass and placed them on her remains in a feeble effort to cover her body.

There is another possible scenario which could have occurred the night of Jean's murder that has never been made public. It was entirely possible that Collins may have indeed had a helper whose name remains unknown to this very day. The reader should remember that the thinking of criminologists at the time when these murders were being committed was that this type of crime was committed by one person.

It is entirely possible that Collins took Jean in his car to the K-Mart Parking Lot which, at that time, was about midway between Ann Arbor and Ypsilanti. Shortly after they arrived, Davis and the third man arrived on the scene in the third man's car. Collins and the third man then dragged the screaming girl from the car to an area in back of the garage where they raped her. She then tried to escape and was

Marjorie was not a disciplinary problem for school authorities, but according to confidential police sources, she was selling dope in school to support her own habit. She acknowledged that she had a drug problem four months before she was murdered.

Like Jean S., this victim also was very much interested in horses. As a girl, she enjoyed being around horses. She worked cleaning out stables so she could ride them. She worked also as a babysitter, and saved her money to buy a horse, which she eventually acquired. Of course, when she became involved in drugs and began associating with that sub-culture quite some distance from her home, she asked her father to sell her horse because she no longer could take care of it.

Marjorie was an excellent babysitter. All the people for whom she worked thought very highly of her until she became involved with drugs. Then her pot smoking, acid dropping, hippy friends began showing up at the places where she worked. In one case, a mother came home unexpectedly and found the word, "fuck" written with a frost spray on the bathroom window. (43.31)

Several times Marjorie told her employer, for whom she babysat and did house-work, that she was going to the party store to get a package of cigarettes. This store was only a few minutes walk from the house where she was working. Instead she went to Pete's Truck Stop located at that same intersection.

This truck stop was reputed to be a "hang out" for marijuana and other drug users. Marjorie would secretly meet her fiance, Morgan, there. They would often times spend an hour or more together. Morgan would hitchhike to get there to meet her. He said that marijuana was not being used there anymore than at several other places he frequented. Morgan also said he used to come to the house where Marjorie was working when her employer was away. Morgan said he gave Marjorie an engagement ring on February 26, 1969. He also said that they had an intimate relationship. (43.31-32,34)

Marjorie's sister, Brenda, said she saw their application for a marriage license. She said not once did Marjorie ever say that she was in love with Morgan. It was her opinion, that she did not love him. If they married it would just have been a means whereby she would get away from all parental control over her. (43.33-39)

The detective who had previously investigated Marjorie's drug selling activities, and who had worked with Marjorie in an effort to get Marjorie to come to the realization that she was wasting the gift of her high intelligence, and who who had tried to get her life back on the right track, stated that Marjorie's parents were opposed to the association that she had with Morgan. (43.35,41)

The victim's home was neat and clean. It was located in a rural area of the southwest corner of the village of Romulus. The house that they were moving to in Flint was the same, as far as cleanliness was concerned. The furniture in the home was inexpensive. The victim's parents were not wealthy people.

The mother of the victim was a very religious person. The father had a problem with alcohol. Mrs. Samson told the author that she was the disciplinarian of the family. She said if someone needed to be punished, she would do it. She did not believe in Marjorie doing any housework in their home. She said she would have enough of that to do when she got married and had her own family. (43.43)

The victim told others that her father beat her. Neighbors said this was not true. It was the opinion of at least one neighbor that the victim told others this to gain sympathy because it certainly was not true. Marjorie was given a considerable amount of personal freedom, probably more than her judgement permitted her to handle. The parents did argue with one another. Mr. S., the victim's father, was drunk much of the time, but did not strike the victim. (43.34)

The victim's sister, Mrs. Brenda S., said her father would often come home drunk. He would become angry and throw things, but he never hit his wife or his daughters. Mrs. Brenda S. said her father was a good provider. They never went hungry. He also gave them a generous weekly allowance which the girls spent horseback riding.(43.33-39)

Morgan M., the victim's fiance, did not like the victim's father or mother. He called the father, "a mean ornery, drunk." And he thought the mother was two-faced. He didn't like it when she called Marjorie and Morgan "drug addicts." (43.34)

In October of 1968, the victim joined the radical Students for a Democratic Society. Marjorie had told her parents that this organization was going to help the country. In reality some of the members of the SDS advocated creating internal strife within the United States. They also printed manuals telling people how to manufacture explosive bombs from common household materials. From the police perspective, it appeared that some people within the SDS were preparing to launch a guerilla warfare attack against the United States.

The victim, if she believed in God, kept these beliefs pretty much to herself. Her girlfriend, Sheila, said she never knew her to attend church. Her fiance said they never talked about religion. The Reverend L. England gave the eulogy at the victim's funeral. She was buried at the Tyler Road Cemetery, located near the intersection of Hannan and Tyler Roads in Wayne County, Michigan.

METHOD OF OPERATION

It is believed the victim did try to hitchhike to her fiance's apartment, possibly from the area of the McKinney Student Union Building in Ypsilanti. She was picked up and taken to the area where she was raped, beaten, murdered, and robbed of her engagement ring and purse. The latter was probably left in the car at the time of the attack.

The murderer then returned to Ypsilanti via the back roads. At a public fishing site just north of Ypsilanti, he searched the victim's purse and wallet and stole all the

44

money he found. He then put some rocks in the victim's purse and threw the purse containing her wallet into the Huron River.

VEHICLE INVOLVED

According to the Ann Arbor police the victim was observed getting into a blue Ford panel truck with flowers painted on the side. Later, the Ann Arbor police advised other officers working on the murder that their sources advised them that the panel was then painted black with both an American eagle and an American flag on the sides. Their information was that this vehicle was being used by "hippies" involved in the drug culture.

CRIMINAL INVESTIGATION

The standard investigative techniques were followed in this case. There were the usual measurements and photographs taken. A stick, several inches in diameter, was found that had an eye lash on it which was similar to the victim's eye lashes in every respect.

The autopsy performed on the victim revealed that the cause of death was due to the severe blows the victim received to both the right and left sides of her head. She had been hit once very, very hard in the area of the right eye and once in the area of the the left temple. She had also been hit on her torso and leg at least eleven times with a belt and buckle. There was an abrasion under her chin in the throat area. There were lacerations inside the victim's mouth. A blue cloth, apparently the victim's blouse, was shoved into her mouth. The blouse forced the tongue up and back against the throat area.

The autopsy also indicated that Marjorie was still alive when a stick was shoved into her vagina about five inches. On the victim's arms were "tracks", needle marks, from her drug use. There was also a laceration on the left nipple of Marjorie's breast. It was believed this was made after death.

Dr. Robert Hendrix, Forensic Pathologist, was unable to provide a time of death other than stating that the victim could have been alive on Sunday, March 23, 1969. He believed that the victim was murdered at the location where she was found, but that she was injured, and perhaps unconscious when she was brought there. (38.)

The United States Weather Bureau at the Detroit Metropolitan Airport was contacted. Personnel there advised that it had rained nearly an inch on March 24, 1969, and nearly two tenths of an inch during the morning before Marjorie's body was discovered. (43.40-41)

An extensive search was made for a van type vehicle which allegedly the victim was observed getting into, but with no results.

Several suspects were given polygraph examinations and were cleared of any involvement in the victim's death.

A detailed biographical investigation was conducted on the life of the victim. This included investigation into any area wherein there might be a possible correlation with the other murder cases. It involved the following areas:

A GENERAL HISTORY: This was simply a brief overview of the main points of the victim's life.

THE EDUCATIONAL RECORD: This included information on where the victim attended school, the activities in which she was involved, whether she had won scholarships, what her intelligence level was, what awards she had won, who were her favorite teachers and her discipline problems, if she had any. To determine this her teachers, the principal, and the classmates in her hometown were interviewed.

Her *EMPLOYMENT RECORD* was examined to determine with whom she worked, and to answer the following questions, "How well did she get along with her fellow employees?" "Did she have any enemies?" "Were there people at work—not employees—she came into contact with who may have attacked her?"

Her *HEALTH RECORD*: A complete medical history of the victim was obtained. This involved a complete investigation from whom the doctor was at her birth, where she was born, up to and including the time of her death.

The *LOVE LIFE* of the victim was closely examined. A complete check was made of all persons the victim dated both past and present. The investigator was looking for someone who had been rejected by the victim, and who may have thought so much of her that he adopted the belief, "If I can't have her no one else will." The investigator was also looking for someone who may have dated more than one of the previous victims, or was acquainted with more than one of them.

What the victim liked to do for *RECREATION* was also investigated thoroughly. Here the investigator was looking for where the victim was spending her recreational time. He was looking for some location, some activity in which more than one victim was involved.

The *HOME CONDITIONS* of the victim were checked as well as those of her neighbors. This was done again to provide the investigator with a "feeling" for the victim which would help him have a better grasp of the case, to learn of any possible suspects, and to correct any erroneous information.

The *ARREST RECORD* was checked on the victim. It was done to determine if there may have been some enemies from a previous arrest, or some enemy while in custody that may have caused the death of the victim.

The victim's *CREDIT RECORD* was examined. This was checked to determine who served her. The investigator was looking for some shop or store where more than one victim shopped.

Other areas which were investigated very thoroughly were: the *CLOTHING WORN AT THE TIME OF THE MURDER*, the *VICTIM'S HABITS*, where she went to *CHURCH*, where the victim had her *HAIR* done, *CLUBS* or *ORGANIZATIONS* of which she was a member, where she did her *GROCERY SHOPPING*, which *LIBRARIES* did she use, her *ART INTERESTS*, her *MENSTRUAL PERIOD*, where she did her *LAUNDRY*, where she took her *DRY CLEANING*, where were her SHOE REPAIRS done, and who were ALL HER KNOWN ASSOCIATES. The investigating officer then included his *COMMENTS* concerning the victim. (43.29-46)

EVIDENCE

Good photographs were obtained indicating the size and shape of the belt buckle used to whip the victim.

OBSERVATIONS

At the time this murder victim was found, it had rained the previous two days and thus helped the murderer by again washing away possible trace evidence.

Once again we have an example of important witnesses lying to the police. In this case, the victim herself told her friend "her parents" brought her to the Ann Arbor-Ypsilanti area. The parents told investigators they had brought her there also.

Later the parents told this writer that they had lied about that because Marjorie was on a form of juvenile probation in Wayne County. One of the conditions was regarding association with others involving drug use in that area. They were concerned if they told the police the victim's brother brought her down from Flint that he would be arrested. Subsequent to this her brother admitted he transported her there.

It's remarkable that in both the case of Jean S. and Marjorie important witnesses who were supposedly their friends and were the last to have seen them alive, lied to the police. *This points to the need not to accept at face value what these witnesses are saying until one probes whether there could be some possible reason why information is being altered.*

Note in both instances just mentioned, the giving of false information to the police was due to the witness' fear of the police. With Jean S. her boyfriend was a deserter, and the witness was afraid he would be arrested. In Marjorie's case, the parents thought their son would be arrested.

Another problem encountered in this case was that Marjorie herself had acquired the reputation as a "con lady". People just didn't know when she was telling the truth. Closely related to this were the people with whom she was associating.

The girl was deeply involved in the drug culture. She had used many different types of drugs including heroin. Her associates regarded the police trying to arrest her murderer as their enemy. When they did cooperate, it was most reluctantly. Nearly all information had to be extracted slowly through long interviews. Then some of the information received had to be viewed with considerable skepticism.

For example, some of the victim's friends were deeply involved in the occult. They held seances using an Ouija Board. Her friend, Sheila, said she had been told that Marjorie did not know her killer personally. Sheila said she had not been able to talk with her friend directly, but she was supposed to come to them at her grave site.

Note also that in this case the victim's sanitary napkin was lying near her body. The fact that most of the murdered women were having their periods became significant in the light of statements made by John Collins—and his apparent attitude towards a woman during her period. Arnie said John Collins could smell when a woman was having her monthly period. (16.) One woman Collins went with said he asked her if she was having her period. When she told him that she was—he replied, "Disgusting". In his warped

48

world of fantasy, he apparently did not believe any woman should date a boy unless she was capable of delivering the only thing he thought any woman was good for—that was to sexually gratify a man.

The evidence has strongly suggested that John Norman Collins was involved in the murder of Jean S., Anne K., Rose P., of Salinas, California, and Karry B. In the latter case, he was convicted of first degree murder. This case will be discussed below. In the case of Rose P., Collins was indicted by a California Grand Jury, but was never extradited for several reasons. One of which was that following his conviction in Michigan he began a lengthy appeal process which required nearly a decade to complete. The authorities in California were uncertain what the impact of these appeals would be upon the proceedings.

The police thought that in the Karry, Anne, Rose, and Jean S. cases, the victims were probably walking and were either picked up by John Collins in a car or on a motorcycle. In all cases the victims were asked if they wanted a ride. The police knew that Marjorie was not afraid to accept a ride with a stranger and that she did use hitchhiking as a common mode of transportation.

Karry B. and Jean S. were also both having their monthly periods when they were murdered. Marjorie was also having her period. Jean S., June M. and Anne K. all had been left lying on their back. Both had two stab wounds to the left breast. The nipple of Marjorie's left breast had been cut after death.

Karry B.'s body was nude except for her sandals, she had brain damage from being hit or kicked, and it appeared an electrical cord had been wrapped around the <u>back</u> of her neck. Marjorie was found nude, she had brain damage and she had abrasions on her neck. Further, both women had objects shoved into the vaginal vault. Karry B. had her panties shoved there and Marjorie, a stick. Also both women, Karry B. and Marjorie had an object of their clothing shoved into their mouth as a gag. Karry B. had part of her gold shorts shoved into her mouth and Marjorie had her blouse put into her mouth.

Therefore, due to similarities between the murders where the evidence strongly suggests that they were committed by John Norman Collins and the murder of Marjorie—it appears quite probable that he killed her too.

CHAPTER VIII

BRIEF HISTORY OF THE MURDER OF DORA B.
(AKA Dale Harum in Michigan Murders)

On April 15, 1967, the victim had gone to a section of the city of Ypsilanti known as "Depot Town". She was infatuated with a boy named Emil K. She regarded him as her boyfriend. Emil, on the other hand, was five years older than Dora. He considered her a friend and a very nice girl. He said he never even tried to kiss her, let alone have sexual intercourse with her.

Near sunset, Emil and Dora walked together to the railroad tracks, after visiting one another in "Depot Town". He left her at the Michigan Ladder Company Factory after they both paused for a short time and waited for a train to pass. He then walked east toward his home along the railroad tracks, while she walked toward the west. (43.56)

Dora saw two friends by the Huron River and asked them what they were doing. They told her they were just fishing and throwing rocks into the water. She talked with them about fifteen minutes. It was starting to get dark. She asked them if they wanted to walk her home. They told her, "No, we live in the other direction. " The boys said she did not act like she was "scared". Dora then left them. She walked along the railroad tracks towards her home about two miles away. According to Raymond P., "It was getting a little dark. " (43.54-55)

Trevor F., a thirty-one year old railroad buff, identified Dora from photographs of her and her sweater that were later shown to him. Thomas was standing on a path about nine yards north of the tracks. This path ran from the tracks to Railroad Street which, at that point, ran parallel with the railroad tracks. He said, "Dora ran down the tracks (toward me) until she came to the path . Then she began walking fast by me. She was all out of breath. "He then watched her walk down the road towards her home. He last observed the victim about five hundred feet west of where he stood on the path. She was walking rapidly along Railroad Street. She was near the Riverside Building which was used to store school buses.

On the other side of the tracks, on Huron Street, which runs parallel with the tracks, but on the south side, he observed an old blue car . He didn't know the make or model. This car was being driven very slowly in a westerly direction. At this point, the cook of the Penn Central Passenger train threw a menu to him from the train. This distracted him from making any further observations concerning the victim. (43.57-58)

Shortly after this incident, Mr. Luke S., seventy-five years old, said he had seen the victim walking very fast toward her home. He knew the victim from having seen her playing with the daughter of his neighbor on previous occasions. He did not see anyone following her, nor did he see anyone else walking in the area or anything unusual.

At 7:30 p.m. that evening, Mrs Anita, thirty-one years old, left her home located on Railroad Street at the intersection of LaForge Road. It would have been at this point that Dora would have turned and headed north on LaForge Road. This was about a block south of where Dora lived. Mrs. Anita was going to her neighbor's house to use their telephone to order a pizza to be delivered. Anita was sure of the time because a television show she liked to watch was just being aired.

As she walked in an easterly direction, she observed two cars parked in front of a vacant house. She saw no one outside the cars. The first car was a maroon or red 1963 Chevrolet. She did not notice the license plates. She said she observed a girl sitting in the car close to the driver. The girl had shoulder length hair. She was wearing a light colored or white blouse. The driver of the car had dark hair. She could see that it was cut square in back. "It was not real long," she said.

She noted the Chevrolet was damaged high on the trunk, as though something had been dropped on it. The car had three tail lights on each side of it. The car was parked headed in a westerly direction. The door on the driver's side was open.

The second vehicle she saw was also parked. It had the headlights on and the door on the driver's side was also open. She described this vehicle as an old dull looking, dark blue, beetle type, Volkswagon. She said she could see two young men in the car. She believed them to be twenty-three to twenty-five years of age. She was afraid to walk by the two vehicles, and so she hid behind a mulberry tree about thirty feet west of her neighbor's house and watched them for what seemed to her was seven or eight minutes. She watched the Chevrolet drive away first. It was driven toward the west. Then the young men in the Volkswagon left in an easterly direction. In about three or four minutes, at the most, the Volkswagon drove by her again and headed west. Shortly after that the Chevrolet came by her.

She said the longest time the two vehicles could have been parked was between ten and twelve minutes because she had made the call and was back home when the pizza was delivered at about 8:00 p.m. At no time did she see the victim and she knew her well. (43.59-60)

Raymond P., Dora's classmate, also observed a Volkswagon crossing the tracks headed north. He said the car, as he recalled it, was light blue in color. He also recalled that it had damage to the right rear. He was standing about eight hundred feet away from the crossing to the east. He said the car got part way across the tracks and then stopped. There were two sets of tracks at the crossing. He did not know, however, why the car stopped. He did not observe anyone either get into or out of the automobile. (43.57-58)

Dora was very much aware of the possibility of being attacked. There was a large apartment complex across from her home. Her mother told her within earshot of others not to walk alone along the road after dark. One of her friends said it was almost as though her mother had a premonition of what was going to happen. (43.57-58)

Dora's close friends from school and their parents all said that it was highly improbable that she would get into a car with a stranger. One of her closest classmates thought she would not even get into a car if there was a woman in the car, unless she knew the lady.

Everyone thought she was so strong that one man could not possibly force her into a car alone. Her classmates and their parents, her brother and mother all believed this, and, therefore, unless some form of trickery or weapon was used, they thought more than one person was involved in this attack.

Anita's husband indicated he felt very confident that if Dora was being chased and made it as far as Railroad Street and LaForge Road, she would have run into their house for refuge.

He also said that several times he had offered Dora a ride when he saw her walking. She always thanked him and told him she'd rather walk.

He also said that the victim was very close to her brother and usually he would usually be walking with her. It was extremely rare for her to walk along the streets at dusk or after dark by herself. (43.56)

Shortly after 10:00 p.m. on April 15th, when Dora did not arrive home, her mother became concerned about her welfare. She began calling Dora's girl friends to try to determine whether she was with them. After meeting with no success in locating her daughter, at 12:46 a.m. on April 16, 1969, Mrs. Carl B. called the Ypsilanti City Police Department and reported her daughter missing. (3.)

After day break, the body of Dora B. was found by Mr. Ernest P. She was lying on her back along the east side of Gale Road between Vreeland and Cherry Hill Roads in section 19 of Superior Township in Washtenaw County.

Her legs were spread wide apart with her toes toward Gale Road. Her genital area was grossly exposed. Her blouse had been ripped apart and part of it was stuck into her mouth as a gag. Her face was a reddish-blue color caused by a heavy electrical wire which had obviously been used to strangle her. At any rate it appeared to this writer that she had been left in the very position where she had died. Rigor mortis then set in, and the victim was in full rigor when the perpetrator(s) moved the body to Gale Road.

There also appeared on the victim's left breast, two or three deep scrape marks. The characteristics of these marks were such that they had the appearance of being made with a beer can opener. These appeared to have been made post mortem. There was no blood. Most investigators thought this was done by the perpetrator(s) to insure that the victim was dead before he transported her away from the scene of the murder.

The victim's shoes were also found laying along Gale Road. One was along the fence row on the opposite side of the road about fifty feet south of the body. The other was along the east side of the road near Geddes Road, sixth tenths of a mile south of the body. There was some speculation that the perpetrator(s) had thrown the shoe found on the west side of the road first before he disposed of the body, then turned the car around in the middle of the gravel road and threw the other shoe out before he reached Geddes Road.

Some investigators thought that there may have been two or more men involved in this murder. They recalled that the victim Jean S. had gotten into a car with three men.

Also supporting the proposition that there was more than one perpetrator was the fact that the perpetrator used heavy wire found at the scene of the murder. It seemed very unlikely that this very powerful little girl would have sat passively quiet, like a lamb being led to the slaughter, while her murderer hunted around a dark house with a flashlight for a piece of wire to strangle her. There were no indications that she had been bound with a rope or anything else. In addition, these officers argued that if the perpetrator had a rope to bind her, why didn't he also use it to strangle her.

There was the possibility that an accomplice had thrown the first shoe out. It was found near Geddes Road. Then the driver threw out her second shoe before the body was removed from the vehicle. They stopped, removed the body, which was now in full rigor, to the side of the road and drove south in the heavy dense fog that was probably in existence when the victim's body was being transported.

Shortly before 11:00 a.m., on April 16, 1969, a deputy sheriff found Dora's orange mohair sweater behind an old deserted farm house at 1888 LaForge Road, north of Ypsilanti. This was less than a mile north of the victim's house. Officers also discovered the location from where the wire had been cut. It was subsequently used to strangle the victim. It had been taken from the barn. Human blood was found in the basement. Also on the steps leading to the basement were fine fragments of glass. These fragments matched the fragments found in the soles of the victim's shoes. This meant she probably was forced down into the cold dark basement. Dora was murdered either in the basement or in the barn. (58.)

VICTIM

The victim of this murder was Dora B. She was born at Beyer Memorial Hospital in Ypsilanti, Michigan, on November 28, 1955. Dr. Paul Wick, M.D. was the doctor in attendance. She was the fourth child born to her parents. She was born two and a half

53

months prematurely. She was the youngest child in her family. She had two older sisters, both of whom were married, and a brother who was a year older than she.

She had blue eyes and light brown hair which had been dyed reddish blond two days before she was killed. She was five feet two inches tall and she weighed one hundred and twenty pounds. She was very strong and could press more weight than her brother. She could press seventy pounds.

She was very well developed physically. While her facial features were those of a thirteen-year-old girl, her body made her appear four or five years older.

The victim associated with a peer group of other youngsters who were from the lower socio-economic strata. Many of them were offspring of parents who came north from the mountainous regions of Kentucky and West Virginia during the Second World War to work at the Willow Run Plant near Ypsilanti, Michigan, which manufactured hundreds of bombers.

The victim had an intense dislike for black people. Probably some of this hatred resulted from her peer group, but much of it did not. Several of her friends related that blacks frequently tried to have sexual intercourse with her, but none succeeded. Black males frequently assaulted her by walking up behind her and patting her buttocks. On one occasion she grabbed a black boy by his head and was kicking him in the legs when a teacher stopped the fight.

In another instance, a black girl accused her of talking about her. Dora, who was sitting in her own seat, denied this. The girl then attacked Dora with her fists while calling her a "white honkey." Dora rose from her seat and then fought with the girl until the girl did not want to fight anymore. Both girls were suspended for this.

Dora was not a trouble maker in the school, but quite capable of defending herself.

Dora's school work was above average, but she was not working up to her capabilities. She had an I.Q. of 133. One of her teachers thought she might have had a hearing problem. The teacher would ask her a question when Dora was looking right at her, but Dora wouldn't answer. It could have been that she was daydreaming.

Dora was interested in art and had applied to an art school for information. She enjoyed drawing pictures of horses.

She was very active physically. She enjoyed riding horses, playing baseball, kickball, football, boxing and wrestling. She prided herself on her ability to do everything that boys who were her age could do. Some of her friends' parents described her as a "tomboy." (43.59-60) Dora also enjoyed reading books, particularly about horses, going bowling, doing modern dances, and going rollerskating.

Like most girls her age, sometimes she had pajama parties at her house. She and her girl friends would stay up all night talking and listening to records.

The victim had very high moral standards. Her mother granted her a large measure of freedom, but this wasn't abused. She did not use drugs of any kind. The only time anyone ever heard her swear was when she became extremely angry with her brother. She would then call him a "shithead." She was a Protestant. She considered herself a Methodist. She also attended both the Baptist and Jehovah Witness Churches on occasion. She did not attend church on a regular basis. (3.0)

The victim's father died of cancer when she was seven years old. Her mother was having an affair with a friend of her deceased husband. This caused considerable embarrassment to the victim. She thought it was wrong for her mother to sleep with a man when she was not married to him, and in fact, he was married to someone else. She cried when discussing this with a neighbor. She would not, however, bring this up to her mother because she did not wish to hurt her mother's feelings. (43.59)

METHOD OF OPERATION

The method of operation used by the killer(s) is not known. What is known is that the victim was picked up on Railroad Street at dusk, probably around 8:00 p.m.

It is extremely unlikely that she would have gotten into a car with a stranger. She may, however, have gotten on a motorcycle because she may not have been as fearful of that as if she were asked to get into a car.

It is also conceivable that the occupants of the two vehicles described above played a role in her abduction, rape, and murder.

It is known that the victim walked down the basement steps at the deserted farm house about a mile north of her home.

It is known that the victim was murdered at that location.

The victim was then quite probably left there for about six or seven hours. Most likely until about 3:00 a.m. At that time the United States Weather Bureau reported the visibility in that area was one sixteenth of a mile, but about 4:30 a.m., the fog started to lift. When the sun rose at 5:52 a.m., the visibility was one and a half miles.

They also advised that the sun had set the previous evening at 7:14 p.m. and the sky was overcast. The temperature on the fifteenth was fifty-nine degrees F, at midnight and dropped to fifty-three degrees at 3:00 a.m.

Then the perpetrator moved the victim from the old farm house to Gale Road where she was later found.

VEHICLES

The suspected vehicles have been described above. The first vehicle was a red or maroon Chevrolet with damage to the trunk. It had three tail lights on each side.

The other vehicle was an old Volkswagon Beetle. It had a very dull finish and had damage to the right rear.

CRIMINAL INVESTIGATION

The standard investigative procedures were followed in this case. The soles of the shoes of the victim were examined. The glass which was found in her soles matched the glass on the steps leading to the basement of the old farm house.

The old farm house was checked for latent prints. Human blood was found down in the basement.

Even while crime laboratory scientists were working at the scene where the victim was found, investigators had taken it upon themselves to begin a search of all abandoned or unoccupied farm sites in the area. It was a completely uncoordinated search.

The cause of death was by strangulation according to Forensic Pathologist Robert Hendrix. He could not provide any indication as to the time of death. Her body temperature was, "way down at the time she was found, and she did not eat supper." (43.54)

The victim was not having a period at the time she was murdered. The smear from the vaginal vault indicated the presence of acid phosphate which would tend to indicate the presence of seminal fluid, but no spermatozoa were found. (58.)

OBSERVATIONS

While this case was technically under the supervision of the Washtenaw County Sheriff's Department, many officers from other departments were involved in the case and worked on it as if it were being handled by their own agencies.

While the crime laboratory personnel were still working the crime scene where the body was found, other investigators and the assistant prosecutor were searching old unoccupied farm houses. This work, in fact, had begun even before laboratory personnel had arrived. It was, however, totally uncoordinated and therefore the most effective use of police personnel was not utilized. Search efforts such as this should be coordinated to prevent needless duplication of effort and to insure the area has been thoroughly covered.

The crime scenes, both where the victim was found and where she had been murdered, had magnificent security to prevent civilians from contaminating them. Unfortunately, the police themselves probably did as much harm as an army of reporters could have caused. We were learning to be more careful, however.

Police officers were quite pleased when the scene where the murder had occurred was discovered. In his exuberance, one police officer boasted to the news media that his department would have the murderer in jail before the sun set that night. While it is good for morale to have a positive attitude, such boasts are difficult to keep. When such statements are made it leads people to believe their help is not needed. In most cases it is far better to make a public appeal for their help.

John Norman Collins, who later was arrested and convicted for the murder of Karry Buchholz, had killed her in the basement of his uncle's house. He also had dated a girl who lived in an apartment across the street from Dora.

The police in this case were going to keep the information that the murder scene had been found confidential. It was thought that then—if another girl disappeared the police would immediately establish surveillance on this location in the event the killer would try to take the victim there. But a police officer talked with a reporter, and the material was printed and on the street before it could be stopped. Again this points up the need in serial murder cases for one person to be the designated spokesperson for all agencies involved. Whether the murderer would have used that location again is difficult to determine. We do know however, that two months later another girl was shot and had her throat cut at an abandoned farm.

With this girl, prior to the thorough background investigation on her, there were many rumors and quite a lot of unsubstantiated information which generally painted the picture of this victim as a thirteen-year-old slut who was copulating with half of the boys in town. Nothing could have been further from the truth. The fact was she had the highest moral values of all the murdered girls. What she was, was a very brave, thirteen-year-old, highly intelligent child, who would never start a fight, but would not back away from one if she was attacked.

As will be observed later, the principle suspect in this case used motorcycles extensively. At no time did officers think that the culprit might be using a motorcycle.

At this stage, investigators were thinking in terms of a perpetrator who was a police officer or someone who was posing as one. They also discussed the possibility of the perpetrator posing as a priest or minister, or that he was forcing the victims into the car at gun point. This was especially considered since June M. had been found in the cemetery shot to death.

This points up the need to always keep an open mind and how very hard it really is to consider all the possibilities even when we are aware of the dangers of getting "tunnel vision."

CHAPTER IX

BRIEF HISTORY OF THE MURDER OF ANNE E. K.
(AKA Audrey Sakol in Michigan Murders)

Shortly before 3:19 p.m. on Monday, June 9, 1969, three young men who were working for a landscaping company turned their pickup truck south into a driveway off North Territorial Road where there was an abandoned ninety acre farm. It was about one quarter mile east of U.S. 23 in section 20, Northfield Township, of Washtenaw County. As they traveled south, they came to a fork in the road. They took the right fork going behind an old barn. Then they saw the body of a young white female who had obviously been murdered. She was lying one hundred and eighteen feet south of the paved portion of North Territorial Road.

She was lying on her back. Her right arm was outstretched at a right angle toward her feet. Her left arm was extended straight at about a thirty degree angle from the left side of her body toward her feet. Her head was facing toward her right side. The victim's legs were close together. The left leg of the victim was bare. On her right leg she was wearing panty hose, which were on up to her right knee. They had been cut through the crotch.

The victim's throat was slashed several times. Some of the cuts were very deep and severed the main arteries in her neck. Some other cuts appeared superficial as though a knife was held to her throat while she was raped. In the victim's right temple, there was a bullet wound. There was also a bullet wound near the tip of the right thumb. It appeared that the victim may have been shot in the right hand as she held out her hand to protect herself when it appeared that she was in imminent danger of being shot. She also had two stab wounds in her left breast.

When found, the victim was wearing a purple blouse. This covered her right shoulder but her left shoulder was bare. The blouse was open exposing the breasts. The front of the brassiere had been cut apart, it was still snapped in back. There was also no covering over the lower torso. She had a bright, multicolored coat wrapped around her feet. A scarf was wrapped around the victim's head. It was a bandana type scarf that circled her head, covering her forehead and the back of the head near the neck. She was wearing silver triangular earrings and a hand made silver ring on the ring finger of the left hand. She had contact lenses in her eyes. (46.2-3)

A blood-spattered white skirt covered the victim's legs. Her panties were laying on the ground near her body. A few feet away from her body was a patent leather pump shoe with a very ornate bow on it.

There was also a rhinestone clasp with the monogram "A" pinned to a yellow and white babushka. (48.108)

The general appearance of the victim was that she had lain there during a heavy rainstorm. She looked drenched. It also appeared that the rigor was in the process of leaving her body. There was little blood found at this location, even when laboratory scientists dug down into the earth under her body.

Missing from the scene were two multicolored buttons from the blood soaked rain coat and one of the victim's shoes. There also was no purse or wallet present.

The victim had no identification on her person. The police had no idea who she was, where she lived, worked or went to school, or anything about her.

INVESTIGATION

The scene where the victim was found was investigated by crime laboratory scientists, the county prosecutor and his assistants, and a forensic pathologist. After handling so many serial murders, the police were now very much aware of the mistakes they had previously made in contaminating crime scenes. In this case, there was good protection and security of the crime scene where the victim's body was found.

The autopsy performed on the victim indicated that the primary cause of death was a .22 caliber bullet fired into the brain. There had been two bullets fired into her head, but only one penetrated the skull. The slugs removed from her head were so badly mangled that they were of no value for positive identification purposes. This did not mean that they were totally useless. While there were many guns that the bullets could not have come from, one revolver it could have been fired from was a High Standard revolver. This became meaningful in light of later information.

There was a significant amount of seminal fluid found in the victim's vaginal vault. It was the opinion of the forensic pathologist that the quantity of fluid, which also contained spermatozoa, could not have come from a single act of intercourse. There had to have been several acts of copulation to have caused such an accumulation of seminal fluid. Dr. Robert Hendrix, the forensic pathologist, said "The victim was either dead or in fear of death within about four hours after she had eaten a meal of leafy vegetables." (46.25)

Because there did not appear to be much blood at the scene where the body was found, as in the murder of Dora B., and the buttons on the coat were missing once again officers launched a massive search for the actual site of the murder.

At about 4:00 p.m. the next day a deputy sheriff observed two loafers side by side on a dirt road leading to the Washtenaw Sand and Gravel Pit on the east side of Earhart Road about one-eighth of a mile south of Joy Road. Upon further investigation, he also found the victim's two buttons from her coat and her scarf with what appeared to be blood on it. He also observed a depression in the ground.

Crime Laboratory scientists were called to the scene. A quarter inch below the surface of the ground the scientists found a large quantity of the victim's blood. A witness who was interviewed told the police that he had observed the loafers on the road at 10:00 a.m. the previous day. The loafers were taken to the morgue and tried on the victim. They fit her. (46.3 & 8)

After a statewide check failed to reveal any report of a missing young woman that matched the victim's description, Investigators appealed to the news media to help get the body identified. A picture was taken of the victim in such a fashion as not to make her appearance offensive to some of the more squeamish members of society. The picture along with her description was published in several newspapers. People were requested to contact the police if they had any knowledge of the identity of the victim.

This paid off when the victim's girl friend and a male student with whom the victim worked closely on photography projects told the police that they thought the victim was Anne K.

The victim's parents were picked up at their home and were transported to Ann Arbor by the Michigan State Police. They identified the remains of their daughter at the morgue in Ann Arbor.

The victim's apartment was secured and thoroughly searched. There were some things that appeared rather unusual. The victim had left both her purse and her wallet, which contained her driver's license, in the apartment. There was a shoe box left out which was not usually done. This apparently was the box from which the purple pumps came. Finally, the victim had been working on some enlargements on a photography project. These were still in the fixing solution in the victim's make shift dark room.

The male classmate who had lent the victim his projector had been at her apartment on Sunday, June 8, 1969, to pick up his enlarger. He was considered a possible suspect. He was given a polygraph examination by the Michigan State Police in Detroit, and he passed it.

A girl friend was interviewed. She said she and Anne had supper together. Anne told her she was going to attend a dance that night at the Depot House. They finished eating around 8:00 p.m. Anne had a large, leafy salad. Her friend took her back to her apartment in Ann Arbor. They arrived there at about 8:30 p.m.

A couple in an apartment in the same building as Anne told the police that at 8:30 p.m. on Saturday evening, as they were leaving the apartment to attend a movie, they passed Anne as Anne was leaving the building. They said Anne was carrying some clothing draped over her arm. They exchanged greetings. This was the last time they saw her alive. (48.115-116)

The United States Weather Bureau at Detroit Metropolitan Airport was contacted for details on the weather conditions that existed in the area on or about the time of the murder. They reported that it began to rain at 8:18 p.m. on Saturday night, June 7, 1969, and continued on through the next day until 5:45 p.m. During this time, there was one short break which occurred at 11:38 p.m. and lasted until midnight.

The weather cleared on Monday, June 9, 1969. It was sunny with a temperature of seventy-two degrees at the time the victim's body was found.

THE VICTIM

Anne K. was born on Christmas day in 1947 at the Elkhart General Hospital in Elkhart, Indiana. Dr. Koehler was the medical doctor in attendance. Anne had two older brothers, one was 13 and the other was 11 years older than she. She was twenty-one years old at the time of her death.

When Anne was a young girl, her parents moved to Bronson, Michigan, where she attended school while her father managed a small hardware store until seven years before the victim's death. At that time, her father moved to the Kalamazoo area, and he worked as a pharmacist in a department store. He had a Master's degree in Pharmacology from the University of Michigan. Her mother also had a Master's Degree in Library Science from the University of Michigan. She worked in a library.

Anne began high school in Bronson at St. Mary's Catholic School. She then transferred to the Portage High School when her parents moved. She graduated from there in 1965. Anne applied for admission to Smith, Wellesley and several other Ivy League Colleges and Universities, but was rejected by all of them in spite of the fact that she had graduated fifteenth of a class of four hundred seventy-nine and had an I.Q. of one hundred and twenty-two, was a member of the National Honor Society, the French Club, and was President of the Social Studies Club. (43.64)

She finally decided to seek admission to the University of Michigan from where her parents had graduated. She secretly was happy that she was going to attend the University of Michigan because a boy named Dave from her high school was also attending there, and she was quite infatuated with him.

Anne began to pursue her academic studies in the fall of 1965. At first, she was going to try to become an English teacher, and English was to be her major subject area. But for reasons which were unclear, perhaps a lack of motivation in that area, she decided to change her major area to art. She decided to become an art teacher. At the time she was murdered, she had more than enough credits to graduate. Only her photography projects remained to be completed so that she could graduate on August 10, 1969. She would have graduated in May, a month before she was murdered, had those projects been completed.

When she met her untimely demise, she was residing with a roommate, Eulalia. The roommate was not present at the apartment much of the time. She was spending most of her free time with her boyfriend who was an engineering student.

Anne had planned an extensive European tour immediately following graduation. She had been accepted for a teaching fellowship at the American University in Cairo, Egypt, but the news of this, unfortunately, came to her parents shortly after her death.

Anne's roommate said she really believed that the victim was not very interested in becoming a teacher. What she truly wanted was to get married, have children and raise a family. Further, she said she was much more interested in social studies than she was in art.

Anne was a white female with brown hair and blue eyes. She wore contact lenses. She was five feet, seven inches tall and she weighed one hundred and thirty-five pounds. She had low metabolism and had difficulty staying awake in class. Her doctor prescribed that she take five milligrams of dexidrene on those days when she attended class.

The victim had a trick knee which was apt to go out on her at anytime. Her parents were surprised to learn, and found it incredible that the night she disappeared she was planning to attend a dance at the Depot House in Ann Arbor. When Anne was in high school, she had to spend six weeks on crutches after she suffered from a dislocation.

She was also not able to participate in either athletics or modern dancing as a result of this problem. (43.63) Other witnesses said the victim did attend dances and she enjoyed modern dances including the twist. (15)

The victim had been taking birth control tablets for over a month before she was murdered. She had an intimate relationship with an Egyptian doctor, with a black male medical student and others. Her neighbors said that many times the black male spent the night in the victim's apartment.

The victim resided in apartment number two at 311 Thompson Street in Ann Arbor. This was a ground floor, four room apartment with a bedroom with bunk beds, a kitchenette, a bathroom and a living room. It was located two blocks from the campus. The victim had been bothered by a window peeker at her apartment.

One night when her roommate was not present, she was in the bedroom when she looked up and saw him. She waited until he was gone then she fled from her apartment, across the street to a male friend's house and spent the night with him. She spent at least two nights at this friend's house on different occasions. Her roommate did not believe they were intimate, and the friend also stated he never had sex with her. (43.64) The Ann Arbor Police Department had no record where the victim had ever made a complaint about the window peeker.

The victim had credit cards or accounts at the following places: She had a Shell Oil credit card. This card had been used on May 29, 1969, when she put gasoline into a friend's car she had borrowed. She had an account at Ulrich's Bookstore in Ann Arbor. She purchased her art and other supplies there for the courses she had been taking. And she also had a credit account at Marilyn's Dress Shop in Ann Arbor. Anne had bought three new dresses at this shop the spring before she was murdered. Since the victim's wallet had been left in her apartment, none of the cards were missing.

At the time Anne was murdered she was wearing a purple long sleeved blouse, a white mini skirt, a coat with red pink, purple, brown and other colored stripes running horizontally around the coat. On the left hand was a band type ring which had been hammered out of metal. On her left ring finger she was wearing a ring with an odd artistic design of wires soldered together. She was wearing a man's gold stick pin with the letter "A" on it in a white head scarf tied around her head. She was wearing white under pants with an orange design of flowers, a black half slip and a brassiere.

The coat that Anne was wearing was bought at Ruby's Clothing Store in Kalamazoo. This was the first and only item used to try to identify her. A check was made at the store to see if anyone there could identify the person to whom the coat had been sold. The salesladies were unable to provide such information.

The fact that the victim had her loafers with her suggested that they were taken for easy walking to and from her destination, while the purple pump shoes, would have been worn once she arrived at her destination. The reader will recall that Anne was wearing one of these pump shoes when her body was found. The most significant point about how the victim was dressed was that she never would have been dressed as she was unless she was intending to attend some special function, such as a dance at the Depot House. (59)

The victim, like June M., also frequented Mark's Coffee House where it was alleged that heavy marijuana use took place. Anne did not use drugs. Even when friends had a "pot" party at her apartment she did not use any.

She generally liked to drink wine, but one night she drank not only wine, but whiskey and beer as well. She became so drunk she vomited and passed out. Another male art student, with whom she frequently worked, brought her to her apartment where her roommate put her to bed. (43.68)

Anne frequently spent a considerable amount of free time at the Student Union Building at the University of Michigan talking with young men. Her roommate said of the Student Union Building, "There are many young black men hanging around the entrance to the Union. These men feel that any girl going there alone, who may stay to read a paper or have an extra cup of coffee, is there to be picked up." She based this opinion on her personal observations of these girls being approached and the comments made to a girl when she entered the Student Union alone. The reader will also recall that this Student Union Building was where June M. put up the note asking for a ride home.

Anne, like June M., attended the same swimming pool on campus. She, like June, had a difficult time controlling her weight. This was also the reason her last meal was a leafy salad.

The victim bought groceries at White's Market on Williams Street just off State Street in Ann Arbor about two blocks from her apartment. She bought wine from a drug store at the corner of State and Packard Streets. From time to time, Tom C., a male friend, would take both her and her roommate to the A & P Store on Stadium Drive to do their shopping.

The victim's roommate said the victim would not talk or ride with everyone, but if she had met a person once before, she would get into a vehicle with them, if she thought he was okay. (43.65,67-68)

The young man that Anne had gone with on photographic projects for the past eighteen months, felt a great deal of affection toward her. He was Jewish and her father was Jewish. They had discussed marriage, but she had told him that she wanted to marry an Egyptian. Yet she offered to let him stay in her apartment when her roommate was not there. She also offered to give him a key. Many times he came to her apartment during the evening hours. On most of these occasions, she was dressed in her nightgown. (15)

Anne underwent psychological counseling for a period of time. She had very little self esteem. She broke off treatment stating that she believed she was better. The doctor did not agree with her assessment. He believed she still had problems. (43.79)

Another Egyptian doctor, who worked at the Ypsilanti State Hospital and who the victim dated, said he thought Anne had a problem in that she could not deal with reality. She did not tell him she had been in therapy. (42.) (43.76)

REMARKS

The cause of death according to the forensic pathologist was a bullet wound in the brain which destroyed the cerebra peduncles. There was a superficial bullet wound on the forehead and the right thumb. There were multiple incisions on the neck with incision of the left jugular vein. There were two stab wounds to the thorax. One penetrated the left ventricle and the other penetrated the pericardial sac. (46.25)

After the finger of suspicion pointed toward John Norman Collins in the subsequent murder of Karry B., several items of evidence, physical, direct and circumstantial, also pointed strongly toward him in this case. Some of these items are discussed below.

On the night of June seventh, the last night the victim was seen alive, John Norman Collins was observed crossing State Street and Liberty Street a short distance from Anne K.'s apartment in Ann Arbor. This witness knew Collins well from intramural wrestling matches. (46.11)

Also on that same day, during the early afternoon, another couple talked with John Norman Collins in Ann Arbor. He was on a motorcycle. It was unknown whether it was his motorcycle or one of those he had stolen. The witnesses said Collins acted much differently than he usually did, for he seemed aloof. He had a "way out" look in his eyes. As they were talking with him, Collins would not look at them, but just kept looking around. (46.11)

John Norman Collins' roommate, Arnold D., said that during the evening hours, on or about June 7, 1969, Collins had picked Anne up and brought her to the apartment house in Ypsilanti where he and Collins lived. Arnold identified the victim from recent photos as the girl Collins had in his room. Arnold said there was a disturbance and Anne K. ran from the apartment building with Collins chasing her.

Sometime later Collins returned to the apartment and Arnold asked him what the problem was earlier. According to Arnold—Collins told him, in substance, that she would not have sex with him.

The white miniskirt the victim was wearing at the time she was murdered was checked for evidence. A wavy boot print was found on the skirt. After Collins was arrested, a pair of fur lined boots with a wavy, rippled sole was seized. The comparison between the print on the skirt and Collins' boots were similar in all respects and different in none.

Blood was found in the one year old Oldsmobile which was registered in Collins' mother's name. Anne K.'s blood contained six major and unique factors. The blood found in the Oldsmobile matched five of the six factors with not one of the factors being different.

In addition to this, Type O blood, the same type as Anne K's, was found on Collins' raincoat in his car. The reader will recall that the night the victim was murdered, it rained all night except for a short, twenty minute period, just before midnight. (46.12)

During the night of March 21, 1969, John Collins and another man broke into a house at 33949 Sleepy Hollow Road in Livonia, Michigan. Collins stole a High Standard revolver and an eight m.m. camera. Both the person involved in the break-in with Collins and Arnold, his roommate, said Collins had the revolver when he went to California shortly after Anne was murdered. When Collins was arrested, the stolen camera was recovered in his apartment, but not the gun. The identifiable characteristics available on the .22 long rifle bullet found in the victim's brain indicated it could have come from a High Standard revolver.

On the morning of July 27, 1969, when the arrest of John Collins appeared imminent, he gave a hunting knife which was eight and one half inches long to his roommate, Arnold.

Collins told him to get rid of the knife. The knife wounds suffered by the victims could have resulted from this knife. (46.14E)

METHOD OF OPERATION

From all available evidence, it appeared that the victim was walking to the Depot House to attend a dance when she was approached by John Norman Collins. Collins quite probably not only offered her a ride, but said he would attend the dance with her. But first he wanted to return to his apartment to change into more appropriate attire.

Once in his apartment he tried to rape the victim. She fought him off and ran from the apartment.

Collins chased and caught her and apologized for his bad conduct. He may have even shed a tear or two to convince her how sorry he really was for such terrible behavior. He then was successful in smoothing things over and told her he would take her to the dance without anymore funny stuff. Also since it was raining, they would now take a car back to Ann Arbor rather than a motorcycle.

It is highly probable that he took Anne to an abandoned farm. He probably pulled out his knife and ripped open her rain coat with such force that he tore off two buttons. He tore open her blouse and cut the front of her brassiere and fondled her breasts. He then cut her white miniskirt from her and ripped her panty hose off one leg. He then took the knife and cut the victim's panties apart at the crotch. He probably then made her completely remove her panties.

Then he probably held the knife at her throat while he had coitus with her more than one time. Quite probably he cursed at her calling her a "bitch". He told her he was going to kill her. He pulled his gun out. She raised her right hand to defend herself. He fired. The bullet hit her thumb and then her head, but did not penetrate the skull. He fired again. That bullet did enter the brain. Anne was then unconscious. He put the gun away and pulled out his knife again.

To be absolutely certain that she would die, Collins then stabbed her twice in the left breast and then cut her throat so deeply that her head was half off.

He left her lay there with blood gushing out until he was sure she was dead. Then he laid out his raincoat in the car and put her body on it.

He transported her to the second area where he took her from the Oldsmobile and laid her body on the road behind the old barn. He took Anne's wet, white skirt and used it to wipe up some of her blood in the car. He did this by throwing the wet skirt on the floor of the car. He then used his foot over the skirt to wipe up her blood. Then he threw her panties, skirt and shoes out of the car.

He then returned to the apartment house in Ypsilanti where he talked with Arnold D.

OBSERVATIONS

Some investigators thought it very unlikely that the victim would have left her apartment voluntarily without her purse, which contained her wallet. However, she was going to attend a dance. It is quite probable that she did not want to have to worry about having her purse or wallet stolen and, therefore, left it in her apartment. In addition, she was already carrying a pair of shoes.

Note that the victim was wearing her pump shoes rather than her loafers. Since she was probably using the loafers to walk to and from the dance, the fact that she had on her pumps tended to indicate that she had been at the dance, or that she was no longer expected to walk any distance.

There was a disagreement between Anne K.'s close friends as to whether she actually had made it to the dance the night of June 7th. Some claimed she was there, but others said it was a different woman who looked like her.

It is possible that the new genetic (DNA) Fingerprinting of the victim's blood, which has been hailed as the greatest advance in crime detection in this century, would have resulted in the odds being one in a million that the blood found in the Oldsmobile that Collins was driving could have been anyone else's other than Anne's. At the time of this investigation, the best that could be achieved was not nearly that significant. In fact, the odds at that time were two hundred to one that it could have come from someone else.

Dr. Hendrix, the forensic pathologist, during a speech to the members of the Michigan-Ontario Identification Association was highly critical of the criminal justice system in Washtenaw County for the failure to charge John Collins with Anne's murder. He believed very strongly that sufficient evidence was available to convict Collins of the murder of Anne too. This will be discussed further below.

Finally, as was stated before, every alibi murder case should be thoroughly investigated.

CHAPTER X

BRIEF HISTORY OF THE MURDER OF ROSE P.

Rose was visiting friends in the Salinas, California, area during her summer vacation. She had made friends with another girl whom we shall call Belle. Belle was the same age as Rose, and she lived near the family with whom Rose was staying. Belle was from Fort Worth, Texas.

On June 29, 1969, a very good looking young white man stopped Belle to ask for directions. She described him as being about six feet tall, square jawed, of wiry athletic build. She said he had dark hair that was trimmed short, but the sideburns were long. He had gotten out of his car to talk with her. He was driving a silver-gray Oldsmobile Cutlass with Michigan license plates.

Belle was only seventeen and she was very, very impressed by the young man. So impressed, that she invited him to her sister's house where they could continue talking. The young man introduced himself as "John." He said he was on vacation with a friend, and that they had brought their own camper-trailer. He told them that he was a senior in college. He planned to complete his studies in the fall, and he hoped to become a school teacher. (19.47-48) (48.237) Belle indicated that John had made a date with her to see her the next day and then left. When Belle later saw her new friend, Rose, she told her all the details about the "neat boy" she had just met. But John never kept their date, and she never saw him again.

Shortly before 1:00 p.m. on June 30, 1969, Rose had left the home of her friends, former neighbors from back home, to mail a letter. In the letter she had written that she was starting to meet some interesting boys, and she wished she could stay there longer. Rose told her hostess that she was going to visit Belle after mailing the letter, and would be back to baby-sit for the children by five o'clock at the very latest.

A witness said that she saw Rose leave the house on East Acacia Street and walk east towards Pajaro, which was the next cross street. (48.240)

Another witness stated that she was driving east on Acacia Street and stopped at the intersection of Acacia and Pajaro for the stop sign. A silver-colored car with dark out-of-state plates, like Michigan's that year, was traveling west on Acacia Street. The driver, whom she described as being a clean cut young man with dark hair, disregarded the stop sign and made a left turn right in front of her , and "burned rubber" as he sped away. The witness stated that she saw a sandy haired young woman sitting beside him. She could see that she was wearing something bright red. (48.243)

Rose never returned to the friend's home where she was supposed to baby-sit. Belle stated that she had not seen her that day. At 7:00 p.m., the friends with whom she had been staying, contacted Rose's parents. At 7:19 p.m. on June, 30, 1969, she called the Salinas Police Department.

Four days later, the victim's mother, at her own expense, had thousands of circulars printed and distributed. They gave the physical description of the missing young woman.

On Sunday, July 13, 1969, two teenage youngsters found the body of Rose in the Pescadero Canyon, just north of the Carmel, California village limits. This is on the Monterey Peninsula about twenty miles southwest of Salinas. The ravine where she was found had very dense underbrush which included a considerable amount of poison oak. The victim was naked except for her sandals which were still on her feet. A belt from her dress was around her neck.

On July 14, 1969, the identification of the victim was made based upon dental records. The friend with whom she had been visiting identified the belt found around her neck as the one Rose had worn on June 30th when she left the house to mail the letter. (48.242)

The cause of death was listed as homicide. The victim had a ruptured larynx. (36.)

THE VICTIM

The victim in this case was Rose P. who was seventeen years old. She was five feet six inches tall. She weighed one hundred and thirty pounds. She had hazel eyes and shoulder length copper colored blond hair. When last seen, she was carrying a large straw tote bag and she was wearing a short, red pants dress with a small floral design. She was a senior in high school. Her parents were divorced. Her home was in Milwaukee, Oregon.

METHOD OF OPERATION

Little factual knowledge is known of the perpetrator's method of operation in this case. What is known was that the victim was picked up while she was walking along the street while enroute to the home of her friend's sister which was six blocks away. The letter she was going to send was put in a mail box. She quite probably got into the car voluntarily after Collins offered her a ride. He then told the victim that he wanted to obtain some article in the trailer. Then he would take the victim to the house where their mutual friend was staying.

He then probably asked the victim if she would like a drink in the trailer. She agreed and went in the trailer. He then raped and murdered her.

During the early morning hours, he transported her body near the location where she was found. He then carried her body into the thick undergrowth of brush where her remains would not be quickly discovered.

The perpetrator then returned to the trailer in Salinas. It was parked in an alley behind a house owned by the eighty year old grandfather of the perpetrator's partner in breaking and enterings. Enroute he stopped near a bridge to dispose of the victim's tote bag and things from her wallet, such as pictures of her friends and her bus tickets. Of course this is only one possible scenario. This one happens to be the writer's based upon the facts as he knows them. Other scenarios may be equally plausible.

CRIMINAL INVESTIGATION

Officers in California made a door to door search of the entire area where the victim had disappeared.

Officers, some who were off duty, helped put up thousands of posters asking for public help in locating the victim.

The victim's tote bag and pictures were recovered by citizens on or about July 1, 1969. The bus tickets, also thought to be hers, were recovered by two sheriff deputies.

A Monterey County California District Attorney's Investigator learned from watching a television news broadcast that John Norman Collins had been under scrutiny for murders in Michigan since his return from California. He began an inquiry on the possibility that Collins was linked to the homicide in California that he had been working on. (48.237)

Officers in Michigan learned that Collins had rented a trailer in Ypsilanti and had traveled to California shortly after June 21, 1969. He and his breaking and entering partner arrived in California near the end of June and stayed through the first week of July. Inside the trailer there were no fingerprints. It appeared as though it had been wiped clean. (48.239)

Michigan officers learned from John Norman Collins' traveling partner that John had been treated for poison oak by a physician in Salinas. Collins physical description also corresponded with the description the doctor gave to California investigators who queried all of the doctors in the Salinas area about anyone who had been treated for poison oak. These queries were made after an investigator, who had been at the scene where the body was found, was affected by it.

When Collins was arrested, laboratory scientists found a piece of fabric about the size of a quarter along the side of the seat of the car that Collins was driving. The piece of fabric had a very unique floral pattern on it. This piece was similar in all respects to the fabric used to strangle Rose, and it was highly probable that they came from the same bolt of cloth.

Detectives at the Crime Center Task Force discovered twenty-two hairs on a dark brown sweater removed from the apartment rented by John Norman Collins. These appeared to be pubic hairs. A Michigan Laboratory Scientist obtained samples of Rose's pubic hair and compared them. It was found that the pubic hair removed from Rose's body was similar in all respects with those found on the sweater allegedly owned by John Norman Collins.

California investigators had a work order receipt from Tolan Cadillac-Oldsmobile Garage in Salinas indicating that repairs had been done on the Oldsmobile Cutlass, Michigan registration RVO101, driven by Collins on July 3, 1969.

When Michigan officials executed the search warrant in connection with the case below, they found a western license plate in the trunk of the silver-gray Oldsmobile.

During the Grand Jury hearing in California, a witness did state that the victim was observed getting into a silver-gray Oldsmobile Cutlass with Michigan license plates. An indictment was handed down. A warrant was issued for John Norman Collins' arrest. Police questioned Collins' traveling companion. He told the police that they had planned to stay in California longer, but after the victim in this case disappeared, Collins wanted to come home early.

Governor Reagan of California requested Collins' extradition to California. Governor Milliken of Michigan, after a lengthy exchange of formal messages, decided to deny such a request. The stated reason for the denial was because Collins was going through a lengthy appeal process, and the Michigan authorities wanted him available in Michigan where he could consult with his attorneys while this was taking place. The real reason for the denial was a concern that, since one cannot predict a jury's decision, the Michigan authorities were worried that if Collins were extradited to California, and then somehow was found not guilty, the Michigan authorities might have some trouble getting him back into a Michigan prison cell where he would continue to serve his life sentence. Monterey County, California, decided to dismiss the warrant for murder against Collins, but would, re-issue the warrant should Collins be set free in Michigan. (48.336)

OBSERVATIONS

There were several very damaging items of evidence in this case against John Norman Collins. First, the piece of cloth fabric found in the metal area in the corner along side the seat, had a very unique floral pattern in it. It was so unique that even a layperson could easily determine, by looking at the belt found around the neck of the victim, and the small piece of cloth found in the Oldsmobile, that they were alike.

Second, the twenty-two pubic hairs which were found on the dark brown sweater were similar to the victim's in all respects and there were no dissimilarities found. This sweater was found in Collin's closet. The pubic hairs on the sweater were difficult to see. In fact, they had initially been missed by laboratory scientists who checked Collins' clothing for hair from Karry B. Detective Janiszewski, who was assigned to assist in putting together the prosecution report, discovered these as part of the process of checking and rechecking to insure the case was ready for trial. The Crime Center then requested a reexamination of the sweater.

It was found that the hairs were not from any victim in Michigan. The investigators requested samples of Rose's pubic hair. Her remains had been buried without obtaining these. Her body had to be exhumed to obtain the samples. Comparisons of her hair were similar in all respects.

By 1993, with the new procedures involving identification through D.N.A., a positive identification as good as fingerprint identification, could have been made in this case.

Third, the fact that John Collins was treated for poison oak infection and the victim's body was placed in an area where there was an abundance of poison oak growing was significant. In fact, the reason investigators began contacting doctors to determine whether they had treated anyone for it was because a detective, working the scene where Rose's body was found was affected by it. The lesson for us here is, if a victim is thrown into an area with considerable poison ivy or oak, we should not overlook this possible avenue of investigation.

Fourth, there can be little doubt that it was John Collins who had taken the friend of the victim home. Let's look at what they knew. He said his name was John. He drove a late model, silver-gray Oldsmobile Cutlass with Michigan plates. He said he was on vacation with a friend with a camper trailer. He said he was a college senior who wanted to be a teacher. It appeared he was in his twenties, he was about six feet tall, he had dark hair which was trimmed short, and with long sideburns. All of the above was true of John Collins. The odds would have to be a million to one that this would have been anyone else other than John Collins.

It would appear to be justified, in an important case, such as this, that arrangements be made for a properly conducted line up and then have the witnesses travel to the state holding the suspect. If at all possible, such witnesses should be sequestered until after the line up has been completed. Short of that, a photo show up could be conducted. It is not known if that was done in this case.

Note that the pubic hairs were found on Collins' sweater. Also note that the victim in this case weighed one hundred and thirty pounds. The abundance of the pubic hairs and their location on the sweater suggested that the perpetrator carried the victim high on his back similar to the manner in which a weight lifter would put the weights on his shoulders and do deep knee bends. This also suggests that rigor mortis may have been in existence at the time he carried her body .

This further suggests that the body was carried to the location where it was found at a time when the temperature was relatively cool, probably on the morning of July the first. During the day it was warm—so warm the victim was wearing only a short pant dress and sandals. It would defy reason to expect the murderer at that time to be wearing a hot sweater. Especially if he was going to carry one hundred and thirty pounds of dead weight. Also at that time, the rigor was probably quite complete. The constant rubbing of the pubic bone against the perpetrator's back while going down the ravine would cause the abundant number of pubic hairs to be uprooted and left on the sweater.

This finally suggests that while John Norman Collins' friend readily admitted being involved in breaking and enterings with him, he was not involved in the murder. If the victim had been carried by two men, the pubic hairs would not have been found on the sweater in the location where they were. Also Collins' friend would not have borrowed the sweater because it would not have fit him. He was a much larger man than Collins.

It is also remarkable that in the Marjorie S. case, her purse had been disposed of near a bridge, and that the same was done with the victim's tote bag in this instance.

It is not known whether the bus tickets which were found were later checked for both the victim's and Collins' fingerprints. Since an investigator cannot predict whether he will need the victim's prints, early in the investigation these should be obtained from her books, papers, or anything else she may have handled. Also, adequate samples of her hair from various parts of her body should be obtained and preserved. Naturally, a check for foreign hair and other substances should also be made.

It was also observed that Collins had in his possession a license plate from another western state. This plate was probably used enroute back to Michigan. He would have done this thinking that if the authorities were looking for him they would be watching for a late model silver-gray Oldsmobile *with Michigan registration plates* which might be pulling a trailer.

Note the parallel with the case below. After the murder of Karry B., Collins sent his friend, Arnie, to the Secretary of State's Office to get another plate For him. He claimed the plate on the motorcycle he used when he picked up Karry was lost. It was, in fact, still on the bike when it was observed by officer Mathewson in the garage at the apartment house where he lived when Davis returned with the plate. It may also have been in Collins' plans to use the western plate while involved in future criminal activity in Michigan.

74

CHAPTER XI

THE COLLATERAL MURDER CASE OF MADELINE P.
(Also investigated by Crime Center Task Force)

BRIEF HISTORY

About midnight on Friday, July 4, 1969, Madeline P. was shot in the head in her apartment. The Ann Arbor Police were called to the scene. They arrived there at 12:20 a.m. An ambulance also arrived and took the victim to St. Joseph's Mercy Hospital in Ann Arbor.

The police found a cold glass of lemonade sitting on a table. There was also two thirds of a cup of coffee on the table. The coffee in the cup was still warm. (67.) Three .22 caliber long casings were found.

Two of the bullets entered the victim's head. One was just under the skin, but the other had entered the victim's skull and was lodged deep inside her brain. This bullet could not be removed and caused her death on July 6, 1969.

Also on the table was a package of Pall Mall cigarettes with only one cigarette removed. Chief of Detectives Olson examined the cigarette package. It had been opened in a very singular way. The foil had not been ripped off as most smokers would have done. Instead it had been cut and folded neatly along the edge of the tax stamp. (50.) (67.) (48.127)

There were no ash trays in the apartment. The victim did not smoke.

The victim's purse containing cash and credit cards was lying in a chair.

The press linked the murder of Madeline P. to the other cases which the task force was working on. For example, the headlines in the Ann Arbor News read, "Wounded Coed Fights For Life". In the lead paragraph, it was reported, "A pretty twenty-five year old university graduate student, fighting for her life in St. Joseph Mercy Hospital may hold the key which will unlock the mystery of the brutal slayings of six young women." (64.1)

VICTIM

The victim in this case was Madeline P. She was a white female born on May 21, 1944. She was twenty-five years old at the time of her death. She was five feet three inches tall, and she weighed one hundred and fifteen pounds. She had blonde hair and blue eyes. She resided in her apartment at 203 North State Street in Ann Arbor, Michigan, while she pursued graduate studies at the University of Michigan. Her Doctoral Thesis was in the area of Social Science.

Madeline worked for the Institute for Social Research at the University of Michigan. She was paid $2.25 per hour. She was doing a study on violence. June M. discussed above also worked at the same institute. (47.)

The victim's home was in Coopersville, Michigan. This is a little town near Grand Rapids. Like June M., a previous victim, she was deeply concerned about poor people and wanted to do something about their plight. (50.)

The Ann Arbor Police secured the crime scene. Michigan State Police Crime Laboratory Scientists were called to the scene. Photographs and measurements were taken. The scene was processed for trace evidence. The most significant bit of evidence found was a good latent print on the coffee cup. Mr. Booker Williams, the assistant prosecutor, put his finger into the cup, as did Chief of Detectives Olson, shortly after their arrival, and discovered the coffee was still warm. (67.) (48.127) The latent print appeared to have come from the right thumb. Three shell casings were found in the apartment. These were from a .22 caliber weapon.

From the bullets recovered from the victim, it was learned that the weapon involved was a V. Bernadelli Gordone.

The Chief of Police in Ann Arbor requested State Police assistance. The Assistant District Commander in Detroit contacted this writer and ordered him to drop whatever he was working on and to proceed immediately to Ann Arbor to give any assistance possible.

Chief Krasny and Detective Sergeant Donald Carnahan briefed the writer fully upon his arrival at the Ann Arbor Police Station. Sergeant Carnahan indicated that the victim had been counseling an ex-con named Ernie Bishop. She had also been working with Pavol S. Pavol was connected with the Students for a Democratic Society. This organization was a very radical group during the sixties. The victim was also acquainted with many students who participated in anti-draft demonstrations.

The writer called the Identification Division in East Lansing. Since it was a weekend, no one was there. Then the Operations Division was called. It was requested that someone from the Identification Division immediately contact the author at the Ann Arbor Police Department.

A short time later, Sergeant Ed Havens from the Identification Division called the author. He was requested by the author to have the fingerprints of Ernest Bishop sent by FAX machine to the Latent Print Unit at the Crime Laboratory in Plymouth, Michigan, if the division had them on file.

Within a few minutes, Sergeant Havens again called the author. He said they did have Bishop's prints on file. In addition, he provided a physical description of him.

"Bishop", he said, "was a Negro male, five-five and one half inches tall. He weighed one hundred and thirty-one pounds. He had brown eyes and black hair. He was born on January 14, 1941." He said Bishop had served time in Jackson State Prison. He had been serving a sentence of ten to twenty years for raping a woman. He was paroled on October 10, 1967. He was arrested again on December 4, 1967, and was again paroled on December 28, 1968. Sergeant Havens said he was sending the prints electronically to the Michigan State Police Crime Laboratory in Plymouth.

The writer tried to contact the laboratory by telephone to tell them the prints were being sent and to request a check of Bishop's fingerprints against the one found on the warm cup of coffee, but it was Saturday and no one was there. They had been up all night working crime scenes. A decision was made to let them rest.

WITNESS INTERVIEWED

Jessica R., a Jewish female, who was also a student at the University of Michigan, was interviewed by the author. She lived in the same apartment building with the victim. They were close friends. Part of the statement that Jessica gave is recorded below.

> It was twenty after eleven (on July 4, 1969). I had turned out the light before I wound the clock. I was in bed with the lights off at twenty after eleven. I was lying in bed and there was a big storm. It was thundering and lightening. I shut one of my windows because the rain was coming in by the pillow. I was lying there for about ten minutes not sleeping. I heard people outside—either footsteps or talking first. I don't remember which. I heard the words, "Get the door open." I got out of the bed and looked out the window.

> What I saw was a boy bending over and picking up a book bag. It was a dark colored boy. A boy was coming back to him. This boy was carrying a guitar. I heard him say, "Are you all right?" Then they walked on. They were walking on Catherine and State Street. I went back to bed.

> I was lying there for ten or fifteen more minutes. I looked out the window when I thought I heard a funny sound. I cannot identify it. Maybe five or ten minutes later I thought I heard Madeline up. I didn't get up to talk with her because I was too tired. Next I think I was falling asleep.

> The next thing I heard was Madeline saying, "Who's there at the door?" I didn't hear any specific name answer, but I may have heard a voice. I can't remember. Then I heard Madeline unlock and unchain the door. I had locked and chained the door to the apartment when I came in. Somebody came in and the door was locked after that person was inside. I tried to hear voices to try to figure out who the person was, but I couldn't. I heard people walking toward Madeline's room. Then I got up and put

77

my ear to the door, to try to figure out who it was 'cause I was curious. I listened for awhile, and I could hardly hear any voices. I gave up and went back to bed.

I started to go back to bed—I never got back to bed. I returned to the door to listen some more. Then I heard something that sounded like a conversation. I tried to recognize the voices. I could not recognize any specific voice, but I thought it was a male voice. So I didn't go out 'cause I was in my nightgown. So I went back to bed. Then I was lying there for awhile, and I heard the bathroom door shut rather loudly. I heard somebody in the kitchen. I heard someone in the refrigerator. Then I heard the bathroom door shut loudly a second time. Maybe a couple of minutes to five minutes, or a minute, I heard something like a big piece of metal that fell and crashed. Then I heard a shot. I think I remember hearing two shots close together after the first sound. They were maybe three seconds apart.

Immediately after that, I heard footsteps out of the apartment. It sounded like male footsteps. It was an even, not real fast pace, like you are walking somewhere and you are late for work. I heard him open the door and shut it. After he shut the door I got out of bed.

I opened my door and walked out into the hall. The hall light was on. I saw the cat looking real scared in the hall. I took a couple of slow walks toward Madeline's room. I heard her breathing real loud and hard—like snoring. Then I knew what happened. I could see from her knees down, like she had been sitting on the edge of the bed. The lights were on in the room. I took the phone into the hall. I was afraid I would faint before I could call anybody.

So I laid down on the floor while I called the operator. Nobody answered. After it rang for awhile, I couldn't get up to look up the police telephone number so I called the co-op. (apartment) (61.)

Jessica did reach the co-op apartment by telephone. She asked a friend to send a man over to protect her because she was in great fear for her life. She also requested that the police and an ambulance be sent to the apartment. Within minutes, three young men came running to the apartment to give aid and comfort to Jessica. A few minutes later the police and the ambulance also arrived.

Jessica told the author that she did not recognize the voice. She thought it might have been "Fred" because he came to visit Madeline once in a while, and she knew that she liked him. (61.)

It was quite apparent to this writer that Jessica was still shaken from the events which had occurred even though this interview was taking place over twelve hours later. She was asked if she would be willing to undergo narco-hypnosis. The writer thought that Jessica may have been subconsciously suppressing information due to the psychologically traumatic experience she had just endured. She consented.

She was taken to the hospital where a psychiatrist who had been working with the task force was going to administer the drug. He examined Jessica. In his opinion she was in no condition for hypnosis. She was too exhausted. Instead he admitted her to the hospital for rest.

On Sunday July 6, 1969, Madeline died from the gun shot wound to her head. The entire task force, about one hundred and fifty officers, were recalled to duty. In addition, the personnel of the Michigan State Police Latent Print Unit were also ordered to report for duty at the Michigan State Crime Laboratory in Plymouth.

When Detective Eugene Weiler of the Latent Print Unit looked at the prints of Ernest Bishop in the FAX machine, he could hardly believe his eyes. He thought perhaps some miracle had been wrought for he had no idea the prints of a suspect on the murder case were being sent. Within a few minutes, he had identified the latent print found on the cup in Madeline's apartment with those which had been sent by Sergeant Havens of the Identification Division. Weiler had other latent print experts also examine the prints too. They all agreed. The print on the cup was Bishop's. Ken Christensen, the laboratory commander then called Captain Walter Stevens in Ann Arbor, and told him the good news. Stevens, the Michigan State Police Second District Commander, advised the Ann Arbor Police.

Meanwhile, the author and another officer interviewed a friend of Bishop's. He told us that he knew that Bishop had been in possession of a .22 caliber handgun, but after Madeline was shot, he had thrown the weapon into a river. He denied any knowledge of Bishop shooting Madeline. But that information along with the knowledge that Bishop had served time in prison for rape, made him a prime suspect. This was sufficient cause for officers to obtain photographs of Bishop from his parole officer. Copies were made for members of the task force and others. Bishop's friend had told officers where he was probably hiding out.

With the news of the identification of Bishop's fingerprints, members of the Crime Center Task Force and others who were on duty that Sunday, set up a tight surveillance ring around the apartment building where Bishop was believed to be hiding. The author and Detective Sergeant Max Little had the "eye". The car was parked about three to five hundred feet from the apartment. The entire area was circled with numerous state police, Ann Arbor police department, and sheriff's department cars.

Shortly before 11:00 p.m. that night, July 6, 1969, the author passed his French night vision binoculars to Sergeant Little. Each officer had been taking turns watching for about thirty minutes. A few seconds later, Little asked, "Did you see that?"

79

"What?"

"Someone just ran between the trees in front of the house."

Rather than giving away the fact that a surveillance was being conducted—the officers chose not to check the person out themselves. Little quickly grabbed the microphone and sent a radio message to the car that was in the same direction as the man who was running. There could have been officers from any force in that car. In some cases, officers from different departments were teamed together. It happened that the officers in the car were Carl Freeborn, the Post Commander of the Ypsilanti Post, and his assistant, Sergeant Chris Walters.

They had seen the man approach and then turn the corner. He was now walking very fast. One of the officers called out to him, "Ernie Bishop?" He replied, "Ya." They placed him under arrest and took him to the Ann Arbor Police Station. A second warrant was obtained to search Bishop's apartment for the gun, but it was not found there. The officers were not accepting the information that the gun had been thrown in the river.

At the Ann Arbor Police Station, Bishop was given the Miranda warnings and interrogated by the Michigan State Police District Commander and the Chief of Detectives of the Ann Arbor Police Department. Bishop confessed to the murder, but would give no reason for shooting Madeline.

Ultimately, Bishop was found not guilty by reasons of insanity in court. He served about five years in prison before he was declared "cured". He was then released and was back on the street again.

OBSERVATIONS

This case was shared with the reader to provide a clear mental picture of what can occur during the investigation of several serial murders by a task force.

This case makes it very obvious that it is not at all uncommon for other murders to occur which the task force must deal with for one reason or another. The usual reason is that there may be a possibility, however slight, that the murder was somehow related to the other serial murder cases.

Another reason this case was significant, was because what happened here flew in the face of the allegations later made by the convicted murderer of Karry B. That murder will be discussed later. In Karry's case, the evidence was overwhelming that she was the victim of a serial killer. She was murdered nineteen days after Madeline P. was found shot in her apartment. John Norman Collins (AKA James Armstrong) years after his conviction, would have a press interview.

During this interview, Collins implied that he had been "railroaded by the police" because they were under social pressure to stop the killings in the Ann Arbor-Ypsilanti area. This is where his reasoning failed him.

If the police were really looking for a scapegoat for all the serial murders, they would have had a tailor made scapegoat with Bishop. He was poor, black, uneducated and had previously served time in the State Prison of Southern Michigan, after being convicted of rape. Contrast his background with that of John Norman Collins. Collins was white, a senior at Eastern Michigan University, tall and handsome. He had attended a Catholic Parochial School as a youth. He was co-captain of his high school football team and vice President of a college skiing club. All in all, he fit the mental picture of the all American boy—not a serial murderer. In other words, if the police were really trying to find someone to blame falsely for the serial murders, it would have been much easier to pin them on Bishop rather than Collins.

Another point which this case makes is that it debunks the myth that there was a lack of cooperation between the various police agencies during the investigation of the several serial murders which made up the totality of the case. It was true that there sometimes were disagreements over criminal investigative techniques, such as when statements should be taken, who should conduct interrogations, and relative to the checking out of alibi statements. And it was also true that a few investigators withheld information from members of the task force. But, by and large, the members of the task force worked excellently together.

Those who point to such behaviors previously mentioned, completely fail to recognize that most police are competitive by nature. Within the same police department, investigators differ on the methodology which should be employed to solve a crime. Also, some investigators like to go slow building a case playing "cat and mouse" along the way. Others, like to adopt the "hit it head on approach". Often times, officers, in metropolitan areas, don't have time to go slow. Investigators develop their own sources of information.

Whether right or wrong—they do not always share their information with others despite the fact they are all playing on the same team. Officers from the same department will sometimes jump into another officer's investigation without knowing all the facts. The primary reason for this seems to be motivated by the so called "glory" of making the arrest. Not infrequently such actions result in losing the case because certain evidence was not obtained. A lack of knowledge by the intruding officer can also result in a botched case.

For example, in one case two officers jumped into a criminal investigation and arrested a suspect in a burglary case. They accused the suspect of committing the crime and tried to run a bluff during the interrogation. They told the suspect that they had found his fingerprints at the scene of the crime. This built up the confidence of the accused because he was fully aware that during the total time he was at the crime scene, he wore gloves.

He knew that the police officers were bluffing. The day was saved when the original investigator came in on his day off and took over the interrogation. He quickly told the suspect that the latent prints had all been checked out. They were all the owner's prints. A short time later, the suspect confessed when the original investigator used the sympathetic approach. The suspect then led police to the place where some of the loot had been hidden.

It should also be remarked that most officers on the force did not believe Bishop murdered any of the other victims. Most investigators thought that the women who were victims of the serial killer were picked up on the street. They appeared to have been selected only because they accepted a ride with the murderer.

There were some investigators who didn't agree, however. They remarked that June M. was involved with the same group of social activists as Madeline P. Further, that Anne K. had also been interested in the same social problems. In addition, she had been intimate with at least one black male. Finally, this was the third woman, within a four month period, who died from gunshot wounds to the head. None of the victims From Ypsilanti had been killed in that fashion. They were all either stabbed to death or died from being struck with a blunt instrument. The problem was, however, that if Bishop was involved, what did he use for transportation?

And when June M. was shot in the head, the murderer also strangled her with a nylon stocking. With Anne K., he slashed her throat so deeply after he shot her, he nearly cut her head half off. In other words, there were multiple causes of death. The murderer wanted to be very sure the victims were dead. In the instant case, there was only one cause of death.

Finally, the .22 caliber bullets from the two victims who had been shot did not match with the weapon used to murder Madeline.

It appeared during this investigation, that it was quite probable that three women all knew a man named Jonas Sobeske. Sobeske was characterized as a 'hippie", took part in civil rights demonstrations with both the victim on this complaint, June M. (a previous

82

victim) and Marjorie S. (also a previous victim). It was Sobeske's wife who was supposed to meet Marjorie S. at the McKinney Student Union Building. She claimed she went there, but Marjorie never showed up. Later Jonas Sobeske and his wife were extremely reticent to discuss her death.

When Ernest Bishop was being interrogated, he asked for a cigarette. He was given a fresh package of cigarettes. Interrogators noted carefully that he opened the package in exactly the same way as the one was found in Madeline's apartment.

CHAPTER XII

BRIEF HISTORY OF THE MURDER OF KARRY B.
(AKA Carol Ann Gebhardt in *Michigan Murders*)

At 11:30 a.m., July 23, 1969, Karry B., a freshman student at Eastern Michigan University at Ypsilanti, Michigan, ate lunch with two classmates, Kim and Sarah, in the Dining Commons on the campus. While they were eating, Karry and Sarah exchanged some food they had on their respective trays.

The women finished eating and left the Dining Commons Building between 12:05 and 12:15 p.m. and returned to their dormitory. Karry told Kim she was going to walk downtown to buy a "fall." This was a hair piece she had ordered the previous day at a wig shop. Karry invited Kim to accompany her, but Kim declined. She had an afternoon class. (45.64) As she was getting on the elevator, Karry talked briefly with another roommate, Paula. Karry told Paula that she would meet her at dinner time. During a personal interview with Paula, she told the author she thought that this was around 12:30 p.m.

A short time later, believed to be between 12:15 p.m. and 12:30 p.m., Karry entered the Wigs by Joy Shop at 18 1/2 North Washington Street in Ypsilanti. Mrs. Pam S., an employee at the shop, had promised to have the wiglet ready for Karry at 12:00 noon. Karry appeared to be very happy. She said to Joy, the owner, "I'll bet that I'm the bravest customer that you have ever had." "Why do you say that?" asked Joy. "Because I've done two things I've never done before. I am buying a wig, and I just met a very nice boy, and accepted a ride on his motorcycle with him."

Joy was greatly concerned about Karry's safety. She asked her, "Haven't you heard about all the girls being murdered in this area?" "Oh, he is very nice, he couldn't possibly do anything like that," Karry replied. "That's probably exactly what all the other girls thought who were murdered. Where is he now?" asked Joy. "He's parked there waiting for me. He's gonna give me a ride back to the dorm," answered Karry.

As Pamela was adjusting the wiglet on Karry, Joy walked toward the door saying, more to herself than anyone else, "Just how nice can any boy be in just two blocks?" She walked out the door of the shop and looked at the young man sitting on the motorcycle thirty feet away from her. Then she went back into the shop.

By now, Karry had her wiglet on and was about ready to leave. Joy was worried. She then said to Karry, "Listen, I have my car parked right out here in back. Let me give you a ride back to the dorm." While Joy was talking, Pam also walked outside the shop to look at the young man with whom Karry had ridden to the shop.

As she came back inside she said, "God he's good looking!" Joy said, "Look, we can tell him that you might mess your wig up riding on the motorcycle." Karry said she wouldn't ride back with him, but would just walk back since it was such a nice day. Karry said she wanted to tell the young man that she was going to walk back.(44.55)

Both women watched as Karry walked back to the young man on the motorcycle. They talked together for a couple minutes. Karry then got on the back of the motorcycle. She had one arm around the waist of the operator and the other holding her wiglet as they rode off, passing within fifteen feet of the front of the wig shop. The motorcycle went south on North Washington. The women watched as the motorcycle then turned and headed west on Michigan Avenue. (44.55)

When Karry did not appear at the dormitory at the scheduled time for dinner, her roommates became quite concerned about her welfare. They contacted Miss Kit. Miss Kit was the House Representative in charge of Downing Hall where Karry was living. When Karry missed the 11:00 p.m. curfew check, Miss Kit contacted the Eastern Michigan University Police and reported her missing. She also notified her parents shortly after midnight on July 24, 1969.

On Saturday, July 26, 1969, at 4:21 p.m., Dr. Conrad M. of 3640 East Huron River Drive, Ann Arbor, Michigan, called Captain Ritter of the Washtenaw County Sheriff's Department and reported that he had found the body of a young woman in the weeds at the foot of a hill near his home. The body was completely nude except for the sandals on her feet. She was lying on her stomach with her legs crossed at the ankles. It appeared as though the perpetrator stood at the edge of the road and threw the body of Karry down the bank. It appeared that she rolled over several times before coming to rest at the bottom. There was no rigor mortis in the body. There was no larvae activity, but there were eggs in some of the body orifices such as the eyes. (44.74)

The Michigan State Police Crime Laboratory at Plymouth was notified. Personnel from there took measurements and made photographs.

The Washtenaw County Medical Examiner also came to the scene. He ordered that the body be removed to the University of Michigan Hospital where the autopsy would be performed by Dr. Robert Hendrix.

Where the body was found was along a private drive—Riverside Drive—in section 36 of Ann Arbor Township. This is a horseshoe shaped drive with several houses along it. Both ends of the horseshoe enter and exit on Huron River Drive. (60)

The following day, Sunday, July 27, 1969, the autopsy was performed. Externally, it was apparent that there were marks around her wrists, ankles and at the back of her neck. It appeared that she had been bound hand and foot with a heavy duty type of electrical cord. At the time of the autopsy, there was maggot activity.

The victim was identified from her dental records and from her fingerprints as Karry.

In Dr. Hendrix's opinion, Karry was either dead or in great fear of death within two to three hours after she had eaten lunch. He put the time of death for investigative purposes between 2:05 p.m. and 3:15 p.m. on July 23, 1969. The cause of death was strangulation and multiple blows which caused microscopic brain injuries. (45.60)

A small amount of alcohol was found in her blood which suggested that she had been given some type of alcoholic beverage shortly before she died.

In Karry's mouth was found part of her gold colored shorts. Karry's mouth appeared burned by some caustic substance such as ammonia.

The victim started having her monthly period on July 20, 1969. Her mother said her periods lingered for ten to fourteen days.

The medical examiner discovered the victim's panties in the vaginal vault. They appeared to have literally hundreds of short clipped hairs on them. They were dirty as though they had been used to wipe up a floor. And they were cut across at the crotch. Also in the vaginal vault seminal fluid was found. It was also on the panties. (45.40)

THE VICTIM

The victim of this murder was Karry B. She was born in Blodget Hospital in Grand Rapids, Michigan, on February 10, 1951. Dr. Virgil Stover of Grand Rapids was the physician in attendance. Karry was the third child born to Ralph and Meredith B. of 136 Guild Street N.E., in Grand Rapids.

She was a white female, eighteen years old. She was five feet one inch tall. She weighed ninety-six pounds with reddish brown hair and blue green eyes. While she had a slight build, she had very strong arms. She also had exceptionally large busts for her size. She suffered from an allergy problem in the spring, and her menstrual periods were exceptionally long. In fact she had been contemplating seeing a doctor about the problem. She had blood type "A". She did not wear glasses. (6) (43.82)

The victim had two older sisters, Beverly, who had her own apartment in Grand Rapids, and Jane, who lived at home. The sisters were nine and seven years older, respectively, than Karry.

The victim's mother worked all her life as a homemaker. The father was co-owner of the Seaway Time Equipment Company in Muskegon Heights, Michigan. This firm manufactured time clocks. Both parents of the victim were very friendly people who tried to provide their daughters with the best training possible, and were devoted to helping others. They hosted exchange students from Chile and Finland. (4) (5) (6) (7)

The victim graduated from Criston High School at 1720 Plainfield Avenue N.E., Grand Rapids, Michigan. She carried a "B" average in the high school subjects she studied. She also studied political science at Grand Rapids Junior College while in high school. She also was a member of the Spanish Club, the high school choir, the Pep Club, and the Homecoming Committee. She was highly regarded both by other students and teachers.

Karry had applied for admission to five universities and was accepted by all of them. Since Eastern Michigan University offered her a teaching scholarship, and since it was located close to where her boyfriend taught high school, she decided to attend there. Part of the discussions which had taken place before she made that decision, involved the killings which had occurred in the area. (43.82)

Her parents were concerned for her safety. They wanted her to attend Grand Rapids Junior College for two years before transferring to a major university.

She was undecided as to exactly what she would like to do for a vocation, but she was giving serious consideration to becoming a special education teacher so that she could help handicapped children. Her main problem was whether she could handle it emotionally. Karry had a large sign over her desk which read, "Karry study." She would study for long hours every night and was having no difficulty with her classes. (43.86-87)

Before attending Eastern Michigan University, Karry worked as a waitress at the Warzburg Coffee Shop in Grand Rapids. She left the job on May 30, 1969, to have a short vacation before she began summer classes at the university on June 22, 1969.

Prior to this, while attending high school, from Thanksgiving 1968 until April 1969, she worked at Gantos Dress Shop.

She had worked at George's Stable in Ann Arbor where she would braid the tails and manes of horses for people who requested it. First, she kept her horse at the Three Gates Stable and then at the Kentree Stable outside Grand Rapids. At the time she was murdered, she was concentrating all of her efforts toward college and was doing no other work.

As far as recreation was concerned, Karry liked to do things that were adventurous. She liked both water and downhill skiing. She learned to downhill ski by starting at the top of the hill. She also enjoyed less strenuous activities such as sewing and collecting stamps.

She had been riding horses since she was five years old. She was an expert in equestrian skills and had won many trophies in horse shows and jumping competitions. She had owned several horses herself. She rigged an exercise apparatus on a swing set in her back yard where she could pull up cement blocks with her arms to help strengthen them so she would be better able to control a horse. She had taken her riding boots with her to the university along with pictures of her trophies, which she had shown to her roommates. (43.84)

In her spare time, she continued to study about horses. She had already acquired a level of expertise which was respected by horse lovers. She was frequently requested to fault a horse for one interested in buying the horse. (6)

Her home environment was excellent. Her parents lived in a two story, green house about forty years old in a middle class, well maintained neighborhood. The home was well furnished on the inside with contemporary furniture. In the basement of the home was a large family room. Her family could have afforded a much more expensive house, but they were happy and quite content in the neighborhood in which they lived.

At Eastern Michigan University, Karry was living in room 307 in Downing Hall. Her roommate was Paula. This was a suite type of arrangement with a bedroom on each side of a study and recreation area. According to her roommate, Karry liked to be around other people. She had requested a double room where she would have another girl in her room. (51)

Karry had no police record. She told her roommate the police caught her and some of her friends with beer in their car. The police just reprimanded them, opened all the beer and poured it on the ground. Karry caught a student who was living with her family as an exchange student stealing something in a store. She warned the student never to do that again because it would reflect badly on her family if the exchange student were caught. (43.86)

Karry did not use marijuana, L.S.D., or other drugs which were so prevalent on college and university campuses during the 1960's. She thought anyone using these drugs was stupid. She would not accept a drink at a party handed to her by a stranger because she feared someone may have put L.S.D. into it. (51)

Karry was a very active young woman. She never just sat around doing nothing. (7)

She was also very clean about her person and dress. During the summer, it was not uncommon for her to shower three times a day. She put on fresh clothing after each shower. She was also very particular about her appearance in public. It would be unthinkable for her to enter a store in her horse riding outfit. In the college dormitory, she would not leave with her hair in curlers. She would sometimes spend a considerable amount of time trying to locate a dress that she liked. After she bought it, she would bring it home and make alterations to provide for her large breasts.

Karry also had a sense of humor, and she liked to tease people. On one occasion, her mother was bending over looking for something under the trailer they were using for camping and Karry took her picture. One time she brought some roses, which she had obviously found growing by someone's house, up to her room. Her arms and hands were covered with scratches. Another time, she presented some of the other girls with some moldy bread she had in her room, all in fun, of course.

Karry sang in the church choir for five years, until she was twelve. Then, since most of her horse shows were held on Sunday, her church attendance fell off.

Miss Gayon, a mentor of Karry's, said she knew that Karry believed in God, but that she did not believe in any particular church. She was thinking about becoming a Roman Catholic, because that was the church which her boyfriend attended. She felt that there were many hypocrites who attended churches. Karry did not attend any church in the Ann Arbor-Ypsilanti area while she was there. (6) (33.) (51)

The victim's fiance was Jonathan Druar AKA Duffy. He was a white male. His date of birth was December 12, 1944. He was also from Grand Rapids, Michigan. He had been going with the victim for over a year before she was murdered. The victim talked about him almost constantly. It was their plan to get married as soon as she finished college. (22) (43.91-92)

Karry, while there was no doubt that she was devoted to her fiance and probably had deep feelings towards him, was also somewhat coquettish. That could have gotten her into some trouble. For example, she told her roommates she was walking to class on a Monday or Wednesday evening shortly before she was murdered when a young man who was lying on the grass in front of a fraternity house called to her. She went over to talk with him.

She said he was a big powerful man who walked with a limp due to what he said was a football injury. He walked her to and from class. She then changed clothes and went motorcycle riding with him. He tried to kiss her, but she would not let him. She told him about Jonathan Druar. He gave her his telephone number and said if she ever changed her mind about Druar she should call him. Karry did not write the number down. Her roommates did not know who this young man was when they saw him. Later, they saw Collins. They said that the young man who talked to Karry that day was not Collins. (43.91) (33)

CRIMINAL INVESTIGATION

Due to the other young women who had been murdered, the investigation into the murder of Karry began very shortly after the report came into the police.

According to plan, during the early morning hours of July 24, 1969, officers began patrolling previously assigned geographic areas in an effort to apprehend the perpetrator as he disposed of the body. The area where the body was found had been assigned to Sergeant McBryde, a motorcycle officer of the Eastern Michigan University Police Department.

Within twenty-four hours after Karry vanished, the two ladies working at the wig shop were interviewed and statements were taken from them. They described the young man that Karry rode away with as a white male, about twenty-two years old, about six feet tall with dark hair with a lock of hair hanging down on his forehead. One thought his hair was curly, the other thought it was wavy.

The women assisted a police artist in making a composite drawing of the perpetrator. Both women described the motorcycle as being like a Honda or Yamaha.

Police obtained a photograph of Karry. The women said that it was positively the same young woman who had bought the wiglet.

Neighborhood stores were canvassed for any additional witnesses who may have seen Karry and the suspect on the motorcycle. Cheri W., who worked at the Chocolate Shop, said she saw Karry and the man on the motorcycle together right in front of the shop. She said she was interested in motorcycles. She didn't pay much attention to the male rider, but she did have a good hard look at the bike. She said it was definitely not a Honda, but rather a Triumph. (44.96)

Larry Mathewson, a young officer, recently assigned to the task force from the Eastern Michigan University Department of Public Safety, also reported that he had observed Collins riding a motorcycle around twelve noon on the day Karry disappeared. Mathewson had just graduated from Eastern Michigan University. He knew Collins. He saw him at a gas station and asked him to be on the look out for a young man on a Triumph motorcycle. Collins said he would do that.

Mathewson talked with Booker Williams, the Chief Assistant Prosecutor who had assumed command of the task force in the absence of the Prosecutor, Mr. William Delhey. Mathewson told him he saw Collins riding his cycle around noon on July twenty-third. Booker told him to try to locate a picture and show it to the women at the wig shop. (67)

Mathewson talked with a girl whom Collins had dated. She gave him two photographs. He showed these to the women, but they would not make an identification. They looked at nearly one hundred photographs in about a week. They consistently said they refused to make a positive identification on the basis of any picture. Repeatedly they said, "We want to see the man." (44.75)

A photo of Collins was also obtained quietly through the Michigan Secretary of State's Office in Lansing. This office handles licensing of drivers in Michigan. Collins had recently renewed his operator's license and his picture was on file. This was an excellent photograph of him in color. There was considerable concern on the part of officials that the American Civil Liberties Union and liberals in the legislature would express great concern regarding the police obtaining someone's picture in this way.

On Friday morning, July 25, 1969, Mathewson took a picture of Karry to 619 Emmet Street where Collins lived. He found Collins in a garage near the rear of the house where he was working on a Triumph motorcycle. Mathewson showed Collins a picture of Karry, Collins said, "Boy, if I ever saw her I sure wouldn't forget her...She's nice." Mathewson also heard Collins and his friend Dylan M. joke about how the police artists' sketch looked like Collins. (44.75)

Mathewson heard Arnie D. walk into the garage and tell Collins he had gotten the plate for him as Mathewson began recording the license plate numbers in his notebook. Suddenly, Collins friendly demeanor changed dramatically. He became extremely angry. "Hey, what are you doing?" he asked. Someone said, "He's just writing down the license numbers." "Let him go play policeman some place else," Collins replied sarcastically. (44.48)

As a result of the sketch and article in the local newspaper, several girls came forward and contacted the Eastern Michigan University Police and reported that this same young man had tried to pick them up. They also positively identified Collins from photographs they were shown.(44.54)(44.94)

Lieutenant Fuller of the Eastern Michigan University Police was aware of the girls who identified Collins, and of Mathewson's observations of Collins around noon on July 23rd. He also recalled the interview with Collins during the investigation of the murder of Jean S. the previous year when Collins denied being with Jean.

Fuller and Captain Mulholland of the Washtenaw County Sheriff's Department met with Williams. They wanted to bring Collins in for questioning. Williams told them that he did not want that done because the police did not know for certain that Karry had been murdered. (67)

On Friday, July 25, 1969, detectives talked with Marcia Torre. She was one of the girls that a man tried to pick up. The next morning, she was shown Collins' picture while she was eating a sandwich. She dropped the sandwich and told Mathewson, "Oh shit. That's him! He's the guy who tried to pick me up." (44.94)

When Karry's body was found on the afternoon of July 26, 1969, the sheriff wanted to leave her body where it was found, have a minimal number of police cars visible at the scene, process the scene as quickly as being thorough would permit, and then establish a "stake out". Prosecutor Delhey rejected the idea of leaving Karry's body out in the elements. He indicated that he did, however, agree with the concept. It was worth a try. Delhey and Williams obtained a mannequin and placed it at the scene after Karry's body had been removed. (17)

That night a "stake out" went into effect. It was made up of nine officers from the Washtenaw County Sheriff's Department, the Eastern Michigan University Police, and the Michigan State Police.

The operation was under the command of Chief Hayes of the Eastern Michigan University Police Department and Lieutenant Bordine of the sheriff's department. The officers were told to report for duty in old clothing and rain gear. They were taken into the area one by one and dropped off. The nearest officer to the mannequin was forty feet away.

Near midnight a heavy thunderstorm occurred in the area. All except three officers either took shelter inside Dr. Conrad's porch or inside unmarked police cars. All three of these officers saw a man running along Huron River Drive. Trooper Botbyl of the Ypsilanti Post said that a deputy told him, "The suspect had gone to the mannequin and had fled on foot on Huron River Drive."

There apparently was a question in Booker William's mind as to whether the footprint found near the mannequin was fresh because he asked Trooper Botbyl to examine the print. Extensive efforts to locate the man—including the use of tracking dogs—were employed. The man never was located. This was according to the investigation and "Special Report on the Stake Out at 3640 E. Huron River Drive in Ann Arbor, Michigan." The report was dated October 29, 1969. It was submitted by Detective Sergeant Maxwell Little.

Early that Sunday morning, July, 27, 1969, Assistant Prosecutor Booker Williams returned to the Crime Center and made arrangements for around-the-clock surveillance to be placed on Collins. Those taking part in this did not have special training or practice. If Collins went anywhere, he was to be followed, but not intercepted. Initially one of the men assigned was an officer who had interrogated Collins on the Jean S. (Jill Hirsch) case and later Mathewson was given the duty of following Collins. Shortly after 11:00 p.m., Collins returned to his apartment. Then two officers, other than the ones mentioned above, arrived to take over the surveillance duty.

Contrary to Booker Williams wishes, these officers who were members of the Crime Center Task Force, broke the surveillance picked Collins up and brought him to the Crime Center for questioning. After reading the required Miranda warnings, Collins agreed to answer their questions.

The officers first questioned him about whether he had tried to pick up any girls on July 23, 1969. He denied that he had tried to pick up any girls. One of the officers told him they had several women who already had identified him as the young man who tried to pick them up. He caught Collins in another lie about whether he was wearing "cut offs" that day. Collins suddenly became very quiet and would not say anything. He just sat there in silence with a blank expression on his face and refused to answer any more questions.

After about fifteen or twenty minutes, he began talking again. He then admitted to the officers that he had tried to pick up girls, but that he had broken no law. He asked, "What was wrong with that?"

Also he told them that on that entire afternoon he had been teaching his friend, Arnold Davis, how to ride a motorcycle. They could check with Davis if they didn't believe him. The officers asked Collins if he would agree to take a polygraph examination to verify what he was telling them. He agreed to do that. Since it was around one in the morning and no examiners would be available until eight in the morning, they took him back home.

The following day, July 28th, when they went to Collins' apartment to take him to the Michigan State Second District Headquarters in Detroit for a polygraph examination, Collins was not there. Collins had retained an attorney who told him not to take the police polygraph examination.

When the author inquired of the officers why they had brought Collins in as they had done, one of them said that they were only carrying out orders from their superior. The supervisor at the time was the shift commander of the Crime Center Task Force Headquarters in the Holy Ghost Seminary between Ann Arbor and Ypsilanti. They were unaware of any contrary instructions from the Chief Assistant Prosecutor, Booker T. Williams. (10)

The evening of June 29, 1969, Corporal Derik Lair and his family returned to their home at 1307 Roosevelt Boulevard in Ypsilanti. They had been away since July 17th on vacation. Collins had been feeding their German Shepherd dog, which was kept in the garage. Collins was also looking after their house.

When Mrs. Lair came into the kitchen, area she immediately noticed scuff marks all across the floor. She had left it freshly waxed and polished. In the basement, she noticed one of her dental technician uniforms was turned around. Upon closer examination, she could see what appeared to be blood on a sleeve. The uniform had been freshly cleaned before they had left. A large Bold box, used as a waste box, a bottle of ammonia, and a can of black paint were missing. There were splotches of paint around the floor. (44.71)

The next day Lair called Collins in Centerline. Collins had no explanation for the paint on the floor. He said he still had the key to the house. He gave no indication that it had been out of his possession. This key was later picked up by Lair. Lair changed the locks on his house and lost the key.

The Crime Laboratory Scientists came to Lair's house. They found blood in front of the dryer in the basement. Dust had been knocked off the pipes as though someone had been suspended from them. Blood was also found splattered on one of the walls, and a damp rag was also found which had hundreds of short, clipped hairs on it. While this was taking place, Collins was observed riding by the house. He didn't stop.

In the laboratory, the microscopic examination of the hairs indicated that they were similar to the hairs found on Karry's panties. Also, the blood found on Mrs. Lair's uniform, in front of the dryer, and on the wall was of the same type as Karry's. (44.62)

Dr. Buzas, who lived across from Corporal Lair, said she had seen the same young man who fed the Lair's dog ride off carrying a Bold box on his motorcycle on Friday morning, July 25, 1969. (44.40)

Detectives interviewed Dylan P. and Lydia Metiva who rode with Collins to Ortonville on Saturday morning, July 26th. They said Collins talked incessantly about the missing girl. Lydia Metiva told Collins that the women working at the wig shop were able to identify the young man on the motorcycle whom Karry had ridden off with on that fateful Wednesday. Collins asked her, "Are you sure of what you're talking about?" She answered, "Yes." But it was as though Collins had not heard her answer, because he asked the same question about five times. Both David and Lydia Metiva thought he appeared visibly shaken by what she had said. Then for about twenty minutes he didn't say anything. He sat in complete silence, as though he was in very deep thought. (43.77-78)

Then Collins told them that the girls were stupid and were not careful and deserved it. He talked about how funny it would be to see a body hanging from a viaduct. Collins said, "I am sure they could find them there." At that time Karry's body had not been discovered. Lydia asked him why the killer would want to leave bodies where they could easily be found. Collins replied, "What good would it be if no one found the body, then you wouldn't get credit for it."

Also during that weekend, Metiva said Collins made an unusual comment about using a baseball bat or club to stick up a woman's "snatch or up her ass."

Metiva said he observed a woman's bra in Collins' drawer. Collins didn't want to talk about that. Metiva said Collins knew how to apply the "sleeper hold" which cuts off blood circulation to the brain and can render one unconscious. (44.77-78)

Arnold Davis, Collins' close friend who also lived in the same apartment building with him, was interviewed. At first, Davis told the detectives he had been motor-cycle riding with Collins during the early afternoon when Karry disappeared, but he quickly told them the truth. He told them that Collins had asked him to lie about the times when they were bike riding together.

Davis related how Collins gave him the knife and that he had observed Collins carrying out a cardboard box which contained women's articles after the police had questioned him. (44.48)

Davis also admitted that he had gone to the Secretary of State's Office at Collins' request, to obtain another plate for Collins, who claimed the one on his motorcycle was lost. In fact, it was still on the bike. Ordinarily, at that time, a person was required to either swear or affirm under oath that such plate was lost. Davis then forged Collins' name. In this case, the Secretary Of State's Branch Manager indicated he did not recall Davis swearing under oath that the plate was lost. (16.)

Davis also admitted that he was with Collins when he stole a Triumph motorcycle on July 19, 1969. He stated that he knew of Collins' ability to switch parts on motorcycles. He indicated that Collins had the ability to completely dismantle a motorcycle and put it back together again. Sometimes Collins was asked to work on other people's motorcycles.

In addition, Davis knew Collins had sufficient cash available to pay the bill for work done on his motorcycle the day before Karry disappeared. Collins left the shop with an unpaid balance. Davis said he had between 50 and 100 dollars. (44.48)

Detectives interviewed Frances C. who stated she had accompanied John Collins to his apartment. She said she and Collins kissed. Then Collins made sexual advances toward her. When she resisted, he beat her with his forearm several times. She was hurt and was afraid of serious bodily injury. She stopped trying to resist. Collins was very angry. He had a difficult time maintaining an erection, but Collins raped her and had an orgasm in her. He then apologized for what he had done. Frances said, "He began crying and told me he could not help what he had done because I was so beautiful."

Another girl, Daphne G. said on Sunday, July 20th, Collins gave her a ride on his motorcycle as she was enroute to the drug store. She said Collins took her to his uncle's house on Roosevelt Avenue. She said Collins laid on the floor and wanted her to rub his back. She wouldn't do it, and told him she wasn't a nurse. Collins was very quiet as though he was in deep thought. That disturbed her, and she told him she would walk to the drug store. As she was leaving, he decided to take her to the drugstore.

This was the same Daphne who saw Collins with Jean S. at 11:30 p.m. on the last night she was seen alive as she walked toward her apartment. (44.33)

Karry Norriss was interviewed. She stated that on the afternoon of the day Karry B. disappeared she had a date with John Collins to go swimming. Collins never kept that date. She also related that she wanted to report Collins to the police immediately after Karry disappeared, but her girl friend talked her out of it. Karry also told officers of Collins' practice of switching handlebars, mirrors, and the license plate from motorcycle to motorcycle. She also said Collins always conducted himself as a perfect gentleman around her, and he used to talk with her in a kind of baby talk.(44.83)

An intelligence officer, code name "Horse", enrolled at E.M.U. and began attending classes. While doing this, he established residence where Arnie Davis lived in a different apartment. He befriended Davis in an attempt to establish the extent that Davis was involved in the murder of Karry and others.

The probable cause for the arrest of Collins was based upon the following facts: On the 31st of July, Forensic Scientists discovered minute traces of blood spattered on the wall in front of the dryer, and on the shirt covering Mrs. Lair's laboratory jacket in the basement of the Lair house. They also discovered hundreds of clipped hairs on the basement floor which were similar to those found on Karry's panties which the murderer had crammed into the vaginal vault. Further, Mrs. Lair said there were black marks all over the kitchen floor indicative of a struggle, which she had not mentioned previously to investigators. Add to this the statements of Dr. Buzas, who said she saw the young man who had been feeding the Lair's dog ride off with a large Bold soap box on his motorcycle. Detectives knew a Bold soap box was missing from the Lair's house. Finally, Davis told detectives that he saw Collins remove a Bold soap box from the trunk of his car. At the time, Davis could see that it contained a woman's purse and other items of female apparel which were disposed of by Collins. A warrant was issued for the arrest of John Norman Collins. He was placed under arrest by Captain Stevens, the Second District Commander of the Michigan State Police, and others. At that time Collins returned the key to the Lair house to Corporal Lair.

Early the following morning, after Collins was arrested, Officer Adams, apparently acting entirely upon his own without any direction from the task force commander, went to the respective homes of the women who were working at the wig shop on July 23rd, when Karry was there. He showed each woman a picture of Collins and asked her if Collins was the man with whom Karry had ridden away. Both women told him the same thing. They had decided some time before to refuse to make any identification based on just a picture. They insisted on "seeing the man in the flesh."

Later, on the day of August 1st, when the line-up was conducted, the two women were brought to a room at the Washtenaw County Jail. Collins' attorney was also present. The women were talking together as those who were participating in the line-up came into the room. The women both identified Collins as he came through the door. The people in the line-up were photographed. The attorney, while present, was not told before the line-up began. (44.93)

Later, during an incamera hearing regarding a photo show up, Officer Began testified that he had shown other "mug shots" along with Collins' pictures to the women from the wig shop. This was a different time than the instance above which involved Officer Adams. Again, the women would not make an identification. During a recess, an assistant prosecutor told Officer Charles to, "just get some pictures out of the mug files and use these along with Collins' pictures that had been shown." The assistant prosecutor and all officers present were fully aware that no miscarriage of justice would result from this action since the women had consistently refused to make any firm identification based on photographs. That afternoon, Officer Began testified that these were the pictures he had shown the women along with Collins' pictures. Immediately after this, a police officer noted they could not possibly have been the same pictures, since the arrest dates on the photographs were about five months after Collins' had been arrested. This was pointed out to Officer Bagen. This testimony was then corrected and the officer admitted he did not know whose pictures had been shown along with Collins' at that photographic show up. Prosecutor Delhey, who was a man of great integrity, was furious that this had been done, regardless whether it was a collateral matter.

The investigation continued constantly after Collins was arrested as detectives working on the case concentrated their efforts on insuring the case was properly prepared.

The extensive background investigations on the victim's lives were completed; backup cases were investigated further and were prepared in event they were needed.

Detectives surreptitiously tried to learn as much as possible about every single jury member on the list without actually interviewing neighbors. Their houses were checked by driving by them. Their cars were examined for bumper stickers that might give some insight into the personal beliefs of the owner. The strategy of the people was to select jurors who were highly intelligent, logical people since the People's case was primarily circumstantial with one part of the case connected like a chain of events to the other parts. Each depended on one another. The type of juror desired was one trained in the hard sciences like engineers or chemists.

When it appeared that Mr. Louisell and Mr. Fink would be representing Collins during his trial, investigators met with other detectives, from the Detroit Metropolitan area, who had worked on cases where defendants were previously represented by these two outstanding defense attorneys.

It was learned that Mr. Fink was a very hard working, intelligent attorney, and his cases were thoroughly prepared. He had attributed much of his success as a defense attorney, and he was very, very successful, to the lack of case preparation on the part of the police officers and prosecutors.

Mr. Louisell, on the other hand, had in the past represented organized crime figures from the Detroit area. They said Mr. Louisell was not a "show boat." He was very smart. His cases were well prepared. He would lay the groundwork to defeat opponents during the appeal process, if he happened to lose the case in trial. The detectives said, "He is a master of the innuendo." When they were asked to explain what they meant, they said, "If a witness testified in a way that damages his case, several days later Louisell would phrase questions to another witness using the previous witnesses' testimony. But the testimony will be misstated to the point where it was now favorable to his client. Thus, it would cause the jury to think that the witness had testified much differently than she actually had done." Detroit officers were very pessimistic about the chances of a conviction due to the complexity of the case and the number of witnesses involved.

METHOD OF OPERATION

Since the perpetrator in the case never confessed, no one can know precisely how he operated. We are in a good position though to make some fairly good assumptions based upon the facts as they were brought out during the investigation.

The day before the murder, Collins was feeling the desire to kill again. He attempted to pick up a victim on that day. He went to the J & J Motorcycle Shop. He left there owing them money so he could return there at any time to establish an alibi. He would even have a receipt to prove the date, but this would not contain a time. After that Collins tried unsuccessfully to pick up several girls, but couldn't get one to go with him.

On the twenty-third of July, again he tried to pick up girls. He had a date with a good looking blonde named Karry N., but he didn't keep it. A possible reason for this was he wanted to have sex, but they weren't having a sexual relationship. Also, he did not want to murder someone who he had come to know and regard as a human being. He was not at all sure he could control himself.

He found an eighteen year old freshman student who liked to flirt and also liked adventure. Collins told her he would give her a ride to the wig shop, would wait for her and would then give her a ride back to her dorm.

When Karry came out of the wig shop, she told him she was going to walk back to the dorm. Collins told her he'd give her a ride back, but first it was necessary to stop by and feed and water his state police uncle's dog. His uncle, he probably explained, was a corporal in the Michigan State Police. He was taking care of his house for him while he and his family were on a vacation up north. Karry's family had considerable respect for the Michigan State Police, and her oldest sister was involved in the State of Michigan District Court System. Karry decided it would be safe to go with him. She quite likely reasoned that if a state policeman trusted the care of his house to him, he must certainly be trustworthy.

Upon arrival at Lair's house, Collins took Karry inside and fixed her a drink and asked her to make herself comfortable while he took care of the dog. Karry could readily see the large picture of Corporal Lair, M.S.P. in his uniform and probably relaxed. He quickly fed and watered the German Shepherd in the garage, and went back inside the house. He may then have either went into his "rub my aching back routine" or he may have sat down beside her and tried to kiss her. Collins then tried to have sex with her, but she resisted his advances and tried to leave. She tried to escape through the kitchen, but he grabbed her. They struggled violently with each other in the kitchen. Collins beat Karry viciously. He ripped Karry's clothes from her body and raped her. Then he forced her down into the laundry room of the basement. He then tied her to the plumbing in the ceiling of the basement. She was suspended in the air with electrical wire. Her shorts were ripped up and part of them were crammed back into her mouth as a gag. He continued to beat her—splattering her blood on the wall and the floor.

Collins then washed up and went to the motorcycle shop and paid the bill and tried to act as nonchalant as possible.

He then returned to the Lair's residence where he tried to revive the victim with ammonia by pouring it in her mouth, but he could not revive her. She was still having her period and may have gotten some blood on the floor and probably on Collins. He wiped the floor up with her panties. He saw a plastic baseball bat nearby. He picked up the black bat and using the handle crammed the now dirty panties, covered with clipped hair, into the vaginal vault.

Collins then left the house and went motorcycle riding with his good friend, Arnie, who he trusted a great deal. He told Arnie, should anyone inquire, to lie about the times they were riding together. Collins also asked Davis to go to the Secretary of State's Office posing as Collins and tell them he had lost his license plate, which was still on the motorcycle, and obtain a new plate. Two days later, Davis carried out his friend's request and acquired the plate for him.

That night he worked hard cleaning up the motorcycle which he and Karry had been riding. He wanted to insure it did not have her fingerprints on it. He also returned to the Lair residence to "feed the dog."

Early Friday morning, after midnight, he disposed of Karry's body near Ann Arbor, off Huron River Drive. He then went to his apartment and went to bed.

Early that morning (still Friday), he returned to the house to finish the cleanup job. He couldn't get the spots, which looked like blood, up from the floor. He was very tired and panic set in. As an English major, surely Shakespear's Mac Beth must have come to his mind, "Out damn spot—out." He grabbed a can of black spray paint and painted over them. He then picked up Karry's clothing from around the basement floor. He put everything in an empty Bold soap box which Mrs. Lair used as a waste box. She had put lint in it from the dryer. He then rode off with the box and returned to his apartment and locked the Bold box in the trunk of the Oldsmobile until he was able to dispose of it the following morning.

PHYSICAL EVIDENCE

The following items of physical evidence were obtained and examined. The cloth gag found in Karry's mouth came from her gold colored Burmuda shorts. These were identified by her mother. (44.23)

Karry's panties had been cut through the crotch with a knife. There were literally hundreds of short clipped hairs embedded into the fabric of the panties. These hairs were examined both microscopically and with Neutron Activation Analysis. Experts disagreed on the value of these examinations. On the people's side, experts said there was one chance in a million that the hair found on the panties came from some place besides the Lair basement floor. The defense said it was not possible to say that based upon averaging the half lives of the various elements from the various known samples taken from Corporal Lair and his sons. (44.26)

Both wet slides and dry slides were utilized to make a microscopic analysis of the fibers found in the victim's panties with the samples taken from the floor. The comparison was similar in every respect and different in none.

The photographs showing heavy duty electrical cord markings on the victim's body were important. Lair had a cord like that in the basement.

Blood samples were discovered on the floor and wall in the basement of the Lair's home and on a shirt covering a uniform. The victim's blood, type A, matched the blood found in the basement. (44.62)

Karry was positively identified by using fingerprints obtained from items in her college dormitory room. Her dental records, acquired from her dentist in Grand Rapids, matched positively. (44.61, 91)

The two Triumph motorcycles with the green and blue gas tanks respectively were also seized and held until after the trial. These cycles were devoid of evidence such as fingerprints. Collins had washed and polished them thoroughly and had switched the parts from one cycle to the other. (44.83)

The replacement license plate that Collins had sent Davis to obtain for him claiming the other plate was lost was seized. (44.75)

Crime laboratory scientists made drawings of the location where Karry's body was discovered, the Lair's basement where she was beaten to death, and also the area in front of the wig shop where witnesses saw Collins ride off with Karry. From there he headed toward the Lair residence on Michigan Avenue. (44.34)

The photographs taken during the line up when Collins was identified by Pam S. and Joy G were used. (44.29)

The order and receipt from the wig shop on the wiglet ordered by Karry were obtained from the owner. (44.33)

WEATHER CONDITIONS

On July 23, 1969, as Karry walked to the wig shop, the temperature was about eighty-one degrees. The wind was blowing out of the southeast between five and twelve miles per hour. The sky was cloudy. There was no precipitation that day.

The high for the day was reached between 2:00 p.m. and 3:00 p.m. when temperatures reached eighty-five degrees. This was about the same time she was murdered. Then temperatures began to fall. By 6:00 p.m. it was at eighty-two degrees.

On July 24th, a very small amount (.07 in.) of rain occurred at 6:00 p.m.

On July 25th, there was a trace of rain at 4:00 p.m. and at 11:00 p.m. until 12:00 midnight .17" of rain fell.

On the 26th of July only .02 of an inch of rain was recorded.

REMARKS

We know that much more rain than was reported had occurred on the night of July 26th during the stake out. This information dealt with that period of time when Karry was missing until her body was discovered.

VEHICLE(S) INVOLVED

Collins offered Karry a ride on a stolen "Trophy Special" Triumph motorcycle. It was one year old. It had been stolen during the late evening of July 18th or the early morning hours of Saturday, July 19, 1969, in Ypsilanti. The cycle had a yellow gas tank and chrome fenders. Collins simply pushed the cycle down the street as though it had run out of gas. Collins then went to another apartment complex in Ypsilanti between 2:00 a.m. and 6:00 a.m. and stole a blue gas tank, seat and battery from a two year old Triumph that he found parked there. Collins then put the stolen parts on the stolen Triumph. The seat and the yellow gas tank were then taken to the Helena Apartments on Emmet Street in Ypsilanti and were left there. The seat was recovered from that location, but not the gas tank.

Arnold Davis, Collins' friend, was with him when all of the above occurred. He also forged Collins' name at the Secretary of State's Office to obtain a license plate for the stolen motorcycle. Collins had another motorcycle similar to that one. It was a green Triumph. It was the plate from that bike that Collins was using when the victim was picked up. (44.48)

The affidavit which Davis signed had an incorrect serial number for the green Triumph also. They had increased the first three numbers by one hundred. (62.)

The opinion that Collins used a Triumph Special with the blue gasoline tank the day he picked up the victim is based upon the following: The witness in the Chocolate Shop, Cheri W., paid little attention to Collins or the girl with him. She was very much interested in motorcycles. From her initial interview, she said the motorcycle was a Triumph with a blue gasoline tank.

Arnie Davis went riding with Collins on the Triumph motorcycle with the green tank. Davis said the Triumph with the blue tank was warm to touch.

Jack Lowry, the mechanic who had put a new chain on the Triumph with the blue gasoline tank, said he talked with Collins on the afternoon of July 23. He said Collins came in with the Triumph motorcycle with the blue tank. He asked Collins whether it was running better with the new chain and Collins told him it was. (44.68)

Later, some investigators were of the opinion that Collins was using the Triumph with the green tank when he picked up the victim. They believed that he used the plate from the stolen bike on the bike with the green tank. Immediately after the murder, they thought he threw this plate away. They were of this opinion because the witnesses at the J & J Motorcycle Shop stated that the motorcycle he was using during the afternoon of July 23rd did not have semi high rise handle bars. The cycle with the green tank also did not have semi-high rise handlebars, but the cycle with the blue tank did have them. Also Pam S., the witness in the wig shop, said the tank was either black or green.

The other vehicle used during the commission of this crime was a one year old (1968) Oldsmobile Cutlass Coach. It was painted black over grey with Michigan license plates RVO101. This car was actually registered in Collins' mother's name. Quite likely that was done for insurance reasons.

The day after Collins' arrest, a search warrant was obtained and executed to search his car. The warrant was based upon the following probable causes: (1) Karry's body was transported approximately five miles away from where she was murdered. (2) Some form of transportation was necessary to take her body from where she was murdered to where the body was found. Undoubtedly, public roads had to be used. (3) This car was constantly available for his use. It was his car. His mother's name on the title was only nominal. And (4) the front license plate from his car had been missing for over a week. (At that time, a front registration plate was required under Michigan law.)

While evidence linking Collins with the murder in California and the murder of Anne K. was found in that car, no evidence was found linking Collins to the murder of Karry. (44.46)

It is not known what type of vehicle Collins used to carry out his crimes. In the case of Anne K., it was probably his car. With Rose in California, it was his car. With Jean S., it was his car. With Karry it was a combination of picking her up with the motorcycle and then using his car to transport her body, wrapped in a blanket to where it was found.

It is believed that Dora B. would never have gotten into a car with a stranger, but she was a very tough, strong, adventurous girl who would have been willing to accept a ride on a motorcycle with a handsome young stranger whom she had seen dating a girl from the apartment complex across the street from her home.

Mona F. was observed rejecting a ride from a man who tried to pick her up by driving into a driveway and blocking her path as she walked. Collins did this frequently when he was trying to pick up girls either with a motorcycle or a car. Did Collins then return to his apartment, get his motorcycle and then return to the area where she was walking? Did she then ride with him on the motorcycle even though she was wearing a tent dress? Did Collins take her to his apartment, strip her clothes from her, and then stab her to death? Did he then transport her body out to an abandoned farm where he threw it on a trash pile? And did he then hide her clothes under some cardboard near the circle drive? No one will ever know what Collins did unless he decides to confess, and that seems very unlikely. It is known that an Expo '67 Canadian Silver dollar was found in Collins' apartment. Collins denied that it was his and that he ever had it. Mona F. did have one just like it that she wore on a necklace.

THE PERPETRATOR

John Norman Collins A.K.A. John Norman Collins Chapman, Bill Kenyon, Don Collins, and Creepy John, was convicted of the murder of Karry B. on August 17, 1970. The jury had deliberated for twenty-seven and one-half hours before reaching their decision.

The jury which convicted Collins, was one of the most intelligent and best educated ever to hear a case in the history of American Jurisprudence. Eight of the jurors were college graduates. Several of those had completed post graduate work. Three of the jurors were engineers.

According to information obtained after the verdict was rendered, the jury had voted on the first ballot to convict Collins of first degree murder ten to two. On the second ballot taken after discussion, the vote moved to eleven to one.

Then for three days the beautiful wife of a University of Michigan Law professor held her ground until finally she was persuaded to change her vote to avoid a hung jury.

There was substantial evidence available to convict Collins of the murder of Rose P. in California and Jean S. (AKA Jill Hirsch) and Anne K. in Michigan.

Collins' parents were married on May 15, 1943, and they were divorced on January 18, 1949, by Circuit Court Judge Calahan in Detroit.

John Collins was born on June 17, 1947, at Riverside in the Province of Ontario in Canada. He was the middle child of Robert and Loraine (nee Gerard) Chapman.

On June 30, 1953, when John Collins was six years old, he became a naturalized American citizen. His mother had moved back into the United States and married Mr. Warner Collins who had a garage in the Centerline area.

Mr. Collins adopted John in 1956. He grew up working with his step-father. It was reported that John was very close to his step-father and cried when his mother and Mr. Collins were divorced. His step-father said John was an adept mechanic, but he was better at working on cars than motorcycles.

John Collins attended a Roman Catholic Parochial School. The sisters thought quite highly of him. It appeared that he was insecure as a child because from time to time he slept with his mother up to the age of twelve. (13)

John was active in sports while in St. Clements High School. He was co-captain of the football team. He was a good athlete. Later in college, he was active in an Alpine Skiing Club.

In the fall of 1965, Collins enrolled at Central Michigan University in Mount Pleasant, Michigan. His older brother lived and worked in that area. In the summer of 1966, however, Collins transferred to Eastern Michigan University in Ypsilanti. He was pursuing a bachelor's degree in education. His major was English. In his papers were found many other works by other students. When he was arrested, he only needed a few additional hours for graduation. He probably could have completed his college studies by taking summer courses. It has also been suggested that the reason he did not, was to avoid being drafted into the army and being sent to Vietnam.

Collins was accepted into a fraternity at Eastern Michigan University and lived in the Fraternity House for a time. It was alleged, however, that his brothers learned that he was involved in thievery, and he was asked to leave before he was caught as it would have a negative impact upon the fraternity.

Collins' personal habits, as far as cleanliness was concerned, were excellent. He always kept himself neat and clean. He did the same with the vehicles he possessed.

104

This was true whether he bought the equipment or stole it. He kept the two "road bikes" in outstanding appearance. They were always clean and highly polished. He also maintained all the vehicles in excellent mechanical condition.

Collins' demeanor was ingratiating. He liked to make people laugh. But one of his classmates, both in high school and at the university said, "He (Collins) had to be popular. If the group would quit laughing at the things he would do, then he would quit associating with them and associate with a group who did laugh at him." (44.99) It appeared Collins had a real need to be the center of attention and required considerable recognition. He frequently liked to help other people. For example, twice in 1969 he took care of his uncle's dog and looked after his house while his uncle (by marriage), his aunt, and two first cousins were out of town on vacation. He also helped his friends by making adjustments on their motorcycles and taught others to ride them. (44.48)

Collins did not smoke cigarettes or use tobacco products, and he drank very little alcoholic beverages. He did apparently use an anxiety reducing drug. When Collins was arrested, a bottle of valium was found on the dresser in his apartment.

Most people who knew John Collins superficially thought very highly of him. He was the epitome of what a young American man should be. He was clean cut and well developed physically. He especially had very muscular biceps. In the September 1969 issue of *Tomorrow's Man*, a picture of John Collins was published showing him flexing his muscles. He posed under the name Bill Kenyon.

At the time of his arrest, John Collins was residing at an apartment house at 619 Emmett Street in Ypsilanti, Michigan. He was six feet tall, weighed about one hundred and seventy pounds, had blue eyes and had dark brown straight hair. He kept his hair well trimmed and combed a lock of it down over his forehead. His teeth were very straight and even and women described him as exceptionally handsome. Many people thought the police had the wrong man.

The witness in the Chocolate Shop said that the motorcycle the man was riding was positively a Triumph. She would not exclude or identify Collins during the line-up. She said she felt sorry for him. Several young ladies were leaving him flowers.

Cpl. Derik Lair of the Michigan State Police thought a great deal of John Collins. Lair was a dedicated police professional who wished to see the state police staffed with outstanding troopers. He was so impressed with Collins that he had asked him to join the Michigan State Police. (44.69)

Collins had coffee with other troopers at the Bomber Restaurant in Ypsilanti. This was a favorite hangout for all the police officers in the area. In fact, the owner of the restaurant had one large round table at the back which was usually occupied by policemen from one or more departments. Officers ate there, and frequently stopped in before, during, and after duty.

It was common practice to exchange investigative information, and there can be little doubt that Collins was privy to confidential information about the progress of the investigations of the various murders the task force was investigating. That source of information would have been diminished, however, when the task force moved its operations to the Holy Ghost Seminary because task force members then did not frequent the Bomber as often.

Collins still spent time motorcycle riding with Sergeant Judd McBryde of the Eastern Michigan University Police Department. Undoubtedly, Collins used his acquaintance with McBryde to try to acquire information regarding the investigation in the same fashion that he tried to obtain information from his state police uncle.

Aside from his study of Dostoevsky's *Crime and Punishment*, there is no indication that he studied criminal investigation or served in any security type work before his arrest.

Beneath this facade, however, was a much darker side of John Norman Collins, of which very few people were aware, including some of his closest relatives. For example, while he was "helping" his Michigan State Police uncle by looking after his dog and house while he was on vacation, he also stored a stolen Bultaco motorcycle in his uncle's garage. Incidents such as this show Collins' uncanny ability to use people for his own gain. (44.69)

In the spring of 1968, before the second victim, Jean S., was murdered, Collins took Pauline L. to the Lair residence during the time he was taking care of it. She said Collins became angry and upset when she refused to have sexual intercourse with him.

In the spring of 1969, he took the beautiful blonde, Karry Norriss to the Lair's house. He had a date with her on the same day he murdered Karry B., but "he stood her up."

Just three days before Karry was murdered, Collins took Daphne G. to the Lair's house. He tried to get her to rub his back for him, but she wouldn't do it.

After July 23rd, Karry Norriss became convinced that John Collins was the murderer and she wanted to call the police. She based this upon the following: (1) John Collins matched the police artist's sketch published in all the news papers. (2) John Collins rode a motorcycle. (3) When John Collins left the area and went to California, the murders in Ypsilanti stopped. (4) While Collins was in California, a girl in Salinas was murdered. (5) On Sunday, July 20, 1969, she saw him and asked him to go swimming with her. He replied, "Why not, if it isn't you, it will be someone else."(6)

After the murder of Karry B., he switched the handlebars and removed the square mirror from his motorcycle. Added to this, of course, was the fact that Collins broke his date with her. (44.83) Karry Norriss' friend, Susan, talked her out of calling the police because she thought Karry Norriss was just very upset because Collins didn't keep their date.

Another young woman, who knew John Collins for several years, was the girl friend of Collins' former schoolmate. She said, "He is very aggressive, and can rationalize anything that he does wrong." She also said, "...He is deceptive." And she related an incident that occurred when she was only fourteen years old. She said he took her to his grandparents' home in Canada. He told her he wanted her to meet them. But when they arrived, the grandparents were not there. She was too embarrassed to talk about it. One can only speculate about what happened there, but whatever it was, it left her with the steadfast belief that, "He would be capable of any crime." She said, "He would only associate with girls to get something from them—either sex or to get them to do his school work." (44.100)

John Collins held most women in very low esteem. He told his aunt, Mrs. Lair, that his mother was a "bitch." Mrs. Lair was surprised and shocked that her nephew would say this about her sister. She said, "John you should never talk that way about your mother. Why did you say that?" He replied, "She goes around the house not properly attired." (44.71)

It is also possible that he knew of the alleged affair that his mother was having with a very prominent Jewish man who owned an exceptionally large clothing store in the Detroit Metropolitan area. In fact, it was said that she was his mistress, but the truth of this was not established.

Collins also, allegedly, attacked and beat his sister, Amy, with a meat tenderizer after he supposedly caught her and another man having sexual intercourse in his mother's house at 7327 Helen Street in Centerline, Michigan. (44.71)

One time Collins allegedly told some of his high school friends when they were near John R. and Brush in Detroit, "Let's get us a whore and cut her tits off and paste them on the car windows." Another time he talked about grabbing one of the girls, tying her up, and dumping her on Belle Isle. (1.)

It's very clear that Collins thought women's primary value was for men to have sexual intercourse with them. For example he told Louise A.W., "God made women for sex." (44.100)

When he tried to have sexual intercourse with another girl in his apartment, she resisted him and asked, "Do you have to take every girl to bed?" He replied, "That's all girls are worth."

On March 9, 1969, he forcibly raped Frances C. in his apartment. Frances met him and thought he was such a handsome young man that when he asked her to go to his apartment to watch television together she assented.

At the apartment, he gave her something to drink. They sat on the couch together and kissed. Then he made sexual advances towards her. She resisted. He threw her to the floor and twisted her arms behind her. Then he hit her several times with his forearm alongside her neck. The pain was terrible. She feared for her life if she continued to struggle, so she quit fighting. He stripped her blue jeans and panties off and his own trousers and tried to insert his penis into her. He had a difficult time because he could not maintain an erection. She said he was very angry. She thought, "The anger appeared to arise more from his inability to maintain an erection—rather than my previous resistance." Finally, he was able to get it in and did ejaculate into her.

Then he apologized to her for raping her. He began crying. He said she was so beautiful he just could not help himself. He tried to make arrangements for a future date. Out of shame, she did not report this information to the police sooner. (44.44)

Collins apparently did not believe that any woman should ever date when she was having a menstrual period. One time he was dating a girl named Genevieve J. She said that one evening he was saying "good night" to her when suddenly he asked, "You're having your period aren't you?" She told him that she was, and he replied, "Disgusting," and he walked away. Arnie Davis, Collins' roommate, said Collins could tell when a woman was having a period. Davis did not know how he could determine this, but he had the ability to do it. (44.48)

Collins also had a dislike for women who pierced their ears. He told Lillian D. that he did not like women with pierced ears. And he tested another young woman about her feelings in that area. (44.112)

Leah W. met John Collins at the Theta Chi Fraternity House in Ypsilanti in September 1968. This was two months after the murder of Jean S. They were at a party. They talked about their common background. Both were from broken homes and were Roman Catholic. Collins then talked about people's actions. He told her, "You should not worry about what you do and never regret anything that you do". He said this was different from what he had been instructed at the Catholic School, and that is why he did not care for what they had to teach. He gave an example about the Ten Commandments and how utterly foolish he thought they were. "Take the Fifth Commandment for example. 'Thou shalt not kill.' I know how to commit the perfect crime." (44.97)

Leah had short hair. John told her she would look really nice with pierced ears. She replied, "I have never really considered them, and I never will."

They talked about their birth dates and astrology. Leah told Collins that his sign was Gemini and that these people supposedly had split personalities. Collins was very interested in this. "Do you think I have a split personality?" he asked. She said, "I don't know." Then they danced and a very peculiar thing happened. First, they danced fast and everyone else was watching them because John Collins was such a good dancer. Then they danced a slow dance, and Leah said, "I was very pleased with the way that John held me, and we danced quite close. After the music stopped, John (Collins) pushed me away. His face appeared very pale. He looked very drained. He said, 'You're a phoney. You're just like all the rest.' " Then they sat down. John Collins stared out the window. After a few minutes, Leah said, "John came to and went back to normal." (44.97)

John Collins statement to Leah about not worrying about what she did corresponds to his belief set forth in a college paper he wrote for one of his classes. In it he said, in substance, "That it doesn't make any difference what society feels is right or wrong. If you want a ring in a store and don't have money to buy it, you can steal it. And if you are holding a gun on a person, it is up to you whether or not to kill that person."

Also in the glove box of Collins' Oldsmobile Cutlass was found Cliff Notes of Fyodor Dostoevsky's *Crime and Punishment*. In that novel, a poor university student murdered an old woman pawn broker with an axe. The student, Raskolnikoff, wrote an article which he later discussed with a magistrate while visiting him in chapter nineteen. The magistrate said that Raskolnikoff, "...Maintained that there are men in existence who can, or more accurately, who have an absolute right to commit all kinds of wicked and criminal acts—men for whom, to a certain extent, laws do not exist."

Raskolnikoff disputed that interpretation. He asked, "Didn't he mean to say that a criminal is urged to crime by the irresistible centrifugal influence?" Then later he amplified his position, "This is what I really maintained: An extraordinary man has a right—not officially, be it understood, but from and by his very individuality—to permit his conscience to overstep certain bounds, only so far as the realization of one of his ideas may require it." (21.184-185)

Collins' former roommate, previously mentioned, who had known him in both high school and college said, "Collins felt that he couldn't do anything wrong." (44.99)

Collins appeared to have bisexual tendencies. It was alleged that Collins associated with a homosexual, Asa S., during his high school days. Asa S. allegedly gave Collins beer and money in exchange for sexual favors.

According to his roommate, Collins told him that "He would like to have sex in the ass." (44.48)

Collins also allegedly tried to sleep with Dylan M. over the weekend that Karry's body was found and the stake out occurred. He also allegedly put his hand on Jeff M's leg on the trip back to Ypsilanti.

Another witness even said Collins had his nephew, Dewey M., play with his penis when they were enroute to a football game. (35) (1)

Collins also allegedly went up to his attic when he was a high school student so he could window peek on a girl who was his neighbor. (35) He also continued to window peek on occasion until shortly before he was arrested. (44.73A) (16.)

Collins did have the ability to rationalize acts and blame others. He had little sympathy for the girls who had been murdered. He thought they were stupid. They should have been more careful. (44.78)

Besides his involvement in the crimes of murder and rape, Collins was also extensively involved in breaking and enterings with his friend with whom he had traveled to California.

After the case was over, several weeks were spent tracking down various owners of the stolen property that he had in his possession and returning it to them.

Collins apparently either had dreams about the murders or was laying the ground work for a criminal defense in that area. One night, sometime between September and December 1968, while working part time at Motor Wheel Company in Ypsilanti— he asked a fellow worker whether he ever had any dreams where girls were taken out, raped, and then killed. (44.98)

Collins' reaction, when he was being interrogated and was caught in a lie, was generally to stop speaking, until he could clearly think about what he was saying.

Collins attitude about the investigation and the ensuing trial could be characterized as the old, "the best offense is a good defense." For example, when officer Mathewson was writing down the serial numbers of the motorcycles in the garage, some of which were stolen, Collins said, " Let him go play policeman someplace else". And again when the author was conducting a line-up with Cheri W., the waitress at The Chocolate Shop. She said from the outset that the motorcycle was a Triumph. Collins asked the author, "You think I killed all those girls don't you?" And finally, when he drove by the Lair's residence several times while laboratory scientists were working on the crime scene there. All of these and many more demonstrate a brazen, bold attitude.

Eight years after the offense, Collins was still lying and denying he killed Karry B. For example, in an interview conducted by Davis Nadeau for the Detroit Free Press, Collins was asked, "Why is John Norman Collins in Jackson Prison?" Collins replied, "...I think there was a lot of tension in the Washtenaw area in the summer of '68 and '69, and I think that the police had a lot of social pressure—community pressure, and I think that they needed a solution to a problem which was several unsolved murders in the Ann Arbor-Ypsilanti area, and I think I happened to be at the wrong place at the wrong time."

Could it be that he was unaware of the arrest of ex-con Ernest Bishop for the murder of Madeline P? The task force played a critical role in Bishop's apprehension. Bishop admitted he killed her. Bishop was a poor, black male who had a previous criminal record for rape. That murder occurred in Ann Arbor just nineteen days before the murder of Karry. If the police were interested in just hanging these murders on someone, why not Bishop? He certainly would have been easier to convict.

Then later, Collins told the interviewer, "...I was engaged to be married that summer, the summer that I was arrested, '69". This was simply another outright lie. Collins was not engaged to anyone.

At first, after Collins was sent to prison, he spent long periods of time in Jackson Prison's extensive law library, and he built a shell around himself. (66.3B)

Then he became involved in athletics and played on the prison football, softball, and baseball teams. He also lifted weights to increase his strength. His weight increased to two hundred and five pounds within the first six years.

He was described as a model prisoner and was granted many special privileges. His cell was located in an honor block where he even had his own television set. His job was managing the prison gym. All during this time he, through his lawyers, appealed to the State Court of Appeals, the Michigan Supreme Court, the United States District Court in Detroit, the Sixth United States Circuit Court in Cincinnati and the United States Supreme Court. All appeals were rejected. (66.3B)

In 1977, Collins was transferred to the maximum security prison in Marquette in Michigan's Upper Peninsula. This was after he was thought to have been instrumental in the escape of Robert Taylor, another convicted murderer. It was learned at that time, that Collins was planning an escape by helicopter. It was also alleged that Collins was heading a drug selling ring inside the prison. (41)

A short time after his arrival at Marquette, Collins and six other inmates tried to dig an escape tunnel. Of those involved, six were convicted murderers and the seventh was serving two life terms for kidnapping and armed robbery. They had tunnelled nineteen feet before they were caught.

Then he was placed into a special cell, F Block, with twenty-two other of the state's highest risk inmates. He spent twenty-three hours each day there.

111

In 1982, he had the approval of the Director of the Michigan Department of Corrections to serve the remainder of his sentence in Canada. Had that occurred it is quite likely Collins would have been paroled in 1985, after serving fifteen years in confinement. However, a fellow inmate alerted the press of this. Prosecutor William Delhey of Washtenaw County, and Beverly Buchholz moved to block such a transfer. With the extensive publicity, Director Brown reversed his decision.

Since then Collins' record has been "pretty good", but corrections officers did discover two hacksaw blades and a drill bit inside his cell. (66.3B)

In 1995, Collins can petition the Governor of the State of Michigan for a commutation of his life sentence. It is unlikely that such a petition will be granted. (66.3B)

Collins was quiet until September of 1988. At that time he launched his offense for either a new trial or a commutation of his sentence in 1995 by the Governor of Michigan. Again many of the things he said were either misleading or were lies created by him to generate sympathy for himself. Let us examine a few of his statements published in the Oakland Press on September 11th and 17th 1988.

Collins was asked whether he felt betrayed by the Lair family. He said, "...Then, when they refused to give their blood types, which was the same type that they found on the (basement) floor...I thought it was a travesty of justice."

The truth was that each member of the Lair family gave a sample of blood for analysis by an English expert in the area of blood analysis.

Collins was asked whether he had ever taken a lie detector test. Collins said, "At one time I did. We had it all set up...he turned it into a charade."

Then he was asked, "Would you take one now?" To which Collins replied, "No, I definitely wouldn't take one now. Not with all the evidence regarding lie-detector tests. They say they are only forty percent accurate."

The fact is that Collins' polygraph examination was arranged by his attorney. It was to be administered by Mr. Alex L. Gregory. Mr. Gregory was part of a three man team comprised of the famous writer Erle Stanley Gardner, and Le Moyne Snyder. Dr. Snyder was a lawyer, medical doctor, and author of the classic work, *Homicide Investigation*. These three men called themselves, "The Court of Last Resort". They carried tremendous influence. Their primary objective was to protect the rights of any person whom they believed was falsely accused of a serious crime, usually that of murder.

Based on what those present told the author, Collins' polygraph test was anything but a "charade". The polygraph had been set up in the judge's private chambers. Collins was brought over to the Washtenaw County Court House for the examina-

112

tion. Mr. Ryan, who was then Collins' attorney, briefly talked with the polygraph examiner with John Collins present in the room. Then Mr. Ryan left and told the detectives standing guard outside the door, that he was going to the (court house) coffee shop. If he was needed, he could be reached there.

The detectives standing guard overheard the polygraph examiner telling Collins that he had here a scrap book which contained many stories about the innocent people that he had cleared (as part of the Court of Last Resort). They heard him tell Collins that if he was telling the truth, he would clear him too. If he was not, it would be reported to his attorney that he was lying. As the examiner was talking to Collins, he moved toward the door and shut it. Then the detectives could hear no further.

A short time later, perhaps fifteen minutes to a half an hour, the door opened again. Mr. Gregory asked, "Where is Mr. Ryan?" The detectives told him down in the coffee shop. Mr. Gregory asked them to go get him and ask that he return to the judge's chambers. The detectives found Mr. Ryan and together they went back upstairs to the judge's chambers. Mr. Ryan went inside alone with Mr. Gregory and John Collins.

They were only inside the room with the door shut for a few minutes. Then the door opened and Mr. Ryan came out and announced that his client would not be taking a polygraph test. He asked the officers to return Collins to the jail.

Collins left the chambers. The officers who were present said he was crying. Some officers who were working at the jail later said Collins cried all that night in his cell.

Years later officers speculated whether this was the reason that Mrs. Collins fired Mr. Ryan and hired Mr. Fink and Mr. Louisell, because Collins had confessed to Mr. Gregory and then could not be put on the stand? Was this the reason Mr. Fink and Mr. Louisell did not put Collins on the stand to testify in his own behalf?

Everyone knows that had Collins then denied murdering Karry. His lawyers could then be disbarred for perpetrating a fraud upon the court.

Mr. Fink, an acknowledged brilliant defense attorney, recently said concerning polygraph , "When we took over, we never opted for one because it would not have been admissible anyhow and we felt it wouldn't have made a difference."

The truth is the polygraph would have made a remarkable difference if Collins were really telling the truth. Even twenty years ago—it was exceedingly rare when a prosecutor continued to pursue a case against an accused when the accused had passed a polygraph examination administered by a competent expert.

In addition to that, a favorable polygraph examination result would be considered as part of the information received by an appellate court in Michigan, and would be considered with other facts in their decision on whether a new trial should be granted. This principle was set forth in People vs. Barbara.

Collins' figure of forty percent validity on polygraph is clearly erroneous. In the report, *Validity and Reliability of Detection of Deception* put out by the National Institute for the Administration of Criminal Justice on page eleven it is written, "However the seven examiners who employed numerical scoring of the charts were significantly more accurate in the decisions (99 percent) than the eighteen examiners who did not use numerical scoring (eighty-eight percent)". In Michigan, which has the highest polygraph standards in the United States, very few examiners do not utilize the numerical scoring system.

Further, the government spends between twenty to thirty thousand dollars training each and every polygraph examiner. Private examiners spend thousands of dollars of their own money for the finest polygraph instruments available. Does Collins really believe private examiners would be willing to spend four to six thousand dollars on an instrument that was no more than forty percent accurate? Common sense tells us otherwise.

Collins said that the state went to a "sewer water tester" from the Michigan Department of Public Health to analyze the hair because, "they couldn't get a qualified person to get up there and say the things they wanted him to say."

Here Collins was making obvious reference to Laboratory Scientist Walter Holz who not only analyzed the blood—but also analyzed the hair found in the basement of the Lair home. Mr. Holz was hardly a "sewer water tester." He was Chief of the Criminalistics Section of the Michigan Health Department. Collins was right about part of his statement—the state could and did find the best experts possible to analyze the hair. In addition to Mr. Holz, the state had the hair analyzed by Dr. Quinn and Mr. Howard Schlesinger of Gulf Atomic Laboratories in San Diego, California. The hair had been analyzed using the most modern technique available at the time—Neutron Activation Analysis.

Dr. Quinn stated that, in his opinion, odds were one in nine million that the hair found on Karry's panties could have come from someplace else other than the floor of the Lair basement. He said that he would be conservative on the witness stand by testifying the odds were two in nine million. Dr. Quinn was backing up testimony of Mr. Schlesinger.

The day that the four neutron activation analysis experts testified in court (two for the people and two for the defense), the validity of the test was never an issue. What was at issue, was whether one could make a comparison between a sample taken from the floor and a sample from the hair found on Karry's panties. What complicated the procedure was the fact that there were hair clippings from three different people on the floor.

The people's experts argued that such comparisons could be made. The defense's experts argued otherwise on the stand, but during the recess, after all the experts had testified, Dr. Quinn showed the defense experts his mathematical computations. During these discussions which involved much highly esoteric language between twelve experts (other experts had been present just to listen)—one of the defense experts conceded Dr. Quinn was correct. It could be done as he had said. Enroute to the airport, Dr. Quinn said to the author, "Dr. Jarvis has taken a position too early. Now he will not back off from it. Someday, over a glass of scotch, he will admit that I am right."

There are many other areas that could be gone into regarding Collins' misstatements and lies, but it would not be appropriate at this time. What is very obvious is that Collins has no remorse at all for murdering Karry, nor does he have any feeling for the great loss he inflicted upon her family. As is so typical with this type of criminal, he sees himself as the victim, and he is obviously continuing to find some woman to use, as he has done all his life.

OBSERVATIONS

Early in the morning, on the day of the line-up, after Collins was arrested, an officer went to the respective homes of both women who were working in the wig shop on July 23rd. The officer said he was carrying out the instructions of the Task Force Commander. Major Myre denied that he had ever told him to do such a thing.

Since the defendant was in custody and was available for a regular line-up, it was improper to do this in Michigan. There were some who said that this was done to insure that both women would be able to identify Collins later that day.

It was fortunate that both women refused to make an identification based upon a photograph. They told the officer the same thing they told the author when they were shown photographs of possible suspects. This was before the investigation narrowed down to John Norman Collins. They said, "This is far too important to make any identification based upon a picture! We want to see the man in the flesh."

The officer's actions and the manner in which the line-up itself was conducted, caused Collins' identification at the subsequent line up to be ruled inadmissible. It is possible that had an identification been made during those early morning hours, the subsequent in court identification could have been rejected too.

The lesson here for those in law enforcement, is that a single photograph of an arrested person should not be shown to a witness just prior to a line-up. It is highly suggestive that the person in the photograph is the person the police have in custody and the one they want the witness to identify.

In the author's opinion, the identification of John Norman Collins by these two women was given a great deal of weight by the members of the jury. While in many instances eye witness identification is unreliable, this case was an exception. Both women were thinking about the young women who had been murdered while they were talking with Karry. Both women went outside to look at the young man on the motorcycle. The owner of the shop was so worried she even offered Karry a ride back to her dormitory.

Both women were chatting together when the line-up of August 1st began. They identified Collins as he came through the door. He followed two other people into the room and there were several other participants who were behind him. This practice could lead to an identification by consensus. This should be avoided. Only one witness should be in the room at a time. That witness should not be brought into the room until the suspect and the other participants are in the room and the line-up has been set. Each participant should be holding a number or be standing directly beneath one. The author believes that having the participants hold cards with the number is preferential to having them stand under a number painted on the wall. The reason for this is it can cause confusion due to the witness looking at the participants at an angle. To understand this, all one has to do is note the difference between the instrument readings in an automobile between the way the driver sees them and the way one sitting in the passenger's seat does.

116

Identifying by number is better than asking the witness to count from the right or left. This again can be confusing. When someone says," The third person from the left", does he mean my left or the participant's left?"

The officer in charge of conducting the line-up should be very careful of what is said to the witness. It should not be implied in any way, that the suspect is even present. In this case, it would have been much more appropriate to ask, "If you see the young man with whom Karry B. rode away from the wig shop with on the afternoon of July 23rd, please let me know which number he is holding." If an identification is made, the witness should be asked to write down the number on a 3x5 card. The card should then be signed by the witness and dated.

In this case, before the trial, the author questioned the witnesses about their identification individually. He asked each woman, "Are you absolutely positive that the young man you saw Karry ride away with was the man you later identified as John Norman Collins?"
"Yes."
"Isn't it possible, just possible, that you're making a mistake?"
"No."
"Do you realize that if you are wrong, we could be sending an innocent boy to prison for the rest of his life?"
"Yes, I realize that, but I'm not wrong." Essentially, this was each woman's response. The women were both unshakable.

The line-up should be photographed as each witness views it. The names of the participants should be recorded along with their position. The suspect should be permitted to pick his own spot in the line-up. The first line-up should have at least six people in it. Try to keep the numbers even. That way no one will ever be in the center. The lighting should be adequate, but not glaring as it will cause participants to squint. The participants do not have to be clones. But the line-up should be fair and governed by common sense.

For example, it would be patently unfair to put a lone white suspect into a line-up with five other black men. If possible, the participants should be dressed alike or very similar. They should be about the same build. That avoids an identification of clothing rather than perpetrator.

After each witness views the line-up, she should be taken into another room. This way there is no opportunity for her to discuss the line-up participants with someone waiting to view it. The line-up participants should then be shifted to new positions. Their positions should be recorded. Again let the suspect choose his spot. Photograph the line-up. When everything is set, bring in the next witness.

In this case when the line-up began, Collins' attorney was standing at the back of the room. He was apparently talking with someone. Later during an in camera hearing, the purpose of which was to challenge the line-up and the in court identification which followed, he testified that no one appraised him that the line-up was about to begin or had begun. Therefore, he was not in a position to protect his client's rights. The participants in that line-up happened to be other prisoners.

After Collins was arrested, he was placed in another line-up at the Washtenaw County Jail. This line-up was related to the Anne K. murder. Officer Mathewson asked his fraternity brothers to participate in the line-up with John Norman Collins because several of them appeared very similar to Collins physically.

Collins and all the other participants wore the standard one-piece jail coveralls. Collins was wearing jail slippers. The witnesses viewing the line-up, however, were unable to see the feet of the line-up participants through the one-way mirror. In addition, and not noticed by the author, Collins was the only person in the line-up without a tee shirt.

Collins' attorney was present. He was asked by the author whether he had any objections to the fairness of the line-up or the procedures being employed. He said, "I'll withhold my objections at this time." The author did point out to him from the viewing room that Collins was wearing jail slippers. Collins' attorney acknowledged that the witness would not be able to see his feet. The line-up was held and those particular witnesses were unable to identify Collins.

In the newspapers the following morning were printed the interviews by members of the press with the fraternity brothers who took part in the line-up. They said the line-up was unfair because they were all wearing shoes and Collins had on slippers. In addition, they were all wearing a tee shirt and Collins wasn't wearing any.

Had an identification been made, the remarks of these fraternity brothers would have been extremely damaging. As it was, their remarks gave the perception that the police were not treating Collins fairly and put the Crime Center Task Force in a bad light and on the defensive.

What occurred there suggests that when feasible only other police officers should be used in the line up. That practice would eliminate erroneous information being related to the public. The true facts have to be explained to the public as a defensive measure and to maintain good public relations.

John Norman Collins and Sergeant McBryde of the Eastern Michigan University Police rode motorcycles together from time to time. McBryde was a motorcycle officer. Undoubtedly, Collins attempted to elicit as much information as possible relative to the investigation of the murders. The area where Karry's body was dumped was the area patrolled by McBryde during "Operation Baby-sit". Collins had a great habit of using people.

For example, he stored stolen motorcycles in his state police uncle's garage. After all, who would look for them there? Collins asked his good friend, Arnie, to forge Collins' name and swear his motorcycle plate was lost. He also asked him to lie about the times when they were motorcycle riding. He wanted Davis to say they had been riding all afternoon, when in fact, he did not return to his apartment until late afternoon. In other words, the reader should take note how Collins had the marked propensity to use people for his own purposes.

The drawing made by the police artist in the Jean S. murder and the composite drawing drawn from information supplied by the women in the wig shop were remarkably similar. In the author's opinion, these drawings left little doubt that the murderer was one and the same person.

This example helps to further substantiate how the eyes of a witness really see selectively. Compare the observations made by the two women in the wig shop. Neither women were very interested in the motorcycle. They were interested in the rider and identified him later quite easily. But they were pushed for information about the motorcycle. On this they were not accurate. They thought it was like a Honda or a Yamaha.

Contrast this with Cheri W., the witness in the Chocolate Shop. She didn't care about the rider. She was interested in the motorcycle and her mind was focused there. At the outset, she said the motorcycle was a Triumph, and she gave an excellent description of it. This was later verified as being correct. The officer that interviewed her indicated in his report, "The girl will be a poor witness".

The defense attorneys had a "field day" with that little phrase. We know what the officer meant. He wanted other officers to know that this witness was shy. She had to be drawn out, and she certainly was not very articulate.

The defense made it sound to the jury that the girl "will not be a good witness FOR THE PROSECUTION". For this reason, officers must be very guarded about what is placed into a police report and how it is worded. Today the defense has access to the police report in nearly each and every case. We must avoid putting something into a report that could be utilized to put the police in a position where they appear to be anything but unbiased professionals. The fact is that the police are about as neutral and unbiased on a case as the defense attorney who has put countless hours into case preparation. The name of the game to him/her is to win the case. The same is true of the police, but the facade of unbiased neutral professionalism must be maintained.

It may be even more difficult for the police than anyone else in the criminal justice system to maintain the myth of neutrality. This is true simply because they have talked with the poor rape victim after she has had her clothing ripped from her body and has been beaten. They have talked with the sobbing parents of a girl senselessly murdered by a serial killer. In other words, the police have experienced these things first hand. A judge or lawyer reads a report and perhaps looks at a few pictures.

In this case, the women at the wig shop were shown well over sixty different photographs of various suspects before Collins was arrested and identified. It is recommended in a major case, that only one officer or two at the most be designated to show the witness photographs. This is because it is important to maintain a good log on the pictures the witness has viewed, the date she viewed them, and the names of the possible suspects. It is critical that the investigator handling these photo show ups knows what he/she is doing. No single photo should be shown. There always should be about eight. If the photograph of the suspect is in color, so should the rest of them. If the suspect is wearing glasses, the others should be wearing glasses. All the photographs should be about the same size. The best guideline to follow is one of basic fairness to avoid a false identification.

The police knew that the identification by the women at the wig shop would be the subject of great scrutiny. It was for that reason the women had their eyes examined to insure that the women would not be vulnerable to attack by defense attorneys.

The police also had learned that the owner of the wig shop had lied on her marriage application about having been married previously. She had a son born out of wedlock. She had lied to protect herself and her son.

The police also learned that the defense was aware of this and was going to attempt to trap her with that information in cross examination. Officers had a discussion with her and tipped her off that it was quite probable that this would happen. The defense did try this, but it was handled excellently by simply telling the truth.

The stake out where Karry's body was found was improperly manned. Three officers were avoiding the rain by staying inside the porch. No one was really in a position to apprehend a suspect who came up to the mailbox by the mannequin. No arrangements had been made to have a blind constructed from which infra-red photographs could have been taken of a suspect. Today, night viewing devices are available for use that only the military had access to at that time. The main lesson taught by this operation is that if it is at all worthwhile to conduct a stake out, officers should be positioned to record and apprehend anyone who returns to the scene. There were officers present that noted the shortcomings of where the officers were being assigned. In fact, they objected verbally, but were disregarded. Instead of calling a tracking dog to the scene, the handler and the dog should be present in the area a short distance away from the stake out crew.

While working the scene, no effort was made to obtain a sample of the insect eggs already present in the body orifices of the victim. These samples should have been taken and placed into chemicals to arrest further development. The time this was done should have been noted. The assistance of an entomologist familiar with the various types of insects in that area and the time span of the various developmental stages could have rendered valuable assistance by providing officers with an expert opinion to help determine the approximate time the victim was left at the body recovery site.

In some cases, where the victim's body has been present at a location for a period of time and has affected the growth of plant life under her body, a botanist can also be of assistance in making a determination on the approximate length of time the victim had lain there.

From a positive viewpoint, assigning officers such as Mathewson to keep John Norman Collins under surveillance was advantageous because he knew Collins and his friends. There was, however, the disadvantage that the officers could be quickly identified by the target. It is suggested that the target be identified by some officer or other reliable person working in cooperation with the police. Then that person or persons should withdraw and leave such surveillance operations to trained professionals.

A good surveillance crew will consist of at least three officers. It is not something for rank amateurs. It requires skill, practice and teamwork. In this case, no effort was made to use the Michigan State Police special team. Possibly, there was a lack of knowledge it existed.

When Collins was brought in for questioning, he should have been served with a search warrant at that time. By picking him up and releasing him, he knew he was a suspect and he was able to dispose of a considerable amount of valuable evidence. This could have been used against him and perhaps would have assisted in solving other cases.

Everything dealing with the time when Collins was picked up should have been executed according to plan. Experienced interrogators, such as a polygraph examiner who would not later be called upon to conduct an examination, should have been standing by. These interrogators should have been well rested and fed and have had a thorough briefing of the suspect and the case before he's brought in for questioning. Experience suggests that afternoon or evening are best. The plan for proceeding with the interrogation should already have been formulated by the interrogators prior to their first meeting the suspect. The interrogator(s) should have been appraised of any new evidence or information discovered during the execution of the search warrant which could be used during the questioning of the suspect. For example, it could have conceivably been very helpful had something belonging to the victim(s) been found in Collins' apartment. It would have put considerable pressure on Collins to confess.

When Collins was first interviewed, notice that he denied trying to pick up any girls whatsoever on July 23rd and that he even had any "cut offs". At that point, the two officers knew he was lying. There had been about seven or eight different young women who identified Collins as having tried to pick them up on that date. After they told Collins this, he refused to say anything for about twenty minutes. He was silent and he thought things through. When he made these denials, a statement should have been taken. He should not have been challenged and shown where he had lied. That gave him a chance to straighten out his position.

The key that Cpl. Lair had given to Collins was later returned to Lair. Since Lair was a state police officer, he was not asked to mark the key as evidence and turn it over to the Crime Center Task Force where it would have been available for trial. Cpl. Lair subsequently changed all the locks on his doors. The key that Collins had returned to him was lost. Fortunately, no issue was made of this during the trial. It seems apparent that because Lair was a police officer, officers overlooked getting this critical piece of evidence. We must be careful to obtain all evidence available.

As the case was being prepared, Cpl. Lair came to the author, who was in charge of the team putting the case together for trial. Due to the tremendous pressure this entire matter was putting on his family, and his wife in particular, he requested that his wife not be called in to testify. He was told that it was not possible to exclude her for many reasons. She observed the scuff marks on the kitchen floor she had just cleaned. She saw fresh blood on a shirt covering her lab coat which she had recently washed and hung up to dry in the basement. She had been the one to cut her son's hair in the basement prior to vacation. Cpl. Lair was very concerned about the impact the entire matter was having upon his wife's emotional state. He told the writer, "All right, I want you to know, if my wife winds up in a mental hospital over this, because you are forcing her to testify, I am holding you personally responsible." Without the testimony of Mrs. Lair, however, the People's case would have been severely weakened. Officers always treated Mrs. Lair as kindly as possible. Officers knew the predicament she was in as far as her feelings toward John Collins. One of the gross errors the defense made was their failure to recognize Mrs. Lair as being a witness very sympathetic toward the defendant. By treating her on the witness stand as a hostile witness, they forced her squarely into the camp of the People.

Notice how Collins reacted towards officer Mathewson. Collins was "Mr. Nice Guy" until Mathewson began writing down the license numbers of the motorcycles. (44.75)

One should have all key evidence ready for court even though it is doubtful that the People can get it submitted into evidence. For example, during the trial there was considerable testimony from witnesses about the bright, shiny, green and blue Triumph motorcycles that John Collins had in his possession. The prosecution had discussed in depth the possibility of getting these motorcycles introduced into evidence. The prosecution finally gave up on the idea. Meanwhile, about twenty miles outside of Ann Arbor, the motorcycles were locked up in a barn. Nearly a year had passed since they had been confiscated. They were no longer as witnesses had described them, but rather they were covered with dust.

To the prosecution's surprise, the defense called for them late one morning during the trial. The People stalled for a time by explaining the bikes were stored outside of town. The court ordered the People to have them in the courtroom immediately after lunch. The bikes were brought into Ann Arbor and were taken to the Washtenaw County Jail where they were quickly washed, polished and transported to the courtroom. The lesson here is that one should not presume what the other side will or will not do, but one should be prepared for any contingency. The bikes should have been readily available.

Observe that the blood tests were typed only and were not carried out to the fullest extent possible. Some scientists sometimes failed to understand the urgency and thoroughness that was required in this particular case. Some scientists, certainly not all, thought of the evidence coming in from Task Force as if it was from any other case. They failed to see the importance of thorough speedy analysis. In some instances, items of evidence were not even analyzed. A rag found in the basement laundry room was covered with clipped hair. It was never examined for blood, hair or anything else. It would have been an excellent control sample to be compared with Karry's panties. This rag was essentially destroyed by mold and mildew.

The remark Collins made to Metiva about using a baseball bat or club to put something into a woman's vagina was significant. Investigators believed that Collins had used the handle of a baseball bat to push Karry's panties up into the vaginal vault after he wiped the floor with them.

Notice that like Albert DeSalvo before him, Collins also knew how to apply the sleeper hold to render a victim unconscious.

John Collins had extensive ability to work on motorcycles. He could dismantle one completely and put it back together again. He would steal specific parts. When Collins went to the J & J Motorcycle Shop on July 22nd, to "have the chain on the motorcycle adjusted" that simply defied common sense. First, it would be illogical because if that's all it needed, Collins could have done that himself. Second, if the motorcycle really needed a new chain he would have stolen it. And third, it was known that Collins had more than enough cash to pay for the chain on the 22nd. It was readily apparent that it was Collins' plan to use the people at the motorcycle shop for his alibi.

Initially the employees at the motorcycle shop said Collins was there between two and three o'clock. The officer who interviewed them did not obtain a statement in writing. The defense attorney later interviewed the alibi witnesses and got them to back their time up to Collins being there between 1:00 and 2:00 p.m.—"the time we usually ate". The special intelligence surveillance squad was called upon to establish the average eating time of the personnel at the motorcycle shop. This costly and time consuming procedure paid off because it verified that they did generally eat around 2:00 p.m. This hammers home the important necessity of obtaining timely, taped or written statements from witnesses while events are fresh in their minds and important facts less apt to be forgotten.

Since most murder cases are not brought to trial for long periods of time after the events occur, it is helpful to provide witnesses with a copy of their statement before they testify to help refresh their recollection. In most cases that was standard procedure for the author in all felony cases. It was not done in this case with most witnesses. The reason for this was, the prosecutor did not want the witnesses' testimony to sound "canned".

One can only speculate about this, but notice how the attacks required Collins to take greater and greater risks. The attack in California on Rose, and the attack on Marjorie S. had both occurred during the day, but never before did Collins sit out in front of a business while witnesses got such a good look at him. In fact, it is the author's personal opinion that if the women would have had a camera in the shop, they would have photographed him. They were that suspicious of him even while Karry was in the shop. Collins, on the other hand, had little fear of such identification.

Note that none of Collins' fingerprints were found in the Lair house, nor were Karry's prints or Daphne G.'s. Collins had taken Daphne to the Lair house the preceding Sunday before the murder of Karry. Collins tried to get her to rub his back. Daphne was very suspicious of Collins because she still remembered that he was the one she saw Jean S. with at about 11:30 p.m. on the night of June 30, 1968.

The property under the control of the Crime Center Task Force was kept in a large room which was securely locked at all times except when an officer working with the Task Force wished to store an item of property or check one out. The items inside the room were stored in areas around the room according to the case. The key to the property room initially was in the possession of the individual shift commander from one of the various departments involved in the investigation. As a matter of practice, these commanders would not accompany all officers into the property room. Two items disappeared from the property room, one was a wrist rocket sling shot and the other was a Montgomery Ward wrench. The author purchased these items so they could be returned at a later date to the defendant's mother.

It is suggested that in future cases a property officer be assigned to each shift, if it is a large task force. These property officers may have other duties as well, but they are primarily responsible for handling evidence and other property. Only these officers should have keys to the property room. They should maintain the records of items as they are checked out for court purposes and as they are returned. Further, one of them should accompany any person who enters the property room.

When property is missing, as it was in this case, it opens the door for the defense to the possibility of the contamination of evidence. This can be made to appear as if the police were negligent in the manner in which evidence was handled.

In a small task force, perhaps it would be better if only one officer was totally responsible for the property room, and he/she alone had the key to it. If someone had to have access to it at night then the property officer would have to be called into duty. It is better to put up with a degree of inconvenience rather than be open to the accusation that evidence may have been contaminated.

Making an Emergency Prosecution Report paid great dividends. The case was thereby reduced to its bare essence. This case was complicated by a considerable amount of scientific testimony and by having many witnesses, but that early report served as the road map for the entire case. This so called "Emergency Prosecution Report" was actually the "nuts and bolts" type report used in all felony cases. It also made it possible to determine the weakest link in the circumstantial chain—Collins' alibi at the J & J Motorcycle Shop.

When officers had more time, a much longer Prosecution Report was prepared. One might say that flesh was put on the bare bones of the earlier report. This contained the following headings and the page numbers where the information could be found:

—Details of the offense
—Victim
—Weather Conditions
—Details of the Investigation
—Scene of the crime
—Arrest information
—Arrest, probable cause for
—Line up number one
—Line up number two
—Money
—Collins' ability to repair motorcycles

Under the heading of "physical evidence," the following was included:
—Blood on the shirt over Mrs. Lair's uniform
—Blood typed by Dr. Hendrix
—Blood in basement of the Lair home
—Cloth found in victim's mouth
—Dental charts
—Hair clippers
—Hair samples
—Hair on basement floor
—Hunting knife
—Hair on panties
—Panties
—Photographs of line up
—Photographs of crime scene
—Photographs of location where the victim was found
—Photographs of the panties by Walter Holz
—Picture of victim
—Receipt for wiglet
—Scale drawing of the murder scene
—Service record for the wiglet
—Shirt Collins' gave to police
—TR 6 (Triumph) motorcycle

This was followed by a list of "Witness Statements" in alphabetical order. Their last names were listed first, then their first names with the page number where their statement could be found. Anyone who was considered as a possible alibi witness had a small (a) in front of their names. There were seventy-one witnesses.

This was followed by sections "Contra alibi at the J & J Motorcycle Shop, Statements made by Collins Concerning the Murders", and "A Summary of Case and Witnesses in Chronological Order".

Discussions with other investigators and assistant prosecutors to learn the pet tactics of defense counselors also proved to be worthwhile. Once or twice Mr. Louisell tried to use his pet trick to turn around unfavorable testimony. Mr. Williams, who not only had a photographic memory, but a mind that could recall conversations like a tape recorder was lying in wait after being warned of such tactics. After an argument over what a particular witness said, it was read back by the court reporter, and the damaging testimony would be repeated a second time. Mr. Louisell dropped that tactic. There was, however, nothing the People could do about Louisell hiring a pretty, young, curvaceous, mini-skirted woman to act as a defense investigator. The prosecution was completely aware that the underlying message for the jury was, "Look, if Collins was so dangerous, this beautiful girl wouldn't sit so close to him or help him."

Investigators often wondered why Collins was getting such favorable press coverage by a major Detroit newspaper, including such things as a large photograph on the front page showing Collins' mother and his sister, Gail, on their knees inside the Roman Catholic Church praying for him. Her own sister was astonished by this. She said, "She hasn't been in a church in years." One morning the pretty investigator was not in court. There were those who tried to make it appear as if she was another victim. An immediate investigation was begun into her whereabouts. A short time later she was located. She had spent the night with a reporter from a Detroit newspaper—the same paper that published the large picture of Collins' Mother and sister on their knees praying as they awaited the jury's verdict. They were later married.

When the Task Force Commander assigned the author the job of preparing the case for trial, he disregarded the possible problems that could result from this because the author was only a detective. It was true that the author had plenty of experience because he worked at the Flat Rock Post, just south of Detroit. That post had the heaviest felony load in Michigan at that time. To assist the author he assigned two outstanding detectives from the Intelligence Section. The result was a success, but there were problems. The main problem was of a management nature. There was a great deal of responsibility delegated, but there was an insufficient amount of authority delegated to go along with that responsibility. The incidents below demonstrate this problem.

For example, the author recognized immediately that the people at the J & J Motorcycle Shop were being used as an alibi. Two or three times the author spoke with the detective sergeant who was dealing with the J & J Motorcycle Shop witnesses. The author requested that the sergeant get statements to nail down the time Collins was there. This was the weak area in the case for the prosecution. Finally, the author went to the Task Force Commander and explained the problem to him. The Task Force Commander then talked with the detective sergeant. By the time we got the written statements, defense attorneys had beaten him to it. The witnesses times were backed up to around one o'clock. This was a change of nearly two hours. This problem could have been avoided had the officer putting the case together been given the authority to order that the statements be taken or permission to take the statements himself.

When the writer contacted laboratory scientists in the Criminalistic Section of the health department, they were not inclined to give his requests high priority, due primarily to his low rank. It was very apparent that initially, they did not understand that the author's role was, from an investigative standpoint, to insure the case was prepared for trial. They did come to understand this at a later time.

While preparing the prosecution report, it was not uncommon for the author to find two officer's reports that were in conflict. This often happened two or three times a day. In most cases, both of the officers had been working on the same incident. To solve the problem both officers would be called in and showed the reports. Most of the time it was simply a matter of their respective writing failing to communicate what was intended. In some instances, however, the difference could not be resolved without further investigation. Taped statements were taken from all witnesses and then these were transcribed. The detectives preparing the prosecution report reinterviewed key witnesses to help the officers get a feeling for the case and to probe how solid the witness would be when he or she testified.

During the trial, one witness stated that he heard screams coming from the Lair house during the evening of July 23rd. Mr. Williams called the author at his house in Flat Rock. The author recommended that, at that late hour, the witness' testimony not be used as it might appear that the prosecutor was grasping for straws. There was already sufficient evidence on record to prove the victim had been murdered there. The testimony from that witness was not used.

Finally, every juror who was seated was voted on by the author, Mr. Williams, and Prosecutor Bill Delhey.

In such cases, when a person of lower rank is chosen for an assignment where it may become necessary to accomplish the mission for such person to issue directives to higher ranking officers, the Task Force Commander should issue a written order explaining his action. It should be brought out in briefings that this person has been given the responsibility to carry out a certain task. Any request that he or she may make, or order given in connection with that assignment should be regarded as coming from the Task Force Commander. While this would not eliminate all the problems, it would be helpful. There will always be the pompous, arrogant officer of higher rank who thinks it is beneath him to do anything he is asked to do by someone of a lower rank. The Task Force Commander will still have to deal with him.

It was doubtful that the big powerful young man who walked Karry to and from her class during the evening and then took her motorcycle riding was the same person with her at the wig shop. First, because he was described as being six feet tall and weighing about two hundred and twenty pounds. The women at the wig shop did not think that the motorcyclist was that big. Second, Karry told the women that she had taken a ride with a nice young boy *she had just met*. She was displaying a bit of daring.

The perpetrator made some revelations about his attitude and thought processes on several occasions when he communicated with other people. Notice when Collins told Lydia W. that he no longer believed the teachings of the Roman Catholic Church. He

127

thought the Ten Commandments, especially the Fifth Commandment, "Thou shalt not kill", was foolish and that he knew how to commit the perfect crime. He was really giving some insight about his personal beliefs. Also, the college paper in which he wrote that it doesn't matter what society believes is right or wrong, a person can do as he pleases, if he is smart enough to get away with it. Then recall, he carried Cliff Notes on Dostoevsky's *Crime and Punishment* in the glove box of his car. Consider that these notes contained excellent, concise statements on the Philosophy of Hegel and the Philosophy of Nietzsche. To Collins, the latter philosophy probably was more meaningful to him. For we find written in these notes: "Therefore, the Neitzsche superman is the one who possesses the strongest will and is able to make his desires and his power dominant over others. Consequently, Svidrigailov can rape a thirteen-year-old girl so as to satisfy his will, he can be the instrument causing the death of a servant or his wife and he can pursue Dounia without any fear of some power punishing him. He asserts his own will in order to gratify his own desires." (21)

Just as two other serial murderers, Leonard Lake and Christopher Wilder, were fascinated and probably influenced by John Fowles' *The Collector* so it was, and is this writer's opinion that John Collins was probably affected by Dostoevsky's *Crime and Punishment*.

The hours that Collins was busy stealing parts off other motorcycles, switching the parts around, and disposing of the old parts provide very useful information. For if he believed that this was the best time to carry out these criminal activities, it is also quite probable that he transported Karry's dead body from the Lair residence to the location off Huron River Drive during a similar time—during the early morning hours.

The manner in which he disposed of the gasoline tank and seat from the stolen motorcycle also provides a possible clue on the method of disposal of the remnants of Karry's shorts, bra, wiglet, and blouse. There could of course be a different method. It is known that there was an incinerator in his apartment building. He was not supposed to use it, but that did not mean that he did not use it.

The primary reason that Collins sent Davis down to get the new plate was because he thought the women at the wig shop may have obtained his license number. After all, he knew they saw him because they both stepped outside the shop to look at him.

This is instructive, however, for it provides a possible investigative avenue. When it becomes clear that one or more of the witnesses may have obtained the license number of a vehicle, or the perpetrator believes they have, measures should be taken to insure the task force is advised of replacement plate applications. What agency is involved varies according to the jurisdiction in which the plate is obtained. The perpetrator may apply for a replacement claiming the plate was lost or stolen and it may not be immediately following the incident. In this case, Collins waited two days before he sent Davis down to get the new plate. A comfortable span of time should be permitted. Even a month would not be too long.

Notice also that Collins himself did not go to get the new plate. His reason for this probably was that he thought the personnel there would be on guard for any person who matched the police artist's excellent sketch. It was a remarkably accurate sketch of the motorcyclist with whom Karry had ridden away.

The lesson for us here is that one should not rely on the description of the person obtaining the replacement plate. If possible, and the author realizes this is not always possible, one should obtain a photograph of the person to whom the plate is registered. Sometimes these photographs can be obtained from the licensing agency through the Driver's Licensing Section or from high school or college year books, or from surveillance crews. Once obtained these can be shown to witnesses for any possible identification. Of course, it is also possible that if the perpetrator was using his own vehicle, and he feared a witness may have obtained his license number, he may wipe the vehicle clean of prints, drive it to a remote location, set it on fire, or simply abandon it, and then report it as stolen. So we must be alert for that too.

Another possibility, especially if the perpetrator has extensive mechanical ability, as Collins had, is to dismantle the vehicle completely and disperse the parts. This was done by Collins with some parts from the stolen motorcycle.

It was interesting to note the conflicting opinions between investigators over which bike Collins was using to pick up a victim on July 23rd. While we will never know for certain, unless some day John Collins decides to tell us, this writer would be inclined to believe it was the stolen Triumph Trophy Special with the blue tank. The facts seem a bit more convincing for this cycle rather than for the one with the green tank. The information from Cheri W., the witness in the Chocolate Shop would have to be given considerable weight. The women in the wig shop were busy taking a long, hard look at the cyclist with Karry, and were consciously aware that he could well be the murderer. The young woman waitress in the Chocolate Shop was interested in the motorcycle, and was not interested in who was riding it. For this reason, she could not either identify Collins or exclude him as the cyclist in front of the Chocolate Shop during the early afternoon of July 23rd.

The reader should recall that three days prior to the murder of Karry, Collins picked up Daphne G., and took her to his uncle's house. At that time, he was using the Triumph with the blue gas tank, barely thirty-six hours after he had stolen it. It appeared quite likely that Collins was searching for another victim on that date. It is quite probable that he also used that same cycle on both the twenty-second and the twenty-third when he was trying to find a victim after his propensity toward sadistic behavior surfaced again.

It is further the author's opinion that he could not control that "urge". It is quite likely that he never understood why he had this desire to commit the brutal acts that he did. He only knew that once these desires came into existence that he had to carry them out otherwise there would be no relief at all. After they were committed he would be all right for a time. Then the feelings—the driving force would return, and he would have to seek out another victim. His problem was that the time period between the murdering of one victim and obtaining relief and the time when the burning urge surfaced causing him to need to murder again decreased rapidly. This resulted in an increased amount of his energy and thoughts being devoted to these urges to commit these acts.

One could argue, "Well, wouldn't this make his behavior so as to render him not guilty by reason of insanity?" The answer, of course, is "No". For Collins could have controlled his behavior. The terrible urge would still have been present, but had his state police uncle been with Collins and Karry in the Lair home, Collins would not have beat, raped, and murdered her.

The search warrant on Collins' car was obtained and executed the day after his arrest. It is instructive to note that Davis told us that he observed Collins remove a Bold box from the trunk of his car on July 29th and dispose of it, the same day the Lair family returned. This quite probably was the Bold box missing from the Lair house which Dr. Buzas observed "the fellow who took care of the dog" ride away from the Lair residence in his hand at around (11:30) eleven-thirty a.m., about twenty-four hours after Karry had been murdered.

Collins put this box in the trunk of his car until he could dispose of it. After the attempt to gain a confession from Collins failed, and he was released, Davis stated that the Monday before he was arrested he saw Collins dispose of both a large Bold box containing a purse, blue jeans, and other articles.

It should be noted that the probable cause which was sufficient for the court to grant a search warrant for Collins' car on August 1 was exactly the same as it would have been if such a warrant had been requested four days earlier, when Collins was first questioned. The dilatory effects of failing to obtain that warrant had a deleterious affect upon the investigation and increased the difficulty of obtaining a conviction later.

The significant point for us to bear in mind for future cases is that if it is at all possible, and one must at least try before saying it is impossible, to obtain a search warrant before picking up the suspect. Do not give him any opportunity to dispose of valuable evidence which could help convict him. It is tacitly implied and we can see from this case, that some serial murderers do keep evidence of their crimes in their apartments, car or other locations so they can have access to them after the crime. The most probable reason for this is that they may fantasize the crime over and over again by looking at and handling items that belonged to the victims.

It is interesting that when Collins carefully removed the Bold box and blanket from the trunk of his car, he took them into his apartment. Then he disposed of them. This tells law enforcement officials that whenever possible get a warrant for all places where a perpetrator may have hidden something.

When executing a warrant, officers should not have tunnel vision. Bear in mind that the perpetrator may have committed other murders of which no one is aware. Ask yourself before executing the warrant, "What other evidence of criminal activity am I likely to find here?"

When executing the warrant, take your time and be very thorough. If you do find evidence of other crimes, don't just take it, if it is not included in the warrant. Leave at least one officer there to continue the search under the original warrant and return to the court. Then return to the scene with an amended warrant. The additional evidence then can be included on the return on the warrant.

It's also very educational to note that while Collins removed the Bold box and blanket from his car, he did not remove a raincoat with blood on it which was believed to have come from Anne K., nor did he get rid of a piece of Rose P.'s dress. He also didn't bother to remove a license plate from a western state quite probably used on the trip returning from California. Collins' remark to Davis about the police looking for a killer, not for stolen motorcycles tend to indicate that he did believe the police suffered from tunnel vision. Note how completely confident and calm he was while talking with Mathewson even though Mathewson could readily see the stolen motorcycles.

There can be little doubt that Arnie Davis helped Collins steal the Triumph "Trophy Special" motorcycle with the yellow gas tank on the night of July 18 or early morning hours of July 19th. Davis acknowledged he was with him all night until six a.m. the next morning. It would be totally unrealistic to believe that Collins would be left to push the large heavy motorcycle down the street without Davis raising a finger to help. Davis later went to the licensing office and represented himself as Collins. He affirmed the motorcycle plate was lost when he knew it was on a motorcycle. He forged Collins' name and listed a phony serial number.

Davis came within a hair's breadth of being prosecuted. The primary reasons this was not done was because the prosecution did not want to turn Davis into a hostile witness. The murder case was difficult enough to prove without handing the defense a witness by arresting Davis on a lesser charge. In addition, while the Secretary of State Board Manager remembered Davis being at the office getting the license for Collins, he had a poor recollection of the details.

Manuel, Collins' friend with whom he had traveled to California, left the state the weekend after Karry disappeared. He took the guns with him. This made Collins so angry that Davis said he flew into a rage. "His face was red. He was almost frothing at the mouth." Collins told Davis that if he knew where Manuel was he would kill him.

Veteran investigators believed that Collins transported Karry's body to the location where it was found during the early morning hours of Friday, July 25. This opinion was based primarily upon insect activity and the belief that *rigor mortis* had left her remains at the time Collins decided to get the body out of the Lair basement.

It appeared that with Dora B. he transported her when she was in full rigor. If he carried her out of the basement of the old farm house, loaded her into his car and then took her to the location where he left her body, that would have been quite a job. It is possible, therefore, that he waited until the rigor left Karry's body so he wouldn't have that much trouble.

It is much more likely, however, that the reason he waited until early Friday morning to dispose of her body was because he knew of "Operation Baby-sit". He wanted to wait at least a day before he tried to get her body out of the basement. He probably believed that it was quite important that he get her body out of there in event his aunt and uncle returned from their vacation during the weekend. It is possible that today a positive identification could have been made using DNA profiling of the blood found in the Lair basement and the seminal fluid found in the victim.

It did not appear to the author that the members of the jury gave a great deal of weight to the testimony regarding the fibers or the hair on the panties, except that there were clipped hairs from several sources, and Mrs. Lair did cut hair in the basement.

From the author's observations the jury was highly influenced by the following: the testimony of the two women from the wig shop who stepped outside to look at Collins. The girl in the Chocolate Shop who said at the outset that the cycle was a Triumph with a blue gas tank. The seven girls who testified that Collins tried to pick them up around noon on the date that Karry disappeared. The fact that Collins had access to the Lair house and he was the only person who had a key other than immediate family members. The evidence that the murder was committed in the Lair house (e.g. the black marks on the kitchen floor which indicated a struggle had occurred there, blood splattered on the wall and floor in the basement which was the same type as the victim. The blood splattered on the sleeve of a freshly washed shirt which had been placed over Mrs. Lair's dental uniform to protect it. The testimony of Mrs. Lair that she used a large Bold box for waste materials which she removed from the washer and dryer. The testimony of Dr. Buzas who observed John Collins ride away from the Lair house carrying a large Bold box. Also the fact that Karry's bra, blouse, what was left of her Bermuda shorts, her purse and her wiglet were never recovered.

Additional damaging testimony was put forth by Arnold Davis. He said that Collins switched parts around on the two motorcycles to disguise their appearance. He sent Davis down to obtain a new plate under false pretenses. He asked Davis to lie about the times they went motorcycle riding on the day Karry was missing. Collins could not account for time on the day that Karry was killed. This and the facts listed above led to his conviction.

Collins did not take the stand in his own defense. Had he done that, the People were prepared to utterly destroy his credibility as a witness by proving that he was a thief and a rapist who had previously beat a young woman into submission using his forearm. The People would have also shown that only three days before Karry was murdered, Collins took another young woman to the Lair house and tried to get her down on the floor with him by telling her his back ached. Ironically neither her fingerprints nor Collins' were found when laboratory scientists searched the Lair house for clues. When Collins wiped everything down to insure Karry's prints would not be found, he also wiped away his own and that girl's too.

It was observed in this case study and it will be observed in several below, that the propensity of serial murderers to flee from authorities at the time of arrest or after they have been in custody, is very strong. Collins, for example, was convicted of first degree murder and was sentenced to life in prison at Jackson, Michigan. There, correction officers alleged that he helped another convicted murderer escape and was planning his own escape. For these activities, he was transferred to the state prison in Marquette where Michigan's most dangerous criminals are held. Again, he tried to escape. Collins, along with a group of other murderers tried to tunnel their way out. Collins and the others were caught. This resulted in Collins' placement in a cell block where he is required to remain in his cell for twenty-three hours per day. He is only permitted one hour each day outside his cell.

REFERENCES

1. Baginski, Dennis. High school acquaintance of murderer. (official police statement): August 1969

* 2. Buzas, Dr. Mary Ann. Neighbor of Lair Family. (official police statement): August 1969

* 3. Bauer, Mrs. Carl. Mother of Dora B. (personal interview): May 1969

* 4. Buchholz, Beverly. Court Reporter in Kent County Michigan and sister of Karry: (personal interview): August 1969.

* 5. Buchholz, Jane. Sister of Karry: (personal interview): August 1969

* 6. Buchholz, Meredith. Mother of the victim. (personal interview): August 1969

* 7. Buchholz, Ralph. Father of the victim and co-owner of manufacturing company. (personal interview): August 1969.

* 8. Blackwell, Anita. Neighbor of Dora B. (personal interview): May 1969

* 9. Blackwell, Tracey. Neighbor of Dora B. (personal interview): May 1969

10. Bunton, Paul. Detective (now Captain) Ann Arbor Police Department. (personal interview): August 1969

* 11. Chilico, Frances. Rape victim of John Collins. (official police statement): August 1969

12. Collins, John Norman. Eastern Michigan University College Paper. 1969

* 13. Collins, Loraine Girard. Mother of John Collins. (personal interview): December 1969

* 14. Collins, Warner. Step-father of John Collins. (official police statement): 1969

15. Cologie, Benjamin R. University of Michigan student. (personal interview): July 1969

16. Davis, Arnold. Close friend of the defendant. (official police statement): August 1969

17. Delhey, William Esquire. Prosecutor of Washtenaw County. (personal interview): 1970

18. De Masellis, Nancy. (personal interview): 1969

19. Dillion, George. "Raped Beaten and Burned: Skinned Alive and Strangled...It Can Happen to Any Girl.", *Detective Dragnet*: Detective Dragnet Publishing Company, New York, New York: February 1971 (pp. 47-48)

* 20. Duffy, Lillian. Student at E.M.U. who thought the artist's sketch looked like Collins. (official police statement): July 1969

21. Dostoevsky, Fyodor. *Crime and Punishment*: International Collectors Library, Garden City, New York: 1953 (pp. 184-185)

* 22. Druar, Jonathan. Fiance of victim. (personal interview): August 1969

23. Eastern Michigan University Police Report of Complaint or Occurrences. (missing person report on Karry Buchholz from Miss Kit): Investigated by Officer Slagenwhite: Ypsilanti, Michigan: July 23, 1969

24. Fitzsimmons, Minnie. Head Secretary Creston High School, Grand Rapids, Michigan: (personal interview): March 1969

25. Flannery, Mrs. Pauline. Neighbor of Skelton family. (personal interview): April 1969

* 26. Foust Charles. Father of Mona F. (personal interview): March 1969

* 27. Foust, Tamara. Mother of Mona F. (personal interview): August 1967 and March 1969

* 28. Frenso, Trevor. Railroad buff. (personal interview): April 1969

29. Frank, Gerold. *The Boston Strangler*: The New American Library, New York, New York: 1966

30. Freeborn, Carl. Staff Sergeant. Post Commander. (confidential report—not to be released to the general public): Synopsis of Homicide—Ypsilanti Post Area: Ypsilanti, Michigan: April 18, 1969

* 31. Green, Daphne. Girl friend of the murderer's fraternity brother. (official police statements obtained by Detective Wm. Canada): August 7, 1969 and July 1968.

* 32. Goech, Irene. Potential victim of the murderer. (official police statement obtained by Detectives Ing and Cowan): August 6, 1969

* 33. Graey, Sarah. Roommate of Karry B. (personal interview): August 1969

135

  *   34. Goes, Joy. Owner of Wigs by Joan Shop in Ypsilanti, (personal interview) August 1969

      35. Hamel, Douglas. Boyhood friend of the murderer. (official police statement): August 1969

      36. Hanna, Roy. Captain Salinas California Police Department. (personal interview): July 1976

  *   37. Heilweil, Martin. Neighbor of Anne Kitze in Ann Arbor. (personal interview): June 1969

      38. Hendrix, Robert M.D.. Forensic Pathologist at the University of Michigan Hospital in Ann Arbor, Michigan. (personal interview): August 1969 and other dates

      39. Holy, Walter. Forensic scientist and head of the Criminalistics Section at the Michigan Department of Public Health. (numerous personal interviews): Winter of 1969/Spring and Summer 1970

      40. Howard, Vern. Detective Lieutenant with the Ypsilanti Police Department. (personal interview): August 1967

      41. Hutchings, Stewart Detective. (personal interview): 1971 and other dates

  *   42. Hassad, Abraham Ph.D. Lover of Anne Kitze. (personal interview): June 1969

      43. James, Earl. *Confidential Biographies on Serial Murder Victims in Washtenaw County*: Michigan State Police, Ypsilanti, Michigan: 1969

      44. James, Detective Earl. et al. Official Prosecution Report. *The People of the State of Michigan vs. John Norman Collins for the Murder of Karen Sue Beineman*: Michigan State Police, Ypsilanti, Michigan: 1969

      45. James, Detective Earl. *Official Prosecution Report: The People of the State of Michigan vs. John Norman Collins: (Schell Case)*: Michigan State Police, Ypsilanti, Michigan: 1970

      46. Janiszewski, Detective Harold. *Official Prosecution Report: The People of the State of Michigan vs. John Norman Collins: (Kalom Case)*: Michigan State Police, Ypsilanti, Michigan: 1970

      47. Kahn, Robert M.D.. Psychiatrist St. Joseph Hospital, Ann Arbor, Michigan: (personal interview): July 6, 1969

      48. Keyes, Edward. *The Michigan Murders*. Reader's Digest Press. New York, New York: 1976

* 49. Kniblesy, Elliot. Fraternity brother of murderer. (personal interview): April 1969

50. Krasny, Walter. Chief of Police, Ann Arbor, Michigan. (personal interview): July 5, 1969

* 51. Lisney, Paula. Roommate of the murdered victim, Karry Buchholz. (personal interview): August 1969

52. Maxwell Detective Sergeant Bert. Ypsilanti Police Department. "Wanted by This Dept.": Ypsilanti, Michigan. July 23, 1969 (sic).

* 53. Metiva, Jeff. Friend of the murderer. (official police statement): August 1969

54. Michigan State Police Official Complaint Report. 26-3634-67: Ypsilanti, Michigan: original date August 7, 1967

55. Michigan State Police Official Complaint Report. 26-3418-68: Ypsilanti, Michigan: original date July 6, 1968

56. Michigan State Police Official Complaint Report. 26-1556-69: Ypsilanti, Michigan: original date March 21, 1969

57. Michigan State Police Official Complaint Report. 26-1643-69: Ypsilanti, Michigan: original date March 25, 1969

58. Michigan State Police Official Complaint Report. 26-2132-69: Ypsilanti, Michigan: original date April 16, 1969

59. Michigan State Police Official Complaint Report. 26-3468-69: Ypsilanti, Michigan: original date June 9, 1969

60. Michigan State Police Official Complaint Report. 26-4427-69: Ypsilanti, Michigan: original date July 23, 1969

* 61. Risner, Jesicca. University of Michigan Student who resided in the same apartment building with murdered victim Madeline Prescott. (personal interview): July 6, 1969

62. State of Michigan Secretary of State Branch Manager. Ypsilanti, Michigan Office. (personal interview): August 1969

* 63. Salinasse, Sylvia. Eastern Michigan University Co-ed. (official police statement): August 1969

64. Treml, William B. *The Ann Arbor News*: "Wounded Coed Fights for Life": Ann Arbor, Michigan: July 5, 1969.

*   65. Watters, Louise A.. Witness who thought Collins was capable of any crime. (official police statement): Fall 1969

66. Willcox, Christopher. The Detroit News: "EMU Co-ed Killer Collins is Riddle After Six Years." p. 3B August 10, 1976

67. Williams, Booker T. Esquire. Chief Assistant Prosecutor Washtenaw County. (personal interview): Summer 1969

68. Winn, Steven and Merrill David. *Ted Bundy: The Killer Next Door*: Bantam Books Inc., New York, New York: 1980

69. Ypsilanti Police Department Complaint or Occurrence Report. (Investigation Re: Karen Sue Beineman's activities at Wig Shop by Detectives Sergeants H.C. Smith and D.G. Howell.) Ypsilanti, Michigan. July 24, 1969

* fictitious name used, not real name

CHAPTER XIII

THE CASE STUDY OF JOHANN SCHARADITSCH AND HAROLD SASSAK

This case occurred in Vienna, Austria, during the early 1970's. The case is instructive in that it demonstrates how a series of crimes that began as robberies can eventually evolve into sexual offenses and ultimately a series of murders. It also teaches that perpetrators of serial murders sometimes do leave fingerprint evidence behind, and through hard police work, and the work of latent print experts, the perpetrator(s) can be identified.

SHORT SYNOPSIS OF THE CASE

During 1971 Johann Scharaditsch and Harold Sassak planned a series of robberies together. All together there were fifty-five of these. At first, they stole only small things—money and jewelry. Later Sassak, in addition to stealing began to beat and rape his female victims. Before they were apprehended fifteen women had been raped, and six women and one man died from injuries they received when they were beaten.

METHOD OF OPERATION

Scharaditsch and Sassak went to apartments occupied by elderly people. Posing as gas inspectors, they told the residents of the apartments that they must come inside their apartments to check for gas leaks which were very dangerous and could cause an explosion if not found. The elderly folks living in the apartments admitted the two "gas inspectors."

While the two "inspectors" were searching for the "leaks," they stole anything that was available to steal. They usually took rings, other jewelry, and money. They would then thank their victims for permitting them to inspect the premises and leave. They would then repeat the process in another apartment.

They became discouraged with the small amount of the loot. They thought that perhaps they might do better if they started beating their victims to force them to turn over all their money and valuables. Then to increase the terror, and for his own personal amusement, Sassak decided to add rape with the beatings. Sometimes a woman was raped in front of her husband if he refused to give them his money or valuables.

The victims were bound with ropes the perpetrators had brought with them. Sassak beat the victims with his fists. Scharaditsch did not take part in either the beatings or the rapes. He confined his activities to stealing.

These criminal activities took place for about one and a half years before they were apprehended by the police.

WITNESS

One elderly wife tried to fight off Sassak as he was raping her. She scratched him across the face. Although beaten, she survived and was able to provide the police with a description of him. She said that Sassak's breath smelled of alcoholic beverages.

EVIDENCE

Laboratory scientists, while processing the crime scene, found a Marlboro cigarette butt that Sassak had flipped on top of a wardrobe. On the butt, the scientists developed an excellent partial latent fingerprint.

CRIMINAL INVESTIGATION

Acting upon the theory that after the rape and robbery, the perpetrators would go to a restaurant and have a drink, one hundred and fifty police officers began checking all restaurants. They made inquiry as to whether anyone had observed a man with a scratch on his face matching the physical description of the rapist/ murderer. They also said that the suspect smoked Marlboro cigarettes.

WHAT LED TO THE ARREST OF THE PERPETRATOR

During the course of this investigation, one thousand two hundred potential persons were investigated by the police. They were all fingerprinted. These known prints were then compared with the questioned partial latent fingerprint found on the cigarette butt. Finally, an identification was made. The latent print was found to have come from Harold Sassak.

ARRESTED PERSON

Harold Sassak, a white male, date of birth October 26, 1942, was the person arrested in this case. Sassak, at the time of his arrest weighed about one hundred kilograms and was one hundred and seventy-five centimeters tall. He did not participate in any sporting activities while he was growing up. He was divorced. When he was arrested he was not armed (nor was he armed while he perpetrated the attacks outlined above). He offered no resistance. When officers questioned him about his criminal activities, he confessed to three beatings and rapes where the women victims later died from these severe beatings. Sassak said he did not intend to cause their deaths.

SENTENCED

In 1972 Sassak was sentenced to life in prison. He could not be convicted of murder under Austrian law because the court believed he did not intend to kill his victims, but only meant to rob and rape them.

Johann Scharaditsch was also sent to prison.

OBSERVATIONS

The Austrian Police worked very hard rounding up possible suspects to obtain their fingerprints to make a comparison with the partial latent fingerprint found on the cigarette butt. In this country under the Constitution of the United States, there is a question of whether it would be reasonable to take a person into custody to take inked impressions of his fingers because he fit the general description of the suspect. In this instance, hundreds of men were taken into custody because they fit the general description of the suspect; he had a scratch on his face and he smoked Marlboro cigarettes. In the author's opinion, it would depend entirely on the personal beliefs of the appeals judge(s) whether the obtaining of fingerprints in this way would be ruled legal or illegal. The entire question would be an issue of whether such action was reasonable. The author would suggest that any prudent man or woman would say that it was.

Clearly a round up of all the males in a town and then fingerprinting them merely because there was the probability that the suspect lived in that town would be ruled unreasonable conduct on the part of the police, even if the perpetrator was found and identified by that method.

One of the observations this writer observed while accompanying the special unit which investigates homicides in Vienna, Austria, was that the police were certainly in no hurry to disturb the body. Another observation was that on every homicide, a police officer who was also an attorney, rolled with the unit. His purpose was to be immediately available should he be needed to render advice or to draft legal papers. Finally, when the investigators go to the scene of the crime, they do so in a van which is a rolling office. The van has a desk with a typewriter and all the various forms needed. If the officers wished to take written statements from witnesses or a confession from the murderer, their mobile office was readily available.

In addition to the above, the highly trained officers of Vienna's tactical unit also responded to the scene. They do this for two reasons. First, to protect the scene thoroughly until forensic scientists could process it. Second, they are there if it is necessary to help search for evidence.

For the most part Vienna's investigative techniques correspond with our own. One exception is that they do not use polygraph in their investigations as is done here, in Japan, Canada, Mexico and in Israel.

CASE AUTHORITY:
Obstlt. F. Maringer
Bundespolizeidirektion Wien
Sicherheitsburo
Rossauer Lande 5
A-1090 Wien (Vienna), Austria

CHAPTER XIV

THE CASE STUDY OF CHRISTOPHER BERNARD WILDER

This case study is about serial murderer, Christopher Bernard Wilder, who was also known as "The Beauty Queen Killer." The case contains several lessons which are significant to those called upon to investigate serial murders. This case exemplifies how the serial murderer may travel thousands of miles, how he may force a hostage to help him acquire new victims, how he may use several different methods of killing his victims, how, even though he may appear respectable, he may be capable of murder, and why it is important to use surveillance after a serial murder suspect is picked up and released, and how the serial murderer will sometimes use innocent people to lie for him to establish a phony alibi. The case also demonstrates the importance of using the media in serious murder cases to both warn and enlist the support of the people and to make a direct appeal to a kidnapper.

SHORT SYNOPSIS OF THE CASE

The murders apparently began in February 1984. Wilder had approached Beth Kenyon, a beautiful twenty-three year old white female. He told her he was a photographer. He talked with her about posing for pictures for him. They began dating. After a few dates, Wilder asked her if she would marry him. Beth told her mother that she was surprised by the proposal since he had never even kissed her before he asked her to marry him. She rejected his proposal, but they remained friends. Beth described Wilder as "the perfect gentleman." Beth had known Wilder for two years before she disappeared. Their first meeting came after the Miss Florida contest in 1982 when Wilder had come back stage to talk with her.

Then on March 5,1984, Beth Kenyon of Pompano Beach, Florida, disappeared. Her parents reported her missing. The parents were so upset with the progress the police were making that they hired a private detective firm to investigate the disappearance of their daughter.

The President of the University of Miami had dated Beth. At the gasoline station where she bought fuel, he was told by the attendant that Beth had come in the day she disappeared and had her car refueled. The attendant said a man about six feet tall, in his late thirties, deeply tanned, with slightly balding brown hair, drove in behind her in a slate grey Cadillac and paid for her gas with a twenty dollar bill. He heard them talking. She asked him, "Who is going to take the pictures?"
"I am."
"Do I look all right?"
"You look fine."

The attendant started to wipe her windshield but she told him, " Forget it. We're in a hurry to get to the airport."

The private detectives, one of whom was a former member of the Federal Bureau of Investigation, obtained a photo album which contained pictures of the various men that Beth had dated. These pictures were shown to the station attendant. He identified Wilder as the man in the Cadillac.

There could be little chance that the witness was wrong. Wilder owned a slate grey Cadillac. He fit the physical description. He was interested in photography. According to the author, this information was given to the police, but still no action was taken. There were no requests that Wilder take a polygraph examination to test his knowledge of her disappearance.

A private detective called Wilder on the telephone and asked him about whether he knew anything about Beth's disappearance. Wilder told him he had not seen Beth for over a month. The private detective also undoubtedly told Wilder that he was identified by the gas station attendant as being the last person identified as being with her.

The private detectives also checked with the Boynton Beach Police Department and learned of Wilder's criminal record.

The private detectives contacted Wilder again. This time at his construction office where he was co-owner of two corporations. Wilder had his secretary give an alibi for him stating that Wilder had been working on a project in Boca Raton during the morning and was in the office during the afternoon on the date Beth was missing. Wilder slipped up during this interview, however. He stated that the victim's car had been found at the airport. That was true, but the police had not made that information public.

On February 26, 1984, a few days before Beth disappeared, Rosario Gonzalez, a white female twenty years old, of Homestead, Florida, was working at Miami Grand Prix track. She was distributing aspirin samples in skimpy red shorts and a tee shirt when she disappeared. A family friend was suspected. He was given a polygraph examination and passed.

The investigation by the police then began to zero in on Wilder. Much of the credit for that belongs to another friend of Beth. He was the only police officer she knew personally. His name was Mitch Fry. Wilder was not placed under surveillance. However, they did want to question him.

On March 16, 1984, there was an article in the *Miami Herald* which stated the police were looking for a Boynton Beach race car driver in connection with the disappearance of two South Florida women. The article did not mention Wilder's name, but it did give his physical description and said that he was a wealthy contractor.

On Friday, March 18, 1984, Wilder called his business partner and told him he was in trouble. He told him that the police wanted to "frame me" for Beth's disappearance. He said, "I don't know anything about it, but the cops don't care. They just want a fall guy, somebody to take the rap. I am not going to jail. I am not going to do it."

Wilder put his three English setters in a kennel he jointly owned in Fort Lauderdale.

He had with him a loaded .357 revolver, extra ammunition, handcuffs, a roll of duct tape, a rope, a sleeping bag, a copy of John Fowles' *The Collector*, and a fifteen foot electrical cord that had been split at the end so each end of the wire could be attached to a woman's leg. He also had an electrical switch whereby he could turn the electricity on and off. He used this device to give the women he kidnapped the shock treatment when they were not dancing for him as he thought they should be. He did this when he held the women captive.

He was driving a one year old Chrysler New Yorker. It was rather plain compared to his Cadillac, Porsche, or one of the other seven or eight cars he had available to him. He also apparently had a considerable amount of money, some photographic equipment, some photo layout work examples, and his business partner's credit card. Then he set out to satisfy his lustful fantasies.

Wilder's first victim appears to have been Terry Ferguson, a white female, twenty-one years old, from Indian Harbour, Florida. She was last observed in a shopping mall near her home. Like the other girls, she was interested in becoming a model. An hour after she was last observed at a shopping mall, Wilder called for a wrecker off state road A1A near Canaveral Groves when his car got stuck in the sand. He paid for the wrecker with his partner's credit card. There was no woman seen in the car, but she may have been in the trunk. About a week later, Terry's body was recovered from a snake infested river about seventy miles west of her home. She was fully clothed. She was identified from her dental charts. A witness identified Wilder from a photo show up conducted by the F.B.I. as the man with whom she had observed Terry talking on the day she disappeared.

Wilder then kidnapped a beautiful nineteen year old blonde coed from a shopping mall near Florida State University in Tallahassee. Subsequent to the kidnapping, she was tortured and raped, but she then escaped. That incident will be discussed at length below under the heading of *modius operandi*. Wilder had taken this victim across the state line into Georgia.

Wilder then murdered Terry Diane Walden of Beaumont, Texas. She was a twenty-four year old nurse who attended Lamar University. She died from multiple stab wounds. Her body was fully clothed. She had been thrown into a canal near a dam. There was no indication that she had been tortured or sexually assaulted. Her car, a three year old burnt-orange Mercury Cougar, was stolen. Her husband stated that she had told him that she had been approached by a man who asked her if she was interested in doing some work as a model two days before she disappeared. Wilder's Chrysler was recovered with blood in it in the Beaumont area.

On March 24, 1984, Wilder kidnapped Susanne Wendy Logan from a shopping mall in Oklahoma City, Oklahoma. She had long blonde hair and a good figure. Her body was found floating in Milford Reservoir by a fisherman. She was half naked. She had been beaten about the face. She had numerous small cuts on her back as though they were made with the tip of a knife. Her pubic hair had been shaved off and the hair on her head had been crudely cut. Her hair was found in the wastebasket of the motel where Wilder spent the night. Her death was caused by a knife being used to stab her above the left breast.

Wilder then drove to Grand Junction, Colorado. On March 29, 1984, he approached Sheryl Bonaventura in the Mesa Mall. Sheryl was eighteen years old and had previously worked as a model on a limited basis. Another woman identified Wilder's picture in a photo show up. He had also approached her about posing as a model. He had his camera with him. Sheryl had a sports car with a "for sale" sign in the window. It is unknown whether Wilder talked with her about her car or a job. Her car was left in the parking lot.

Later that same day, Wilder and Bonaventura had lunch in a restaurant one hundred miles south of the place where she had been abducted. She told a waitress who she was and that she was headed to Las Vegas to be a model with another girl. The waitress could not understand why this young woman was telling her these things.

That evening Bonaventura and Wilder spent the night in a motel at Durango. Bonaventura's naked body was found thirty-six days later near a rest area in Utah. She had been stabbed several times, once in the heart, and shot in the chest too. It was believed that she was murdered on March 31, 1984.

On April 1, 1984, at the Meadows Mall in Las Vegas, Nevada, Michelle Korfman who was seventeen years old was taking part in the *Seventeen* magazine cover competition. She was also very interested in a modeling job. Her father had even paid to have a professional photographer take photographs for her portfolio.

While the contest was taking place, the shutter on one camera was accidentally tripped taking a picture of Wilder sitting there watching the competition. Later Wilder was identified during a photo show up as leaving a store with Korfman. Wilder had approached eight other women that afternoon about a modeling job. They were supposed to meet him in front of Caesar's Palace, but he never showed up.

Wilder had arrived in Las Vegas on March 29, 1984, paid cash for a room at a downtown motel, and had signed in under his own name. He moved to another motel on the next night. The police in that area were investigating three other murders that occurred on earlier dates where subsequently the finger of suspicion pointed toward Wilder.

Wilder then traveled to California. On April 4, 1984, he contacted a sixteen year old girl who had just filled out a job application at Hickory Farms. He offered her one hundred dollars if she would pose for some pictures for a billboard ad he was shooting. She went with him to a beach to shoot "a few test rolls." This was about ten miles north of the girl's home in Torrance, California.

After she had posed for one roll, she said she had to go home. Wilder became enraged. He pulled out his revolver, stuck the barrel in her mouth, and told her, "Your modeling days are over." He then tied her up and drove two hundred and thirty-seven miles Southeast to the small town of El Centro. He was still driving the orange Mercury. He took the victim, Tina Marie Risico, inside a motel room he had rented. He tied her to the bed and sexually assaulted her. The police knew she had been abducted by Wilder because the manager at Hickory Farms picked his picture out of a photo show up.

At The Behavioral Science Unit at Quantico, Virginia, Wilder was profiled as a "...classic serial killer." This was someone who was a compulsive murderer who goes on killing until he is stopped. Typically a handsome white man in his thirties, the serial murderer roams constantly looking for women, children and the elderly, any stranger who is in some way weaker than he is. Another trait of the serial killer, and one that makes him so hard to identify, is his urge to drive long distances, often following an aimless itinerary. It is not unusual for a serial killer to drive between 100,000 to 200,000 miles in a year.

After Wilder had been put on the F.B.I.'s Ten Most Wanted List, and after there had been considerable publicity about him in Florida, the manager of a dating service came forward and told the police he had a video tape Wilder had made in 1981 after he had been put on probation for the rape of a fifteen year old Tallahassee girl. On the tape Wilder indicated he wished to meet young women no older than their early twenties. The tape tended to show that Wilder was "a consummate actor who could slip into any role in order to elude the massive manhunt that had been launched to find him." The tape was broadcast to serve as a warning to women should they chance to come into contact with Wilder.

On April 10, 1984, Dawnette Sue Wilt, a sixteen year old high school student was filling out a form at a clothing store in a mall when she was contacted by another teenager. The latter asked her to step outside the store while she fetched the "manager." Wilder, who was posing as the store manager, asked Dawnette to accompany him to his car where he had some forms to sign. At the car, he pulled a gun from his briefcase, bound Dawnette's arms and legs, and put duct tape over both her eyes and mouth. Tina Marie then drove the Mercury while Wilder assaulted Dawnette. She was abducted from Merrillville, Indiana, just south of Gary.

She was taken to a motel in Ohio where she was sexual assaulted and tortured. The next day they traveled through Pennsylvania into New York. While Dawnette was kept bound and gagged in the car, Tina and Wilder looked at Niagara Falls and took photographs. Then they proceeded on to a motel southeast of Rochester, New York.

*Wilder has also been called a "Spree Killer."

146

Dawnette was then raped and tortured for a second night. After he was finished, he told the girls he would kill them both if either tried to escape.

The next morning on television, Wilder saw an appeal made by Tina's mother to Wilder to free her daughter. Wilder reacted immediately by saying, "We're getting the hell out of here." He took both the girls to the car, but Dawnette was bound and gagged and put into the back. Wilder left the area on the back roads. He traveled to a wooded area fifty miles south of Rochester, New York. There he promised Dawnette that she would not be hurt if she did what he told her. He took her out of the car and into the woods. At first he tried to suffocate her by pinching her nose while she still had her mouth sealed with tape, but she twisted her head loose. Then he pulled out his knife and stabbed her twice in the chest and twice in the back. Dawnette, being an intelligent Hoosier, played opossum, and Wilder left her for dead. After Wilder had gone, Dawnette got up and walked down a road until she met a man who took her to the hospital. She was able to tell the police that Wilder said he would not be taken alive, that he was still driving the Orange Mercury, and that he was headed for Canada.

Wilder then went to Eastview Mall near Victor, New York. This was back toward Rochester. There Wilder had Tina approach a thirty-three year old woman just getting out of her two year old Pontiac Trans-Am. Tina asked her to come over to their car, which the woman did. Wilder then forced the woman into the Mercury. He gave Tina the keys to the Trans-Am and told her to follow him, which she did. He drove the woman to a gravel pit where he shot her between the shoulder blades. She died. This victim's name was Beth Dodge. Wilder then abandoned the Mercury at the gravel pit and fled in the gold Trans-Am.

Wilder took Tina Marie to Logan International Airport where he bought her a plane ticket, and gave her a wad of money, and told her he did not want her with him when he died. She then flew to Los Angeles.

Wilder stopped to "help" a nineteen year old woman whose car had broken down along an expressway in Massachusetts. After he drove by a gas station, and she objected that he did not stop, he threatened her with a gun. When he was forced to slow down near an exit, she rolled out of the car and escaped.

Wilder disposed of a small suitcase, his camera, spent casings, the floor mats from the car and various other items that belonged to victims. He proceeded into New Hampshire where he made preparations to cross the United States/Canadian Border. He then drove into the little town of Colebrook where during a scuffle with a New Hampshire Trooper, who was investigating him, he was shot to death with his own gun and died instantly.

The police suspected Wilder of other murders in addition to the ones mentioned above, but clear and convincing evidence of his involvement does not exist.

The perpetrator of these crimes generally operated in the following manner: He approached a young woman at a beauty contest, or filling out a job application, and asked her if she would like to pose for a magazine layout that he was doing. Sometimes he offered her a considerable amount of money if she would just pose for some "test pictures". He would ask the young woman to accompany him to his car where he would show her some of his work. At his car he would either pull a gun on the woman, or as happened with one university coed, he punched her hard in the stomach. He then forced her into the car where he bound her hand and foot with ropes. He then put duct tape over her eyes and mouth. He then put the victim in a sleeping bag and went to a motel where he left her in the car until he checked in.

He then carried the victim out of the car like a sack of grain into the motel room. Inside the room he removed the ropes and the tape across the victim's eyes. In one instance, he put Super Glue on the victim's eye lids to seal them shut and then used an electric blow dryer to dry them. He then forced the victim to perform fellatio upon him. He raped the victim. He then put the ends of an electric wire on the victim's legs and made her mimic aerobic dancers he liked to watch on television.

He shaved off the victim's pubic hair. Most of the young women he abducted had long hair. He cut their hair and threw their tresses in a waste basket. He told them he wanted all of his girls to have their hair cut like the girl in the movie *Flash Dance*.

After Wilder was finished with them, he would generally murder them. In some cases, the victims may have been murdered in the motel room by being suffocated with a pillow. Sometimes he took the victim to a remote location where he stabbed the victim to death. In one case, he both stabbed the victim and shot her. It should be remarked that this was a victim who told a waitress her name and told her they were headed for Las Vegas.

He threw the bodies of some of his victims into the water, rivers or man made lakes. Some victims were left near rest areas along highways. One victim was left near a gravel pit.

Wilder had access to several different vehicles that belonged to him. Undoubtedly he used his Cadillac or Porsche to influence his young, impressionable victims that he was a professional photographer. He even had a special room prepared in his house for taking pictures. While on his murderous crime spree, the vehicle he used was a Mercury which attracted little attention. He would use stolen plates on the car. He later obtained a high performance car—a gold Trans-Am. That vehicle definitely could and did attract police attention.

There were no indications that Wilder had studied law enforcement or been involved in security work. He did take his clothes to a woman tailor whose husband was a police officer. Undoubtedly he used this woman as a contact to talk with her husband to acquire information regarding how an investigation was progressing.

As the joint owner of two corporations and a dog kennel, some police officers may have thought Wilder was a honest, responsible citizen. Therefore, he would have a degree of influence within the criminal justice community unless someone checked into his criminal history.

WITNESSES

Four of the victims Wilder abducted managed to survive. One woman escaped by running into a motel bathroom and then began screaming and pounding on the walls causing Wilder to flee. Another victim was stabbed in her chest and back yet survived and was able to give the police valuable information as to which direction Wilder was headed. Another victim was put on a plane with a one way ticket back to Los Angeles. And one victim rolled out of the car along an expressway and escaped.

There were several witnesses who identified Wilder in photo show ups as the last person to be observed with a particular victim.

EVIDENCE

When the New Hampshire State Police Troopers attempted to arrest Wilder, he was in possession of a murdered victim's car.

The Mercury owned by another murdered victim was recovered from the area where the owner of the Trans-Am was found.

Troopers recovered the gun that had been used to shoot at least two of the victims.

Credit card receipts could be used to put Wilder in certain areas on certain dates.

Police had a photograph taken of Wilder at a beauty show where a victim disappeared shortly thereafter.

CRIMINAL INVESTIGATION

The investigation focused on Wilder after it was learned that he was the last person who was observed with Beth Kenyon. He had lied about being with her, and knew her car had been left at the airport when that information had not been released to the general public.

The police were able to track Wilder's movements through his use of his business partner's credit cards. The police had Wilder's fingerprints and his photograph from his previous arrest on a sexual assault charge. They also had good psychological data on him from two evaluations connected with that previous arrest. Both of the doctors indicated that Wilder required a structured environment. One doctor, however, regarded Wilder as psychotic and thought he should have been confined. The other doctor however, did not believe that Wilder was of any danger to society.

The police also had a video tape of Wilder which had been made in connection with a dating service. Wilder indicated during that interview that he wanted to date younger women—no older than their early twenties.

The police consistently used the photo show up in an efficient manner while tracking Wilder.

The police used the media to good advantage to alert the citizens of the United States to the danger of Wilder and to enlist their support. The victims stated that Wilder saw one Mother's appeal for her daughter. It caused Wilder to flee the area immediately. That victim was later put on a plane and flown home.

PERPETRATOR

The serial murderer in this case was Christopher Bernard Wilder. He was a white male, who was born on March 13, 1945, in Sidney, Australia. His mother was a citizen of Australia and his father was a career navy man. Wilder was five-feet eleven inches tall and weighed one hundred and eighty pounds. He had brown balding hair and blue eyes. Most of the time, he wore a beard.

Since Wilder's father was in the navy, after the war, Wilder came to the United States where he lived around bases on both the East and West Coasts. Wilder graduated from high school. He completed a carpenter's apprenticeship which he started when he was sixteen years old. Wilder was the oldest son in the family. He had three younger brothers.

Wilder admitted window peeking for about three years. This occurred when he was eleven to thirteen years old. He had been involved in a gang rape when he was a teenager in Australia. He had been married for a very short time after he graduated from high school. When he returned to Australia, he was arrested again for the sexual assault of two young girls. He jumped bond. When he was going through the psychological evaluation to determine if he was sane enough to stand trial and to provide the judge with some guidance regarding sentencing—Wilder told the psychologist that he masturbated twice a week. HE USED THE MENTAL PICTURE THAT HE WAS RAPING A GIRL TO ACHIEVE CLIMAX. HE HAD BEEN DOING THAT FOR " THE PAST COUPLE OF YEARS." This was eight years before his attacks led to murder. He told the doctor that he did not use these fantasies in general anger or anything like that. As events subsequent to that interview were to demonstrate, it is very doubtful that he was being truthful when he made that statement.

Also during that interview, Wilder stated that HE RATIONALIZED THAT IT (the slapping of a sixteen year old girl and forcing her to commit fellatio on him) WAS *NOT* WRONG, but he realized that he had created problems for his "current particular victim." He said on the day he committed the offense he was feeling down and that it all happened like it was in slow motion. Then he said to himself, there is no way to stop this unless he put his victim in a hole and went away.

Wilder did sometimes date women his own age. One thirty-two year old woman, who had been intimate with Wilder off and on for over two years said that one evening she was in the jacuzzi with Wilder when a strange look came over his face. He told her to get out of the water immediately and leave. He would not tell her why, but said he did not want to hurt her.

Another time the same woman stated she awoke one night to find Wilder standing at the foot of her bed. Wilder had a key to her apartment. She asked him what he was doing in her bedroom. What did he want? Wilder told her that he did not know. He said he did not know what he was doing there and did not know even how he had gotten there. He also told her about taking pictures of young girls. He said he could not explain why he was doing that. It was like a sickness. He said he could not stop. It was something he had to do.

Most people who knew Wilder, but were not aware of his criminal record, thought Wilder was a perfect gentleman. This included his associates with whom he liked to drive a race car. Wilder also loved his dogs and went to great extreme to insure that they received proper care.

WHAT LED TO THE ARREST OF THE PERPETRATOR

A check was made by a citizen at the gasoline station where the victim usually bought her gas. The attendant there gave a physical description of a man fitting Wilder's description and driving a Cadillac of the same color that Wilder owned. An album of men the victim had dated was shown to the attendant. He identified Wilder. The attendant recalled that the victim would not let him wash her windshield because she was in a hurry to get to the airport. The victim's car was recovered from the airport. Wilder slipped up in an interview with a private detective and told the detective her car was left at the airport. That information was not made public. The attendant also heard the victim ask who was going to take the picture and Wilder told her that he was going to take it. Wilder had a considerable amount of photographic equipment and was an amateur photographer.

As the finger of suspicion was pointed strongly toward Wilder and police were looking for him, an article was published in the newspaper that a contractor who drove race cars was being sought. Wilder fled the state of Florida and began a tour throughout the United States that left bodies of tortured and murdered women in his trail until he took his own life to avoid arrest by a New Hampshire State Trooper.

It appeared as if when the police were closing in on Wilder he had decided to go on a rampage of rape and murder and to fulfill his lustful fantasies before he took his own life. It is remarkable that he was able to travel from one side of the nation to the other without being stopped by the police. There did not appear to be any deliberate plan to cross into Canada. If there had been, he would not have waited until he was in some remote area to do it, but would have crossed over at some busy area such as between Detroit and Windsor.

It appeared that both the student nurse and the woman in her thirties were murdered solely for their respective cars. In the first instance, Wilder knew that the Florida State University student who escaped told the police what kind of car he was driving, so he had to get rid of his Chrysler. In the second case, he had been driving the orange Mercury for a long time. He thought he might be involved in trying to escape from the police, and he wanted a high performance car. In the opinion of the writer, that is why he murdered the owner of the Trans-Am.

In one murder, Wilder returned to the parking lot where the victim's car was parked. He got into the car and drove it to a bar where he went in and had a drink. The lesson here for police is that a stake out should be placed on the victim's car if it is discovered a short time after she is reported missing. In the event that the perpetrator comes to her car to either search it or steal it, officers can be ready to apprehend him.

Once again when the finger of suspicion was pointing toward Wilder, no police surveillance was established. It is the author's opinion that this should have been done prior to any interrogation or tip off to him that he was a suspect. This type of error has been made in several serial murder cases. This permitted the killer to get rid of evidence or to flee.

With regard to Tina Marie Risico, there must have been some special reason why Wilder did not murder her. It is possible that her mother's appeal to Wilder saved her life. It is obvious, however, that he came to regard her differently than the other girls. This was demonstrated by using her to help him abduct other victims and having her drive the Trans-Am. He knew it could go so fast he could not catch her, if she had decided to escape.

It was noticed that Wilder tried to get rid of any evidence before he was going to try to cross the Canadian Border.

The two girls missing from Florida early in 1984 probably never will be found. As was observed, he was throwing the bodies of his victims in snake infested rivers and also into lakes. It is quite possible that he threw the girls into Florida rivers where their remains could have been eaten by alligators.

Looking at the diversity of Wilder's method of operation is instructive. It teaches that one should not be too hasty in stating that a particular murder was or was not connected to a particular serial killer based strictly on his method of operation. For example, Wilder killed some victim's by suffocation, some died of multiple knife wounds, one was knifed and shot. It was remarkable, however, that Wilder did not shoot any of the victims in the head.

Wilder also did not follow any consistent pattern in disposing of his victim's remains. Some bodies were thrown into rivers, others were left behind rest areas, and one was left in a gravel pit. Another victim who survived, was stabbed and left for dead in a woods. Wilder did not attempt to bury any of his victims.

It is the author's opinion that whenever the attack by a serial murderer appears more severe and brutal than previous attacks, it could mean that something went awry in that particular attack or in the attack immediately preceding it. For example, it was observed in the instant case study that the victim who was both knifed and shot had told a waitress who she was and where she was being taken. It will be noted below when the case study of the Boston Strangler, Albert DeSalvo, is taken up, that after an aborted attack on a sick German waitress, who screamed and bit DeSalvo on the finger, that the attack on the next victim was much more ferocious. He pounded her head to mush.

It was observed that Wilder's tailor's husband was a police officer. Wilder probably selected her and used her to obtain information about the investigation efforts. Note from the case above that Collins also used his contacts with officers to obtain information on the progress of the police investigation. Convicted serial murderer Edmund Kemper of California made it a practice of hanging out in a bar frequented by off duty police officers. He even bought them drinks. He acquired information by listening to them talk. Also, serial murderer David Alan Gore of Vero Beach, Florida, had a police scanner in his house which he used to monitor police whereabouts.

It was also noted how Wilder asked his secretary to lie for him to help him establish an alibi to extricate himself from a difficult situation. As was seen above, John Collins asked his friend, Davis, to lie about the times they had been motorcycle riding. It will be observed in many other serial murderer cases that the serial killer likes to use people. Therefore, to get someone to lie for him is second nature. Some other serial killers who tried, or in fact did, get others to lie for them were Richard Hansen, Kenneth Bianchi and Gerald Gallego. Since a secretary is frequently asked to lie for her boss by telling people he is not in, when in fact he really is in, but for one reason or another does not wish to talk with that particular person, and since her job may be at risk if she does not lie for him; it is suggested that she be contacted away from the work place. Then, at the outset, it should be explained to her what is being investigated and the seriousness of obstructing justice. If possible, try to keep what she has told you as confidential.

Finally, as was stated before, every alibi in a serial murder case should be thoroughly investigated.

CASE SOURCES

The analysis of this case was based upon the book, *The Beauty Queen Killer*. This was written by Bruce Gibney. The book was copyrighted in 1984. It was also published that same year by Pinnacle Books, Inc., 1430 Broadway, New York, New York 10018.

Fry, Sergeant Mitch. Coral Gables Police Department. Coral Gables, Florida. (telephone interview): August 3, 1990.

Ressler, Robert K., Supervisory Special Agent, F.B.I. (ret.)
American Academy of Forensic Sciences Workshop: Anaheim, California, February 19, 1991.

CHAPTER XV

THE CASE STUDY OF KENNETH ERSKINE

This case is about Kenneth Erskine. It occurred in England during the early spring and summer of 1986. The primary lessons taught by this case are the value of fingerprint or palmprint identification and the necessity to sometimes put forth great perseverance and maximum effort to identify the guilty person. That was what our British colleagues did when they manually searched through the palmprint files to make the identification. Incorporated in that was the tacit lesson that palmprints were important. Had the English police failed to take the perpetrator's palmprints when he was previously arrested there would, of course, have been no possibility of subsequently identifying the palmprint found in a victim's room.

The case also brought to light the very strong likelihood that the perpetrator was engaging in negative fantasies.

Another point this case makes was that the perpetrator had a criminal record, but like the Boston Strangler, he had been convicted only on a burglary charge, not a sexual offense.

SHORT SYNOPSIS OF THE CASE

This series of murders occurred on the South side of London, England. The first murder victim was a white female. She was only four feet eleven inches tall and only weighed about seventy-five pounds. She was a spinster who had devoted her entire life to the teaching profession. She loved cats and had several of them in her apartment. She was seventy-eight years old. She was suffering from a hearing disability. Her body was found in her bed by two friends who had come into her apartment to check on her. They found her lying on her back. Her hands had been folded across her chest. She had on a floral night gown which was completely buttoned and reached all the way to her feet. There were contusions around her eyes. There appeared to be finger marks on her neck. The autopsy revealed that she had been raped and strangled. There did not appear to be any sign of forced entry into her apartment. The police did not find any clues. The body of the first victim was found on April 9, 1986.

At about 1:30 a.m. on June 9, 1986, a sixty-eight year old white widow was attacked in her apartment in an area of London called the "Angell Town Estates." This area was built during the 1960's , but was suffering from neglect. This was a high crime area about two miles from where the first victim had lived. People had heard this victim scream, but no one came to help her.

At approximately 11:30 a.m., the victim's grandson came to check on her and found the victim lying naked on her bed. She was dead. There were finger marks on her throat. There was a large bruise on her chest, as though the perpetrator had put his knee on her chest while he strangled her. The victim's legs were spread apart, and there was blood on the sheet. Again, there was no sign of forced entry into her apartment. The police discovered a good latent palmprint on the window ledge which indicated the perpetrator was not wearing gloves.

A check was made with the palmprints on file via a manual search, but no match was found. Teams of detectives talked with older women and warned them against opening their door to someone they did not know.

On June 28, 1986, at a hostel for the elderly in the Clapham District of London, an eighty-three year old white female was awaken from her sleep by a very light tapping on the window, which had the curtain drawn. Shortly after that, a large rock was thrown through the window. The perpetrator crawled through the window and entered the apartment. She could hear the person saying in a soft voice, "Kill--kill." The woman screamed as loud as she could. Other people got up and began trying to locate from where the scream had come. She said that he stood there in the room for a moment before he decided to flee. This woman was not injured.

At 4:00 a.m. on that same day, the police were called to the Sommerville Hastings Home, another home for the elderly which was a short distance from the Clapham District.

Shortly before that time, the staff observed a young man prowling in the halls. He was described as being between twenty and thirty years of age. He was of medium height and build. He had dark curly hair. They had tried to talk to him, but he fled.

Upon checking the rooms, they found a ninety-four year old former judge lying on the floor. His pajama trousers were pulled down around his ankles. He was the victim of an act of sodomy. He had been strangled to death.

In another room, a former colonel in the Polish Army, was found dead on his bed. This man was eighty-four years old. He also was the victim of a homosexual act, and he had been strangled to death.

The police responded by interviewing everyone who had any contact with the elderly in the area where the murders had been committed. That effort, however, did not yield any positive results.

The police then got a break from a retired engineer who lived in the area where the murders had occurred. He related the information only after he was promised that his name would be kept anonymous.

He said a couple nights prior to June 28, 1986, he was awakened by the sound of someone moving around in the corridor outside his room. The perpetrator entered his room. The victim was looking at him. The perpetrator motioned for him to be quiet by putting his finger up to his lips. The victim attempted to press a button to summon help, but the intruder pounced upon him and grabbed him by the throat, and pulled him across the bed away from the alarm button. The attacker sat on his chest. He kept his hand on his throat. His other hand was over the mouth and throat so the victim could not breathe. He was unable to holler. The man kept saying, "Kill-kill." He could see that he had a grin on his face which the victim described as making him appear like "the very devil."

The perpetrator jerked him out of the bed and threw him up against the wall. The victim played dead. The ruse worked. The perpetrator left. The victim was in great fear that if his attacker found out he was still alive he would return to kill him. That was why he had not come forward sooner. He was able to provide the police with a good description of his attacker because he had seen him through the glass door as well as when he was in his room.

In Paris, France, there had also been a large number of attacks upon elderly people so a check was made there, but it was decided that there were just too many differences in the crimes for them to have been committed by the same person.

On July 8, 1986, after an eighty-two year old white male had not been observed around his apartment, the neighbors called his daughter and asked that she check on him. She found her father dead in his bed. The bed sheet had been pulled up to his chin. There were finger marks on his neck. He had been the victim of sodomy. His bank book was missing along with three hundred pounds. His pictures had been turned toward the wall or laid face down. No clues were found.

On July 12, 1986, when another seventy-five year old man was not observed around his apartment, the police were called. The officers broke in and found the victim dead in his bathroom. He had been strangled, and he also had been sodomized.

On July 20, 1986, another seventy-five year old male victim was found sodomized and strangled on Overton Park Estate. The victim in that case was a recluse and was bedridden. The police found an excellent palmprint on the wall. Once again for two days and two nights they made a manual search for a match of the palmprint. On July 22, 1986, the palmprint was identified as being that of Kenneth Erskine.

On that same date, however, the perpetrator raped and murdered another female victim. She was another elderly woman; an eighty-two year old white female who was slightly hard of hearing. She had left her window open, and the culprit climbed through the window. He had forced the woman into the bedroom, stripped her clothing from her, raped her, and then strangled her. She was found the next morning.

Police learned that Erskine was getting a Social Security Check. They queried that department when and where he was to pick up the next check. When he picked it up, they arrested him.

The police found he had a bank account where he had deposited three hundred pounds the day after one of the victims had been killed and had his money stolen.

Erskine was examined by psychiatrists. They stated that he had reached a stage of development equal to an eleven year old. They could provide no reason for his acts except to say that he enjoyed killing.

THE ARRESTED PERSON

Kenneth Erskine was a child of a mixed marriage. He was twenty-four years old at the time he was arrested. He did not have any home, nor did he have a job. His mother and father forced him to leave home when he was sixteen years old after they had grown tired of his violent acts. He was getting into constant fights at school. He had stabbed a teacher in the hand with a pair of scissors. He had been exposing himself to middle aged and elderly women. He was sent to a psychiatrist, but attempted to kill him with a knife. At that time, he was into drug use. He hallucinated and thought he was Lawrence of Arabia. When he was eighteen years old, he was involved with an older man in a homosexual relationship. In 1982, he was sent to prison for burglary. In prison it was learned that he was a gifted artist, but his pictures were of old people lying on a bed. Their mouths were gagged, and knives protruded from various parts of their bodies.

Later, Erskine's pictures were such that it was not possible to determine whether his subjects were young or old. But then he returned to the theme of drawing older people again. In these pictures, the bodies were on fire and their faces had the look of terror.

It was the belief of the police that Erskine had a hopeless memory. They felt that he could not retain information any longer than approximately an hour.

SENTENCE

On January 11, 1988, Erskine was charged in Old Bailey with seven murders and one attempted murder. He was tried and found guilty of all charges. The court sentenced him to seven terms of life imprisonment for each of the murders and one term of twelve years for the attempted murder. Further, the judge said that the prisoner should not be considered for parole until he had served at least forty years. Therefore, he should not be considered for parole until he is in his sixties. That was the longest prison sentence ever imposed on a person in Britain for the crime of murder.

WHAT LED TO THE ARREST OF THE PERPETRATOR?

During the processing of the crime scene where one of the victims had been attacked, the forensic scientists found an identifiable palmprint on the wall. A manual search was made of the palmprint files. An identification was made by comparing the print found in the victim's room and the known print in the files. The perpetrator was identified by the matching palmprint. Information was also received from a witness who survived an attack by playing dead. He identified the perpetrator. The perpetrator was subsequently arrested and convicted. He admitted he had stolen things from the rooms, but denied murdering anyone.

The use of fingerprint evidence in serial murder cases has not been too successful in the United States. It was heartwarming to see that it was essentially through the very difficult task of searching and comparing palmprints of criminals in their files that our British colleagues were able to bring an end to Erskine's murder spree. Most of the perpetrators in this country very carefully try to wipe down the scene. That does not mean we should quit trying. The search should not be limited to the crime scene. Investigators should always search the murderer's vehicle or any other location where the victim may have been in an attempt to obtain her prints to prove she was inside the culprit's vehicle or apartment. All thoroughness should be used to prevent missing prints. In a case like this, Automated Fingerprint Identification System would have been valuable had the police found the latent print from a finger.(3.)

This case points out how important it is to have the complete confidence of the citizens. The police obtained a very good physical description from the victim who had played dead. This is why a *very carefully planned* appeal should be made to the people asking for their help in the matter. If the people believe that their help is not really needed, most citizens would just as soon stand back and let the police handle the matter. But if it is a very serious series of murders, and if they are made to believe that the police's back is to the wall and the public's help is really needed, they will come forward to give a hand.

It was observed that this person, like the Boston Strangler and Harold Sassak in Vienna, Austria, started out by committing burglaries and gradually the criminal acts became much more serious and involved sexual offenses.

One must ask oneself whether a government is really doing its job when a man who tried to stab his teacher with a pair of scissors and later attempted to stab his psychiatrist with a knife is permitted to be with the other members of society. In the author's opinion, Erskine should not have been on the street. Rather, he should have been confined and denied the opportunity to commit the murders outlined above.

It was remarkable that four years before these murders, while Erskine was in prison, his drawings reflected a hatred of older people. It appeared that he was possibly fantasizing in his mind at that time what he would like to do to them. It seems to be a fairly common practice of the serial murderer to picture these criminal acts in their mind long before they are carried out. It appeared as though Erskine had a great deal of anger and hatred possibly toward his parents for forcing him out of their home. In the opinion of the author, the imagining of brutal acts toward the elderly cannot be overemphasized.

In Maxwell Maltz, M.D., F.I.C.S. classic work called <u>Psycho-Cybernetics</u>, he pointed out the power of the subconscious mind to accomplish positive goals. Anyone who has ever tried these techniques cannot deny that they work.

In the author's view, what Doctor Maltz subscribed to was a form of self hypnosis. It is suggested that if these techniques can work to accomplish positive goals, causing the conscious mind and body to carry out the wishes of the subconscious mind of a person, then it would follow if the person had engaged in mental imagery of a negative nature, the result may be totally beyond something he would be capable of understanding. It would be predictable only when one who was trying to understand him knew the form of mental imagery in which he was engaging.

Based upon this case and many others, the author suggests the possibility that the phenomena of self hypnosis may play a role in at least some of these killings. This could happen because of the following: First, it is known that serial murderers tend to fantasize sadistic acts toward women while they masturbate and at other times.(2) They often use detective magazines and books about bondage to help reinforce their fantasies. Second, the only real differences between what the serial murderer does when he fantasizes and what the athlete does when he "visualizes", which in the opinion of the author can be a form of self hypnosis, are in the end result and in possible awareness of what one is doing. Third, such self hypnosis uses the power of the subconscious mind to carry out the behavior. In sporting events, the athlete would be consciously aware of what he was doing. (1) The serial murderer, since this is the result of action by the subconscious mind, may not be cognizant of the true role his fantasies have played in his criminal acts. Fourth, the thoughts of negative behavior could have originated in the mind of the serial murderer, or they could have been suggested to him from some outside source. It would be the author's view that in most instances, they originate in the mind of the killer. Fifth, it would appear that certain circumstances would have to be present in order to trigger the negative behavior. The circumstances should be consistent with the fantasy, and the perpetrator must believe that such negative behavior was not wrong. Hence, self hypnosis would account for why some serial killers cannot explain their actions and why it was almost as though a third person committed the crime.

Could it be that this is what Solomon meant when he wrote in Proverbs 16.30: "He (an evil man) shutteth his eyes to devise froward things: moving his lips he bringeth evil to pass"? This does not mean that the serial murderer does not realize he has committed the crime and has no fear of detection.

The perpetrator's subsequent attempts to avoid arrest by destroying any incriminating evidence or by fleeing from the police, in some cases, may simply be a matter of self-preservation.

The writer would also like to point out that Park Elliott Dietz, M.D., M.P.H., Ph.D., does not believe that self hypnosis exists. Therefore, if he is correct, it is clear that the writer's theory would have little merit.

CASE SOURCES

1. Beauchine, Ronald L., First Lieutenant (ret.) Michigan State Police. Telephone Interview. August 7, 1990.

2. Printky, Robert M.D., "Fantasy May Fuel Serial Killers," *The Indianapolis Star*, January 19, 1989.

3. Versailles, John. Captain. Michigan State Police Crime Laboratory. Telephone Interview. August 7, 1990.

4. Westwood, Philip., "Seven Victims of the Whispering Strangler," *Front Page Detective*, February, 1989.

CHAPTER XVI

BRIEF HISTORY OF THE MURDER OF A.S.

The series of murders which were attributed to Albert Frank DeSalvo, which the news media called, "The Case of the Boston Strangler," began on Thursday, June 14, 1962, when the body of A.S. was found dead in her apartment. This was Flag Day.

At 7:49 p.m. on that date, officers who had been on routine patrol were dispatched to apartment 3F at 77 Gainsborough Street in Boston, Massachusetts. This area is called the "Back Bay Area". A.S.'s son had called the police. His mother had been depressed. He thought she had committed suicide. It appeared to him, when he walked into his mother's apartment, that she had hung herself in the corner of the bathroom with the cord of her bathrobe, and her body had then fallen to the floor into her living room.(3.19)

A.S. was found lying on her back on a runner near the door to the bathroom, with her head nearest the door. She was wearing a blue housecoat, which was spread open exposing her nude body. Both her legs were spread apart forming an angle of nearly forty-five degrees. Her left leg was bent at the knee, and her genitalia was clearly exposed.(3.19)

A.S. had been strangled with the cord of her bathrobe. It had been knotted tightly about her neck with a bow under her chin. There was a quantity of blood under her head.(3.20) She had been hit on the head with a blunt instrument. No semen was found in her vagina. Her facial expression appeared serene.(2.139)

The bathtub in A.S.'s apartment was partially filled with water, her slippers were beside the tub, and her dentures were soaking in a glass of water on a shelf in the pantry. Her steel-rimmed glasses were laying on the runner next to her body. Her white purse was also laying on the floor near her. The contents had been dumped out on the floor. The apartment appeared as though it had been ransacked.

The contents of a wastebasket were strewn about on the floor. Drawers had been pulled open and obviously searched and then pushed partially back. The drawers formed an angle like a pyramid, with the lower drawers pulled out the furthest distance. (3.23)

A.S.'s son told the police that he thought two broaches and two necklaces were stolen (3.35), but that was all. The victim's gold watch was found on a shelf in the bathroom. Later, the jewelry, which was thought to have been stolen, was found in the apartment.

Initially some of the officers did believe that the death of A.S. was a suicide, others thought it was a rape-murder, others believed it was a house breaking and entering, where A.S. surprised the burglar, was then struck, raped, and murdered to prevent a later identification of the perpetrator.

The person living directly below A.S.'s apartment was taking a nap, and was awoke at 6:10 p.m. by a bumping sound similar to the sound of someone either moving furniture or dancing in the apartment above him.(3.21)

VICTIM

A.S. was a white female, fifty-five years old, with brown bobbed hair. She appeared younger than her age. She was of Latvian descent. She had the reputation of being shy and retiring. Those who knew her doubted that she would have opened a door to a stranger. She had been divorced for over twenty years. She graduated from a university as an agronomist. This is a branch of agriculture dealing with field crop production and soil management. She had two children, a son and a daughter. She worked as a seamstress to put her son through the University of Maryland. Her son had lived with her after he had graduated up until a month before her death. (2.139) (4.19,20,22,23)

METHOD OF OPERATION

DeSalvo, the confessed murderer of A.S., did not know her before he killed her.(2.177) There was no indication that he had any contact with her at all, nor was there any evidence that he had planned the crime for any length of time prior to its commission. He did take a lead weight with him from his car into the apartment where A.S. was living. Also the clothing which he wore at the time of the murder could have resulted from a plan to murder. In his statement regarding the murder of A.S. , DeSalvo said to his wife, "I said I was going fishing. That was my excuse for getting out of the house. I had a fishing net. It was weighted down with three lead pipes, and a fishing rod in the back of my car." (4.288)

He drove across the Mystic River Bridge into Boston, and then drove down St. Stephen's Street. He parked his eight year old, green, Chevrolet coach in front of St. Anne's Church. There was no indication that the church had any deterring affect upon him. DeSalvo got out of his car and walked around the corner into Gainsborough Street. With his car out of sight, he selected 77 Gainsborough, one of the four story brick apartment buildings that lined both sides of the street. He walked up the steps and entered the building. (4.288)

DeSalvo said he was wearing a raincoat over a charcoal colored sports jacket. In his pocket, he carried one of the lead pipes he had removed from the fishing net. It was quite apparent that he intended to use the pipe as a weapon. At some point in time, he put gloves on his hands. He said that he had stopped at apartment 3F and knocked at the door. A.S. answered the door.

DeSalvo told her, "I was sent to do some work in your apartment." She let him in and was leading him toward the bathroom, telling him what work needed to be done in her apartment when he hit her from behind with the pipe. As she was falling to the floor, he put his arms around her neck, and they fell together on the floor. He removed the belt from her robe and strangled her with it. He told his attorney, F. Lee Bailey, that he had sexual intercourse with A.S. before she died, but there was no evidence that she had been raped. (4.288) There was no seminal fluid found in her vagina, but there were bruises which tended to indicate she had been sexually manipulated with some hard, blunt edged object, such as a soft drink bottle. (2.139)

DeSalvo talked of having an abnormal sex drive. He frequently only needed to touch a woman, or girl, in order to have an ejaculation. As will be seen below, this helps explain why he derived so much pleasure from his activities by taking women's measurements.(4.336)

DeSalvo, after killing A.S., went into her bathroom to wash the blood off, and noted that he was wearing gloves. He consistently spoke as though some third party had committed the murder. He found another raincoat and put it on, even though the sleeves were short.

He searched the apartment, but said he really did not know what he was looking for in the drawers. He thought it might have been something he had done to make it appear like a burglary, but he wasn't really certain.(4.295)

He then left the apartment building. He claimed a policeman was passing by as he walked out the door. He said he was not afraid, worried, or had any anxiety about being apprehended. It was as though someone else had committed the murder. In his confession he said, "It was all the same thing, always the same feeling. You was there. These things were going on. And the feeling after I got out of that apartment was as if it never happened. I got out and downstairs, and you could of said you saw me upstairs, and as far as I was concerned, it wasn't me. I can't explain it to you any other way. It's just so unreal...I was there. It was done. And yet if you talked with me an hour later, or half an hour later, it didn't mean nothing. It just didn't mean nothing."(4.321)

Furthermore, when discussing his activities as the "Measuring Man," where he posed as an agent for a modeling agency and traveled about measuring ladies, he said,"...I'd go into the apartments day after day. I used to know the police were right there. Some of the women complained (about DeSalvo), three or four patrol cars shooting right by me, looking for me, and yet I still got out of my car and walked right in front of them and did these things, knowing they were there."(4.325)

After leaving the apartment building where A.S. had lived, he went to an Army-Navy Surplus Store where he bought a white shirt. He claimed he had picked up a black male who was to provide an alibi for him in the event someone were to question him about why he was walking into a store without a shirt. The black man was to say that DeSalvo had been caught in bed with another man's wife, and he had to flee without his shirt. After obtaining the shirt, he dropped the black man off where he wanted to go and headed toward the Atlantic Ocean.

DeSalvo drove his car to the Lynn Marsh, an Atlantic Ocean inlet. He claimed he waded out into the mud and threw his bloody shirt, jacket, and raincoat, which he had cut into small pieces, into the Atlantic Ocean. It should be noted here that prior to leaving A.S.'s apartment, DeSalvo had removed his bloody clothing and had wrapped them in his raincoat which he rolled up into a bundle before he carried it out of the apartment. As he was leaving the marsh, he noted another man watching him about one hundred yards away on the shoreline. DeSalvo got back into his car and drove home.(4.239)

DeSalvo gave a slightly different version of his method of operation to Dr. James Brussel. To Dr. Brussel he said, "She shut it (the water going into the tub) off when I came in. We went into the parlor through the bedroom. It had a pretty bedroom set...European Oak. There was a record player playing long hair music...We sat on the sofa talking. She turned away to walk to the kitchen, which was very dark, and it came to me all the sudden...the feeling...Jesus, like now! Inside...I'm ready to explode...Like right now I feel it. I had a piece of metal (a chunk of lead) in my pocket. I use it when I go for lobsters on the net. The next thing I know I hit her on the head, and she fell on top of me, and blood ran all over me...on my jacket...on my T-shirt. She just kept lying on top on me, and blood kept running down on me. I got up and had to put the thing around her neck."

Brussel asked him what thing he was talking about, and why did he think he had to put it around her neck? DeSalvo replied, "The blue cord from her robe. I looped it three times and then I tied it. I went to the waste basket and emptied it out. I put my jacket and shirt in it. I wiped the blood off me. I looked for something to put on. I recall I went to a metal cabinet, which had twenty dollars on top of it and took it...That's the only time I ever stole anything from any of these women...Right? I found a raincoat. It was tight on my arms, but I put it on. As I crossed the street, two cops in a car passed me. It must have been because there were so many people they did not notice me. I got into my car and took off the coat. I drove to Tremont Street.

I picked up a colored man and asked him to get in, and he did. I told him I had some trouble. I had a girl and I had shacked up with her, and her husband came in, and I had to leave without my shirt. I asked him to go with me to get a shirt in case they wouldn't believe me in the store. He said he would. I found an Army-Navy Store and went in and bought a shirt. He stayed in the car." (2.177-179)

DeSalvo also told Brussel that in addition to ripping and cutting up the bloody clothing he was wearing, he also tied some of the pieces of clothing up with rocks and then threw them into the ocean at the Lynn Marsh. He did not tell Brussel that he had worn a raincoat into the victim's apartment building, which would have meant that the reason for wearing this coat was to conceal the lead pipe he was carrying and to enable him to discard the coat and change his physical description in the event he had to flee from the scene of the crime. DeSalvo began his statement to Dr. Brussel by saying that he remembered (when he murdered A.S.) that it was hot, in the afternoon, and in the summer.(2.177)

VEHICLE INVOLVED

DeSalvo used a vehicle in this case to transport him to the crime scene area, to travel to a store where he could buy a new shirt after the one he was wearing at the time of the murder got blood on it and to dispose of evidence (i.e. his bloody clothing) after the murder was committed. The vehicle was about eight years old. It was a green Chevrolet coach. He parked this car a short distance away from the crime scene and then walked to the scene. While DeSalvo was still in the United States Army, he attempted to use the ruse on a woman that he had just chased away a prowler from her house. She obtained DeSalvo's license number which had led to DeSalvo being questioned by the police. From that time on, DeSalvo was wary about someone getting his license number.

EVIDENCE

There was no significant evidence found at the crime scene which would positively link Albert DeSalvo to this crime.

OBSERVATIONS

There was no forced entry into the victim's apartment. He conned her into letting him in by talking with her about doing repair work for her. He was obviously very articulate and a very convincing person. Those who knew the victim well told the police that it was highly unlikely that she would admit a stranger into her apartment, but the fact was that she did admit a perfect stranger.

The presence of uniformed police officers had little, if any, deterring affect upon DeSalvo. DeSalvo appeared to have been totally committed to carrying out his attack. Probably the only thing that would have prevented the attack on A.S. was if someone else had been in the apartment with her. DeSalvo then would have sought another target probably in the same building. If one was not found in that building, then one in a nearby building would have been selected.

When DeSalvo entered the apartment building, he was wearing his raincoat. According to him, it was a hot summer day, late in the afternoon. The sun was shining. Apparently the raincoat was worn so he could conceal the lead pipe he carried into the apartment to hit the intended victim with, to avoid getting the victim's blood on his clothing, and to change his appearance should that be necessary when fleeing the scene.

There were at least two significant witnesses on this case that were apparently not located. First, the black man that DeSalvo picked up after the murder was even asked to provide an alibi for him should DeSalvo be questioned about entering the Army-Navy Store to buy another shirt after the one he had been wearing at the time of the murder became covered with blood. Second, the man who stood along the shoreline and watched him as he ripped and cut up his shirt, jacket, and raincoat, and tied some parts of the clothing up in rocks and threw them into the ocean. While hindsight is always twenty-twenty, perhaps an appeal made to the public asking them to help the police locate any persons who may have observed anyone acting in a suspicious manner that afternoon might have been productive.

DeSalvo's remarks about the two police officers passing him in their car as he was coming out of the apartment building where he had just committed the murder of A.S. is significant because in some of these cases the perpetrator is tripped up by officers on patrol. Rarely do they leave evidence at the scene that links them directly to the crime. Most of these types of criminals are far too cunning for that type of error. Note the efforts DeSalvo went through to avoid leaving any evidence. Note how he carried his bloody clothing from the scene, and the disposing of the clothing in the ocean. Because of this, officers on patrol should be on constant alert for anything which just doesn't make sense. If they stop vehicles for traffic violations in areas where these serial murders are being committed, they should take advantage of the "Open View Doctrine," and they should look into the driver's car for any possible bloody clothing or any other physical evidence of the commission of such a crime while they are approaching the driver. They should also take a good look at the driver of the car for blood on his trousers, shirt or shoes.

It was also noted how cool DeSalvo was under pressure, if there was, in fact, any pressure on him. He did not panic when he got the victim's blood on his clothes. Instead he looked in the cabinet and wore a different raincoat out of the apartment even if the sleeves were too short.

If DeSalvo was telling the truth about seeing the officers, had they checked DeSalvo out because he was wearing a raincoat on a bright, hot, summer day—a raincoat that did not fit—they might have apprehended a murderer. Those few serial murderers who have confessed generally concede the first murders they committed were when they were most vulnerable because that was when they were the most apprehensive and most apt to make mistakes. After a few murders, they become better at what they do.

When DeSalvo saw the officers, he was carrying a bundle of bloody clothing. Perhaps the officers did see DeSalvo, but thought "There's another kook wearing a raincoat on such a hot day" or perhaps they were responding to a complaint. But the bottom line was, however, had DeSalvo been apprehended at that time his murderous activities would have been cut short and twelve women would have been permitted to live out their lives and the many assaults which later occurred on other women would not have happened.

CHAPTER XVII

BRIEF HISTORY OF THE MURDER OF M.M.

Two weeks after the murder of A.S., on June 28, 1962, the body of M.M. was found dead in the apartment where she had lived. It appeared that she had been dead two or three days at the time when the police investigated her demise. The apartment where M.M. had lived was only a short distance away from the apartment building where A.S. had been murdered. When she was found, she was lying on a couch on her back. The contents of her purse were on the floor. She did not appear as though she had been sexually molested or physically harmed in any way. The apartment had not been disturbed to any noticeable degree. It appeared that the victim had died of heart failure.

THE VICTIM

M.M. was a white female, with gray hair. She was eighty-five years of age. The apartment where she had lived and wherein she was found dead was located at 1435 Commonwealth, Boston, Massachusetts.

INVESTIGATION

Both the police and the Medical Examiner were of the opinion that M.M. had died of natural causes. Photographs were taken of her apartment. Later, after DeSalvo had been apprehended, detectives reviewed the photographs of this case which had been taken during the investigation. Subsequent to this, the photographs were shown to Albert DeSalvo, and he admitted he had been in the apartment and had caused the death of the victim when he attacked her.

EVIDENCE

There was no physical evidence, nor any other type of evidence, to link Albert DeSalvo to this crime. It was only through the confession of DeSalvo that the police came to the knowledge that a crime had, in fact, been committed.

METHOD OF OPERATION

DeSalvo said, "I walked up to the second floor of the building, and I knocked on the door of the corner apartment. This old lady opens it. I said, 'I got some work to do in the apartment'. We went in together and sat down. I was in an armchair, she in a rocking chair...She got up from the rocking chair, turned around...she was talking nice—and I don't know what happened. All I know is that my arm went around her neck. I didn't even squeeze her..., and she went straight down. I tried to hold her. I didn't want her to fall on the floor..."

After she slumped to the floor, DeSalvo picked her up and put her on a green couch. He knew she was dead. He assumed the police would think she had died of natural causes.

DeSalvo dumped the contents of the victim's purse out and searched through them, but claimed he did not steal anything He also denied sexually molesting the victim in any way. (4.351-353)

OBSERVATIONS

When DeSalvo spoke with M.M., he used the positive approach on gaining entrance to her apartment. He told her, "I've got some work to do in the apartment." He left her little choice regarding whether she wanted the work done. It appeared, however, that in the area where he was conducting his criminal activities, there were many old apartments, most of which quite probably needed some work done in them. DeSalvo used this knowledge to his advantage .

It was noted that when DeSalvo was making this confession, he talked about how he did not want to let the victim fall to the floor. This was a bit of a paradox. His intent was to murder the old woman, yet after she died of heart failure, probably the result of extreme fear, he didn't want her to fall on the floor. He could have told his interrogator this merely to show that he was really a considerate human being capable of deep feelings towards other people.

The photographs taken during the investigation of this case proved to be invaluable. It was through the examination and review of the photographs that the police began to suspect DeSalvo had caused M.M.'s death, but they would never have been able to prove it in court.

DeSalvo told his attorney that the age of the victim had little to do with whether she was a suitable target for a sexual attack. DeSalvo indicated that the primary criterion was that the target was a woman.(1.152)

It was noted that while DeSalvo, did not tie his customary knot around the victim's neck because he knew she was dead, he still dumped out the contents of the purse and did not return them to it even though he would have known that this might have been a tip off that this was not a natural death.

It was observed that following the murder of M.M., DeSalvo did *not* pull out M.M.'s dresser drawers. This would tend to suggest that his statement about trying to make the murders appear that they had been committed in connection with a burglary or robbery was probably true.

CHAPTER XVIII

BRIEF HISTORY OF THE MURDER OF H.B.

On July 2, 1962, the police in Lynn, Massachusetts, received a report regarding H.B. Friends and neighbors were concerned about her well being since no one had seen, nor heard from her, since the previous Saturday, June 30, 1962. At that time she was observed taking some trash to an incinerator. Shortly after 8:00 a.m., a neighbor heard someone take the two bottles of milk, which had been delivered to her apartment earlier that morning, inside.

H.B. lived on the second floor of an apartment building. The door was equipped with a chain, a bolt, and a Yale lock. There were no indications that there had been any forced entry into the victim's apartment.

The apartment had been searched. Every drawer in the bureau had been pulled open. All the blinds had been closed so no one could see through the windows.

Upon investigation, the body of H.B. was found laying face down on her bed. Her legs were apart. She was nude except for her pajama top, which was over her shoulders. A nylon stocking was tied around her neck with the knot tied at the nape of the neck. Her brassiere had been looped under the stocking and a bow was tied under her chin. She had been sexually assaulted.(4.23) Traces of seminal fluid were found all the way down her thighs, and on one knee.(2.140)

It was the opinion of the investigating officers that she had been strangled in the kitchen and then carried into the bedroom. Further, they believed, if only one perpetrator was involved, he had to have been exceedingly powerful, for H.B. was a large woman. It was known by relatives that H.B. owned two diamond rings. These were missing. Investigators thought they had been removed from her fingers.

THE VICTIM

H.B. was a white female, who weighed about 165 pounds, and was described as being heavy set with large breasts.(4.291) She resided in apartment 9 at 73 Newhall Street in Lynn, Massachusetts. She wore glasses. She was a retired practical nurse, who did handle a private case on occasion. Her friends knew her as a very sturdy, energetic woman. (4.27) She was sixty-five years old at the time she was murdered.

She had been married for a brief period when she was thirty years old, but the marriage had been annulled. Her hobby was telling people their fortunes with cards. She could play the piano well and enjoyed music generally. During evening hours she attended concerts both in Boston and Lynn.

EVIDENCE

The police found seminal fluid on the victim. It is not known whether there was an effort made to blood type this fluid. It was also noted that the perpetrator tied a unique knot around the victim's neck. This knot had an extra half hitch in it.

METHOD OF OPERATION

DeSalvo said that on Saturday morning, June 30, 1962, he had told his wife that he was going out on a job. He had a cup of coffee at a restaurant near his home. He then went to Lynn, Massachusetts. He drove through the back ways, in and out, and around. He said, "That's the idea of the whole thing. I just go here and there. I don't know why." He went to the 73 Newhall Street apartment building. He had been in this building previously. He parked his car and started up the backstairs, but he saw someone, so he reentered through the front door. He went to the second floor and knocked on the door of the apartment. (4.290)

H.B. answered the door. She was dressed in her pajamas. He told her, "I'm going to do some work in the apartment." "This is the first I've heard of it," she replied. "I'm supposed to check all the windows for leaks, and I'm going to do some interior painting," DeSalvo said. "Well, it's about time," she commented. "You've got milk bottles here," DeSalvo said. According to him, he reached down and picked up the milk bottles and was very careful about the manner in which he handled them so he would not leave any fingerprints. He claimed that H.B. took the milk and put the bottles on top of the refrigerator.

DeSalvo stated that he made small talk with the victim first by talking about the picture of a young woman whose picture he observed on the television set. Then he told her,"Your ceilings need only one coat of white paint. I'd like to check the windows in the bedroom too."

They walked into the bedroom together. DeSalvo said, "While she was pointing (toward a window), I grabbed my hand right behind her neck. She was a heavy set, big breasted woman—" The interrogator interrupted him, and asked, "Did you have to bend over to grab her?" DeSalvo told him, "No, we were standing near the bed. She went down right away. She fainted—passed right out."

DeSalvo removed H.B.'s glasses with one hand while holding her by the neck with the other hand. She went down on her knees against the bed. Blood was coming from her nose.

DeSalvo then pulled the window shades. He then said,"...I picked her up, took off her pajamas—the buttons popped—I took everything clean off. She was unconscious. I got on top and had sexual intercourse." The interrogator again interrupted him and told him to think carefully.

173

DeSalvo then said, "I do remember biting her on her bust, possibly other parts of her body too—her stomach maybe—right? I'm trying to see if I have intercourse with her . . . It's possible. Then he strangled H.B. with her bra and then added the nylon stocking. Then he went into the bathroom and wiped the sweat off his face.

He searched the apartment. There was a chest under H.B.'s bed which he was unable to open. He went to the kitchen and obtained a knife. He attempted to pry the chest open, but the knife blade broke off. He then threw the knife down. He left the apartment at 10:20 a.m.(4.293). A friend of the victim had attempted to call her at 10:00 a.m., twenty minutes before DeSalvo departed.

DeSalvo claimed that for the next six hours, "Well, I was just riding around (in the old green Chevrolet previously mentioned)—like in the middle of the world". Then at 4:20 p.m. on that same day, he attacked N.N.

OBSERVATIONS

Note that DeSalvo went to the second floor of the building where H.B. resided. The apparent reason for this was to avoid being observed by the larger number of people going in and out on the first floor. It is, of course, also possible that there were no single women living on the first floor.

Again DeSalvo used the positive approach to gain entry into the victim's apartment. He said, "I'm *going* to do some work in your apartment." "...I'm *supposed* to check all the windows for leaks, and I'm *going* to do some interior painting." He did not give the victim a choice.

His knowledge and use of practical psychology would tend to make him a difficult subject to interrogate because he could see through the various ploys used by an interrogator.

DeSalvo's interrogator demonstrated a lack of training and experience in the art of interrogation. One should not constantly interrupt the suspect during the questioning. And he should not correct the person when he relates inaccurate information. For example, in this case DeSalvo stated he had sexual intercourse with the victim. Yet no seminal fluid was found in H.B.'s vaginal vault.

It was interesting how DeSalvo tried to present himself in the best light whenever possible, and sometimes this was quite ironic. For example, he related to his interrogator that he removed the victim's glasses as she was falling to the floor so they would not break. He murdered the victim, but he was quite careful not to break her glasses in the process.

There was no indication that DeSalvo knew the victim prior to the crime.

DeSalvo was familiar with the area where he was committing the attack. He had previously been in the apartment building where the victim lived. He frequented these apartments as the "Measuring Man" and while he was breaking into them.

DeSalvo was exceptionally brazen, a rather common characteristic among serial murderers. He spent over two hours inside the victim's apartment, including twenty minutes after someone had tried to call the victim. He obviously did not have any excessive fear of being apprehended.

Since there were no latent fingerprints found inside the victim's apartment, it can be assumed that DeSalvo either wore gloves or carefully wiped everything down before making his departure.

There was no indication in the literature whether the bites on H.B.'s body were sufficient for identification purposes or whether an effort was made to carry out such an identification during the investigation of DeSalvo as the perpetrator. In other words, there were no indications that a known sample was obtained. And if there was one, there was no indication that an attempt was made to identify DeSalvo by this means.

Sometimes bite mark evidence can play a very significant role in the identification of the perpetrator. A good example of this will be observed in the Ted Bundy Case in Florida which will be discussed below.

CHAPTER XIX

BRIEF HISTORY OF THE MURDER OF N.N.

Shortly after 5:00 p.m. on June 30, 1962, N.N. returned to her apartment at 1940 Commonwealth Avenue, Boston, Massachusetts. She had been out of town visiting friends and was scheduled to have supper and spend the night with her sister in nearby Wellesley Hills.

N.N. lived on the fourth floor. She opened the windows because it was so hot and put on a light housecoat. She then telephoned her sister and told her she would be there for supper at 6:00 p.m. As they were talking on the telephone, N.N. told her sister, "Excuse me, Marguerite, there's my buzzer. I'll call you right back." The time then was 5:10 p.m. Her sister had also heard the sound of the buzzer over the telephone. N.N. never did call back as she had promised she would do.

When N.N. failed to arrive at her sister's house by 7:30 p.m., her brother-in-law called the apartment superintendent and requested a check be made to determine whether N.N.'s car was still in the parking lot. It was there. The superintendent was asked to check N.N.'s apartment to determine whether she was ill.

The superintendent went to N.N.'s apartment and knocked loudly on the door. When he received no response, he opened the door with his master key. The apartment appeared to have been burglarized. The drawers were pulled out and possessions were strewn about the floor. He observed, however, that a set of sterling silver was untouched. As the superintendent peered through the bedroom door, he saw the nude body of N.N. lying on a hooked rug.

Her feet were toward him. Her legs were spread apart. She lay dead with her eyes open. Her pink housecoat and her slip had been pushed up to her waist. Her vagina was exposed. She had two nylon stockings tied around her neck so tight they had cut her flesh. There was a unique knot, with an extra half hitch, tied under her chin. The ends of the stocking on the floor appeared to have been arranged like a bow. She was wearing a watch on her left wrist and was wearing blue sneakers. She had been criminally assaulted.(4.24-25)

Something had been placed into her vagina. Semen was observed on her thighs and around her vagina, but the pathologist later found no seminal fluid inside her vagina.(2.140)

A thorough check was made of N.N.'s belongings, but nothing was found stolen, despite the fact that there were some very expensive articles in the apartment.

There was no sign of any forced entry into N.N.'s apartment.

EVIDENCE

Seminal fluid found on the victim, and the unique knot tied around the victim's neck were the primary evidence found at the scene of the crime.

VICTIM

N.N. was a white, female, of fragile build, age sixty-eight, with gray hair. She had been a widow for twenty years before her death. She dated no one. She was the retired chief physiotherapist at the Memorial Hospital. She wore glasses. Two mornings every week she contributed to the elderly charity patients at St. Patrick's Manor, and had been treating a seventy-five year old man in Webster. Her hobbies were music and photography. The only man who had ever been observed in the victim's apartment was the painter who worked there three years prior to her death. The cause of death was strangulation.

METHOD OF OPERATION

DeSalvo murdered H.B. in the morning in Lynn, Massachusetts. He then spent the remainder of the day just driving around.

Late in the afternoon, he parked his car in the parking lot next to the apartment building where the victim lived. He entered the victim's apartment building through the front door. He pressed a buzzer for an apartment on the third floor, but received no response. He saw the name, N.N. _____ over an apartment on the fourth floor. He pressed that bell twice. The buzzer sounded, and he went inside. He was going to take the elevator to the fourth floor, but hid out of sight when he saw it was descending with a woman passenger. He then decided he would take the stairway.

On the second floor, he stopped and knocked on the door of the apartment he had rung in the first place. A woman answered the door. There was another woman standing behind her who DeSalvo assumed was her sister. He tried to talk with the woman, but said, "She was batty as all hell...I could see right away I wasn't making any sense to her." He then continued up to N.N.'s apartment.

N.N. called out and asked him, "What do you want?" He told her he had come up to check the windows for leaks. The previous night it had been raining. N.N. asked him, "Who sent you here? Did the superintendent, Mr. Bruce, send you?" DeSalvo told her that he did. She said, "Well, I don't know anything about it." DeSalvo then said, "Look, you can call him up." She replied "Oh all right, but make it fast because I'm leaving. I'm on my way out."

DeSalvo checked out the windows in the apartment until he came to the bedroom. There he stopped and just looked toward the window. N.N. asked him, "What's wrong?" He replied, "I don't want to wrinkle your curtains—will you check that window?" As she took her eyes off DeSalvo, and turned to check the window, DeSalvo grabbed her from behind. He said, "She fell back on me on the bed, on top of me. I was in this position, my feet around the bottom of her legs. I'd almost swear that it was here that she took her fingernails and dug into the back of my hand. It didn't bleed. She pulled the skin and then she stopped. You must have found skin under her fingernails!!!"

The interrogator asked DeSalvo how he knew she got skin under her fingernails and he said, "Because it was off me. She kept doing it until she...went."

DeSalvo indicated that he then slid out from under her, picked her up, and put her on the floor. DeSalvo did not know if she was alive when he did that. He bit her on the breast. He put a belt around her neck, but it broke near the buckle when he pulled it tight. He then put a silk stocking around her neck which he knotted three times. He then took a wine bottle and shoved it up her vagina. He then searched the apartment. He claimed he really did not understand why he did that, but he assumed it was to make it appear like a burglary. When the telephone rang, he left the apartment. He stopped on the stairs when he saw a woman getting into the elevator.

Outside the building, while walking to his car, he passed two elderly women carrying packages. He then got into his car and drove home. He arrived home shortly before 6:00 p.m. (4.294-297)

REMARKS

DeSalvo in describing his feeling just prior to attacking N.N. said, "Well, as her back was turned to me, and I saw the back of her head, and I was all hot, just like your going to blow your head off—like pressure right on you... not her face, seeing nothing, but the back of her head, right? Everything built up inside me!!! Before you know it, I put my arm around her and that was it. And from whatever happened through that time. I can remember doing those things. As for the reason I did them, I, at this time, can give you no answer."(4.296-297)

Dr. DeRiver, while discussing "Sadistic Piquers, Snipers, ect." wrote what could possibly be an explanation for DeSalvo's feelings at the time he attacked N.N. Regarding sadists DeRiver wrote, "These individuals are thrill seekers—dangerous criminal degenerates of whom it is safe to say ninety-nine percent will progress and become lust murderers; in which case a killing is no longer accidental, but premeditated."

"Such individuals have no thought, no mercy, for their victims. Their lust for blood may even assume the nature of vampirism. They maim to appease a perverted appetite and to inflate an insecure, weak ego. Frequently they are peeping Toms (voyeurs) and will "case" the home of their intended victim, waiting for the proper time to strike. Still others in this group may act purely on the impulse of the moment, when the abnormal urge strikes them, if they happen to see a suitable victim. In either case, the ego—or "I" element takes predominance and must be gratified; the consequences, the possibility that they may fatally injure or kill the victim is not even considered."

"Prompted by a frustrated, revolting ego, the perverted sexual impulse presses to express itself in positive action with such force that both the intellect and will become its obedient servants. Such actions, therefore, in many instances might be called impulsory rather than rational, in that the intellect is by-passed and the will merely serves as a rubber stamp without benefit of proper psychic rationalization." (3.48-49)

POLICE ACTION

The police took the following actions when it appeared that they were confronted with a serial murderer.

1. All detectives were immediately assigned to homicide.

2. All known sexual offenders were ordered rounded up.

3. A check was made on every male person between the ages of eighteen and forty who had been released from mental institutions two years previous to the murder of N.N. Special attention was given to those suffering from paranoia with mother hatred.

4. A public appeal was made to women to (a) keep their doors locked, (b) allow no strangers to enter their apartments, (c) report all prowlers or anyone observed behaving in a peculiar manner, especially in those areas where women were living alone.

5. An emergency number was established for people to contact the police twenty-four hours every day with information regarding the murders.

6. The floors of the apartments where the murders had occurred were swept thoroughly for any pieces of trace evidence, such as fibers.

7. Two broaches and a necklace were reported stolen from A.S.'s apartment. Sketches were made of these and sent to all police departments in the State of Massachusetts. In addition, every pawn shop within a fifty mile radius was checked for the missing jewelry. (It was later learned the jewelry had not been stolen.)

8. The Federal Bureau of Investigation was contacted. It was requested that Special Agents of the F.B.I. conduct a seminar to better prepare the local police to deal with this complex subject. Special Agent Walter Mc Laughlin conducted a seminar for about fifty investigators on the various forms of sexual perversion, their relationship to different categories of sex crimes, the personalities of sex criminals, the symptoms of their illness, and the deep compulsions that could drive them, often despite themselves, to commit criminal acts.(4.37)

OBSERVATIONS

The unusual knot that was tied was as though one were tying his shoes, but instead of just intertwining the two ends of the string once, it was intertwined twice before making the loop and tying the knot.

It was observed that although two women on a lower floor of the same apartment building where the victim lived had seen DeSalvo, he was not in the least deterred from murdering N.N. This seems to be an excellent example to which Dr. DeRiver was referring when he wrote, "The perverted sexual impulse presses to express itself in positive action with such force that both the intellect and will become its obedient servants."

Note that DeSalvo remarked to his interrogator, "You must have found skin under her fingernails." This indicates that DeSalvo was aware that in a murder investigation that the police do check under the victim's fingernails. He was knowledgeable of this area of criminal investigation.

Earlier in the day, DeSalvo spent considerable time in H.B.'s apartment, but on this murder, it appears that he spent probably less than an hour at the scene of the crime. It is logical to assume from this that he did not lose track of time while engaged in his criminal acts. By returning home at his usual time for supper, he was helping to keep himself above suspicion.

When the police made sketches of the broaches and the necklace, which were thought to be missing from A.S.'s apartment, and sent this information to all police agencies within the state of Massachusetts, this was time and money that was not well spent. Also time was wasted checking pawn shops within a fifty mile radius. This was so because the jewelry never was actually stolen from A.S.'s apartment and was later found in it.(4.35)

All the police actions undertaken were standard police practices in effect at the time. Though the thought was clearly there and the police were on the right track, the one thing that was not done which may have begun to bring DeSalvo into the investigation was a check on those persons arrested for attempted breaking and entering and assault and battery where women were the victims. This was because on May 4, 1961, DeSalvo was, in fact, convicted on those charges. He was sentenced to serve two years for those offenses. The sentence was later reduced by both the court and the parole board. He actually served only eleven months of the twenty-four month sentence.

At the time of his incarceration, he was diagnosed as having a sociopathic personality. This simply is a person who manifests anti-social behavior. Two months after his release from prison, he murdered A.S.(4.240-241)

CHAPTER XX

BRIEF HISTORY OF THE MURDER OF I.I.

On August 21, 1962, Mrs. I.I.'s sister tried to call her, but was unable to reach her at her apartment. The apartment was on the top floor. I.I. had lived there for over thirty-five years. She had moved there with her husband when the area was quite fashionable. At the time I.I. was murdered, the area was quite run down, and it was frequented by sexual deviates.

After Mrs. I.I.'s sister could not reach her, she made a telephone call to the apartment manager. She requested that he make a check on her sister. The manager sent his son to the top floor to check on I.I. There was no response when the son knocked on the door of I.I.'s apartment. He then opened the door with the pass key his father had given him to use in the event he needed it. When he opened the door, he observed that I.I. had been attacked, and he caused the police to be contacted.

The first officer on the scene reported, "Upon entering the apartment, the officers observed the body of I.I. lying on her back on the living room floor wearing a light brown night dress which was torn (open) completely exposing her body."

"There was a white pillow case knotted tightly around her neck. Her legs were spread apart approximately four to five feet from heel to heel, and her feet were propped up on individual chairs. And a pillow, less the cover, was placed under her buttocks..."

Her ankles were locked into position between the vertical wooden rungs of the backs of two dining room chairs. The body had been placed similar to an obstetrical position. The feet were facing the entrance to the apartment to enable anyone entering the apartment to see the body as soon as the door was opened. It was as though this were done in an attempt to shock anyone who came in by such a gruesome sight.

It appeared that the victim had been dead for about two days, which would have put the day of her death on the preceding Sunday. Her sister said she had last talked with I.I. on that Sunday at about 1:00 p.m.

The apartment had been thoroughly searched, but it did not appear that anything had been stolen. There was money in the victim's purse and her gold watch had been left behind. There were no signs of forced entry into the apartment.

The cause of death appeared to be that of manual strangulation.

VICTIM

The victim, I.I., was a white female, seventy-five years old. She weighed about one hundred and sixty pounds. She was short with a stocky build. She had gray hair with black streaks in it. She was of the Jewish faith and spoke with a Hebrew accent. She resided on the fifth floor, the top floor, in an apartment building located at Seven

Grove Street in Boston, Massachusetts. She had lived there for over thirty-five years. She was a widow. She shopped daily for her small needs. She made weekly visits to the Massachusetts Memorial Hospital where she was being treated for a skin aliment. She rarely left her home during the hours of darkness. About the only exception to this was to attend a concert in the Esplanade in Boston, which was only a short distance from her home.(4.38-39)

CRIMINAL INVESTIGATION

Standard police criminal investigation methods were used.

It was decided to withhold as many details as possible about the crime from the public. This was done in the event the police were questioning a suspect, if he slipped and made a statement about something that only the police and perpetrator would know, they would have their man.

METHOD OF OPERATION

DeSalvo said on Monday, August 20, 1962, that he was driving around aimlessly thinking about the crime he was about to commit.

He parked his car on Grove Street and went into the apartment where I.I. lived. He did not know I.I., and had not singled her out before he killed her. He rang about four different bells before someone buzzed the door so he could go inside. He went upstairs. When he got to the top floor, I.I. was waiting for him on the landing. She was looking down over the railing.

DeSalvo told I.I. that he was going to do some work in her apartment. He said he could see from the look on her face that she did not trust him so he told her, "If you don't want to be bothered by me going in, I won't bother you." I.I. then told him, "But I don't know who you are." He talked further with her, and once again played his mind game. "If you don't want it done, forget it. I'll just tell them you told me you don't want it done," he said. Then he started slowly walking back down the stairs, giving her plenty of time to think it over so she would change her mind. "Never mind, come on." DeSalvo had won again. He entered her apartment.

He said, "We went into the bedroom to check the windows, and when she turned around—I did it. My right arm around her neck—she went down. She passed out fast. I saw purplish dark blood. It came out of her right ear. I saw it more clearly when I put the pillowcase around her neck. I think I had intercourse." But the fact was that DeSalvo was not really sure about having sexual intercourse with I.I.

F. Lee Bailey, DeSalvo's attorney, was puzzled by this attack on a seventy-five year old woman. To him it obviously just didn't make sense because she was not sexually attractive. DeSalvo told him, "(SEXUAL) ATTRACTIVENESS HAD NOTHING TO DO WITH IT. SHE WAS A WOMAN."(1.152) When this certain time comes upon me, it's a very immediate thing. When I get this feeling, and instead of going to work, I make excuses to my boss. I start driving, and I start in my mind building this image up, and that's when I find myself not knowing where I am going."

184

After murdering I.I., he then searched her apartment, but claimed he did not steal anything.

Then he returned to I.I.'s body. He spread her legs apart and put them on two chairs he had pulled away from the table. He could not give any explanation why he had done this.(4.299-300) He only said, "I just did it."

EVIDENCE

There was no significant evidence found at the scene of the crime.

OBSERVATIONS

Again DeSalvo demonstrated his ability to "con" his way into a victim's apartment. The victim was wary and very much aware of the murders of other elderly women which had occurred in the area. DeSalvo again was capable of "reading" his victim. His ability to do this quite likely played a role during his interrogation because he was probably better able to "read" the attorney, who was inexperienced at interrogation, than vice versa. It was observed that DeSalvo was quite adept at making the victim feel guilty because she did not trust him.

Also underlying his technique, was the latent threat which was, "If you don't want the work done on your apartment, don't blame anyone later except yourself for its run down condition."

Again he used the positive approach by not asking the victim if she wanted the work done, but rather by telling her that he was there and, "I'm going to do some work in your apartment." As usual he wasn't offering the victim much choice. This was all very significant. It was clearly part of his method of gaining control over his victim without initially utilizing a weapon such as a knife.

CHAPTER XXI

BRIEF HISTORY OF THE MURDER OF J.S.

On Thursday, August 30, 1962, ten days after the murder of I.I., at 4:30 p.m. the body of J.S. was found murdered in her apartment. J.S. was a registered nurse who worked the 11:00 p.m. to 7:00 a.m. shift at the Longwood Hospital. Due to fear, she had recently moved to the first floor apartment at 435 Columbia Road in Boston, Massachusetts. She was murdered before she could finish unpacking. This was the opposite side of the city from where I.I. had lived. One of the primary reasons she had moved to the new apartment was because a bus stopped right in front of the apartment. She had been walking a considerable distance in darkness before she had decided to move.

Her body was found in the bath tub in the kneeling position. Her face was down under about six inches of water. Her bare buttocks were exposed. She was wearing a cotton housecoat which had been pulled up over her shoulders. Her girdle was pushed up above the waist. Her panties were down around her ankles. She had been strangled with two of her own nylon stockings which had been tied together.

It appeared that she had been murdered in another room and then her body was carried into the bathroom. The apartment had obviously been searched, but nothing was stolen.

The pathologist believed that J.S. had been dead for about ten days before she was found. He based this opinion upon the decomposition of the body. A determination of whether the victim had been sexually assaulted could not be made.(4.43,44)

VICTIM

J.S. was a white female, sixty-seven years of age, with gray bobbed hair, of 435 Columbia Road, Boston, Massachusetts. She was about five feet seven inches tall and weighed about one hundred and fifty pounds. She was of Irish descent and had an Irish accent when she spoke. She had the reputation of being a hard working, efficient, registered nurse. She did not date and was not known to have any male companionship. (4.43,300)

METHOD OF OPERATION

Two days following the murder of I.I., DeSalvo stated he murdered J.S. He bragged that he talked his way "in fast." J.S. was in the process of moving into the apartment. He said, "...I saw all these cartons. Things were not set up. I knew what I was there for...whatever it came to...that was it."

DeSalvo asked J.S., "Have you got straightened out yet? Thought I'd drop in because I've got some other places to do. I'm going upstairs later this afternoon. I want to check a few things out to make sure they're in order..."

DeSalvo said he went through the apartment. When he looked into the living room he commented, "Boy they didn't do a good job there." J.S. replied, "No, they left a mess." Then she looked into a closet.

DeSalvo said, "I was behind her. I put my right arm around her. We both fell back on the floor. She struggled and struggled. She was so big there was nothing to grip hold of. She finally stopped struggling. It took about a minute and a half—I put a scissors grip..."

He was not certain whether he had sexual intercourse with her, and he was completely unable to give any explanation as to why he had placed the victim's body in a bathtub.(4.301)

CHAPTER XXII

BRIEF HISTORY OF THE MURDER OF S.C.

On Wednesday, December 5, 1962, at 12:30 p.m., S.C. left the Carnegie Institute of Medical Technology for her apartment, which was located on the fourth floor at 315 Huntington Avenue, Boston, Massachusetts. This apartment was along a busy, commercial street in the "Back Bay" area, two blocks from where A.S. had been murdered.

S.C. was scheduled to be present at 2:00 p.m. on that same date to have her picture taken, along with other members of her class at the institute. No one knew why she had left the institute early, but she was not present for the photograph sitting.

Shortly before 2:30 p.m., as she was writing a letter, wherein she had indicated the time to her boyfriend, she was apparently interrupted as her sentence was incomplete.

At 5:30 p.m. when one of her two roommates returned to her apartment, the body of S.C. was found dead on the living room rug. She had three of her nylon stockings, which had been tied together, and were then tied so tight around S.C.'s neck they were difficult to see because they were buried into her flesh. There was a knot under her chin. Her white slip and elastic belt were also tied around her neck. A gag had been stuffed into her mouth. She was on her back. Her bathrobe was open exposing her body which was nude except for the black stockings held up by a garter belt and loafer shoes. Her legs were spread far apart exposing her genitals. It appeared her bra had been ripped from her body. Her glasses were broken. The glasses and the bra lay near her body. It appeared there had been a struggle.

Investigators found a sanitary napkin laying behind a chair. It appeared as though this had been removed from victim's body and thrown there.

The apartment had been ransacked. The bureau drawers had been searched. Their contents were left in disorder. The perpetrator had searched through a collection of classical records which were in the corner of the living room.

There was no sign of forced entry into S.C.'s apartment. The double lock on the door had apparently been opened voluntarily by S.C.

The autopsy which was later conducted on the victim revealed the presence of seminal fluid inside the vagina. The cause of death was by strangulation.(4-49-51)

VICTIM

S.C. was a very beautiful black female, twenty years old, who wore glasses. She was about five feet ten inches tall, weighing about one hundred and forty pounds and was described as being, "Well built."(1.152) She also had long black hair and dark brown eyes.

She was very cautious and insisted upon having a double lock put on the door of the apartment. It was thought by her roommates that she would not open the door to a stranger. If she did not recognize someone's voice, she would have asked him what kind of car he drove to verify his identity.

She was very fond of cooking, and she enjoyed doing that for her boyfriend. She had a premonition about being murdered by the Boston Strangler. The very day she was killed she had expressed her fear of him even though there had not been a murder for three months.(4.51)

WEATHER CONDITIONS

The day S.C. was murdered, it was raining. It had snowed the previous day. The snow had turned to slush.(4.49)

CRIMINAL INVESTIGATION

The standard criminal investigation procedures were followed.

Seminal fluid was found both inside the victim's body and on the rug next to her body. It is not known whether an attempt to blood type the fluid was made. (4.51) (2.143)

WITNESS

While interviewing tenants in the apartment building, Mrs. L. told the police that at approximately 2:20 p.m. she answered a knock at the door of her second floor apartment in the same building where S.C. had lived prior to her untimely demise. A man, whom she described as being twenty-five to thirty years of age, with honey colored hair, average height and weight, wearing a dark colored waist length jacket and dark green slacks told her, "My name's Thompson. The super sent me to see about painting your apartment." Mrs. L. replied, "We're not due for painting." As she was saying this, the man walked right by her into the apartment, looked into the living room, and then into the bathroom, giving her the impression that he was fully aware of how the apartment was laid out, before he returned to her. He then said, " We'll have to fix that bathroom ceiling." Then catching her by surprise, "You know, you have a beautiful figure! Have you ever thought of modeling? With your form—" Mrs. L. interrupted him by putting her finger to her lips warning him to be quiet. In a rough tone of voice the man then asked, "What's that for?" "My husband is sleeping in the bedroom," she lied.

The man's demeanor changed rapidly. "Maybe I have the wrong apartment. Perhaps it's the one down the hall," he said. He then left the apartment so quickly he nearly ran into Mrs. L.'s five year old son, who came through the door.(4.51)

DeSalvo said the day he murdered S.C. was his wedding anniversary, and he took the day off from work. He drove around as usual, finally parking his car near 315 Huntington Avenue. He said, "I was wearing green pants and shirt, and I talked to a woman in the building first—not S.C."

He stated that he knocked on her door. When she answered it, he told her his name was Thompson. He said, "She was a colored woman. She wore glasses. This woman had a piano in the room. I was trying to con her by telling her she was very pretty." He indicated that the reason he left her apartment so quickly was because he saw that she had a son, not because she had told him her husband was asleep in the bedroom.

DeSalvo then went to the lobby where he checked the names under the bells for unmarried women. He saw the names of three women, including S.C. under one of the bells. He wrote these names on the back of his hand with a pencil. Then he went to apartment 4C where S.C. was residing via the back stairs. He knocked on her door.

S.C. answered the door. He told her that he was there to do some repair work on the apartment. She did not want to let him in because her roommates were not there. She tried to convince him they would be home shortly. DeSalvo estimated the time to be about 2:35 p.m. when he entered her apartment. He said, "I gave her fast talk. I told her I'd set her up in modeling. I'd give her twenty to thirty dollars an hour." While he was talking, he claims he told her to turn around so he could see how she was built. When she turned around, he grabbed her from behind with his right arm.

He pulled her down from behind, and they landed together on the setee, with her body on top of him. He wrapped his legs around her legs in his customary scissor hold. He claimed she did not struggle at all.

After she was unconscious, he removed her sanitary napkin and threw it behind a chair. He then had sexual intercourse with her.

When she started to regain consciousness, he got two nylons out of the drawer to keep her from screaming. No mention was made of the gag in her mouth. He then succeeded in strangling her even though she fought for her life.

After he murdered S.C. DeSalvo said, "...I'd set there looking to find something, looking through photographs like I was looking for someone...It didn't take no more than five, ten minutes. This is what I feel. It could have been half an hour, but it seemed like five or ten minutes."

As DeSalvo left the apartment, he did not feel any remorse whatsoever. He asked himself, "What am I doing here? I got to get away...I never ran when I left a building. Even when I saw people, I nodded to them very politely. I never met anyone when

I walked out. I was just plain lucky. But he added, "When I came across a person, I never let him get to see me, and I don't get to look at him too fast. I don't duck, but I put my hand up to my face. I never let them see me directly."(4.304)

POLICE ACTION

In response to the murder of S.C. and the increasing public demand that something be done to protect the women in the community, the police took the following action:

Police in soft clothes rode buses and subways which had been used by some of his victims.

Taxi cab records were checked for anyone who was dropped off or picked up in the general vicinity of the several crime scenes.

People having occupations or any professions which might use such a unique knot with the extra half hitch that was tied around the necks of the several victims were sought out.

Officers began an investigation into the personal lives of each of the victims. The objective here was to determine whether there was some person who was commonly known by several victims.

Homicide detectives went from house to house, street by street, in an ever widening circle away from each crime scene. They were using a questionnaire consisting of standard questions. They asked women, "Did you know the deceased? Did you see anyone suspicious in this neighborhood at the time of the crime? Have any of your friends told you anything out of the ordinary? Have you had any unusual incidents while living here?

PSYCHIATRIST'S PROFILE

After studying each of the murders, the psychiatrists gave the police the following profile on the Boston Strangler:

He might be a Dr. Jekyll and Mr. Hyde personality.

He may work at a menial job.

He might appear quiet and well adjusted when actually he is a psychotic sex pervert suffering from the most malignant form of schizophrenia. A disease in which he lives in a world of fantasy which he thinks is real.

If he is not caught, he will kill again because his obsession will give him no peace.

The forces driving him will, sooner or later, cause him to make a mistake, and he will be caught.

He looks like any other person on the street.

He probably has a routine nine to five job and is committing the murders on the way home from work.

Due to his method of operation, it is doubtful that his fellow employees or neighbors suspect him.

OBSERVATIONS

While these murders were being investigated, it came to the attention of officers that a man posing as a medical doctor would call ladies on the telephone and make them believe that they had previously met him at a party. The ladies would invite him to come to their respective apartments. He had sexual intercourse with between forty to fifty women using that strategy. The women then never saw him again. He was apprehended. This clearly demonstrates that during the time period that a serial murderer is active, there will be no shortage of potential victims who take foolish chances with their lives and who willingly open their doors to him.

One of the problems the police encountered during this investigation was that there were several people who thought that this was an excellent opportunity to get even with their enemies, or to play a joke on one of their friends, by sending an anonymous letter to the police identifying a certain person as a suspect. Of course each of these persons had to be investigated. This took valuable time away from the investigation. It also could have the effect of jading an investigator's attitude to the point that when a real, bona fide suspect was being investigated, he would not receive the attention he deserved, and thus it would be possible for the perpetrator to evade detection. This is why a check system must be devised to take a second look at how a tip was cleared.

Again DeSalvo talked of how careful he was to put his hand up to his face so no one could really get a good look at him, but it should be carefully noted that even though DeSalvo was observed by another woman prior to the murder of S.C., he was not deterred in the slightest from committing a murder in that apartment building. This points out two very important facts to any investigator. First, the murderer is very brazen. One would believe that once he was clearly observed in a certain apartment building that he would not follow through and commit a murder. This attitude will also be observed in the perpetrators in other cases and will be pointed out then. Second, and very significant for investigators, is the fact that the perpetrator may have attempted to murder another woman other than the victim in the same building or area where a victim was killed. An all out effort should be made to seek out any other potential victim because she may be able to provide the police with a physical description of the murderer. This should be accomplished by means of a door-to-door canvas and by using the media.

It is not known whether the police attempted to have DeSalvo identified in a properly conducted lineup after his arrest as the, "Green Man". An attempt should have been made to do this by Mrs. L., to help verify that he was the murderer.

During the questioning of DeSalvo, his interrogator asked him if he expected such a healthy, strong girl like S.C. to pass into unconsciousness so quickly. DeSalvo replied, "I didn't expect anything. Whatever happened—happened!"

Regarding the profile given to the police by the psychiatrists stating that the perpetrator would continue to murder and would eventually be caught because he would make a mistake, assumes that when that mistake was made it would be recognized by the police. If the murderer does make a mistake and the police do not apprehend him, the cost of that mistake could easily be the lives of one or more women. This will also be observed in other cases.

With the murder of S.C., it appeared that there was a drastic change in the method of operation of the Boston Strangler. This was because S.C. was so young, only twenty years old, as compared with all the previous victims who had been much older. This caused such a rift between police investigators that some investigators refused to believe murder of S.C. was committed by the same person who murdered the previous victims. They began to refer to "The Second Strangler." But we later learned that despite the differences in age and race, there was only one man responsible for all the murders. What investigators did not understand was that, to DeSalvo, the only thing important was that his victim was a woman. This points out the difficulty that investigators are confronted with when dealing with these types of cases. In many other types of crimes, the detective is capable of putting himself into the shoes of the criminal to help him solve the crime. With this type of criminal, it is nearly impossible to think as he has done because the killer does not live in the real world, but in a world of fantasy which is as real to him as the world in which other "normal" people exist.

It was noted that DeSalvo obtained the names of targets from underneath their respective buzzers in the apartment building in which they lived. He then wrote their names on the back of his hand. Officers who may apprehend a suspect in an apartment building, or even a distance away from it, should check the suspect's hands and notes in his pockets for writings that would indicate he had targeted one or more victims.

In most criminal investigations, police quite typically ask a potential witness whether he had seen anything unusual or out of the ordinary. Since serial killers are masters of blending in with their surroundings and show little emotion, investigators should also ask witnesses about what was observed or heard that could have any possible bearing on the murder.

Women, who are living alone, frequently use their first initial rather than their first name below buzzers and on mail boxes. If a serial murderer is slaughtering women in an area, the writer suggests that single women be asked to use their father's name rather than their own .

CHAPTER XXIII

BRIEF HISTORY OF THE MURDER OF P.B.

On Monday morning, December 31, 1962, about a month after the murder of S.C., the body of P.B. was found in her apartment at 515 Park Drive in Boston. This also was in the "Back Bay" area. She was found in her bedroom. She was lying face up on the bed with the coverlet drawn snugly to her chin. Her eyes were closed. Her head was turned slightly to the right. Her arms were by her side, and her legs were together. There were three nylon stockings around her neck. They were knotted and intertwined with a silk blouse. P.B. was wearing only the top of her imitation leopard-skin pajamas. These had been pushed up to her shoulders, and she was naked from there down. There was evidence of sexual intercourse.(4.56)

There was no indication that a forced entry had been made into the apartment. A partially filled cup containing coffee was found in the living room. There were no latent fingerprints found on the cup. The handle of the cup was toward the left indicating whoever drank from the cup may have been left handed. Again the apartment had been thoroughly searched.

The Medical Examiner was of the opinion, based upon how the body of the victim had been left in the bed, that the victim had been murdered during the heat of passion; then when the passion subsided, the perpetrator was sorry and contrite about having killed her. The Medical Examiner stated he observed this often where an angry husband killed his wife and then was remorseful after he had done it.(4.57)

VICTIM

P.B. was a white female, twenty-three years of age with dark eyes and brown hair. She had been employed as a secretary with Engineering Systems, Inc. P.B. was, in fact, one month pregnant at the time of her death. She was unmarried. The cause of her death was that of strangulation. (4.56)

INVESTIGATION

The standard criminal investigation was conducted with nil results.

Persons in the building were interviewed. The building superintendent told police he had observed the victim at about 3:30 p.m. on Saturday, December 29th. She was washing clothes in the laundry room. An hour later, he observed that the machine that she had been using was empty. It was assumed that she had finished washing her clothing sometime prior to 4:30 p.m.(4.57)

Laboratory Scientists discovered trace evidence of soot on the nylon stockings used to strangle the victim.(4.307) The janitor of the building immediately became a prime suspect in the murder of P.B., but he was later cleared of any suspicion by a polygraph examination.

METHOD OF OPERATION

In his confession, DeSalvo stated he had left his home early Sunday morning, December 30th, for work. He was working for a construction company at that time. His job was to light kerosene burners so newly poured cement would not freeze. He had completed this work in Belmont and then went into Boston.(4.306)

Sometime before 8:00 a.m., he parked his car on Beacon Street in front of a laundromat and walked to the apartment building where P.B. was residing. He entered the building. He noted that the names of three girls were on the door. He said he had been in that particular apartment at least four times previously when other girls lived there. He did not knock, but rather slipped the lock and opened the door quietly. As he entered the apartment, the bells rang from a Christmas decoration P.B. had placed on the door. This awoke P.B., who got out of bed. While holding a blanket in front of her, she confronted DeSalvo by asking, "Who are you? What do you want?"

DeSalvo bragged about this by saying, "I gave her fast talk. I said I was one of the fellows living upstairs." He then asked her where her girl friend was, using the name of one of the girls he had read on the door. P.B. told him they were out of town. She had to stay behind because she had to work Monday morning. DeSalvo indicated that she had believed the story about him living upstairs. She made them both coffee. DeSalvo offered to go out and buy some donuts, but she did not want him to do that. (4.304)

DeSalvo claimed they sat in the kitchen for a few minutes, and then they went into the living room. P.B. put on some Christmas records on the phonograph. As they sat there talking he said, "...I was looking at her and getting worked up. I went over to her. I was on my knees." She told him, "Take it easy!" He then told her, "Nobody is here! Nobody can hear you!" According to DeSalvo, P.B. then became angry. She told him, "If that's the way you're going to talk, you better go right now!!!" He then grabbed her with his arm around her neck, and she fell back on top of him. She passed out a short while later.

He ripped her pajama bottoms off her body. He picked her up and carried her into the bedroom where he raped her. Then he strangled her.

REMARKS

During the interrogation, DeSalvo said, "I don't know if I did this, well, for a sex act, or hatred, or for what reason. I think I did this, not as a sex act, but out of hate for her—not her in particular—but for a woman. After seeing her body, naturally the sex act came in...There was no thrill at all."

When his interrogator asked him why he had covered her up, DeSalvo replied, "She was so different...I did not want to see her like that—naked—and she talked to me like a man. She treated me like a man."

As is frequently the case, the police, while this and other serial murders were being investigated, were confronted with the murder of a teen aged girl whose body was found in an alley. That case was solved two weeks later.

P.B. was actually the seventh victim of the series. The public as a whole was very disturbed and frustrated that the police were unable to stop these murders. They were contacting their politicians, who in turn, were calling for an investigation of the police to determine why the murderer was not apprehended. The Chief of Police then was forced to defend the actions already taken by his men by providing a detailed accounting of the work performed to demonstrate that the police were doing all that was humanly possible within the law to solve the crime.

For example, he told them that over 5,000 Massachusetts sex offenders had been checked out. Every inmate had been screened at the Center for the Treatment of Sexually Dangerous Persons. Thousands of persons had been interviewed. Four hundred suspects had been checked out. This included checking out their alibis. The heel and hand print found in I.I.'s apartment had been checked against 500,000 known prints. And hundreds of tips from all over the world were being received and these were being checked out as rapidly as possible.(4.60)

While the Chief was making this news release, he talked in terms of two or more murderers. He did this because of the apparent different age groups of some of the victims, the different race of at least one of the victims, and the different manner in which the victim's body was left in this case.

OBSERVATIONS

The importance of having current data available on the work completed by the group handling the investigation was clearly demonstrated here when the Chief of Police was forced to give an accounting to the people who were expressing worry and frustration because the murderer had not been caught. Since serial murder cases sometimes go on for a long time, in some instances years, the police must be in a position to tell the citizens what efforts they have made to solve the case.

It was a mistake for the Chief of Police to talk in terms of more than one murderer. While it is understandable for him to draw that conclusion because of the difference in age groups in some of the victims, the difference in race with one of the victims, the fact that some of the victims had been entered sexually while others had not been, and the contrast in which the body of P.B. had been left at the scene and most of the others, there was only one killer involved. This would tend to incite additional fear within the community. Of course the advantage was that it tended to take some of the pressure off the police because they were not just after one perpetrator, but several.

From an investigative point of view, this case demonstrates that a serial murderer may leave a victim's body in a different position because there was some change in the interaction between him and the victim. In this case, DeSalvo said the victim treated him like a man, and he did not want to see her lying there naked. Notice that even though there was a change in the interaction, he still murdered her.

In a broader sense, this case points out that there may be some significant differences in the method of operation and yet the crimes are committed by the same person. One possible reason for this could be that many times those who are involved in these types of crimes are connected with the criminal justice system, either directly or indirectly, and are students of criminal investigative methods. DeSalvo had been trained as an Army Military Policeman and read true detective stories.

The soot found by the laboratory scientists was very significant, for it tended to tie DeSalvo to this crime when there was no evidence other than DeSalvo's confession to do this.

The observation regarding the possibility of the user of the coffee cup found in the living room being left handed was very good, for DeSalvo was left handed.

CHAPTER XXIV

BRIEF HISTORY OF THE ATTEMPTED MURDER OF G.G.

During the early afternoon of February 18, 1963, a white male, described by the victim as being thirty to thirty-five years old, who weighed about one hundred and seventy-five pounds, knocked on the door of the apartment where G.G. resided. G.G. arose from her sick bed and answered the door. She told him, "Go away! I don't feel well. I've got a virus. Come back some other time." DeSalvo told her, "I've got to turn off the water in the bathroom." He said his fellow workers were on the roof, and they would give him the signal.

Reluctantly G.G. admitted the man into her apartment. While they waited for the "signal," the man removed his air force type jacket and draped it over a chair. He then told her, "You're very pretty. You could be a model." G.G. said, "It's hot in here," as she walked over and opened the front window. The man told her, "No, you better not do that ," as he quickly closed the window she had just opened. G.G. then opened a back window. The man then told her, "There's some dirt on the back of your coat." G.G. turned her head around and looked down at the back of the red coat she was wearing over her nightgown.

As she was trying to determine where the dirt was that the man was talking about, he suddenly, and without warning, grabbed her around her neck. But she fought back by kicking, screaming and biting into the man's finger, which she would not release, even though the man promised her he would let her go. Finally, she did let go. This meant she could scream all the louder when she didn't have the man's finger in her mouth. The man released her, grabbed his jacket from the back of the chair where he had hung it, and ran out the door.(4.310)

VICTIM

G.G. was a twenty-nine year old white, female, with dark brown hair and eyes. She was a native of Germany and worked nights as a waitress. She was a well built,very attractive, physically strong, and obviously determined young lady. At the time the attack occurred, she had been sick in bed with the flu and had been taking sleeping pills. Because of the medication she had been taking, she could recall the physical appearance of her attacker only vaguely. This also made it impossible for her to later identify Albert DeSalvo.(4.155,309)

METHOD OF OPERATION

The information which Albert DeSalvo gave to his interrogator corresponded with what the victim had said. DeSalvo, in addition, claimed that as he fled from the apartment building, he hollered to the two workmen, "Quick, he's upstairs! Look at my hand! I couldn't stop him. You've got to stop him! He's coming down!" The men then ran up the stairs. DeSalvo, this time, did not walk calmly away from the scene.

He ran past his car which was parked half way down the block, around the corner and into an alley. He removed the jacket and threw it down. He then walked back to his car in his T-shirt, got in, started the car, and retrieved the jacket.

To establish an alibi, he immediately drove to his attorney's office in Chelsea. The attorney met DeSalvo and wanted to shake hands with him. DeSalvo had to act like he was angry, for his hand was still bleeding, and he had wrapped it in a handkerchief and kept his hand in his pocket.

REMARKS

During DeSalvo's confession, DeSalvo was obviously not pleased with his proficency during the attempted murder of G.G. He brought out the things he could have done, but did not do.

For example, DeSalvo, a former champion boxer, said he could have hit the intended victim with his fists and knocked her out, but he did not. He said he had a knife with him and could have laid her open, but did not.

It was while he was discussing the failed attempt to murder G.G., that DeSalvo told the interrogator that one of the reasons that the police could not catch him was because he himself never knew where he was going until minutes before the attack.

OBSERVATIONS

Notice how DeSalvo, as he was fleeing the scene of the crime, ran past his car rather than immediately getting into it. This was to avoid the risk of someone getting his car's registration number which could be traced back to him. He had remembered the lesson well when he had been caught while in the U.S. Army as a result of a woman recording his license plate number.

DeSalvo obviously changed his appearance by removing the jacket before returning to his car.

When he was nearly caught, he played the old game, "They went that a way," with men who could have captured him.

DeSalvo was again very brazen and bold. While he did run from the scene, he quickly gathered his wits and went to his attorney's office to establish an alibi. And what better alibi witness could one have than an Officer of the Court. We shall see in other cases where serial murderers like to use alibi witnesses.

In this writer's opinion, the reason DeSalvo began his murderous career by killing older, possibly more frail women, was to build confidence in his abilities to carry out his crimes . He knew where older women were living and where he would be more apt to find young women living in apartments, for he had been in many of the victim's apartments several times previously when he was pulling burglaries, and in his role as the "Measuring Man." Note in the following case where he reverts to attacking an older victim. Note also the viciousness of the attack, as though he was taking out his hatred and aggressions on the victim for his failed attack in this case. It was as though he once again had to rebuild his confidence before he could attack younger women.

It is unknown whether any attempt was later made to have the two workers who came to G.G.'s rescue try to identify DeSalvo.

It would appear that in failed attacks, such as the one here, police would have had the best opportunity to obtain physical evidence such as fingerprints. This would be true simply because the criminal fled the scene rapidly without the usual opportunity to wipe away prints and clean up other trace evidence.

CHAPTER XXV

BRIEF HISTORY OF THE MURDER OF M.B.

On Saturday, March 9, 1963, the body of M.B. was found murdered in her apartment in Lawrence, Massachusetts. Lawrence is twenty-seven miles outside of Boston. It appeared that her head had been covered with a sheet, and then she had been struck repeatedly with a blunt instrument. Investigators did not consider this particular murder part of the same series of murders due to differences in the methods of operation.(4.311)

VICTIM

M.B. was a white female, sixty-nine years old, stocky build with gray hair. Prior to her death, she resided in an apartment at 319 Park Avenue, Lawrence, Massachusetts. M.B. suffered from a severe case of asthma. It was so bad that she was forced to sleep sitting in a chair so she could breathe.(4.313)

METHOD OF OPERATION

DeSalvo said when he walked into M.B.'s apartment building, he saw a brass pipe about nine inches long laying behind the door. Again he was wearing gloves. He picked the pipe up and put it in his back pocket. He knocked on M.B.'s door. She answered the door. He told her that, "We got to paint the kitchen." He told her that he had to see it. She let him in and they both went into the kitchen. As they walked from the kitchen with M.B. leading the way, DeSalvo said, "I hit her right on the back of the head with the pipe. She went down. She had on a blue square-print house dress with buttons. She was gray haired—a big woman. Her things were ripped open. Her busts were exposed. I got a sheet from a chair and covered her. I kept hitting her and hitting her... Her head felt...it felt like it was all gone."

DeSalvo had a fork in his back pocket. He thought he'd picked this up from the kitchen table. He stated, "I remember stabbing her in the bust, the right one...and leaving it (the fork) in her ."

He then left the apartment.(4.312)

INVESTIGATION

Again standard investigation procedures were followed, but with no meaningful results.

REMARKS

DeSalvo was able to provide details of the victim's apartment of which only the murderer would have been aware. Since M.B. did sleep in a chair covered by a sheet, his comment on where he had obtained it had particular significance.

It was during the interrogation on this case, that DeSalvo stated that he did not use alcoholic beverages.

OBSERVATIONS

Serial murderers frequently fantasize their criminal acts over and over in their minds before they actually carry them out. When the attack does not proceed as pictured, and the intended victim fights off the murderous intentions of the killer, one can only imagine the frustration and pent-up anger that the murderer feels.

Note in this case that it apparently took DeSalvo a time period of three weeks before he carried out another assault. Note also the viciousness of the attack. Imagine placing a sheet over the victims head so he could pound her head again and again until nothing was left of the skull except mush.

During the three week interval, DeSalvo must have analyzed over and over again what had happen in his failed attack upon G.G., and what he should have done to bring her under his control. When he did renew his criminal activities, it would appear that he once again murdered an elderly, sickly women to regain confidence in himself. And when he did kill her, he overcompensated, as far as force was concerned.

This case should teach us that when a serial murderer fails in an attempt to murder a woman, as was done with G.G., the attack which follows may be extremely vicious and brutal as a result of overcompensation for his previous failure.

It was observed that the left handed DeSalvo stabbed this victim in her right breast with a fork. This malicious act was obviously not meant to kill her. As we will observe in other cases, when DeSalvo did want to murder his victim with a knife, he stabbed her in the left breast (to his right side).

CHAPTER XXVI

BRIEF HISTORY OF THE MURDER OF B.S.

On May 8, 1963, at 7:00 p.m., the victim's boyfriend checked on her after receiving a note which indicated that the victim failed to appear for choir practice in the morning as well as for rehearsal in the afternoon. He went to her apartment in Cambridge, Massachusetts. He opened the door with a key which she had previously given to him.

He observed the victim on the convertible sofa bed in the combination living room / bedroom. She was nude except for a lace blouse draped about her shoulders. She was lying on her back with her legs spread apart. Her right leg was on the sofa, and her left leg was hanging over the edge between the bed and the wall. Her wrists had been tied behind her. A nylon stocking and two handkerchiefs, covered with blood, were tied together and were knotted around her neck. There was blood also on the victim's chest and her neck. There was a cloth over her mouth. There was also another cloth inside her mouth. Her eyes were closed.(4.64-65)

B.S. was a twenty-three year old, white female, with dark brown hair, who resided at Four University Road, Cambridge, Massachusetts. She was attending Boston University as a graduate student. Her master's degree was to be in rehabilitation counseling. She was scheduled to receive her master's degree in June 1963.

The victim suffered from impaired hearing. She, therefore, always sat at the front of her classes so she could hear the professor. She had received extensive voice training for singing. She was a member of the Second Unitarian Church and sang in the church choir. She was also rehearsing for an opera in Brookline, Massachusetts. She intended to go to New York for an audition with the Metropolitan Opera.

B.S. had previously worked as a music therapist at the Walter E. Fernald School for Retarded Children at Waverly, Massachusetts. While she was earning her master's degree, she spent two days every week working as a rehabilitation counselor at the Medfield State Hospital.

INVESTIGATION

Although it appeared that the cause of B.S.'s death was by strangulation, the autopsy indicated that the actual cause of death was by stabbing. She had been stabbed a total of twenty-two times. Eighteen of these stab wounds were in the left breast. The wounds were clearly in the form of a bull's eye target. There were two circular patterns with a final stab wound in the center. There were four stab wounds in the victim's throat. It was estimated that the victim had been dead about two or three days before her body was discovered. A bloody knife with a four and a half inch blade was found in the kitchen sink. The nylon stocking and the handkerchief around the victim's neck were not tied tight enough to have resulted in her death.

Police found the Sunday newspaper dated May 5, 1963, on a chair. Sunday was the last day she had been seen alive. She had spent that day busy with several activities. At 9:00 p.m. she met her girl friend at a restaurant for a late night snack. At eleven o'clock they parted company. Her girl friend was the last person, other than the murderer, to have seen her alive.

The murder appeared to fit the pattern of the other murders. The only thing which did not fit the pattern was the stabbing of the victim. Police thought that it was possible that he could not kill B.S. by strangling her because she had such strong throat muscles which were highly developed by singing. So he stabbed her to death.

In the victim's typewriter was page eighteen of her master's thesis. It was entitled, "Factors Pertaining to the Etiology of Male Homosexuality." It was believed that she may have been interviewing someone in connection with the subject matter of her thesis. There were no other notes found, and the police doubted that she would have been typing the thesis without notes of some kind.

Police departments in the area were advised of the details of the victim's murder via teletype by the investigating officers.

All investigative efforts by the police failed to produce a viable suspect.

METHOD OF OPERATION

DeSalvo said he had been painting a house in Belmont, Massachusetts, when he found a knife while searching through some drawers and had stolen it. This knife had a blade which came straight out of the handle when a button on the handle was pushed.

A few days later DeSalvo went to Cambridge. He said he had been in the apartment where B.S. had lived at least five or six times before as the "Measuring Man."

He rang the bell in the vestibule, walked up, and knocked on her door. B.S. opened the door. He thought she was reading his lips when he talked to her.

He told her, "I got to do some work in the apartment." She asked him, "Can't you come back later?" He told her that he could not. "Oh well, come in and get it over with," she said. After DeSalvo closed the door, he pulled out the knife. Even though she was a hearing impaired person, she probably was able to hear the sound of the knife blade snapping into place. This sound probably had a shocking affect upon her.

DeSalvo ordered, "Don't scream, and I won't hurt you. I want to make love to you..." She interrupted DeSalvo and said, "I won't let you!" Then DeSalvo made her think he would not rape her. "I won't have intercourse with you. I'll just play around with you and go," he said. "Promise me you won't get me pregnant. You will not rape me," she demanded. "No, I'll just make love to you and leave," DeSalvo promised.

She told him it was all right, but she wanted to wash first. She walked into the bathroom with him following close behind. After she washed, they went into the bedroom where she was forced to lie down on the bed. DeSalvo tied her wrists behind her. He put a gag in her mouth and then tied a cloth around her mouth so she was unable to scream, but yet was still capable of talking. He tied a blind fold over her eyes. He also closed the windows so no one could hear her if she screamed. He also pulled the shades. There was low light in the room.

After DeSalvo fondled B.S. he said, "Then I was going to have intercourse with her anyway, and she began talking, 'You promised. You said you weren't going to do it to me -don't!-don't! I'll get pregnant!' The words kept coming and coming. I think because she couldn't hear me saying, 'Keep quiet! Keep quiet!' I can still hear her saying, 'Don't do it! Don't do that to me!' Just like hearing something over and over again. She made me feel so unclean the way she talked to me. Everything I was doing to her, she just didn't like it. And she wouldn't keep quiet. I'd do one thing—she did not like it. I'd do another—she didn't like it. I did have the knife out. I promised I wouldn't hurt her. I had put the knife on the edge of the coffee table. The typewriter was there. She said she wouldn't scream, but she started to get louder and louder and louder. She was stripped naked on the bed and her hands were under her...Her hands were tied underneath her. I put the handkerchief over her eyes so later when you found it you thought it was around her neck. It was to cover her eyes... You know what happened? I stabbed her three, four, maybe five times."

His interrogator asked him, "You strangled her?" " No, she did not get strangled. The stuff you found around her neck, I told you...She was stabbed two times right over the heart, right in the throat and neck," he said. Later he added, "I held her breast. I reached over, got the knife...and I stabbed her in the throat. She kept saying something. I grabbed the knife in my left hand and held the tip of her breast, and I went down two times hard." Earlier he had said, "...Once I did it once...I couldn't stop. I kept hitting her with that damn knife."

He told his interrogators that B.S.'s conduct reminded him of his wife. He said he loved his wife on the one hand, but hated her on the other, because she made him feel lower than an animal when it came to having sex.(4.355-357)

OBSERVATIONS

B.S. was trained to deal with mentally disturbed people in her master's program. She had been working with mental patients two days every week. Yet, she was completely unable to handle DeSalvo. It was obvious that she could not bring DeSalvo under control by simply talking with him.

Note that in DeSalvo's warped mind, he apparently pictured himself a great lover. He erroneously thought he would be capable of exciting the victim. Even though he was using force she would still be receptive to his desire to have sexual intercourse. It has been the author's experience in interrogating numerous rapists, that it is not uncommon for many of them to view themselves in this fashion. Frequently, they feel that women just need a little extra persuasion. Oftentimes, this persuasion takes the form of a gun held to the woman's head or a knife held to her throat.

DeSalvo was obviously enraged when B.S. did not agree with his sexual advances and tried to hold him to his worthless promise not to rape her.

From the standpoint of criminal investigation, this case is significant. An investigator might have been led to believe that this murder was not connected with the others in the series because the victim was stabbed to death rather than having been strangled. A serial killer may use different means to dispatch his victims.

Second, an investigator might draw the conclusion that the murderer was right handed since the stabbing occurred on the left side of her breast. DeSalvo did have the knife in his left hand, but stabbed B.S. so the knife would pierce her heart. Therefore, one should be exceedingly cautious when drawing any conclusion about whether the perpetrator is right or left handed based on the location of the stab wounds. If the stab marks are in the right breast of the victim, and it appears that the murderer was facing the victim, is would be a good assumption that the perpetrator used his left hand, but no assumption should be made if the stabs were into the heart area.

The bull's-eye pattern on the victim tends to indicate she was dead or dying when they were made. At any rate it would appear that the victim was not struggling at the time she was being stabbed, for if she had been thrashing about, it is unlikely that DeSalvo could have made such a pattern. Observe DeSalvo's inclination to close windows, which he also did in the case of the attempted murder of G.G., so no one could hear the screams of his victims. Note also how he pulled the shades. Again from an investigative standpoint, when handling a murder where the victim has been killed inside a house or apartment, if windows are closed and shades drawn, it would behoove laboratory specialists to check those areas closely for latent prints. This would be especially true during the summer months.

It was also noted that DeSalvo again changed his method of operation after the aborted attack on G.G. In the attack just prior to this, he went back to attacking an older woman. In this case, he once again attacked a young woman, but it is remarkable that he did not wrap his arm around her neck and have her fall on top of him, nor did he smash her skull in with a pipe. This time, he tried a knife to bring the victim under control. He did this immediately after gaining entrance to the apartment. He apparently thought it was necessary to con his way inside so no witness would spot him in the hallway with a knife and call the police.

DeSalvo undoubtedly gave considerable thought to changing his method of attack. He probably went over what he was going to do mentally hundreds of times before he attempted to carry it out. What would appear different from his mental picture was that the victim in this case did not respond in a fashion that he had thought she would, and this angered him.

It will be also noted below that when DeSalvo was later apprehended as the "Green Man" that his tactic was essentially the same as it was here except he broke into the apartment and permitted the victim to live following raping her. In that case, the victim was married and her husband was working when the attack occurred.

CHAPTER XXVII

BRIEF HISTORY OF THE MURDER OF E.C.

Throughout the summer of 1963, there was no criminal activity by the Boston Strangler. Then on Sunday morning, September 8, 1963, E.C. ate breakfast with Mrs. M., as was her usual custom, before she attended worship services. During breakfast both women talked of how someone had tampered with the door to their respective apartments. Mrs. M. said that at 9:10 a.m. someone put a key in the door of her apartment and tried to open the door. When the key did not work, the person left.

After breakfast, at 10:35 a.m., E.C. returned to her own apartment to prepare to attend worship services at nearby St. Theresa's Roman Catholic Chapel.

When E.C. did not knock on Mrs. M.'s door enroute to church by 11:15 a.m., as she usually had done, Mrs. M. tried to telephone E.C. to warn her that she was going to be late. There was no answer.

At 1:00 p.m. Mrs. M. and another neighbor checked on E.C. Mrs. M. had a key for the apartment where E.C. was living. They found E.C. dead. She was sprawled across the bed. She was still dressed the same way as when she had eaten breakfast two and a half hours earlier.

E.C. had two of her nylon stockings knotted together around her neck. The knot had the extra half hitch. The front of E.C.'s housecoat had been ripped open with such force that three buttons had popped off, exposing her left breast. Her night gown had been pushed up. Her right leg was extended on the bed. The left leg was placed at almost a forty-five degree angle. It was dangling over the side of the bed. She was nude and grossly exposed.

The murderer had put E.C.'s panties in her mouth as a gag. He had tied another stocking around the victim's left ankle. The knot there was also the double half hitch. This was the knot that was typically used by the "Boston Strangler."

The evidence seemed to indicate that the victim had been assaulted in an unnatural manner. (4.82-84) There were savage bite marks all over E.C.'s body, including the genital region. There was seminal fluid found in the victims's vaginal vault and between her breasts.(2.145)

The apartment door was locked. Her possessions had been searched. The contents of her purse had been dumped on her couch, and the purse was on the floor by the bed.(4.82-84)

VICTIM

E.C. was a white female, about five feet five inches tall, with blond hair and blue eyes. She was very petite. She was born on September 6, 1905. While she was fifty-eight years old at the time of her death, she appeared to be about fifteen years younger than her actual age. Prior to her death, she resided in an apartment building at 224 Lafayette Street in Salem, Massachusetts. The apartment in which she was living was located on the first floor of a five story building.(4.82)

E.C. was divorced and was dating Mrs. M's son, who was working at the time she was murdered.

E.C. was employed on the assembly line at the Sylvania Electric Company.

INVESTIGATION

The usual investigation was conducted with negative results. The only evidence found was a fresh donut which was on the rear fire escape. None of the tenants said they had either thrown or dropped the donut there.

METHOD OF OPERATION

In his confession, DeSalvo stated on the morning of September 8, 1963, before entering the building where E.C. lived, he had gone to another apartment located over a store. He said he talked with an elderly woman there, but fled when he heard someone else talking inside the apartment.

He then went to the apartment building where E.C. resided. He looked at the names under the various bells for a woman living alone. He saw E.C.'s name and rang her bell. He said she unlocked the door to permit him to come inside the building.

He knocked on her door. She asked him who was there and what he wanted. He told her, "The superintendent sent me to check the leak in the bathroom." He told her that, "There's water seeping through your windows, and I want to check behind the curtains." She let him in and apologized for her caution. She told him, "You don't know who can be knocking at your door these days. How do I know you're not the Boston Strangler?" DeSalvo said he replied, "Look, if you want me to leave...I'll leave!!!"

She told him she didn't have much time because she was getting ready to go to church. They went into the bathroom. E.C. complained about the paint peeling, and then said, "I don't see any leak." From behind her, DeSalvo pulled out a knife and put it against her neck and told her, "Don't scream! I won't hurt you." She asked, "Okay...you're not the Strangler are you?" DeSalvo lied, "No, I just want to make love to you." He then took her into the bedroom. She told him, "I can't, have intercourse. I am not well." He then asked her, "Okay, will you blow me?" "Yes, but please don't hurt me," she replied. "Okay," DeSalvo agreed.

DeSalvo told Dr. Brian that he then took a pillow from the bed and told her to kneel on it. During his confession, he indicated that the victim took the pillow from the bed and kneeled on it at the foot of the bed. He sat on the end of the bed while she performed the act. DeSalvo said, "Before coming she reached over and got a white Kleenex tissue and finished it off with her hand. After that, DeSalvo claimed that she got up and he made her lie on the bed. He then tied her hands in front of her.

The interrogator asked DeSalvo how did he manage to keep the victim from screaming while he bound her. DeSalvo replied, "I told her when I left I'd tell someone she was tied up in there."You give me time to go." She promised not to make a sound. No mention was made of the fact that DeSalvo had stuffed the victim's panties into her mouth.

DeSalvo said he then took a pillow and put it over her face. He sat on top of the victim's tied hands and straddled her body on the bed. He then strangled her to death with his bare hands. She attempted to bounce him off, but she lacked sufficient strength to do it. He then took the nylon stocking from the drawer and tied them around her neck. He left the apartment completely undetected.

REMARKS

DeSalvo gave two different versions of some of the details regarding what occurred during the attack on this victim. The first, regarding the pillow has already been mentioned. The second version was related to the time when the victim's hands were tied. DeSalvo told Dr. Brian that he made the victim lie on the bed. She did this, and he tied her hands in front of her. He told Bottomly after she performed the act of fellatio, she had turned her back to him while she replaced the pillow on the bed. DeSalvo said that when she turned her back to him, he grabbed her. He tied her hands in front of her with a pair of her nylons. Then he put a pillow over her head and strangled her.(4.272,317)

The questions regarding whether it was DeSalvo who left the fresh donut on the fire escape and whether he had tried to gain entrance earlier in the morning by using some type of key were not resolved.

DeSalvo did not acknowledge raping E.C. after she had oral sex with him. Since he had an enormous sexual appetite, it is possible that he also raped her. But it is also possible that the seminal fluid found in her vaginal vault came from her boy friend. Since seminal fluid was found in the victim's mouth, it would appear logical to assume that she was murdered a short time after she had oral sex.

OBSERVATIONS

When DeSalvo was engaged in his activities as the "Measuring Man", he would frequently offer to go out and get the donuts while the "prospective model" would make the coffee. Also recall that he had offered P.B. to go out and buy some donuts before he murdered her. DeSalvo liked donuts. This could account for the donut found on the fire escape.

It was observed that there were significant parallels which can be drawn between the murder of E.C. and DeSalvo's attack as the "Green Man" that eventually led to his arrest. In the latter case, he broke into the victim's apartment. In the case of E.C., both E.C. and Mrs. M. stated someone had tried to enter their respective apartments. When the woman was attacked by the "Green Man," he used a knife and held it to her throat. He stripped her panties from her and stuffed them into her mouth. In the instant case, E.C.'s panties were found inside her mouth . Around the left ankle of E.C. was found a nylon stocking which could have been used to tie the victim's legs apart on the bed. The "Green Man" tied the victim "spread eagle" on the bed, and he loosened the victim's bounds on the wrists and legs before he left her apartment. As the "Green Man," DeSalvo repeatedly told the victim not to look at him . With E.C. he claimed he put a pillow over E.C.'s face before he strangled her. Finally, as the "Green Man, " he kissed and bit the victim and then raped her.(4.241) E.C. had what Dr. Brussel described as "savage bite marks all over her body." Apparently there were no photographs taken of the bite marks with a ruler in the photographs, nor was there any attempt to link DeSalvo to this murder using the bite mark evidence. It appeared, from the fact that her night gown had been pushed up, that E.C. had also been raped.

The significant difference between his activities as the "Boston Strangler" and his later activities as the "Green Man" was, of course, that while operating in the latter capacity, he permitted his victims to live, and in fact even apologized to at least one of his victims.

From a criminal investigation standpoint, this case would strongly suggest that while it is true that a serial murderer's actions may become increasingly bolder as he seeks increased excitement and thrills, he may also revert to a serial rapist with a method of operation that closely corresponds to a case, or cases, where he has murdered a victim. This means that investigators working on serial murders should pay close attention to any future rape cases occurring in their area where there are close similarities in the method of operation in the rape case and one or more of the serial killings. Naturally, the method of operation of all known rapists should also be examined for parallels with those on serial murders which occurred prior to the killings, but no former rapist should be eliminated as a suspect simply because his method of operation while committing a rape differed from the murders.

CHAPTER XXVIII

BRIEF HISTORY OF THE MURDER OF J.G.

On Sunday, November 24, 1963, the body of J.G. was found on her bed in her one room apartment at Fifty-four Essex Street in Lawrence, Massachusetts. This town was located about twenty-seven miles from Boston. The victim had been a teacher for the Sixth Grade Class at the Lutheran Church Sunday School. She had failed to appear on that Sunday to teach the class.

Through investigation, it was determined that she had been murdered shortly after 3:30 p.m. on November 23, 1963. At 12:30 p.m. on that Saturday, the landlord had contacted her about collecting the rent. Later, at about 3:25 p.m. on that same day, a man knocked on the door of an apartment directly above the apartment in which J.G. was residing, and asked where she lived. When he asked about her, he mispronounced her first name. The man was told that J.G. lived in the apartment below. At 4:00 p.m. a friend attempted to call her on the telephone, but no one answered the phone.

J.G's body was found lying at a diagonal angle across the bed. She was nude except for a pink blouse bunched up around her shoulders. Her legs were spread wide apart. The left leg was extended directly forward. The right leg was almost at a right angle. It dangled over the edge of the bed. She was wearing a slipper. Her blouse had been ripped apart with such force that four buttons had popped off. There were teeth marks on J.G.'s left breast. She had been strangled. There were two nylon stockings intertwined with the victim's black leotard. The knot had been tied with the extra half hitch, the same as had been used to strangle the other victims. The apartment had been ransacked, but there was no sign of forced entry.(4.85)

VICTIM

J.G. was a white female, twenty-three years old. She wore glasses. She was about five feet six inches tall, was physically well built, but with a plain face. She worked as a designer for a firm creating motifs for upholstery, tablecloths, and trays. This firm was located across the street from the Lawrence General Hospital.

The victim was very conservative in her dress. She considered most print dresses far too gaudy for her to wear.

The victim was very wary. She did not even permit the landlord into her apartment to collect the rent. When she rented the apartment, she wanted to be certain that it was a respectable place to live. She insisted on knowing about all the tenants living in the apartment building before she moved into it.

J.G. was an extremely hard working, thrifty, clean woman. In addition to her regular work, she usually scrubbed the floors in her apartment on her hands and knees until they were spotless.

214

She was very reserved and quiet. Her entire life, up until the time when she was murdered, was entirely devoted to her work as a designer and her work and service to God. She did not even date anyone.(4.85,314,315)

INVESTIGATION

The usual investigative techniques were employed.

Witnesses were interviewed. From these interviews, it was learned that the victim always kept her blinds closed as she had observed a man in another apartment watching her through binoculars. It was also learned that the day before J.G. was killed that someone had been prowling in the hallways of the apartment building.

A witness, who resided in the same apartment building as the victim, described for the detectives the type of clothing and the physical appearance of the man whom had asked for the location of J.G.'s apartment. However, he could not provide a description of the man's face because the man rubbed his nose in such a manner that he prevented his face from being observed. He indicated that a few moments after he had talked with this man, he heard the door below open and close. (4.85-87)

There were no latent prints found. This writer doesn't know whether the bite marks on the victim's breast were of sufficient quality that they could have been used for later identification purposes.

SUSPECT

The witness described the suspect who knocked on his door and wanted to know where the victim lived as being, "About twenty-seven (years old) with shiny pomaded hair, wearing a brown jacket, a dark shirt, and dark green slacks."(4.86)

METHOD OF OPERATION

DeSalvo stated that two months prior to murdering J.G., he was in the area and had observed the figure of a woman in an apartment across the street from where J.G. lived. He went there on November 23rd in search of a victim, but no one was home. He then went across the street to the apartment building where J.G. lived.

He checked the names on the mail boxes. J.G. was the only single woman he found. The remainder were either businesses or married couples. He went upstairs and talked with a man and asked him where she lived. He said he was very careful about not permitting this man to get a good look at his face. He said, "I kept my hand over my face and kept talking and walking away at the same time. I just kept going. I wanted to get away from him period." He was told she lived in the apartment below.

DeSalvo said he knocked on the victim's door. She opened it only slightly. He then told her, "The super sent me to do some work in the apartment." DeSalvo said he could see she was nervous, "...But I kept talking to her. I said there were repairs to be done in the bathroom." J.G. replied that she did not know about it and asked, "Who sent you?" DeSalvo again told her,"The super." She finally let him into the apartment.(4.314)

DeSalvo said he walked directly into the bathroom. She followed him, but would not go into the bathroom with him. DeSalvo said he told her, "See that's bad." She just stood outside. Finally using some of his manipulative street psychology, he told her angrily, "Well—look at it!!! I mean this is your place. If you want it fixed, then I'll fix it for you. If you don't want it fixed, I'll leave right now!!!"

DeSalvo said that she then told him that she was expecting some company and someone was coming to pick her up for dinner. As she was telling him this, she stepped into the bathroom.

DeSalvo then pulled out his knife. The victim tried to escape, but DeSalvo said he grabbed her. He claimed he told her. "Don't scream, and I won't hurt you. Now walk over to the bed!"

At knife point, DeSalvo forced the victim to lie on the bed. But when he was going to tie her up, she resisted him. He put the knife away. He said she got up from the bed. He heard someone walk by in the hall. He told her to be quiet, and she did not say anything as the person in the hallway walked past.

He was apparently behind the victim as he then said, "I put my right hand right around her neck and pulled her backwards on the bed. She was on top of me...and she passed out. I got from underneath her. I took off her clothes. I ripped off her blouse. Her busts were large, thirty-eight, very smooth, hefty, well built, beautiful body, but she had no face. Five feet six and a half...I'm sure I stripped her naked. That's how I see her in my mind...her head...the bed not made up...the legs over the edge of the bed towards the door. I played with her busts. I know I possibly may have bitten her...not to draw blood...possibly on her body. I just had intercourse with her, and that was it. It was very fast... all over within a matter of ten minutes, maybe fifteen, from the time I went in. It only took two minutes to talk with her...right? It only took a minute to a minute and a half to get her to the bed...right?"

DeSalvo stated that he acted very quickly because she was expecting someone to pick her up to take her to dinner. He said as he was leaving the victim's apartment, there was someone else leaving another apartment too. He closed the door, waited until that person had gone, and then left the building himself.

DeSalvo said that he then drove to his home in Malden, Massachusetts where he washed up, played with his children, ate supper, and watched television. He said while he was watching television, there was a broadcast about the victim being murdered.(4.315)

OBSERVATIONS

A criminal investigator might think that the perpetrator of a rape and murder would not ask someone where a potential victim lived in the same apartment building and then immediately go to her apartment and carry out the crime. As was observed here, that is exactly what DeSalvo did .

From this case, once again we can observe the extreme boldness, almost recklessness, of this type of thrill seeking killer. But note that while he was very brazen, DeSalvo was thinking of avoiding detection by keeping his hand in front of his face and backing away while talking to the man who lived directly above the victim. This was done deliberately to obscure his facial features. It was observed that although there was great risk involved in doing this that perhaps this increased risk may have added to the excitement of carrying out the murder, as well as when the victim told him someone was coming to take her out to dinner. DeSalvo then acted quickly and was in and out of the apartment in about fifteen minutes.

Many times while investigating a serial murder case, the criminal investigator will be told that the victim was extremely wary and would not have opened her door to a stranger. We will hear similar stories about the victim not getting voluntarily into a car with a stranger, but as we have observed in this case, a good con man is frequently more enterprising and has greater ability than he is given credit. Of course, as we shall observe in other cases, sometimes the perpetrator(s) will use the ruse that he is a police detective. But the basic lesson for us here is that a victim can be manipulated into permitting a complete stranger to enter her residence even when she is very cautious.

DeSalvo began his attack in this case by first pulling a knife. But when the victim would not permit herself to be tied up, probably even at the risk of having her throat cut, DeSalvo said he put the knife away. He then reverted to his earlier method of knocking out the victim by using strangulation to cut off the blood supply to the brain. Then he ripped the victim's clothing off while she lie unconscious. He bit the victim on her breast and other parts of her body. He then raped her and strangled her with nylon stockings he found in the victim's drawers.

DeSalvo probably thought it was necessary to "con" his way into the victim's apartment for at least two reasons. First, he did not want to create any disturbance in the hall where there would be the risk of someone seeing him who might call the police. Second, he wanted to get inside the victim's apartment and get the door closed. This would make it less likely that her screams or pleas for help would be heard. His actions in other cases, where he closed windows and told victims, "Don't scream and I won't hurt you," and his action of putting the victim's panties in her mouth, all tend to show he was afraid that his victim would scream or yell.

The very short period of time necessary to carry out the crime in this case tells us the potential problems that might confront the criminal investigator if a suspect comes up with an alibi, which many of these types of criminals have a propensity to do. The less amount of time required to commit a crime, the easier it would be for the criminal to establish an alibi for that time period, and the more difficult it would be to refute that alibi.

Here again in this case we observed that the victim worked across the street from a hospital. It was remarkable that a high percentage of the victims were connected directly with the health science field or worked near hospitals, such as the instant case.

In future cases like these, which are occurring in apartment buildings, women living alone should be warned by the police that they should not admit a stranger into their apartment. If someone comes to their apartment and says he must have entrance to do work inside, emergency or otherwise, he should not be admitted unless there is verification from the building superintendent. Women should also be aware that a man may knock on her door and feign injury to get her to unlock the door. This is the same trick that has been used successfully by perpetrators of armed robberies of armoured trucks to get drivers to violate company policy. The driver has unlocked the door of the truck only to find the supposedly injured person sticking a gun in his face. Such a trick may work even better with women because it may appeal to their caring and maternal instincts.

Police should also warn women to refrain from listing their names on mail boxes, below bells in apartments, in telephone books, in city directories and anyplace else in such a manner that it would tip off either a serial rapist or serial murderer that there is a single woman residing in the apartment. It was observed in the study of this case that DeSalvo never attacked a woman where either another man or second woman was present. Single women shouldn't publish their addresses with their telephone numbers.

It was observed that there appeared to be a discrepancy in DeSalvo's statement. He stated, in substance, after he had murdered the victim he went home and later that night saw it on television about the killing of J.G. This would have been November 23, 1963. According to the literature, her body was not found in her apartment until November 24th. Therefore, it would appear that DeSalvo could not have possibly watched anything on television on the night of the 23rd related to the murder of this victim. (4.87,315)

218

CHAPTER XXIX

BRIEF HISTORY OF THE MURDER OF M.S.

At 6:10 p.m. on Saturday, January 4, 1964, M.S.'s two roommates returned to their third-floor apartment at 44A Charles Street in Boston, Massachusetts.

They unlocked the door and found M.S.'s body in bed in a propped up position. Under her buttocks was a pillow. Her back rested against a head board. Her head was tilted to the side and rested on her right shoulder. Her eyes were closed. There was what appeared to be seminal fluid dripping from her mouth onto her right breast. Both her breasts and lower extremities were exposed. Her knees were bent and raised, her legs were spread apart, and a broomstick handle had been inserted into the vaginal vault. There was a steak knife laying on the bed. There was also what appeared to be seminal stains on the blanket.

Around M.S.'s neck was a charcoal colored stocking tied with a tight knot which had the extra half hitch, the knot which became known as,"The Strangler's Knot". Covering the stocking was a scarf tied in a large bow. Over that, loosely tied, was a pink and white flowered scarf. Next to the victim's left toes was placed a "Happy New Years" card.

THE VICTIM

M.S. was a white female, nineteen years of age. She resided at 44A Charles Street in Boston, Massachusetts. She was described as a friendly young woman who loved music. She had previously worked at the Cape Cod Hospital as a Nurse's Aide. She had just begun working at a bank. She had moved to Boston from Hyannis, Massachusetts, to attend college about a month before she was murdered. She was a Roman Catholic girl of Irish descent.(4.87) The victim seemed to have an inner conflict. On the one hand, she wanted to be a free spirit with unrestricted freedom and little responsibilty, but on the other hand, she wished to marry and raise a family.(4.202)

THE INVESTIGATION

The standard criminal investigation was conducted. Pictures and measurements were made of the murder scene. Detectives interviewed the victim's roommates, friends, and neighbors. The crime scene was processed for latent fingerprints, fibers, and other forms of trace evidence.

Boston was an Irish-Catholic city. M.S. was an Irish-Catholic girl. The public demanded that the police apprehend the murderer, and the pressure upon the law enforcement community increased. This political pressure resulted in the Attorney General of the State of Massachusetts stepping in to coordinate the various investigations which were being handled by several police departments, and to make available resources not previously accessible to investigators. Listed below were the steps taken by the Massachusetts Attorney General in response to the public outcry for results, not excuses.(4.92-93)

A Special Divison of Crime Research and Detection was established in the capitol. Its function was, not to take over the investigations, but rather to coordinate all investigations. This was to compensate for the problems of six separate police departments and three different district attorneys involved in the investigations.

The Attorney General wanted skilled men assigned full time to work toward solving these series of murders. This was in response to the problem of having skilled investigators diverted from the investigation to handle other cases. For example, at 1:00 a.m., a few hours after the body of M.S. was discovered, and the investigation of her death was in high gear, one of Boston's very best detectives was pulled from investigating her murder so he could be assigned to another murder which had just occurred.

The Attorney General appointed an Assistant Attorney General who had the reputation as a top notch administrator to head the coordination effort. He had no experience as a criminal investigator nor as an interrogator.(4.94)

The Assistant Attorney General appointed a veteran Massachusetts State Police Detective to assist him. It is presumed that this was done to make up for his total lack of knowledge of criminal investigation.(B.S.95)

All information possessed by each police department on the respective murders was requested by the Attorney General's Office. This included information on every strangling, every victim, every suspect, and every piece of information on each case.(4.94-95)

This information was then organized and then analyzed by officers and other specialists.

A special hot line was established where the public could call in information directly to officers working on the various murder cases.(4.95)

A special post office box was established for people to send in anonymous tips to the police.(4.95)

As additional material was received, five copies were made of each report. One was for the master file. The second was for investigators working on the cases. The third was for the Boston Police Department's Homicide Bureau. The fourth was maintained in the Massachusetts Identification Bureau. And the fifth copy was used by the Medical-Psychiatric Committee.(4.95)

A Medical-Psychiatric Committee was established. This was comprised of experts from several different professional fields. There was a psychiatrist with a background in sex crimes, an internist, the medical examiners who did the autopsies on the various cases, and a physician with experience in clinical anthropology who formed the initial group. Later other experts were added to the group including additional psychiatrists, a chemist, and a graphologist. The primary function of the Medical-Psychiatric Committee was to evaluate information in the various casebooks, (i.e. the eleven books formed after all the data on all the cases were received), analyze evidence as it developed, and attempt to produce a psychiatric profile, a character, and a personality sketch of the killer or killers.(4.96)

A computer firm in Concord, Massachusetts, which was involved in the nation's space program, volunteered its services and brought into use a digital computer. The firm worked in conjunction with the Massachusetts State Bureau of Identification. They first focused on the victims. Every important date in each victim's life, every name in their address books, every place where they had worked, every restaurant where they had eaten, every concert which they had attended, every hospital where they had either worked or had been a patient, or had visited, every school they had attended, the names of their classmates, the churches where they had been confirmed, the names of their teachers, the names of every clerk who had waited on them in various shops and department stores, their doctors, dentists, and other professionals, including accountants, who had made out their income tax returns, were fed into the computer.

Later, other categories were also added because it was believed that these would be significant. These included the victim's race, religion, occupation, hobbies, clothing worn at the time of attack, the date and approximate time of death, the day of the week, the position in which the body was left when found, the type of room where the victim was found, where the victim was found in the room, whether the window blinds were up or down, and every physical variable. (4.98-99) Known homosexuals whom the victims knew were also put into the data bank.(4.175) Nine months after the death of M.S., there were 35,000 items which had been processed through the computer.

Similar material regarding every suspect was also put into the data bank. This included the suspect's environment, his relationship with his mother, with women in general, his sex habits, and any abnormal facet of his behavior. The idea behind all of this information was, of course, the hope by investigators that at some point, some juncture, the life of the suspect would cross one or more of the victims. Naturally, the more victims with whom a particular suspect was acquainted,the better suspect he became. It would, therefore, provide investigators with some direction, or as some veteran detectives say, "Something to hang their hat on." (4.99)

A Boston industrialist and some of his friends offered to have a mystic brought in who allegedly solved twenty-seven other murders in seventeen different countries. It was argued that since orthodox police methods had failed for one and a half years, what would be lost by trying something unorthodox? The police agreed to at least give the mystic a try. The police worked with the mystic who said the murderer washed his hands in the toilet, slept on the floor, never took a bath, dressed like a priest, and was a pervert—a homosexual. The mystic also indicated the murderer had an unusual nose.(4.108) After departing from Boston, the mystic was arrested for impersonating a Special Agent of the Federal Bureau of Investigation.(4.131)

Arrangements were also made with the Chief Psychiatrist at the local hospital who was making forensic evaluations to give special attention to any individual who was singled out by the Assistant Attorney General who was heading the special unit. This had to be handled in such a way that the constitutional rights of the patient were protected. If a patient were singled out, no detailed notes were made during subsequent interviews. Suspicious material was forwarded to the Assistant Attorney General. The Chief Psychiatrist was brought up to date concerning the series of murders.

UNITING THE INVESTIGATORS

One of the first actions taken by the Massachusetts State Police Detective Lieutenant was to act as liaison between the various departments working on the several murders. He invited all detectives who had been involved in the investigations, all crime scene technicians, all fingerprint experts, stenographers, artists, and chemists to a meeting where each and every case was reviewed so everybody would know with what they were dealing, to determine whether there was something that had been overlooked during the course of the investigation, and essentially to determine whether there was something that should have been done, but was not.

Next the Massachusetts State Police Detective Lieutenant established a closer relationship with a private detective agency that had been quietly helping in the investigation by employing means that could not be employed by a governmental agency. The agency had extremely sophisticated eavesdropping equipment, special photographic equipment to photograph in the dark, the ability to intercept mail, rent apartments next to suspects, pose as medical doctors, make use of the criminal elements of society and other related activities.

Third, the Detective Lieutenant's Unit considered the emphasis which was placed upon the homosexual community by psychiatrists. This occurred due to the links with homosexuals by both young and old victims. Because of this, as was previously mentioned, the names of homosexuals were fed into the computer.(4.174-175) It was also a generally held misconception by those in law enforcement, during that time, that homosexuals hated women, and were, therefore, considered very good suspects where women had been tortured and murdered.

EVIDENCE

Three Salem cigarette butts were found at the scene in an ash tray. The girls smoked Marlboros.

A small, metal, alloy washer was also found at the scene. It was examined both chemically and microscopically and was found to have been manufactured in Japan by the millions.

Also found at the scene was a piece of charred paper about the size of a thumb nail. This paper was later identified by the crime laboratory as having come from the 1963 Boston Telephone Directory. It was page 307 on one side and 308 on the other side. It also contained the names Treg to Tucker and Tucker to Tuiler respectively. Considerable work went into trying to develop a suspect from the names listed, but without any success.

WITNESS

A lady school teacher observed a man at about 2:50 p.m. through the window of M.S.'s apartment on the day M.S. was killed. She said the man stood motionless. He appeared to be tall and was looking straight ahead. The sunlight was shining on him. His hair appeared reddish-brown.

REMARKS

This witness was later unable to identify DeSalvo as the man she had observed in the victim's apartment.

PROFILE

The profile that the committee developed was not unanimous. The majority of the committee members believed the older women were murdered by one man. But they believed the younger women were murdered by one or more men who, they believed, would be found in the circle of their acquaintances, most probably unstable members of the homosexual community. (4.166)

The committee chairman and his colleagues had this to say of the character of the strangler:

> Generally the sex murderer contains within himself an excapsulated core of rage directed at an important figure in his early life—usually a dominant, overwhelming female. To cope with his rage, he engages in powerful, sadistic fantasies in which he kills this figure. The sex murderer differs from other psychotic killers in his ability to keep his terrible day dreams to himself. He keeps quiet about them; he exhibits no odd behavior. Thus he is able to move among friends and fellow workers without calling attention to himself. Chances were that he might appear bland, pleasant, gentle, ingratiating—even compassionate. Because of the training given

223

him by the hated female figure, he would most likely be neat, punctual, polite, in brief, the personality most often seen in confidence men, homosexuals, and in many normal lower class men. No one would think of him as crazy. (4.167)

The committee thought that certain stresses brought about a sadistic impulse too great for him to cope with, and such impulsiveness could trigger him to murder. The loss of his mother, being forced to leave the house, being fired from his job, OR *ANYTHING THAT COULD CONTRIBUTE TO HIS LOSS OF SELF ESTEEM, OR ANYTHING THAT MADE HIM FEEL A LOSS OF MASCULINITY COULD TRIGGER THE IMPULSE.*

The murderer would be in a deepening depression. The only way out would be by venting his rage in an act of murder in a special ritualistic, fetishist manner characteristic of his particular illness. It would be both sadistic and loving. It was believed he would continue to murder until he was caught.

His mother, the committee believed, would be a sweet, orderly, compulsive, seductive, punitive, overwhelming woman. She may go about half exposed in their apartment, but punish her son severely for any sexual curiosity.

The murderer's father, they thought, either was dead or had deserted the family before the boy reached puberty. At any rate, the murderer was not close to his father.

The boy grew up to feel that women were a fearful mystery...The murderer might have attempted sexual relations with a woman, but was successful only if he could imagine himself beating and torturing her. All of these acts were done to re-establish a seductive fantasy aimed against a mother he had feared.(4.168)

The committee also believed that the murderer was at least thirty, perhaps older, that he was neat and orderly in that he left no prints, and that he was probably single, separated, or divorced.

Further, the committee was of the opinion that the reason the murderer left the victims in such shocking positions was an attempt to degrade them and to make it appear that they tried to entice him. This was a tribute to his masculinity that he wished to possess.

The committee thought that since all of the murders, except two, occurred during the weekends, and mostly during the summer months, the killer might be a college student or a teacher.

The committee also noted that although the Italians were one of the largest ethnic groups in the Boston area, not one single girl of Italian descent had been killed.

Dr. James Brussel, in his minority report, thought the Boston Strangler was either Southern European (Italian) or of Spanish stock since murdering by garroting was associated with such backgrounds. BRUSSEL DISAGREED WITH THE MAJORITY. HE WAS OF THE OPINION THAT THE MURDERER HAD CURED HIMSELF

WITH THE MURDER ON THIS CASE (M.S.), AND HE WOULD NOT KILL AGAIN. FURTHER, IN HIS OPINION, THERE WAS ONLY ONE MURDERER.

METHOD OF OPERATION

DeSalvo said he knew the apartment where M.S. lived, as he knew all the apartments on Charles Street. He claimed that he had been in and out of all of them during the seven years before his arrest. Most of the time this was done as the "Measuring Man."

According to DeSalvo, as indicated in his confession, during the midafternoon of Saturday, January 4, 1964, he knocked on the door of the apartment where M.S. lived. M.S. opened the door with a small knife in her hand. DeSalvo told her, "I came up to do some work in the apartment." She said, "I don't know anything about it. My roommates are out." She gave her permission for him to enter the apartment so he could show her what had to be done.

DeSalvo said they went together into the kitchen "...That's where I put the knife to her," he said. "Don't scream and I won't hurt you." With the knife at her throat, he forced her into the bedroom and made her lie on the bed. He then tied both her wrists and her feet. He claimed he then put a gag into her mouth and put a sweater over her head. M.S. told him, "It's hot under this...I can't breathe too well—"

As so frequently occurred, the Assistant Attorney General who was totally inexperienced in the art of interrogation, interrupted DeSalvo and asked him how she could talk if she had a gag in her mouth.

DeSalvo then changed his story and said she did not have a gag in her mouth. He said he had intercourse with her after he had tied her up and ripped off her clothes. He then got on top of her (straddling her) and sat on her hands so she could not scratch him, and then he strangled her with his bare hands. He kept the sweater over her face while he did this so he could not see her until she was dead. He then cut her hands free and flushed the ascot, which he referred to as a scarf, down the toilet.

He then returned to the bedroom, picked M.S.'s body up and carried her to the other bed and placed her on her back. He removed the sweater from her head. He then sat on M.S. and masturbated until seminal fluid was ejaculated into her face. Then he tied the nylon stocking around her neck and added the blouse. DeSalvo could not recall how long he was in the apartment.(4.318-321)

DeSalvo stated he wore gloves after he murdered the victim and ejaculated on her. He said as he was leaving he saw a broom, which he picked up and placed the broom handle into the vaginal vault of the victim. DeSalvo then left the apartment totally undetected.

OBSERVATIONS

The steps taken by the Attorney General of the State of Massachusetts have become, for the most part, the same steps taken by task forces confronted with serial murders today. They are, therefore, very important.

It was regrettable that DeSalvo's name, along with information on him, was not put into the computer's data bank. While sex offenders, homosexuals, and paroled mental patients were entered, information on DeSalvo was not entered because he was previously convicted on charges of attempted breaking and entering and assault and battery. Both of those charges came about from his activities as the so called, "Measuring Man." The assault and battery conviction was the result of the unlawful touching of young women while taking their measurements for a nonexistent modeling job with a phony agency. The attempted breaking and entering charge came about as he was trying to break into a nurse's apartment, who was working, and who he had previously measured. He had also been charged with lewdness, but he was found not guilty on that count.

While he was incarcerated on the above charges, DeSalvo was given another psychiatric examination. He was diagnosed as having a sociopathic personality.(4.240) This is defined by Webster's Dictionary as, "...characterized by asocial or antisocial behavior or a psychopathic personality."

The lesson for us in future investigations where we are using the computer to help us is to remember the old saying of computer people, "GI-GO," meaning garbage in garbage out. The computer cannot help us if we fail to provide the necessary information for the data base. What we need in these types of cases is information on each and every perpetrator who has been arrested, not necessarily convicted of, a sexual motivated crime. Several states by law require police officers to submit Sex Motivated Crime Reports. This report is valuable because in some instances when one is reviewing a police arrest report, it may not appear, at first blush, that the arrest was for a criminal act that was really sexually motivated.

Since Albert DeSalvo did not smoke, the three Salem cigarettes found in the ashtray remains a mystery. It is unknown whether these cigarette butts were sent to the crime laboratory with a request that an attempt be made to determine blood type from the saliva left on the cigarettes.

Despite the Attorney General's statement that this was not a take over of their respective investigations, in a larger sense this was not true. Subsequent to Albert DeSalvo confessing that he was the Boston Strangler, while being held on criminal activities as the, "Green Man", he was interrogated by the Assistant Attorney General in charge while two veteran police officers sat outside the room for hours.

It is a mistake to think that because one has practiced law in a court room or read a book on criminal investigation or on interrogation, that *ipso facto* one becomes a criminal investigator or criminal interrogator. While it is true that there are scientific concepts that one must know to be effective in those fields, it is also true that there is much art involved. In this case, although through no fault of the police, the Assistant Attorney General was poorly equipped by education and training to interrogate DeSalvo. It is clear from the literature where time and time again he interrupted DeSalvo when he was giving questionable or erroneous information rather that waiting until DeSalvo had given the full statement and then questioning him about these inconsistencies. His practice was, and would be, uniformly condemned by anyone who knows anything about interrogation.

It was observed that while various information from the scene of each of the murders was fed into the computers, it was not put into the computer whether the windows were opened or closed. This was probably because most of the murders did not occur during the summer months, but we have seen from the aborted attack on G.G. and others that DeSalvo did make a conscious effort to make certain the windows were closed so no one could hear the screams of his victims.

Notice in the instant case that the fact that the victim answered the door with a small knife, probably a paring knife, did not deter DeSalvo from his carrying out his attack in the slightest degree.

The profile given to the police to look for a man who appeared normal, was clean, polite, was pleasant, perhaps even appearing gentle and ingratiating, and may even appear to be compassionate, was single, over thirty really was very little help to investigators because there were hundreds upon hundreds of men who lived in the Boston area who would fit into that category. The significant thing here for investigators to keep in mind when interviewing someone who may be a serial murderer is that the chances are good that he will appear normal in every way. Further, however, where some type of a "con" story was used to get the victim into a position where he can exert physical control over her, the chances are excellent that the perpetrator will *not* be some person who is blatantly weird, ugly, and possesses the opposite characteristics from those in the profile.

Where it appears that the assailant used force to immediately take control over the victim this may indicate several things. For example, in those cases where the victim was a hitchhiker, or where she answered the door and was immediately confronted by a man with a knife or a gun, or where her house or apartment was entered and the perpetrator then attacked her at an opportune time, the attacker then will generally not be handsome, and his intelligence level be difficult to predict.

The profile regarding the perpetrator's mother did not seem to fit DeSalvo's mother at all. She did not appear to be a seductive, overwhelming woman who went about her domicile improperly attired. Nor did she appear to be a woman who was bent on mentally castrating her son or one who he feared, but as will be observed in other cases, there are other serial murderers whose mothers fit that very picture.

The profile on the father of the perpetrator was on target. They had indicated that the father had either died or deserted the family before the boy reached puberty. DeSalvo's mother divorced his father due to the frequent abuses she suffered by his hand. In addition, prior to their divorce, he had left the family in dire straits while he served time in prison. This absence of the father, due to whatever reason, may be much more significant than most experts think. For reasons not entirely known this seems to play a prevalent role in the lives of those who later become serial murderers. It may be that when some young boys are raised without the presence of a male role model who they can respect, where the mother is a dominate, overwhelming woman, she may unknowingly influence her son to resent the fact that he is a male. Like the "Stockholm Syndrome," since he can do nothing about the situation in which he finds himself, he comes to identify with her. If he is beaten down, demoralized, and mentally castrated, he comes to believe the best course of action is to join her, if he cannot beat her.

Of course in the above case, if the boy has a very strong fiber, he may rebel strongly against her, come to hate her, and become a very violent person who enjoys getting into fights in bars and brawling whenever possible. His fighting activities help reinforce his self concept of his own masculinity.

There may be, however, those who may follow the advice that Macbeth received from his wife before he murdered Duncan, and act like a flower on the surface, but a serpent underneath. They pretend to graciously submit to the wishes of the overwhelming female whom they fear, but this creates a rage in them so great that at some point it sets in motion a release mechanism so terrible that the only means to get some relief is to kill a victim symbolic of the female that he fears on the one hand and loves on the other. But upon completion of their dastardly act, they discover a short time later that the feeling has returned, and they must kill again to get further relief. It may have been in this case that the overwhelming female may have been, not DeSalvo's mother, but rather his wife.

DeSalvo indicated sometimes he had to work fast, sometimes within fifteen minutes, because his wife was watching him. He always wanted to be home when she expected him. He tended to blame his problems on her. He said, "If she would have given me the proper sex I wanted, at least treated me like a person and not degraded me all these times, I wouldn't be going out to find out if I was a man or not...I couldn't understand why she, who (sic) I loved, treated me like dirt."(4.326)

DeSalvo talked about this as the reason he had stabbed B.S. repeatedly. He said:

> It was Irmgard (his wife). I grabbed her right by the throat. She made me feel so low, as if I was asking for something I shouldn't have, that I wanted something dirty. *I wanted to kill her that night!* Asking her to make love was asking a dead log to move. It was always do it quick, do it fast, get it over with. She treated me lower than an animal...I loved her so much, yet I hated her. I was burning up. How many nights I would lie next to her, so hot, so wanting to be loved and to love her—and she would not...She (B.S.) reminded me of her..." (4.357)

Since it is quite natural for most serial killers to always blame someone else for their problems, one should take the above statements of DeSalvo with "a grain of salt." Nevertheless, this natural inclination of the serial killer is not without some value to the law enforcement community. This tendency should be turned against the killer during an interrogation of him. Under the heading of an "emotional appeal," casting the blame upon someone else would probably be the only appeal that might lead to a confession other than the logical approach.

CHAPTER XXX

ACTIONS LEADING TO THE CAPTURE OF THE PERPETRATOR

On March 17, 1961, Albert DeSalvo, whose activities caused him to be labeled as, "The Measuring Man" was arrested and charged with Lewdness, Assault and Battery, and Attempted Breaking and Entering, Confining and Putting in Fear, and Engaging in an Unnatural and Lascivious Act. When he was arrested, numerous police units, including detectives, were working the area in Cambridge where numerous house breakings had occurred. DeSalvo was observed trying to break into an apartment. He fled, but officers threatened to kill him if he didn't stop. DeSalvo surrendered. The police recovered a screw driver which was two feet in length, and he had skeleton keys and a jack knife in his jacket pocket.

After his arrest, when he was questioned by the police, he told them that just before he was apprehended, he had attempted to break into an apartment where two nurses lived. He had measured them, as he had many other women living in the area, for a job with a fictitious modeling agency. He said, "I just wanted to get into the apartment and wait for them to come home." The detective asked him why he wanted to do that, but DeSalvo would give no further explanation.

DeSalvo was convicted of only Assault and Battery and Attempted Breaking and Entering. The court ordered a psychiatric examination. The expert opinion regarding DeSalvo's mental condition was that he had a sociopathic personality.(4.242)

On May 4, 1961, approximately one year before the murder of A.S., DeSalvo was sentenced to prison for a year and a half. Unfortunately for poor A.S., the Parole Board reduced DeSalvo's sentence to eleven months due to his good behavior while he was confined. In April 1962, Albert DeSalvo was released from prison. Two months later he would murder his first victim.(4.240-241)

Between June 14, 1962, and January 4, 1964, DeSalvo murdered thirteen women in the Boston area which came to be called "The Boston Strangler" murders.

On one day, May 6, 1964, between 9:00 a.m. and noon, he had attacked four different women in four different towns.

On October 27, 1964, at about 9:30 a.m., a twenty year old coed, who had been recently married, was sleeping in her bed at her Cambridge apartment. Her husband had just left for work a short time before.

Something caused her to wake up, and she saw a man standing in the doorway of her bedroom. He told her not to worry that he was a detective. As he was speaking, he was moving toward her. She told him to leave her room immediately. He pulled out a knife and held it to her throat and told her, "Not a sound, or I'll kill you." He removed her panties and stuffed them into her mouth. He stripped her naked and used her clothes and her husband's pajamas to tie her spread eagle to the bed. Then he kissed and fondled her body and had sexual intercourse with her. While he was doing this, he repeatedly instructed her not to look at him. After he finished he asked her, "How do I leave this place?" She told him how to find the front door. He then bent over her with his head turned to one side so she would have a difficult time seeing his face. He loosened her bonds so she would be able to free herself. Then he told her, "You be quiet for ten minutes. I'm sorry." Then he left.(4.241)

The young lady did, however, get a good look at him. In fact, she told the investigating detectives that she would never forget his face. The detectives asked the victim if she would work with the police artist to make a sketch of the man who had attacked her, and she agreed to help. Upon completion of the sketch, one of the detectives studied it a bit and told the others present with him that the sketch looked like the Measuring Man, also known as Albert DeSalvo.(4.242)

The detective contacted DeSalvo by telephone and asked him to come into the Cambridge Police Station on November 3, 1964. He came in as requested, but denied any knowledge of the attack on the young coed. The victim, however, identified him. He was arrested, photographed, fingerprinted, and arraigned. His bond was set at $8,000.00, which was paid and he was released.

DeSalvo's mug shot was then sent to all police departments within a six state area. Within thirty-six hours, DeSalvo became a major suspect in several other cases where women had been tied up and sexually molested.

Apparently for the first time, officers were acutely aware of the type of person with whom they were dealing. They did not call and ask him to come into the station, rather they went to his neighborhood and waited for him to come home.

Again DeSalvo attempted to flee. He lived on a dead end street. When he realized that he was driving into a police trap, he tried to put the car in reverse and back out, but his way was blocked, and he was arrested again.

This time he confessed to officers that he had done some very bad things with women. He said he had a gun, but it was a toy. He also admitted using a knife, but denied killing anyone. He said he needed and wanted help.(4.242)

Subsequent to this, women in New Hampshire, Rhode Island, and Connecticut also identified DeSalvo as their attacker. The label, "The Green Man," was then given to DeSalvo because of the green working man's clothing that he wore while engaging in these criminal activities.

This time when DeSalvo was arraigned, the court sent him to the Bridgewater State Hospital for another examination. This would have been at least his third during his life. The Assistant Attorney General contacted the Director of the hospital and requested that special attention be given to him to determine whether he would have been capable of committing the murders done by the "Boston Strangler." It was quite apparent that at this point the investigators working on the serial murders considered him a suspect.

A Boston Detective traveled to Bridgewater to question DeSalvo in connection with the murders. The investigators were interested in DeSalvo because of the obvious similarities between his activities as the "Green Man" and the method of operation of the "Boston Strangler." In addition, the police had learned that on the day P.B. was murdered (12/30/62), a man was prowling the hallways of the apartment building where P.B. lived dressed in green clothing. Also information was received from another informant who claimed that DeSalvo had held a knife to her throat, blindfolded her, tied her up to a bed, and raped her.

It is not known whether an attempt was made to put DeSalvo into a lineup to determine whether the witness could identify him as the one prowling the hallways. It is also not known whether DeSalvo had used the special knot, with the extra half hitch which was used in the stranglings, to tie the young wife to the bed. Nor is it known whether that same knot was used when the other women from other states were assaulted. DeSalvo did habitually use that knot to tie his shoes.

At the Bridgeport Hospital, the detective was blocked in his planned interrogation. It was learned that DeSalvo now was represented by an attorney, and he did not want to question him without the attorney being present.(4.256)

DeSalvo had told another prisoner that he was the Boston Strangler. DeSalvo was interested in having a book written about his crimes so his wife and family would be provided for during the coming years. He had also confessed to his attorney that he was, in fact, the "Boston Strangler". He related information to him that only the real murderer would have known.

An arrangement was worked out for DeSalvo to plead guilty to the crimes he had committed as the so called, "Green Man." He agreed to confess to the crimes he committed as the "Boston Strangler" in exchange for the State of Massachusetts' promise that prosecution would not be sought on any of the offenses and that DeSalvo should receive medical treatment. By doing this, DeSalvo avoided the possibility of being executed.

The fact was that the police lacked the evidence to convict DeSalvo beyond a reasonable doubt on any of the murders attributed to the "Boston Strangler." All of the witnesses connected with the murders were either unwilling or unable to identify him. There was no significant physical evidence available. Only his confession, where he related information that only the murderer could have known, tied him to the crimes.

In summary, the primary factor that resulted in DeSalvo's identification as the perpetrator of the murders on this case was his arrest for an attack where the method of operation was nearly identical except that the victim was not killed. The importance of the police artist's work in the case, the identification of the sketch by the detective as "The Measuring Man " (DeSalvo), the identification of DeSalvo by the victim after he was arrested, the sending of DeSalvo's mug shot to a six state area, the identification of DeSalvo by the victims in those states, and the cooperation of an outstanding defense attorney who made it possible for the police to close their books on this case cannot be over estimated. It brought so much pressure to bear on DeSalvo that he knew he was not going to be released from custody. One could say he had three reasons for confessing. First, the possibility of making money to support his wife and children. Second, he said he wanted medical help. And third, and most importantly, he was afraid of the death sentence.

232

OBSERVATIONS

The lesson here for investigators working on serial murder cases is to watch for crimes with a similar method of operation which may occur in your jurisdiction or in an area near you where the only difference may be that the victim, for some unknown reason, was not murdered. DeSalvo's method of operation was very similar while functioning as the "Green Man" and as the "Boston Strangler". The primary difference, of course, was that as the latter he murdered and as the former he did not.

Dr. Brussel demonstrated great insight when he told his colleagues after the murder of M.S. that he did not believe that the Boston Strangler would kill again. It was his view at the time that the Strangler had cured himself. It is unknown just what exactly the good doctor based his opinion on, but he was correct. Perhaps it was the viciousness of the attack or the manner in which he left the body with a New Year's Card placed beside her toes to taunt the police.

It was observed in the assault upon the coed, DeSalvo told her he was a detective. He apparently said this to keep her from screaming until he could get close enough to her to put the knife to her throat and get control over her.

CHAPTER XXXI

PERPETRATOR

The perpetrator of this series of murders was Albert Henry DeSalvo. He was born on September 3, 1931, in Chelsea, Massachusetts. He was the third of six children born to Frank and Charlotte (nee Roberts) DeSalvo. DeSalvo was five feet eight and one half inches tall. He had hazel eyes, crew cut black hair, and a beak like nose. He was solidly built with broad shoulders and a narrow waist. He had a thin mouth which slanted down to the left. He had a heavy beard and most of the time he appeared as though he needed a shave.(4.286-287) He resided with his wife, Irmgard, and their two children at 11 Florence Street Park, Malden, Massachusetts when he was apprehended.(4.333)

DeSalvo's father had been arrested eighteen times. Five of these arrests were for non-support, five times for assault and battery upon his wife, and on charges of breaking and entering and larceny. In 1943 and 1944 when Albert DeSalvo was twelve and thirteen years old, his father was in jail. Also in 1944, after having been married since she was fifteen years old, Albert's mother divorced his father. One year later she remarried. (4.341) During most of Albert's formative years, the family was very poor and lived mainly from welfare. During this time, the family received about sixty-three dollars per month upon which to exist.(4.340)

Albert's mother had extremely poor eyesight.(4.343) She was unable to see well from about 1930. This was prior to Albert's birth. Her poor eyesight no doubt permitted Albert to get away with things he should not have been permitted to do, and, therefore, would have had little parental supervision when growing up. A social worker who checked out DeSalvo's home remarked, "...There is little here for the boy (Albert)—only hardship and a loose-living environment. It might be well, and only fair to the boy—were he placed in a reasonable environment for the time being or until his parents come to realize that they have a responsibility to their children."(4.346)

In spite of the hardships, which one would expect when a family is expected to exist on such limited financial resources, Albert was always his mother's favorite child, and he always went out of his way to visit her, if only for a few minutes.(4.328)

It should also be noted during his formative years, Albert DeSalvo began to manifest what some would term sadistic tendencies. He would capture a cat and a dog and put them inside a box with a divider in the middle. He would then starve the animals for several days. He would then remove the divider to watch the two animals tear one another apart. He also enjoyed shooting cats he found roaming the back alleys with arrows after he learned how to shoot a bow and arrow.(4.364)

Albert DeSalvo began school when he was six years old. During his early school years, he suffered from some medical problems. He had tonsillitis and some other childhood diseases. Because of these illnesses, he missed a great deal of school. He failed the second grade and was put into a special education class when he was in the fifth grade. Albert claimed he was put into this class for talking. (Too much talking at improper times) There can be little doubt that Albert was not retarded in any way. In fact, his intelligence level may have been above average. Albert did not have any serious disciplinary difficulties.(4.347) DeSalvo stated he ran errands for his teachers and, although he never received good grades, he managed to get by this way. Based upon this writer's review of the literature, it is his opinion that DeSalvo did not have a high regard for education and his teachers were unable, or did not care, to motivate him.

DeSalvo earned extra money by cleaning porches and emptying and cleaning garbage pails for women.

Albert liked to swim. As a boy, Albert claimed he was afraid to fight and said he ran away from fights. However, this must have been only when the other boy was about his size and he was risking taking a beating because when he was twelve he got into his first serious trouble beating up a newsboy.

Albert and another boy beat up and robbed a newspaper boy. Initially the boys both claimed that an older boy made them do it, but Albert later confessed that it was their idea. He said it was a spontaneous act. "We didn't plan anything. We were just walking up the hill and saw the paper boy and robbed him," he said, "Then we split the money." For this offense, Albert was judged a delinquent minor and was given a suspended sentence.(4.241)

About five months later, he was apprehended again with another youth for breaking and entering a house and stealing twenty-seven dollars worth of jewelry. This arrest could have been one of the reasons DeSalvo was reluctant to later steal items of property from the victims he murdered. On December 29, 1943, when Albert DeSalvo was twelve years old, he was sentenced to the Lyman School for Boys. His older brother, Joseph, had already been there several times during the previous four years. Albert spent his thirteenth birthday in that school. He was released from custody on October 29, 1944.

While he was there, Albert DeSalvo was given what would be the first of at least three psychiatric examinations that he would undergo during his life. At that time, it was reported that his I.Q. was ninety-three. One should question the validity of the score of this examination due to the circumstances under which such an examination was administered. It is questionable how motivated Albert DeSalvo was to do his best on such a test under the circumstances of his environment. The evaluation also indicated that he feared his father, and was an easily led person who was highly suggestible.(4.342)

Albert DeSalvo's sexual activity began when he was only a young boy. DeSalvo told his attorney, when he was nine or ten years old, his brother walked into the bedroom and caught a girl performing fellatio upon him. DeSalvo also told his lawyer that when he was fifteen the mother of one of his male friends engaged in sexual acts with him and taught him every type of sexual perversion. DeSalvo claimed he could last a long time and was driven to reach sexual satisfaction without rest.(4.364)

In 1948, when Albert DeSalvo was sixteen, he graduated from Williams Junior High School at sixty-two Fifth Street in Chelsea, Massachusetts. His teachers there hardly had any recollection of him, which indicated that either there was a high turnover of teachers or DeSalvo was not much of a problem child.(4.347)

DeSalvo then went to Cape Cod where he worked in a motel as a dishwasher for the summer. He spent most of his free time on the roof where he could look directly into some of the windows of the rooms. He watched couples making love. This would sexually arouse him, and he would masturbate repeatedly. After puberty, voyeurism had become a regular means of sexual stimulation and fulfillment for him.(4.365)

On September 16, 1948, after he turned seventeen, he enlisted in the United States Army. His mother apparently agreed to this decision, for at that time a boy that age could not enlist without parental consent. DeSalvo was sent to Germany as part of the occupying force serving there following World War II.

On October 17, 1950, he refused to obey an order and was given a court martial. He was found guilty and was fined fifty dollars. From then on, his record in the army was spotless.(4.347)

He bragged to his lawyer about some of his accomplishments in the army. He said he was always, "Spit and Polish". He always kept his uniform the sharpest and made Colonel's Orderly twenty-seven times. There was at least one other motivating factor for DeSalvo that had absolutely nothing to do with devotion to duty. He indicated that by being the Colonel's Orderly this provided him with the time he needed to look around for women during the day, especially other soldier's wives. (4.365)

Much to his surprise, he found that he had a talent which he did not know he possessed prior to joining the army. While in Germany, he was persuaded to enter the boxing competition as a middleweight. He fought his way to the top and eventually became the U.S. Army Middleweight Boxing Champion of Europe. He held that title for two years.(4.347)

Also while in the army, he was assigned to a tank outfit and suffered an injury to his left arm which was supposedly partially paralyzed. When he was discharged from the army, he received twenty percent disability for that injury.

On December 5, 1953, at the age of twenty-two, he married a German girl named Irmgard from the Frankfort area. They had met at a dance and dated over three years before they decided to get married.

In April 1954, DeSalvo, after serving five years in Germany, was ordered back to the United States. He was assigned to Fort Dix, New Jersey.(4.347)

On Monday, December 28, 1954, a woman was reading in her bungalow at about 9:00 p.m. Her husband was at work. A man knocked on her door and asked if she saw the prowler looking through the window. She told him she had not seen the man. The man told her that he would look around, which he did. He then told her that the prowler was gone. He also told her his name was Johnson. She became suspicious when he asked her when her husband was coming home. She shut the door, locked, and bolted it, and awoke her children and dressed them.

"Johnson" then returned to his car and sat in the driveway for about ten minutes. Then he drove away, but returned in a short time and parked in the driveway again for an additional ten minutes. She was so afraid she wrote the license number of "Johnson's" car down and fled with her children to a neighbor's house. She reported the incident to the Wrightstown Post of New Jersey State Police.

The license plate registration was traced to Sergeant Albert DeSalvo, United States Army, who was stationed at Fort Dix. State Police Troopers questioned DeSalvo. He admitted that he had been the man at the woman's house. He told the officers that he was only trying to find a place to rent when he observed the prowler and was only trying to help. The Troopers had nothing with which to charge him, and he was released from custody.

On Monday, January 3, 1955, a young mother was starting to prepare supper at about 2:00 p.m. She left her nine year old daughter and two younger children at home while she went to the store for some quick shopping. When she returned home, her daughter told her a soldier had been there for the rent. Since the mother owned the house where they were living, she thought this most peculiar. Her daughter went on to tell her how the soldier came into the house and felt her chest and genital areas. The little girl said she told the soldier to stop and he told her, "I won't hurt you." She said the man had a nose like Jimmy Durante. She further stated when her little brother came into the house, the soldier ran away like someone was chasing him.

When the young mother reported the above incident to the New Jersey State Police, the Troopers recalled the previous incident involving an army sergeant, and ultimately arrested DeSalvo. The little girl and her brother both identified DeSalvo as the man who had molested the little girl.

Once again, DeSalvo claimed that he had only been looking for a place to rent. He completely denied that he molested the little girl, but did admit he touched her on her shoulder.

On January 4, 1955, the Grand Jury indicted DeSalvo for Carnal Abuse of the little nine year old girl. The bond was set at $1,000.00 which was posted, and DeSalvo was released from custody .

Later the mother refused to permit her little girl to testify against DeSalvo. She claimed she feared the publicity and the mental trauma which might result to her daughter from such an ordeal. The Prosecutor was left with no other choice but to drop the charges. With all charges dropped, the army also dropped any consideration of the matter, and on February 15, 1956, Albert DeSalvo received an Honorable Discharge from the United States Army.(4.349)

On February 14, 1958, DeSalvo was arrested for the breaking and entering of a house where money was stolen. At that time he was living in Chelsea.

In 1959, he returned to Germany with his wife and daughter. His wife wished to visit her parents. DeSalvo stated during their two month stay in Germany, he had plenty of money from breaking into a number of cafes. He was also busy with phony contests so he could feel women while he was taking their measurements at post exchanges. He posed as a representative from Stars and Stripes, and he was selecting girls for the, "Best Sweetheart of All Contest"(4.322)

As was previously mentioned, in March 1961, DeSalvo was arrested for activities similar to his, "contest" in Germany. He was known before his arrest as the "Measuring Man". He served from May 1961 until April 1962, in the Middlesex County House of Correction. At that time he was fingerprinted and photographed. (4.241) These photographs became extremely significant at a later time when he was involved in criminal activities and was known as the "Green Man". Then he posed as a detective and sexually attacked a newlywed coed. That offense led directly to his arrest and confinement in a state mental institution. During that time, he admitted to other patients in the hospital, his defense attorney, and subsequent to this, to an Assistant Attorney General of the State of Massachusetts, his crimes when he was known by the media as the "Boston Strangler."

OBSERVATIONS

Several other aspects about the perpetrator, Albert DeSalvo, are remarkable and are included here as a matter of general information concerning him. In a few instances some remarks previously made are also included here for the reader's convenience of having them at one location.

DeSalvo did not drink any alcoholic beverages, use tobacco in any form, nor are there any indications that he used drugs.

DeSalvo's wife was a devout Roman Catholic. He was not a member of any church or any organized religion, but sometimes he did take his children to church. After he was apprehended, he asked to speak with a priest. He told the priest he was thinking about becoming a Roman Catholic. It was apparent that, in the main, DeSalvo had little faith in any religion, nor little compassion for those who did believe, for in one instance he parked his car in front of the Roman Catholic Church to go to an apartment building to murder a woman. And in another case, the victim told him that she was getting ready for church when she permitted him to come into her apartment. He strangled her with his bare hands.

DeSalvo had very few guilt feelings after he committed a murder. He claimed he did not understand why he murdered. He indicated that once he left the victim's apartment, it was almost like some other person had killed the victim.

DeSalvo was very conscious of not leaving any physical evidence behind at the crime scene such as fingerprints. There are some psychologists and psychiatrists who believe that these types of murderers really have a desire to be caught. If this were really true, most police would dislike encountering a serial killer who did *not* want to be caught. It is a foolish assumption to believe that a person committing these types of crimes really has an inner desire to be caught and may, therefore, make Freudian-type errors to turn that wish into reality. In fact, the best opportunity to arrest a serial murderer is shortly after he begins to kill. The reason for this is that he has not yet perfected his method. He is nervous. This is the time he is most apt to make mistakes that the police can use to apprehend him. The problem is at these early stages the police are not geared up to deal with a serial murderer. They are apt to be making mistakes too, and he may slip through their grasp. The longer a serial murderer continues his activities, the better he becomes at what he is doing. The one thing that can trip him up then is he is frequently seeking greater and greater excitement and thrills. This may cause him to become more brazen and bold and take increased risks. This increased sense of bravado may also cause him to make mistakes which will ultimately lead to his arrest.

DeSalvo had been trained as a military policeman in the army, and he read detective magazines. These things may have helped him avoid making mistakes which would have led to his arrest.

As time went on, DeSalvo's criminal acts became more brazen, and he appeared to delight in taunting the police. For example, he placed a "Happy New Year's card near the toes of one of the victims. *IT SHOULD BE NOTED THAT HE REACHED A POINT WHERE IT APPEARED THAT HE CURED HIMSELF OF THE NEED TO MURDER*

HIS VICTIMS, AND DR. JAMES BRUSSEL PREDICTED THAT THIS HAD OCCURRED, BUT HE CONTINUED TO RAPE.

DeSalvo kept himself in good physical condition. While he was receiving twenty percent disability from the Veteran's Administration for allegedly having a partially paralyzed left arm, he managed to do twenty-five push-ups morning, noon, and night while a patient in the Bridgewater State Hospital.

DeSalvo would take precautions against being later identified. He sometimes wore dark glasses. Other times he kept his hand partially over his face, pretending to scratch his nose, while he talked with people in the apartment building where he was going to commit a murder. On at least one occasion, when he was receiving information from a person who later might be a witness against him, as that person was telling him where the victim lived, DeSalvo was backing away from him. This made it more difficult for the person to later make a positive identification. In fact it made it so difficult, that no subsequent identification was made by anyone who was not a victim.

Additional police presence did not deter DeSalvo from carrying out criminal activity. DeSalvo walked by police officers while enroute to buildings where he was going to commit crimes. *IN THIS WRITER'S OPINION, WHAT WAS EFFECTIVE AGAINST DeSALVO WAS OFFICERS WORKING IN THE AREA IN SOFT CLOTHES RATHER THAN IN UNIFORM.* It should also be noted from what was written above that Albert DeSalvo was not deterred in the least by talking with someone in the apartment building other than the victim. Police investigators should not conclude that a perpetrator would not be so stupid as to ask someone in the apartment building where a certain young lady lived and then go kill her. That is exactly what DeSalvo did. This also points out the need for a very thorough search for witnesses in any apartment building where the victim lived and was murdered.

While it was probably true that the very sight of uniformed officers on patrol in the area where crimes were being committed made the public feel that the police were doing something to protect them, this was, in fact, really a false sense of security. The truth was that this may have even helped DeSalvo because then he could have seen where his opposition was located, and he was always watching for the police, even though he did not let them deter him from his objectives. DeSalvo said he always also had kind of a sixth sense that told him when the police were watching him.

DeSalvo was QUICK TO USE AN ALIBI to cover his criminal acts. For example, after the aborted attack on G.G., the German waitress, who bit his finger, he managed to escape. DeSalvo immediatedly went to his former attorney's office. He had to pretend that he was angry at his former attorney because the attorney wanted to shake hands, and DeSalvo could not do this because his hand was wrapped and the finger was still bleeding profusely.

Also in another instance when the murdered victim's blood was on his shirt, he picked up a black man and asked him to provide the alibi that DeSalvo had been caught with another man's wife and fled from her home leaving his shirt behind. The black man was asked to vouch for DeSalvo's story should anyone question him regarding why he had no shirt to wear into an Army-Navy Store. As it turned out, no one questioned DeSalvo about it.

Again, when he had escaped from the Bridgewater State Hospital, when a police officer asked him whether he was DeSalvo, DeSalvo told him that his name was Johnson, an alias he had also used while in the army, that he lived in a nearby apartment, that his wife was home, and he could check with her should he like. The officer did not check into this further. Everything that he told the officer was a lie. He would have probably tried to flee if the officer indicated he was going to verify his story. *SERIAL MURDERERS LIKE TO USE THE ALIBI TO GET THEMSELVES OFF THE HOOK. OFFICERS WORKING ON THESE TYPES OF CASES SHOULD VERY CAREFULLY CHECK OUT ANY ALIBI THAT A SUSPECT GIVES.*

DeSalvo by working around his own house, being home with his family during the evening hours, and working hard on the job was able to place himself completely above suspicion as being the Boston Strangler. This included his wife, mother, employer, former attorney, and parole officer. Only his brother, Joseph, seemed to be aware of the possibilty of a problem.

DeSalvo's brother indicated Albert DeSalvo required much sexual activity. He said that he knew there was trouble when Albert began carrying a knife. It would appear that he was one of the very few who could have called the police with a tip, but his brother was so anti-police it was unlikely he would ever have done that. In fact, he later aided his brother after he had escaped from the Bridgewater State Hospital.

It did not appear that DeSalvo wore extra clothing for the sole purpose of changing his appearance while fleeing the scene. However, it was noted that DeSalvo did remove a jacket he was wearing and left it in an alley while he walked back to his car, which a short time previously he had ran past, so no one would get the license number of his car or its make and color. He obviously wanted to change his appearance before he even tried to get into his car.

In another instance, after his own clothing had blood on it, he found a raincoat in the apartment where the victim was living, and he wore that from the apartment. The tipoff that an observant patrol officer might have had was the coat did not fit him. The sleeves were too short.

DeSalvo read newspaper accounts and watched television and listened to radio news reports. When an appeal was made to turn himself in and officials would try to get him some help, DeSalvo stated he knew he needed help, but claimed he would not turn himself in because he thought he would be locked up for the rest of his life, and he was concerned that there would be no one who could take care of his wife and children. There may have been some truth to that because he discussed with his attorney having a book written about his case to raise money for his family. Whatever good the above appeal was to stop the murders, it was probably nullified because the Governor's Office also made a release stating the murderer, if caught, would probably be executed. The significant point for police officers to keep in mind is that serial murderers do watch, listen and read about what is being said about them.

DeSalvo, when he was apprehended as the "Measuring man" and as the "Green man", tried to avoid arrest by fleeing from officers. In the former instance, shots were fired. In the latter case, he tried to escape in his car, but the escape route was blocked. There

241

were several officers present and escape was futile. It was interesting to note that he did not try to flee the country. He obviously had a passport.

DeSalvo was quick to blame his wife for all his sexual problems. In other words, she was to blame for her failure to provide him with sufficient sexual intercourse and making him feel that the sexual act was dirty. The truth, however, was that he was involved in perverse, abnormal sexual acts from childhood. His wife said it was impossible to satisfy him. During work days, it was not uncommon for him to have sexual intercourse with her four times a day, and on weekends as many as five or six times. DeSalvo thought his wife was frigid because she did not want to engage in sexual intercourse more than this. (4.243)

In addition to the above, DeSalvo indicated he relieved himself at least four or five times each day. Sometimes he said he could be overcome by the feeling that he was burning up inside. He would fantasize about a woman and picture her in his mind as he drove down the road in a daze. He would wonder what her body would be like. Sometimes, just through his fantasies, he had an ejaculation. But in a few minutes, the burning desire would return. He said sometimes, after a victim had been located, and he was in the process of attacking her, he would have an ejaculation just by touching the female body of his victim while he was tying her up, measuring her, or feeling her thighs. "Sometimes," he said," after I had raped a woman, I cried, and told her I was sorry."(4.335-336) That statement was verified by at least one of his victims. Another serial murderer, John Norman Collins, acted in the same fashion towards a victim he beat and raped, but did not kill.

DeSalvo's victims were all randomly selected. He didn't know them and had never seen them before. He did, however, know the geographic area where he committed his criminal acts extremely well. He had been inside several of the apartments where he committed the murders several times in connection with other criminal activities such as burglaries, and measuring women for phony modeling jobs.

It was interesting to note that DeSalvo was obviously an exceptionally fine boxer, yet he did not knock even one of his victims out by hitting her, nor did he punch G.G. when she fought off his attack, nor did he so much as slap one of his victim's.

A further possible reason for DeSalvo's good conduct after he was in trouble for disobeying an order was that for a good deal of the time, from 1950 until 1953, there was armed combat taking place in Korea which would have been vastly different duty from that which he was experiencing in Germany. If he were involved in any additional trouble in the army while in Europe, he would probably have been sent there.

It was observed that DeSalvo stuck with the story about the prowler while he was serving in the United States Army assigned at Fort Dix, New Jersey, and was questioned by the State Police there. He indicated he only wanted to help. Of course, if this were really true, there would have been no need for him to tell the woman his name was, "Johnson". The troopers in that case had nothing with which to charge DeSalvo and were forced to release him. The lesson DeSalvo learned from that incident was not to park his car at any location where a witness could obtain a license number which could later be traced to him.

DeSalvo was difficult to interrogate during his later years. It was apparent that he stuck with a story, even when it did not make sense. It was only when the circumstances were such that he thought that it was in his best interest to tell the truth that he finally did so. It was clear that he did not do this out of any remorse for the the murders he had committed. No, it was patently obvious that his primary motive for confessing was due to what he regarded as self preservation. Probably if the State of Massachusetts did not have the death penalty, even though it was not being used at the time of DeSalvo's arrest, he would not have confessed to the murders he had committed or been cooperative with authorities at all. This has also been true of other serial murderers. Donald Miller, a mid-Michigan serial killer, was arrested for rape. He had been the primary suspect in a series of four murders after he had taken and failed a polygraph examination administered by Lieutenant Maynard Markham of the East Lansing Michigan Police Department. Miller finally made a confession and told the police where the bodies of the victims he had murdered could be found in exchange for the prosecution dropping a first degree murder charge against him and charging him with manslaughter. Like so many other serial murder cases, there was very little evidence against him that could have been used to obtain a conviction for murder. He also was convicted on the rape (First Degree Criminal Sexual Conduct) charge. In Chicago, a serial murderer, William George Hierens, exchanged a full confession for a promise that the prosecution would not seek the death penalty against him.

REFERENCES

1. Bailey, F. Lee, LL.B. . *The Defense Never Rests:* Stein and Day, New York, New York: 1971

2. Brussel, James A., M.D. *Casebook of a Crime Psychiatrist:* Bernard Geis Associates, U.S.A.: 1968

3. DeRiver, J. Paul, M.D., F.A.C.S. *Crime and the Sexual Psychopath:* Charles C. Thomas, Springfield, Illinois: 1958

4. Frank Gerold, *The Boston Strangler:* The New American Library, New York, New York: 1966

5. Sifakis, Carl, *A Catalogue of Crime:* The New American Library, New York, New York: 1979

CHAPTER XXXII

THE CASE STUDY OF THEODORE ROBERT BUNDY

Theodore Robert Bundy was one of the most notorious serial murderers who ever lived. Between 1974 and 1978, it is believed by authorities that Bundy murdered thirty-six girls and young women. Before he was executed, he confessed to about twenty sex related murders. He strongly denied his guilt to any crimes until just a few hours before his death. Even then it appeared that he was holding back additional crimes to use them as a bargaining chip to stay out of Florida's electric chair. This is his story.

THE VICTIMS

The murders began on Thursday, January 31, 1974, in Seattle, Washington. Five young women were living together. That evening one of the women observed a prowler. The next morning one of the women was missing. She was twenty-one year old Lynda Ann Healy, a white female who was five feet seven inches tall, 115 pounds, with brown hair parted in the middle, with blue eyes and pierced ears. Healy was a college coed.(15.7)

A police report was made out on the missing woman. Officers found her bed was made, but upon pulling the covers back, and examining the sheets, they found blood on them. The victim's nightgown was hung in her closet. It had blood on it too. Some of her clothing and her back pack were missing. A search was conducted, but no trace of her was found.

Less than a month before, there had been another young woman who was badly beaten in her apartment which was in the University District about a mile and a half from where Healy disappeared. That woman had apparently been left for dead. The perpetrator had shoved a speculum into her vagina. The woman recovered, but she had no recollection of the attack. Both of these attacks occurred in basement apartments.

On March 12, 1974, Donna Gail Mason, a coed at Evergreen State College in Olympia, Washington, left her dorm to attend a concert three hundred yards away. It was 7:00 p.m. and floodlights lit her way along a winding path. She disappeared. Five days later her friends reported her missing to the campus security police. Bloodhounds tracked her to a parking lot before they lost her scent.(15.10)

On April 17, 1974, at Central Washington State College in Ellensburg, Washington, an eighteen year old named Susan Elaine Rancourt disappeared shortly before 9:00 p.m. from the campus. Susan had been a high school cheerleader. She liked to jog with the campus police. Her nickname was "Miss Prudence Pureheart". (13.60-63)

Three months later, two different women reported that a man with his arm in a sling and a metal device on his finger had dropped something and then asked them to help

244

him. In one instance, he was in front of the college library. In another, he dropped a package. One of the women said he was driving a yellow Volkswagon with the front seat missing. The two women just didn't think what they had observed was important.

On May 6, 1974, Roberta Kathleen Parks, a freshman college coed, disappeared from Oregon State University in Corvallis. She had left her dormitory for a late evening walk to the Student Union Building. Like the other times when women disappeared, there was not a trace of evidence.(15.15)

At 2:00 a.m. on June 1, 1974, Brenda Ball left the Flame Bar with a man. No one remembered him. She too disappeared. This was in the suburbs of Seattle.(15.16)

On June 11, 1974, Georgann Hawkins had left her boyfriend's fraternity house around midnight for the sorority house where she lived. It was believed that she never made it inside her door. She too disappeared without a trace.

On Sunday, July 14, 1974, at Lake Sammamish in King County Washington, Janice Ott, aka "Sunshine Girl", went to the parking lot to help a man, who identified himself as "Ted", put a sailboat on top of his car. That was at 12:30 p.m. She disappeared.(15.20-21)

About 5:15 p.m. on that same date and at that same place, the man with the sling was back trying to get another young woman to help him put a sailboat on his car. At approximately that same time (4:30 p.m.), Denise Naslund disappeared after she went to the public toilet at the park. Beside Naslund and Ott, at least three other women were approached by the man with his arm in a sling that day.(15.21)

The police made an appeal to the public for any witnesses asking them to come forth. One woman came forward and told them in confidence that she heard the man tell Ott that his name was, "Ted". This information was made public. Then other women came forward. The matter became known as "The Ted Case". The witnesses said "Ted" wore different clothing on his two trips to the park. One said he wore jeans, but several others said he wore tennis shorts. Witnesses also gave different descriptions of the color of his sling and his physical description.

At the end of July 1974, an appeal was made urging the abductor to do some deep soul searching and to turn himself in to the police.

A $5,000 reward was offered by the local newspaper for the arrest and conviction of the perpetrator.

Detective Bob Keppel assembled the information from the witnesses and gave it to a police artist who made a composite sketch.

Since witnesses thought "Ted" had an English accent and referred to playing racquetball—the police thought "Ted" might be a Canadian.

The police had 3,000 Volkswagon cars in Washington owned by a person with the first name, "Ted".

On September 7, 1974—a Saturday—the skeletal remains of both Ott and Naslund were found just four miles east of Lake Sammamish State Park along Interstate 90. The cause of their deaths could not be determined. The police also found the remains of an unknown person.

The police hired a team of psychiatrists who tried to provide a profile as best they could with the limited information that was available. They told the police they were dealing with a sexual psychopath. He would be characterized by certain typical traits, including a lack of remorse. He would tend also to be an extrovert, likeable, engaging, have high intelligence and motivation. In short, they thought it very likely that the killer would appear perfectly normal. They said the secret to the uniqueness of his personality was his hollow, conscienceless core. Further, since the killer has no guilt—he tends to murder again and again.

On October 12, 1974, seventeen miles from Vancouver, Washington, not far from the Oregon border (130 miles south of Issaquah where Ott and Naslund were found), a deer hunter found the skeletal remains of two women. One woman was eighteen year old Carol Valenzuela. She was last observed alive on August 2, 1974, at a welfare office in Vancouver where she had gone for food stamps. The other woman had been murdered about six weeks before Valenzuela. She remained unidentified.

In the fall of 1974 at the Intermountain Crime Conference, investigators from Utah, California, Washington, Oregon, Wyoming, Idaho, and Nevada met to exchange information. The first item of business on the agenda was the mysterious disappearances and deaths of young women since 1969. There were about ninety of them, and most of them were unsolved.

During this conference the representative from the Murray Police Department (Utah) reported that a young woman was approached in a shopping mall by a man who was posing as a detective. On a pretense she accompanied him in his car. They were supposedly going to the police station to file a report. A short time later he tried to put handcuffs on her and attacked her with a tire iron, but she escaped. She described his car as a "light-colored Volkswagon" with a deep scratch on the door on the passenger's side.

On the evening of October 18, 1974, Melissa Smith, the daughter of the Midvale Police Department Chief disappeared. Her body was found in a canyon in the Wasatch Mountains near Salt Lake City. She had been beaten on the head. The cause of death was strangulation with one of her nylon stockings. Acid phosphatase was found in her vagina. The pathologist thought she had only been dead between forty-eight and seventy-two hours.

On October 2, 1974, Nancy Wilcox, a Salt Lake City, Utah cheerleader also vanished. Debbie Kent, another high school student, disappeared on November 8, 1974. Both of these girls were later found dead. They had been beaten about the head and strangled.

On October 31, 1974, Laura Aime, a white female, seventeen years-old who lived with a girl friend in American Fork, Utah vanished. Laura was a high school drop-out. She weighed one hundred and forty pounds and was six feet tall. She talked with her mother nearly every day. She liked to hitch-hike. She left a park shortly after midnight and disappeared. Her mother did not report her missing until five days later. The officer told her to put an ad in the paper. The officer apparently did not believe that Laura was dead, and he thought this was a good way to encourage Laura to contact her parents who were worried about her welfare.

On Friday, November 8, 1974, Carol Da Ronch, a white female eighteen-year-old high school graduate of Murray, Utah (near Salt Lake City) went to a shopping mall to shop and socialize. A man approached her. She described him as wearing a brown leather jacket, green trousers and reddish brown patent leather shoes.(10.50-53)

He excused himself and asked her if she had a car parked in the Sears Parking lot . She told him, "Yes" . He asked her to tell him the license number of her car. She told him what it was. Then he told her that a Sears customer reported a prowler who was trying to break into her car. He asked her to go with him to check her car to see if anything was stolen from it. As they walked toward her car, he told her that his partner had probably apprehended the suspect. As they approached her car, Carol grew suspicious and asked to see the "officer's ID". He laughed in a way to make her feel "kind of dumb". She unlocked the car and checked it—nothing was missing. He then asked her to unlock the door on the passenger side. She questioned his request. She saw him try the door to see if it was locked. He then escorted her inside the mall. He told her his partner must have gone to the police station. As they left to go there, she again asked what his name was. He told her, "Officer Roseland, Murray Police Department". He then went to the door of a laundry building near the mall and knocked. Getting no answer he told her, "They must have taken him to headquarters." He told her he thought she should really sign a complaint at police headquarters.

They then walked up to a beat up, light colored, Volkswagon with a tear in the top of the seat. Again, she asked to see his identification. The man then took out his wallet and flashed a gold badge so fast that she could not read what was written. He opened the car door for her and asked her to put on the seat belt. She told him, "No, it makes me nervous. I don't want to put it on." But Carol did get into the car, and they drove away from the mall. Carol could smell alcohol on his breath. Suddenly, he drove up over a curb near a school and stopped. She asked what they were doing. She opened the door and got a foot on the ground as the man put a handcuff on her right wrist. She struggled. The man tried to get the cuff on her left wrist but accidentally locked both cuffs on the right wrist. Carol screamed and scratched. He drew a pistol and told her, "If you don't be quiet, I'm going to kill you." She jumped out of the car anyway, and the man dropped the pistol as he tried to hold her. He attacked her again. She saw a crowbar and grabbed it. He pinned her against the car and took the crowbar away from her. She broke loose and ran into the path of an oncoming car. Carol jumped on top of a woman in the car. Neither person in that car saw Carol's attacker.(15.46-50)

The police checked the handcuffs, her car, and the door knob of the laundry building at the mall for latent prints, but they did not find any.

At 7:45 p.m. on that same day (11-8-74), a man described as a white male, six feet tall, 180 pounds, with brown wavy hair and a mustache, very good looking with light dress slacks and patent leather shoes asked Arla Jensen if she would come out to the parking lot at the Viewmont High School with him and "try to identify a car for me". The school was conducting a play and she was involved in the supervision and coordination of the play. She told him she was busy and that she would try to find someone else to help him, but he was very insistent. "It'll only take a few seconds. I just need to find out whose car this is." She said she was sorry, but she had to work. About thirty minutes later she saw the man again. She asked him if he had found someone—he didn't reply—but followed her with his eyes.

After the break in the play that was taking place, Arla tried to walk past the man again. He blocked her passage down the hallway. He told her how nice she looked and once again asked her to help him. She told him that her husband might help him. The man then allowed her to pass.

Debbie Kent left the play shortly after the man had also left. Then, before the play was over, the same man returned to the play, "The Redhead". Mrs. Jensen said his hair was now mussed up and he was breathing heavily. The man left at 10:30 p.m. when the curtain calls began. Debbie Kent's car was still in the parking lot, but no one had seen her or knew of her whereabouts.

Debbie's parents made a personal report to the police. The police thought they were crazy because she only had been missing for two hours. The parents explained that their daughter would not have left them stranded at a play because her father was recovering from a heart attack. The police took the report from them, but did not begin the investigation into Debbie Kent's disappearance until the following morning.

The next morning (11-9-74), the police found a handcuff key just outside the door of the school. The key fit the handcuffs that Carol Da Ronch had on her right wrist when she escaped. One informant said Debbie Kent was involved in drugs and had gone to San Francisco. The police developed a suspect, William Madsen. Mrs. Arla Jensen viewed his police photograph (mug shot), but she wasn't certain, she wanted to see the man in person. When she saw him in person (where he worked), she still wasn't certain, so he was given a lie detector (polygraph) examination and passed it. This man also had a Volkswagon.

On Wednesday, November 27, 1974, a couple was on a picnic when they found the body of Laura Aime in the American Fork Canyon. When her parents' inquired about whether the body found was their daughter, they were told—at first—that the body found was too short to be their daughter. Her own father could not recognize her by looking at her face. He did, however, identify her by a scar from a horse riding accident when her left arm was ripped by barbed wire. The identification was confirmed by her dental records.

At this point, the police believed both Melissa Smith and Laura Aime were abducted and held somewhere before they were murdered. Both victims were naked when found, both had been sexually assaulted, both had been bludgeoned on their heads, and both had been left in the Wasatch canyons.

The father became angry when officers from another police department came to the house asking the same questions that were previously asked by officers from another police agency. He was left with the impression that there was competition between officers which was impacting upon the investigation. He wanted the Salt Lake City Police Department Homicide Squad called in to help in the investigation because of their greater experience in death investigations.(4.O)

According to the mother of the victim (Aime), officers from other departments investigating similar crimes called her and requested her to telephone local departments and advise them about her missing daughter. She was left with the conclusion that the officers from the department investigating her daughter's death were not sharing the information with police officers from other departments. She also claimed that she went to the department for an interview about her daughter and was kept waiting for two hours because the officer with whom she was supposed to speak was giving a lecture at the university.

A witness on the 13th of December 1974, told the police he had seen a "ratty-looking, light colored Volkswagon" leave the High School parking lot at about 10:30 p.m. the night Debbie Kent vanished. The witness did not see anyone in the car.

In Seattle, Washington, Melanie Pattisen, Ted Bundy's girl friend, reluctantly reported him to the police as a possible suspect because (1) the person used the name "Ted", (2) Bundy had a Volkswagon, (3) the murders in the Seattle area stopped and started in Utah where Bundy had gone.

Caryn Campbell, a registered nurse, disappeared from a ski lodge after she had gone to her room to get her magazine. She was last observed getting on the lodge's elevator in the lobby. This was at Snowmass Village in Colorado on January 12, 1975. On February 17, 1975, her body was found off Owl Creek Road between Aspen and Snowmass Village. She was nude. Indications were that she was murdered between two and five hours after her last meal. The causes of death were head injuries associated with exposure to cold. The test for acid phosphatase from a sample taken from the victim's vaginal vault was positive. This test was indicative that seminal fluid was present.

In March of 1975, some forestry students were exploring a region of Taylor Mountain off Route 18, five miles south of Interstate 90. This location was less than twelve miles from where Janice Ott and Nasland were found. The remains of Lynda Healy, Susan Rancourt, Roberta Parks, and Brenda Ball were also found. They were all identified by their dental work. All these women had vanished over a five month period from widely separated locations in two states. Their bones were turned over to a university anthropology professor with a request that he help identify them.

King County and Seattle Police formed the Ted Task Force under the command of a captain from the King County Police. Regular news conferences were conducted.

In Vail, Colorado, on the night of March 15, 1975, Julie Cunningham, a white female, who was twenty-six-years old, left her room between 9:00 and 9:30 p.m. to meet her room-mate at the town mall. She disappeared. All the men whom she had dated agreed to take polygraph tests. All test results were negative.

A month later in Grand Junction, Denise Oliverson disappeared around 3:00 p.m. on Sunday afternoon. She had been bicycle riding. Her bicycle was laying on the railroad tracks under a bridge. The bicycle was not checked for latent fingerprints by investigators. The bike later disappeared from police custody.

On April 15, 1975, Melanie Suzanne Colley, who was a white female eighteen year-old Nederland High School student, disappeared on her way home from school. Her body was found eight days later along the Canyon Road by some workers. This location was fifteen miles from where she had disappeared. She had a pillowcase over her head. Her hands were tied in front of her. Her blouse was ripped, and her jeans were pulled down. She had been hit at the base of the skull with a rock.

On July 1, 1975, in Golden, Colorado, Shelley Robertson failed to come in for work at her father's print shop. Shelley also liked to hitchhike. Two students found her body on August 23rd in an old mine shaft. She was nude and had been bound with duct tape. They also found a wrapper from a package of ham and a beer can.

On July 4, 1975, at about 5:30 a.m., Nancy Baird, who worked at a gas station along Utah 84 near Bountiful disappeared. Her locked car was left at the station.

In Seattle the Task Force Commander called a press conference and told the people they had investigated 2,877 people with the name of "Ted". They were terminating the Task Force.

CHAPTER XXXIII

BUNDY'S ARREST AND CONVICTION

On the morning of August 16, 1975, at about 3:00 a.m., Sergeant Bob Hayward of the Utah State Highway Patrol observed a grey Volkswagon drive by his house. Hayward observed the car later parked by a curb. Hayward decided to investigate, and the driver attempted to flee without lights, but was apprehended. The driver was Theodore Robert Bundy, 565 First Avenue, Salt Lake City. Probably because he did not want the officer to look into his Volkswagen, Bundy got out of his car and walked back to the unmarked patrol car. Bundy appeared totally calm, but his behavior had triggered a "red flag" in the sergeant's mind. This "red flag" always occurs when a person gets out of his car and comes back to talk with an officer. In this instance, the circumstances would have been exacerbated due to Bundy's attempt to avoid being stopped by the officer. The sergeant obtained Bundy's permission to search his car. In the car, Sergeant Hayward discovered a rope, gloves of different makes, ice pick, strips of torn sheets, a pair of handcuffs, a flashlight, a box of black plastic garbage bags, and a pair of panty hose with eye, nose, and mouth holes. Bundy was released on $500 personal recognizance bond. Actually, that meant that he was released solely upon his promise that he voluntarily appear in court. He was not required to deposit any cash. Bundy told Officer Hayward that he had been at a movie, but he gave the name of a movie that wasn't playing.

The Highway Patrol Sergeant's brother, who was one of the officers involved in investigating the murders in Utah, was notified. Bundy was discussed at the regular meeting by the group of detectives the following Tuesday morning. One of the detectives reviewed the files which contained information from Robert Keppel in Washington which indicated that they had "several" tips on Ted Bundy, but Bundy did not appear to have been involved. He came from a good family and he worked for the governor's campaign. He also had a degree in psychology from the University of Washington. Bundy had moved to the Salt Lake City area to attend law school. Keppel sent a picture of Bundy. Another Utah detective had also talked with Bundy's girlfriend. Two days later, Bundy was arrested. Bundy appeared relaxed and cooperative. He joked with officers in the interrogation room. He probably called them by their first names. Bundy provided a flimsy excuse for every item that had been found in his car. When the detectives asked Bundy for permission to search his apartment, Bundy tried to appear like a cooperative, confident person with nothing to hide. Bundy gave the police permission to search his apartment.

In the apartment, a detective took a gas credit card receipt. (He wanted the number) Bundy denied that he had ever been in Colorado, but detectives found a Colorado brochure and a Colorado road map with an "x" by the Wildwood Inn at Snowmass. Bundy gave them permission to photograph the Volkswagon. On August 22, 1975, Bundy retained an attorney and his cooperation stopped.

On August 25, 1975, preparations were underway to subpoena phone bills, law school records, bank statements, and Ted Bundy's gasoline credit card records.

Ted Bundy's picture was in a photo show-up which was viewed by Carol Da Ronch. She pulled out Bundy's picture and said it looked something like him. She thought if she saw her kidnapper in person she could identify him. They first took her to the law school campus, but Bundy was not located. They then tried another photo show up using driver's license photographs because the Da Ronch attack occurred close to the date Bundy renewed his license. Carol identified him.

Bundy was then targeted for very close scrutiny. Meanwhile Bundy had his VW painted, replaced the torn seat, and had gotten new hubcaps. Carol Da Ronch identified the car from a scratch in the door. In Colorado, it was learned that Bundy had bought gas in the same geographic area where three of the girls were murdered. It was also learned that Bundy was using three different plates while he was buying gas. Two of these were from Utah and one was from Washington.

On September 10, 1975, a 24-hour surveillance was placed on Bundy. Bundy made a huge joke of the surveillance. He wrote down their license numbers and photographed them. At no time did he demonstrate any fear, but the police report indicated he was very nervous and was not attending any classes. Bundy sold his VW and cancelled his credit card.

A detective from Salt Lake City flew to Seattle and interviewed Bundy's girlfriend. She said she suspected Bundy because: (1)the composite in the newspaper resembled Bundy, (2) he was never with her when one of the murdered victims disappeared, (3) she saw a sack of women's clothing in his apartment, (4) he had a pair of crutches, (5) he had stolen plaster of paris from a medical supply firm where he worked, (6) he had an oriental knife in a wooden sheath ,(7) he had a lug wrench which was taped on one end, (8) he also had a meat cleaver, (9) he was involved in petty thievery, (10) he lied to her, (11) Bundy wanted to tie his girlfriend to the bed, (12) Bundy wore a fake mustache on occasion. Not mentioned by Bundy's girlfriend during those interviews with the police was that Bundy's name was Ted, and he drove a Volkswagen.

On the morning of October 1, 1975, Ted Bundy was served with a court order to appear in a lineup at 9:30 a.m. on October 2, 1975. The officer said that Bundy looked afraid for the very first time. At the lineup all three of the witnesses were together, but there were spaces between them. The witnesses were told, "If you recognize anyone, write that number on your slip of paper. If you don't, leave it blank. Put your name on the top.

The eight men in the lineup were brought into the room to their assigned positions. Bundy had his hair cut short and parted on the other side of his head and looked almost like a different person. All of the women identified Bundy. Bundy was arrested and charged with aggravated kidnapping and attempted criminal homicide. Bond was set at $100,000.

On October 30, 1975, the court reduced Bundy's bail to $15,000. This meant that by paying a bonding company 10 percent of the bond ($1,500) the company would post the remainder, and Bundy would be out of jail.

Bundy's attorney advised him to refuse to answer any questions shortly after his arrest and all further meaningful interrogation was effectively blocked.

On November 13, 1975, police from Washington, Utah, Colorado, and California met in Aspen, Colorado, to discuss Theodore Robert Bundy as a possible serial murderer for the crimes in their areas.

Robert Keppel gave his colleagues a personal profile of Bundy. *Only two* of eight witnesses identified Ted Bundy as being the man at Lake Sammamish. The net result of the meeting was that the officers had little evidence with which to work.

On November 20, 1975, Mrs. Bundy paid the money for the bail and her son was released.

On November 21, 1975, the preliminary hearing began which lasted for five days. At the end of the hearing the charge of attempted homicide was dropped. Bundy returned to Washington, but was kept under constant police surveillance. Bundy toyed with the police. He talked with them and offered them coffee.

In January 1976, Bundy's attorneys moved to suppress both the photo array and the lineup identification of Bundy. The lawyers based their arguments upon the "impermissibly suggestive manner" the police used in conducting both the lineup and the photo array. The motion was denied.

On January 28, 1975, Detective Thompson of Utah was advised by the FBI that from the debris vacuumed from Bundy's car, two head hairs were microscopically identical to Caryn Campbell, the Michigan nurse, and a pubic hair matched with Utah victim, Melissa Smith.

A woman identified Bundy as being in the area of the elevator the day of January 12, 1975, when Campbell disappeared.

While preparing the case of the kidnapping of Carol Da Ronch for trial, Prosecutor Dave Yocom was interviewing Bill Edwards, Bundy's drinking buddy. Edwards said that Bundy told him while Bundy was drunk, "Well, I abducted three girls, and they're trying to get me for it." Edward's wife also heard Bundy say that, but neither of them thought it was important because of Bundy's drunken condition. Edwards later changed his story.

On February 23, 1976, the trial by the Court (the trial by jury having been waived) of Bundy began. Bundy was convicted of aggravated kidnapping. Bundy's friends were outraged. They thought Bundy was being railroaded.

During the presentence investigation, Bundy told the investigator that Carol Da Ronch was under extreme pressure to make an indentification. He indicated that she would not have been able to make an identification based upon the three to five minutes she spent with her abductor.

Mrs. Bundy caused letters to be sent to the judge on her son's behalf.

Both prior to and following the trial, the results of the psychological experts were generally indicative of a well intregrated person.

Bundy was questioned by police officers regarding the murder of Caryn Campbell near Aspen, Colorado, on January 12, 1975, with his attorney present. Bundy was vague in his answers and claimed he could not remember things that any innocent person would have quickly acknowledged. Bundy was asked point blank whether he killed Campbell, Bundy denied it by saying, "I certainly didn't kill anyone anywhere, and I—wherever it was—I didn't kill anyone."

Bundy also took to the offensive during the interrogation by lecturing the police on tactics of harassment and attempting to build public sentiment against him.

Dr. Gordon Barland examined the taped interview of Bundy using the Psychological Stress Evaluator, an instrument which is claimed by its inventors of being capable of measuring micro-tremors in the voice when a person lies, but concluded that perhaps the recording was inadequate.

Bundy still strongly maintained his innocence. He told the detective he would appeal the verdict in the Da Ronch case as far as possible.

Following the conviction, the FBI Laboratory made an identification of another hair found in Bundy's VW. It was similar in all respects to Da Ronch's hair and different in none. The microscopic examination of hair is circumstantial only. It is not positive identification like DNA or fingerprint evidence.

Bundy objected to the court about psychological tests being conducted at the Utah State Prison. He wrote to the judge, "This is really a conflict between two people, yourself and me. You *believed* that I was guilty, and I *knew* I wasn't." He did not admit to the psychiatrists and psychologists that he had abducted Da Ronch. Bundy did admit he had not attended the movie, "The Towering Inferno". He excused his lying by calling it a "regretable subterfuge".

On June 30, 1976, Bundy was sentenced to one to fifteen years in prison after he made a tearful appeal about what the criminal justice system was doing to him and how his life was being ruined by it.

Bundy began serving his prison term in July 1976. His attorney whined that the police had railroaded Bundy because they thought that Bundy was involved in other murders. The attorney filed an appeal, but on August 16, 1976, his appeal was denied.

Since Bundy was a convicted felon, The Church of Jesus Christ of Latter Day Saints excommunicated him. The effect of that would bar the further support of Bundy by the Mormons.

While Bundy was in prison, he gave free legal advise to other prisoners, continued to study law, and the Mormon religion. For exercise he lifted weights. He also planned an escape.

In a surprise "shake-down" search of Bundy's cell, Bundy was caught with a forged Social Security card, a map, airline schedules, and a sketch of an Illinois driver's license by guards.

Bundy was indicted in Colorado for the murder of Caryn Campbell, R.N. Bundy fought extradition for a time. But in January 1977, he waived extradition, and on January 28, 1977, he went to Aspen, Colorado, to stand trial.

A week before the then 30 year-old Bundy arrived, his mother had called the Sheriff's office to determine what kind of accommodations her son would have while he was in jail there. Later she would send him a radio.

Bundy was very congenial to everyone at the jail until he asked for something he could not have—then he became quite obnoxious.

Bundy was bound over to stand trial for murder at the preliminary examination. An eye witness who originally stated that she saw Bundy standing near the hotel elevator the night Campbell disappeared could *not* identify Bundy. She identified the undersheriff instead.

Bundy was transferred to a county jail 40 miles away in Glenwood Springs, Colorado. He had moved to act as his own attorney and was permitted to do so. He asked for a haircut and dental care, three meals each day, a typewriter and typing table, use of the law library, clean sheets and pillow cases, file folders, services of his own forensic experts, a private investigator and the right to talk with other prisoners. He usually worked 16 hours per day and walked 3 miles.

CHAPTER XXXIV

BUNDY'S ESCAPE & ACTIVITY IN FLORIDA

Bundy tried to get the police to be lax toward him. He objected to the caution sign over his cell door. Eventually many officers did relax their vigilance. On June 7, 1977, Bundy escaped. He jumped from the second story window of the court house. He was recaptured in a stolen car six days later.

Bundy escaped again on the evening of December 30, 1977. He stole a car from a parking lot that had the keys in it. He had driven the car only a short distance, when the motor stopped. He was able to hitch a ride into Vail, Colorado, where he caught a bus for Denver. He got a plane in Denver and flew to Chicago. He then caught a train for Ann Arbor, Michigan. He arrived there at 10:30 p.m. on New Year's eve. He spent New Year's Day in a bar watching the Rose Bowl game and sipping gin and tonic drinks until he got drunk.

Bundy left Ann Arbor, Michigan, and traveled to Tallahassee, Florida. This is where Florida State University is located. He had one-hundred and sixty ($160) dollars left when he arrived. He obtained a room on campus and began stealing credit cards, a television, a typewriter, a bicycle and other things he needed. The other people living in the apartment later told the police that Bundy changed his appearance daily by wearing glasses with different frames and every day he combed his hair differently.

He met another young woman who lived in his apartment building. They had coffee together and later he took her out for a lavish dinner which included wine. He used a stolen credit card to pay for the meal. He apparently did not try to have sexual relations with her, and he conducted himself like a perfect gentleman during their date.

Shortly after 2:00 a.m. on Sunday, January 15, 1978, at the Chi Omega Sorority House on the campus of Florida State University, Bundy launched another assault on four young women, Karen Chandler, Kathy Kleiner, Lisa Levy, and Margaret Bowman. All of the young women had been severely beaten with a club. (pieces of bark were found in their respective rooms) Levy and Bowman had been strangled to death. The sorority house where this occurred was located four blocks from where Bundy lived in an apartment called "The Oaks".

On the wall in Bowman's room, investigators observed a bloody palm print. A pair of Hanes panty hose with one leg cut away and cut at the band was found. It had been prepared previously to use as a garrote.

Chewing gum was found in Levy's hair. A bloody Clairol bottle was found. The nipple of her left breast had been bitten off. It appeared that the perpetrator had entered through the back door of the sorority house. At the hospital, a laboratory scientist (Winkler) took photographs of bite marks on Levy's buttock while the medical examiner held the ruler next to the bite marks. The medical examiner then cut the tissue which contained the bite marks away and placed it into saline solution. Dr. Wood found blunt trauma to the anal and vaginal cavities along with some odd pinpoint bruises to her uterus. These bruises were caused by the insertion of the Clairol bottle into the vaginal vault.

A young woman was entering the sorority house as Bundy was escaping. The physical description which she gave to the police was that of a dark skinned white male or a light skinned black male, five feet eight inches to five feet ten inches tall, and in his early twenties. He was supposed to be wearing a navy blue jacket, light colored trousers, and a knit ski cap. When the police put the broadcast out to the units on patrol, they added that his clothing should be blood splattered. The witness thought the man whom she had observed was a man who previously dated one of the sorority sisters on a steady basis. He also was a university student. He was the primary suspect. At a subsequent time, that student was asked to submit to a polygraph examination. The student took the polygraph (lie detector) examination, and it was the opinion of the polygraph examiner that he was telling the truth. He was, therefore, cleared of further suspicion of being involved in committing the murders.

While the police were busy dealing with the crisis at the sorority house, four blocks away Bundy entered another apartment building at 431 A Dunwoody Street through a window. This building was also occupied by young women who each had their separate apartments. One of the girls, Cheryl Thomas, had been attacked, and Bundy's mask was found in her bedsheets.

When the news of these heinous crimes were broadcast across the United States, a police officer from the State of Washington called the police in Florida and told them that he thought the guy who murdered the girls was Ted Bundy. Forty investigators were assigned to the case, but after leads began to diminish, the number of officers assigned to work on these murderers were reduced to thirteen.

Six days after the murders, Dr. Richard R. Souveron, a forensic odontologist from Coral Gables, Florida, went to Tallahassee to evaluate the tissue excised from Levy's buttock. Specifically the police wanted to know whether the expert could make an identification with a suspect. The doctor's first concern was the condition of the evidence. Then he learned there had been some mistakes made in the method used to preserve the tissue samples from Miss Levy.

On February 6, 1978, Bundy stole a two-year-old white Dodge van in Tallahassee. He also stole a license plate from another car and put it on the van. He then went to the Jacksonville area.

On February 8, 1978, at the Nathan B. Forrest High School in Jacksonville, Bundy attempted to pick up fourteen-year-old Leslie Parmenter. Her brother also witnessed the incident. They recorded the license number of the van as their policeman father had taught them to do. It was 13D 11300.

On the morning of February 9, 1978, at the Lake City Junior High School, Kimberly Diane Leach a white female, twelve years-old, wearing jeans and a football jersey was in class. She asked to be excused to go to the home room where she said she had left her purse. She disappeared. That same night Bundy was back in Tallahassee.

The day after that (February 11, 1978), he fled the area after a profile of the Chi Omega killer was published in the paper. He attempted to steal a car, but was caught in the act. When the police officer questioned Bundy, he told the officer that he had just come out to get a book and the lock stuck (on the car he was stealing), Bundy had the stolen plate (13D 11300) in his hand. He told the officer he had found the registration plate. As the officer returned to his patrol car to make a radio check on the plate— Bundy ran away.

The morning of February 12, 1978, Bundy stole another car and drove it across town to another parking lot where he stole a ten-year-old Volkswagon. Later that same day he stole another Volkswagon that was six-years-old. Then he headed toward Pensacola, Florida.

On Monday morning (February 13, 1978), Bundy ate at the Crestview Holiday Inn. He paid for the meal with a stolen credit card with a woman's name on it. He was confronted by the waitress. She got the license number on the stolen car he was driving as he was leaving the restaurant. A few minutes later, Bundy stopped and bolted a new set of license plates on the car, but got stuck in the sand. Bundy waited until it was dark. Then he went to a gas station and had a tow truck pull the car out of the sand. Then he continued on his journey into Pensacola.

On Tuesday, February 14, 1978, Bundy spent the day on the beach and left for Mobile, Alabama, that evening. He was part way there when—for some inexplicable reason— he decided to turn around.

CHAPTER XXXV

BUNDY'S ARREST AND CONVICTION IN FLORIDA

At about 1:30 a.m. on the morning of February 15, 1978, Patrolman David Lee observed Bundy driving out of an alley in the stolen Volkswagon. It was past closing time and Patrolman Lee did not recognize the car. He made an inquiry on the vehicle and learned that it was stolen. The officer signaled the driver to pull over to the side of the street. Bundy stopped the car and got out of it. It appeared to the officer that Bundy was going to cooperate. Suddenly, with no warning, Bundy actively resisted arrest, which included Bundy punching the officer in the jaw before the policeman subdued him and placed him into the patrol car. Then Bundy told the officer, "I wish you had just killed me there on the street."

Bundy gave the officer the name of Kenneth Misner. He said he did not mean to hurt the officer. He only wanted to run away. A search of the car which Bundy was driving yielded a pile of stolen credit cards, identification cards, and photographs.

After the newspapers reported the arrest of Misner (Bundy) in Pensacola, the real Misner learned of his "arrest" while he was eating breakfast two hundred miles away. When Bundy was confronted with this information by the police—he still refused to give his real name.

Bundy asked for medical attention for the injuries he sustained at the hands of the Pensacola Patrolman David Lee during his scuffle with him when he tried to escape. Bundy began to rapidly deteriorate both physically and mentally. He was chain smoking cigarettes. He cried as he talked on the telephone and was bent almost double in a chair. Bundy finally then told the officers his real name.

Bundy, the supposed Mormon, asked to speak with a Catholic priest. It is not known what Bundy told the priest, but it is known that the priest told Bundy to refuse to answer police questions and to leave his defense to his attorneys.

In spite of what his attorneys and the priest had told him, Bundy wanted to talk to the police. He told the police he had worn gloves when he stole the cars. Bundy would not talk about the white van, but he would not deny that he had stolen it. As Bundy rambled on, the detective realized that he did not have enough tape to make a complete recording of the interview with Bundy. The three detectives involved in the interview, therefore, had to try to reconstruct what Bundy had told them. The interview lasted all night.

At 7:30 a.m. an attorney from the public defender's office came to the Pensacola Police Department. She wanted to see Bundy. The police told her that Bundy was sleeping—which was not true. Bundy apparently talked a great deal without giving the police any information of real substance about the women he had murdered. It was apparent that he wanted to work out a deal which would: 1) save his life and 2) get him out of the State of Florida. It was equally obvious that the officers were not prepared to negotiate any deals with Ted Bundy.

Bundy was immediately suspected of murdering and beating college women in Tallahassee, and that was where he was taken. At that same time, Colorado authorities were trying to extradite him to face charges on the Caryn Campbell case, but Florida authorities made it quite clear that they were not going to release him to anyone until they were finished with him.

The police continued the investigation by checking credit card records. They also had Bundy's fingerprints on the license plate which had been observed on the stolen white van by the policeman's daughter.

For security reasons, Bundy was placed in an all steel cell with 25 watt lighting. He was not permitted to have any exercise or visitors.

The officer who found the stolen white van took extraordinary measures to protect it for evidence. He had it towed to a secure place where it was vacuumed. Bloodstains were found in it.

The police in Utah sent complete dental records along with x-rays of Theodore Bundy's teeth. They also sent several photographs of him to the police in Florida.

Nita Neary was contacted by Florida authorities in Indiana. She told the Tallahassee investigator that the mug shot (of Bundy) was a "pretty definite resemblance" to the man whom she had observed at the door of the Chi Omega house. The entire conversation of the photo show up was recorded.

A sample of Bundy's blood, hair (from head, legs, and arms) were obtained by court order.

Bundy began to complain again about having to wear heavy leg irons, the lack of exercise and the poor lighting in his cell. He also resented the sheriff opening and photo copying his mail and being denied access to the media.

Bundy asked the court to permit him to spend three days a week in the law library and access to the media, but the court denied his motion.

Bundy had confessed to the theft of the 21 credit cards which he had in his possession when he was apprehended. Witnesses identified Bundy as using a stolen credit card, and a handwriting expert said that the credit card receipts had all been signed by the same person.

On April 7, 1978, the body of Kimberly Leach was found under an old shed about thirty five miles from her home by a Florida State Trooper. Her body was badly decomposed. It was impossible to determine whether she had been sexually assaulted. The cause of death was homicidal violence to the neck region. Bundy refused to talk about Kimberly's death.

On April 27, 1978, a warrant to obtain an impression of Bundy's teeth was executed by officers. Bundy hollered and physically resisted, but his teeth were photographed and waxed impressions obtained anyway.

Another twenty-four year-old suspect who confessed to the murder of a mother and her daughter in Florida was given a polygraph examination on the Chi Omega and Kimberly Leach murders and passed them.

Four months after the murder, the forensic odontologist received the photograph of the bite mark on Lisa Levy's buttock with a ruler in the photograph just below the bite mark. This meant that a comparison could then be made with the impressions taken from Bundy. With the aid of an enlarger, the bite marks were now printed precisely at life size. The photograph—even though many consistencies appeared— was enhanced by using a computer. By comparing configuration, relative heights, and the irregularities of Bundy's teeth with patterns in Levy's skin, the experts came to the opinion that the bite marks were made by Ted Bundy.

Bundy concentrated his efforts on trying to put off his trial for auto theft and credit card forgery. Bundy did not obey the court order to give a sample of his handwriting to the police.

Bundy was kept from the press on the basis of fundamental fairness to "protect Bundy from Bundy". However, on July 27, 1978, the indictment was read to Bundy for two counts of murder and three counts of attempted murder by the sheriff in front of the news media. Bundy used the opportunity to criticize the sheriff for attempting to use the occasion to get votes. Bundy also, once again, strongly denied that he had murdered anyone.

On July 31, 1978, Bundy pled not guilty to the charges in court. On that same date he was indicted in Lake City for the premeditated design to effect the death of Kimberly Diane Leach.

A woman in Seattle, Nancy Hobson, was working two hours each day to clear Bundy. She would talk with him a half hour each week. She tried to convince the news media that the police did not have a case against Bundy. She had schooled herself well in the various inconsistencies that seemed to be present.

Bundy stalled the trial by stating that he had not had time to prepare for it. Bundy had obtained discovery rights—which might be compared to playing a game of poker and getting to see what kind of hand your opponent is holding. There were 119 possible witnesses for Bundy. Bundy summoned the witnesses to a holding room at the jail for depositions—testimony under oath subject to cross examination. Bundy frequently disagreed with his attorneys.

Bundy got the judge disqualified due to the excessively "intolerable adversary atmosphere" between the defendant and the judge.

During the pre-trial hearing the defense planned to attack the bite mark evidence in three ways. First, they would try to discredit the bite mark analysis. They didn't expect much success since the appellate courts have regularly upheld such evidence. Second, to attack the known evidence specimens taken from Bundy on the basis of the lack of probable cause for the search warrant. Part of this depended upon their ability to discredit Nita Neary. And third, to attack the methods of the doctor who made the match.

The defense attack plan failed. Two orthodontists testified that the bite marks on Levy's buttocks were made by Ted Bundy.

The defense witness countered that the evaluation of bite mark evidence was subjective. He produced three other sets of teeth. The prosecutor had their expert examine the three sets of dental models. The People's expert was of the opinion that none of them were consistent with the bite marks found on Miss Levy.

Judge Cowart admitted the bite mark testimony along with other relevant items, such as the photographs, into evidence. There were eleven other states that also admitted such evidence.

On May 31, 1979, Bundy was given the opportunity to plead guilty to second degree murder—which would have kept him out of the electric chair. At first it appeared he would accept the offer but he changed his mind saying, "I know that I face death if I am convicted... but there are some principles that are more important than the fear of death. I simply am not guilty."

Probably to drag out the proceedings, Bundy fired his attorneys, claiming irreconcilable conflict.(15.296)

Bundy's attorneys had petitioned the court to have Bundy examined to determine if he were competent to stand trial. He was examined by Emmanuel Tanay of Detroit and Hervey M. Cleckley. Cleckley was the world's leading authority on the psychopathic and sociopathic personality disorders. Both psychiatrists believed Bundy was competent to stand trial.

Due to pre-trial publicity in the Tallahassee area—the trial was moved to Miami. At the start of the trial Bundy introduced many motions. Among them were: 1) the lighting conditions in his cell were poor, 2) the television camera in the court room, and 3) funds for an expert to help with the jury selection.

The judge apparently thought—probably correctly—that the defense was dragging out the proceedings. He ordered night sessions. The jury consisted of seven men and five women. The majority of them were black, middle-aged and middle-class people. The trial lasted for five weeks. The jury was sequestered—they were not at liberty to go home and their conversation and information sources were restricted—during all of that time. At the outset Bundy was pleased with the jury selection. He thought it was quite likely (and he was correct) that the foreman of the jury would be Rudolph Treml, an engineer.

After the trial began, and the jury was sequestered, dozens of depositions were made public for the first time. Many had been sealed for over a year. The press was particularly interested in the depositions taken from the three detectives who stayed up all night and interrogated Bundy after his arrest in Pensacola. Detective Norman Chapman recalled that Bundy had told them, "Fantasies are controlling part of my life." Bundy had told Chapman, "...In order to control my fantasies I had to do things which were very much against society although the act itself was always a 'downer.'"

Bundy had told them that his "problem" surfaced for the first time in Seattle. Bundy said he was walking toward his girlfriend's house. He indicated that there was a girl on the street ahead of him that aroused a feeling in him that he had never had before. *He wanted to possess her by whatever means necessary.* He followed her home until she entered the house—then he never saw her again.

Bundy became a voyeur while attending the University of Puget Sound Law School. While others who rode with him were in class taking notes—Bundy was peeking in windows.

Bundy told the detectives that he liked Volkswagons because they were cheap to drive and the seats would come out (so he could carry bodies easier). Bundy said sometimes the cargo he transported was damaged and sometimes it was not.

Bundy was able to get by with very little sleep—usually only three hours per night—and he used the early morning hours to drive long distances.

Bundy would not confess to the Carol Da Ronch kidnapping. He said he had worked hard on the appeal and did not want to ruin it. He did say regarding Da Ronch, that she was "lucky she got away".

Bundy believed that he had learned to control "the problem" while he was in jail in Colorado and in Utah. This belief made him think he had conditioned himself to control the problem in event he could escape. He was confident that he could survive in the outside world. Bundy admitted after he had escaped from the jail the problem resurfaced. "It wasn't controllable. I guess I have a fool for a doctor." (Like a lawyer has a fool for a client when he chooses to represent himself). He told the investigators that his activities extended over six states and involved victims in three digits (at least 100 victims). Bundy wished to avoid publicity.

When Bundy went on trial for the murders of Lisa Levy and Margaret Bowman at the Chi Omega sorority house, the prosecutor's case rested upon three things: 1) the eye witness identification by Nita Neary, 2) the bite marks found on Lisa Levy's buttock, and 3) the two head hairs found in the panty hose mask.

Bundy argued with his lawyers and took an active role in defending himself. He obviously was extremely confident of his own abilities. Nonetheless, Bundy was convicted.

Bundy continued to deny his guilt until a few hours before he was finally executed—nearly eleven years after he committed the murders.

A witness who saw Kimberly Leach being led to a white van thought the man with her was an angry parent. A rare fiber with four colors from the van's carpet was found on Kimberly's jersey and on Bundy's blazer. B type blood—the same type of blood that Kimberly Leach had—was found in the van (13.326). It was for the murder of Kimberly Leach that Bundy was ultimately executed.(1.0)

CHAPTER XXXVI

ASPECTS OF THE CRIMINAL INVESTIGATION

VEHICLE USED

Bundy preferred to use Volkswagon "Beetles". He gave as his reasons for this that the car was very economical to operate. It could travel for long distances on a tank of gas. He also liked the way the front seat could be easily removed. Based upon what he had told the detectives who interviewed him, he clearly implied that some of the victims he transported in the Volkswagen were dead or dying.(15.302)

The author has owned three "Beetles". From personal experience on fishing trips, the author has learned that they are capable of crossing very rough terrain, like miniature tanks.

WITNESSES

Carol Da Ronch was the key witness who brought the focus of the investigation squarely upon Bundy. Posing as a police officer, Bundy had tried to kidnap her, but she escaped from his car.

Nita Neary observed Bundy leaving the Chi Omega Sorority House after he had assaulted four women—killing two of them by strangulation.

Two of eight witnesses (25 percent) identified Bundy as the man who was overheard telling a young woman his name was "Ted" at the beach of Lake Sammamish in Washington.

One witness identified Bundy as standing by the elevator in the ski lodge in Colorado on January 12, 1975, in connection with the murdered Michigan nurse (Caryn Campbell). However, she was not able to identify him in court.

CRIMINAL INVESTIGATION

Early in the case, it appeared that Bundy had not provided the police many clues that caused the investigation to be focused upon him. This was despite the fact that he picked his victims up at a crowded beach where there were hundreds of people who had seen him.

It appeared that the multi-agency meetings with representatives of law enforcement agencies from several states were very helpful in providing an exchange of information.

The focus of the investigation really zeroed in on Bundy after Carol Da Ronch escaped from him. Bundy was very confident and was sure of himself. He permitted the police to search his apartment and car. In the apartment, the police found a Colorado map and a Colorado brochure. Yet Bundy claimed he was never there. The police also found a credit card receipt. Using the number on the receipt, they learned Bundy had not only been in Colorado, but had refueled a short distance from the ski lodge from where Campbell disappeared.

The investigative work of both the Utah State Trooper and the Pensacola City Police Patrolman was outstanding. After Bundy tried to "punch out" the Florida police officer, the beating he received by the officer who was attempting to subdue him, seemed to have a saluatory effect upon Bundy. Following that incident, Bundy was not his usual cocky self. It was at that time that he appeared to be vulnerable to a good interrogator.

The policeman's children who obtained the license number of the stolen van which Bundy was driving proved to be extremely valuable. This action should stand as a tribute to their father who had taught them to do that. The children put Bundy in the area where Kimberly Leach was murdered.

The officer who caught Bundy in the act of trying to steal another car, with the stolen license plate in his hand, also did well to protect the plate for prints. Bundy's latent prints were found on that plate.

The crime scenes were generally processed according to standard police operating procedures. One of the most valuable actions taken was the photographs of a bite mark on the victim's buttock with a ruler below the bite mark. Ordinarily such photographs are taken by medical examiners or their assistants, not by the police scientists (re: the Chi Omega attack).

The hairs that were found in Bundy's car from Campbell and Smith were significant. The hair found in the panty hose mask were also significant. These hairs were from Bundy.

EVIDENCE

The evidence available has been previously mentioned, but it will be repeated here to aid the reader.

Bundy's girlfriend said that Bundy drove a tan Volkswagon. His name was "Ted". He had bandage material (plaster of paris) in his medical cabinet. He was not with her when all of the victims disappeared.

Two eye witnesses (of eight) identified Bundy at Lake Sammamish State Park in Washington. The witnesses provided information for a police artist's sketch which was a remarkable likeness to Ted Bundy.

One of the witnesses overheard Bundy tell a woman that his name was "Ted" (at Lake Sammamish).

An eye witness (Da Ronch) whom Bundy tried to kidnap while he was posing as a police officer, later identified him in a police lineup.

Police found two hairs in Bundy's car (after Bundy had thoroughly cleaned it). One was similar in all respects to Campbell's hair and the other was similar in all respects to Melissa Smith's pubic hair.

Bundy gave the police an exculpatory statement. He claimed that he was attending a movie on the day a crime had been committed. A check by the police determined such a movie was not showing at that particular time.

The identification of Bundy's Volkswagon was made by Da Ronch whom Bundy kidnapped and attempted to murder as she escaped. Carol Da Ronch identified the car from a long scratch in the door. Bundy had painted over the scratch without sanding it down.

A Utah State Trooper searched Bundy's car after Bundy tried to flee to avoid arrest. The trooper found a pair of handcuffs and a tire iron with one end taped.

Bundy was observed attending a play. Bundy left the play at about the same time as a victim. Bundy reentered the auditorium near the end of the play in a disheveled state, and he was breathing heavily. The victim was never seen alive again.

A credit card receipt that was found in Bundy's apartment indicated that Bundy was lying when he claimed that he had never been in Colorado where one of the women (Campbell) was killed.

An eyewitness identified the profile of Bundy as the man who was leaving the Chi Omega Sorority House where two women were murdered.

Bundy had bitten a victim (Levy) whom he had murdered. A photograph of the bite mark with a ruler in it was taken. This evidence was very damaging to Bundy during the trial.

Bundy lost his panty hose mask in the bed of one of the victims. This mask had two of Bundy's head hairs in it.

Bundy lost his chewing gum in one of the victim's hair.

Eye witnesses identified Bundy as the person who used stolen credit cards in the area where a victim was murdered. It was the opinion of a document examiner that the signature used on all the forged receipts was signed by the same person—Bundy.

Bundy was caught in the act of trying to steal another car. He gave the officer the stolen plate with his latent prints on it. Then he fled on foot. The number on the plate was the same number the police officer's children had noted.

POLICE ACTIONS TAKEN

Essentially, standard police investigative techniques were used by the police while they were investigating the several murders that made up this case.

WHAT LED TO PERPETRATOR'S ARREST

Bundy posed as a police officer. He tricked a young woman into getting into his car at a shopping mall on the subterfuge that someone had been seen breaking into her car. She was very suspicious. She asked him to show her his police identification. As they were traveling down the road, supposedly going to the police station, where the thief was being held, Bundy snapped a handcuff on her wrist. They struggled. As she tried to escape, Bundy accidently put the other cuff on the same wrist. She (Carol Da Ronch) jumped from the car and fled with Bundy chasing her while trying to murder her with a tire iron which had been taped around one end of it.

Bundy was subsequently apprehended by a Utah State Trooper when Bundy attempted to flee from a residential area at night by driving without his headlights turned on. The trooper found handcuffs and a taped tire iron in Bundy's car.

Bundy was ultimately convicted on the Da Ronch case after she identified Bundy in a lineup. He subsequently escaped from Colorado where he was going to stand trial for the murder of a Michigan nurse. Bundy then went to Florida via Chicago and Ann Arbor, Michigan.

Shortly after midnight on February 15, 1978—after closing hours in Pensacola, Florida, a patrolman noticed an orange Volkswagon in an alley. The driver aroused his suspicions so he file checked the vehicle and it had been reported stolen. The driver, Bundy, resisted arrest by trying to knock the officer unconscious. This resulted in Bundy being roughly handled by the officer, and Bundy was ultimately subdued. He was found to have a large number of stolen credit cards and other pieces of identification. He gave an alias, claiming he was a Florida track star. Bundy was, at that time on the FBI's 10 Most Wanted List. He was identified by his fingerprints.

Trace evidence linked Bundy to other murders in Florida that he had committed.

CHAPTER XXXVII

ARRESTED PERSON

Theodore Robert Bundy aka Theodore Robert Cowell, Theodore Robert Nelson, Kenneth Misner, Chris Hagen, and Ralph Miller, was born out of wedlock at a special home for unwed mothers on November 24, 1946, in Burlington, Vermont. His mother's name was Eleanor Louise Cowell. His father's name is unknown, but it may have been Lloyd Marshall, a graduate from Pennsylvania State University. Marshall was a veteran who was born in 1916. Bundy learned his mother and father were not married from his own research in 1969. Bundy was very close the his maternal grandfather, whom he called "Father". He called his mother "Eleanor". He was brought up referring to her as his older sister.

The early years of Bundy's life were spent on the Northwest side of Philadelphia. At first Bundy used his mother's last name, Cowell. Later by court order, Eleanor Louise Cowell had her son's last name changed to Nelson.

During 1950, Eleanor Louise Cowell moved across the country to Tacoma, Washington. She was apparently active in church affairs because she met John Bundy at a Methodist Church social gathering and married him on May 19, 1951. John Bundy adopted Theodore Nelson, and he was then called Theodore Bundy.

Bundy played football when he was ten and eleven years old. In Junior High School, he participated in track and won a bronze medal in hurdles. He was involved in several activities, but never stayed with anything for an extended period of time. He played in Little League Baseball. He was a member of the Boy Scouts of America. Bundy was very self conscious when he showered after athletic events. He would not shower in an open area with the other boys. Bundy was also on the student council, and the high school cross-country team. He did not have a steady girlfriend in high school.

Bundy had a "B" average in high school. One teacher described him as being highly motivated. He had planned to attend college and go to law school.

Bundy met an older student at the University of Washington. She came from a wealthy background and may have used her money to intimidate him. This beautiful woman rejected Bundy which resulted in a very traumatic period during his life.

Bundy's initial major was in intensive Chinese. He had obtained a scholarship to study that subject. However, he apparently lost interest and changed his major subject area.

Eventually, Bundy graduated with a degree in psychology in 1972 from the University of Washington.

Bundy worked in political campaigns. He posed as a newspaper reporter. At public meetings, Bundy would rise and ask embarrassing questions about the previous love affairs of the democratic candidate.

Bundy also was employed by Seattle's Crime Prevention Advisory Commission. He reviewed Washington's hitchhiking law and worked on a white collar crime project. He had also became familiar with police reports of violent assaults. He was a finalist for the Director's job, but another person was chosen instead. Bundy then started to work for the King County Law and Justice Planning Office. He worked on a project dealing with recidivism and the effectiveness of correctional institutions.

In 1973, Bundy apprehended a purse snatcher in a mall.

During the summer of 1974, Bundy worked in the State Department of Emergency Services in Washington.

No one could call Bundy physically lazy. He worked in a lumber mill as a fork lift driver. He stacked boxes at a Safeway store. He bussed dishes in a hotel. He parked cars at a yacht club. He worked as a legal messenger, a shoe salesman, a cook's helper, a dishwasher, in a medical supply firm, a security guard, and later, he was the night manager of a dormitory while he was in Utah. He was fired from this latter job because he was drunk.

In 1974, Bundy was finally accepted by the University of Utah Law School. He had applied three times before he was finally admitted. He did not study hard. He did not socialize with his classmates. He did become well acquainted with his professors. In law school, his grades were mainly B's and C's.

He had a sexual relationship with Wanda Handcock who lived in the same apartment building.

Also in Utah, Bundy was baptized and joined the Mormon Church (The Church of the Latter Day Saints of Jesus Christ). He taught in their Sunday School.

On Saturday nights, however, he smoked marijuana and Winston cigarettes and drank with Bill Edwards who lived in the same apartment building as Bundy. That routine continued until one morning he slipped into Edward's apartment unannounced and awoke one of Mrs. Edward's lady friends from her sleep by pinching her crotch. Bundy tried to keep his religious activities separate from his activities in the apartment where he lived.

Bundy's friends in the State of Washington, in the Mormon Church, and in the apartment where he lived, initially believed Bundy was innocent and would be ultimately cleared of all criminal charges. Bob Keppel, an investigator from King County Washington, described Bundy as a self-serving manipulator who lied at will, stole goods from his employers, and stole his girlfriend's cars.

Bundy's mother could not bring herself to believe that her son confessed to some of the murders he had committed right before he was executed. She still referred to him as "our beloved son".(12.0)

At the time of his first arrest, Bundy was described as a white male, 145-175 pounds, six feet tall. He had blue eyes and brown wavy hair.

After Bundy was convicted of kidnapping Carol Da Ronch on June 22, 1975, the psychological report on him was received by the court. The report was divided into positive and negative lists. On the positive side were "high intelligence, no severely traumatizing influences in childhood or adolescence, few distortions in relationship with mother and stepfather, no serious defects in physical development habits, school adjustments, adequate interest in hobbies and recreational pursuits, average environmental pressures and responsibilities" and "no previous attacks of mental illness".

On the negative side the report indicated, "According to the psychological and psychiatric evaluations, when one attempts to understand Mr. Bundy—he becomes evasive." "The defendant (Bundy) is somewhat threatened by people unless he feels he can structure the relationship...passive-aggressive features were also evident. There was hostility observed on the subject's part directed toward the diagnostic personnel, even though Bundy would carefully point out that it was not aimed directly at those responsible for his evaluation."

Regarding Bundy's scores on the MMPI, they appeared to reflect Bundy as having a "relatively sane profile" but indicated "a fairly strong conflict was evidenced in the testing profile, that being the subject's fairly strong dependency on women yet his need to be independent. Mr. Bundy would like a close relationship with females, but is fearful of being hurt by them. In addition, there were indications of general anger, and more particularly, well-masked anger toward women."

Bundy was supremely confident of his mental ability, and he thought the police were dumb. At the Oaks where Bundy lived after escaping from Colorado—Bundy told another man during a drinking spree that he (Bundy) was a lot smarter than the police and could get away with anything he wanted.

CHAPTER XXXVIII

OBSERVATIONS

Bundy was probably the most vulnerable shortly after his arrest by Patrolman Lee of the Pensacola Police Department. It was fairly obvious that Bundy thought the police were intellectually no match for him and he could commit any crimes he so desired. He felt quite confident that he could talk his way out of any problem with which he was confronted.

For example, when interrogated about his activities on the night a crime was committed, he thought if he'd tell the "dumb cops" he was at a movie—they would never check it out, but they did. Again, when he was questioned about the stolen license plate in his hand by the patrolman when he was about to steal another car—he simply told the officer he found it. When the officer ran a file check on the plate, he discovered it was stolen. Bundy fled. And when Bundy was found in possession of handcuffs in his trunk—he told the officer he found them in a dump.

Like many serial murderers, Bundy appeared relaxed and cooperative when police questioned him. Bundy's denials used strong words,(e.g. steal and murder rather than take or kill), but weren't totally specific. For example, he told a Mormon friend, "I've stolen some stuff in my life, but have never assaulted *Anybody*, kidnapped *Anybody*, or murdered *Anybody*." "Murder" is a strong word. It is not used often by the real murderer, but Bundy used it. But when Bundy talked about not doing these things— notice that he did not use Carol Da Ronch's name— he used "Anybody". Bundy could have been and probably was playing a mental game here. While he did kidnap Da Ronch and tried to murder her, he did not kidnap and try to kill a person whom he called "Anybody". The point the author would like to make is this. Most criminals are vague, defensive, and leak non verbal cues that indicate deception. Most serial murders of the "organized" type are talkative, cooperative (initially) make specific denials, and sometimes use very strong words to describe their criminal acts. And there is little defensive behavior. All in all—from just talking with them—they look and sound like truth tellers. They also appear completely normal. They do have a natural inclination to get out of trouble by using an alibi. And the best way to trip them up is to *always* check the alibi of any suspect. And do not be taken in by their polite, clean cut manner.

It was noted that one of the agencies turned over the remains of one of the victims to a university professor. The police agency later requested the Federal Bureau of Investigation's Crime Laboratory to evaluate the evidence, but they would not do it because there was a possibility that the evidence was contaminated.

Time and time again polygraph examiners played a significant role during these investigations by clearing innocent suspects. For example, all of Julie Cunningham's boyfriends were examined and successfully passed polygraph examinations. Denise Oliverson's boyfriend was given an examination and passed it. And another very good suspect, Jake Teppler, was given examinations on the murders of Julie Cunningham, Denise Oliverson, and Caryn Campbell and passed them.

Denise Oliverson's bicycle should have been processed for latent prints (in Grand Junction.) There was no indication this was done. The bicycle should also have been carefully protected against loss.

When the trooper apprehended Bundy in Utah, Bundy had handcuffs, a taped tire iron, strips of a white sheet, and a rope. Those things are not typical burglar tools. The fact that Bundy carried these items tends to show that he planned these crimes in advance. The only thing that was required was a victim.

Bundy even gave officers permission to search his Salt Lake City apartment and photograph his Volkswagon. The lesson here is that the police should take full advantage of the cocky attitude displayed by the serial murderer. Have the "Permission to Search Form" ready to sign, pull the form out and have them sign it. Of course, if reasonable cause exists and there is time to get a search warrant—that is what should be done. Why take the chance and risk letting a murderer escape because of some technicality? The courts traditionally have placed a heavy burden upon the police to show that any waiver of rights has been intelligently made. Therefore, if the murderer was drunk or under the influence of drugs it could be argued that he was in no condition to make an intelligent waiver. Or if the murderer lacked the mental capacity to understand what was taking place—that issue could be raised. One of the few things that an investigator can count on in a serial murder case is that there will be a legal challenge at any time when the police conduct a search where any evidence is discovered that would incriminate the murderer. The moral is, whenever possible—get a warrant. Of course, the warrant itself could be challenged—but it is much more difficult.

It bears repeating—whenever a warrant is obtained—if at all possible execute it quickly and allow the suspect as little advanced warning as possible that would permit him time to dispose of incriminating evidence. In addition, before executing the warrant, give some thought to what else might be found there of an incriminating nature. In other words, keep an open mind and keep your eyes open for anything else present and avoid "tunnel vision".

If reasonable cause exists, this writer suggests that a warrant be obtained and executed before the serial murder suspect is questioned. Time and time again the serial murderer is questioned—then released. This gives him time to get rid of any incriminating evidence he might have in his car or dwelling. Then, sometimes, a police surveillance has been placed on the suspect, and the suspect has been forewarned and, therefore, it yields no results.

The author suggests that the surveillance be placed on the suspect before he is interviewed—this writer would suggest that such interviews be conducted in a way that would not overly arouse his suspicions. Remember, this criminal type thinks the police are so dumb that they can't catch him anyway so one should take full advantage of that attitude.

Again—if a surveillance team is used—this is no time for rank amateurs. Send in your first string against him. If that isn't done—the chances are great they will be "burned" (identified as police officers) in the first few hours.

Regarding the lineup conducted on Bundy, one should think about the problem that can occur when all the witnesses are in close proximity to one another and are viewing the lineup at the same time. Isn't it true that if the suspect does something during the lineup, if one person is viewing it—possibly only that person's identification is effected? If all the witnesses are watching it—such an act could impact upon all of the witnesses.

For example, during a lineup this writer was conducting on a serial murder case, the murderer asked this writer, "You think I killed all those girls don't you?" He thought the witnesses were already behind the one way mirror and by saying that—he would ruin the entire lineup. The fact, however, was that none of the witnesses had been brought into the room to view the lineup.

The instructions which preceded the lineup during which Ted Bundy was identified were excellent. The witnesses were told, "If you recognize anyone, write that number down on your slip of paper. If you don't—leave it blank. Put your name at the top." Since it is frequently disputed what these instructions were—it is recommended that the instructions be written down and then recorded as they are read. Before the lineup actually begins, advise the counsel representing the suspect that the lineup is about to begin. As mentioned elsewhere—the witnesses should be brought in one at a time and not be permitted to form some sort of identification by consensus.

It should be noted that Bundy tried to convince the pre-sentence investigator that the girl (Da Ronch) was being pressured by the police to identify him as the perpetrator.

It is remarkable that John Norman Collins also used very similar language when he claimed that the police were under social pressure to find a scapegoat for the series of killings that had occurred in the Ann Arbor-Ypsilanti area. Collins said the women at the wig shop were under a lot of pressure to make an identification.

Observe Bundy's efforts to escape. After he had escaped once by jumping out a court house window and was recaptured, he was successful again when he was under more stringent security. How did he do it? First, some person or persons unmentioned or unknown provided Bundy with enough money to pay for his escape. Bundy flew from Colorado to Chicago, took a train to Ann Arbor, Michigan, and then took a bus to Florida. Officials at the jail thought Bundy only had about seven dollars on his person.

Dame Fortune (or the devil) continued to smile upon Bundy the night of his escape. He found clothing in the jailer's apartment that he changed into before he stepped out of the building after he had dropped from the ceiling of the jail into the adjoining apartment.

Besides money, someone had also supplied Bundy with some type of saw blade that he used to cut the welds on the overhead light fixture.

What can we learn from this escape that will help us in our future dealings with serial murderers? Well—we should recall that serial murderers seem to have a propensity to escape or try to escape. Bundy, Albert De Salvo (the Boston Strangler), John Collins (Michigan Murders), Gerald Gallego, William Heirens, Donald Miller and Chris Wilder are a few of the serial murderers who escaped, attempted to escape, or fled to avoid arrest. Serial murderers are high escape risks and should be treated accordingly.

Corrections officers should be aware that serial killers will act cooperatively and friendly to get guards to relax their vigilance. Serial killers may be manipulative both outside and inside of jail. Note how Bundy complained about the food as his excuse for not eating. His real goal was to lose weight so he could slide through the opening in the ceiling when the light was removed. Notice also how he complained about the noise and the poor jail conditions, probably *ad infinitum* and *ad nauseam* until he was transferred into the cell at the end of the row with the light he could remove. Note how by not eating—when he was served breakfast and didn't get up to eat it—they didn't become suspicious. This provided Bundy with valuable time to get out of the area. High escape risk prisoners should not be permitted to have maps, an accumulation of food, flashlights, insect repellent, a compass, and their clothing should be "hunter orange" coveralls and slippers. They should be dressed for inside the jail, not outside it. A new photograph should be taken of the prisoner every 6 months or sooner if he drastically changes his appearance. They should be subjected to frequent shake down searches and to constant surveillance with closed circuit television cameras. They should not be permitted to have any money, but be issued script instead with which to buy things.

Some might say that these people are presumed innocent until they are proven guilty and should be treated accordingly. But let us remember also that after Bundy escaped, he murdered two more women and a girl and brutally beat several others.

There must be a balancing between societies' interest to be safe from the predatory attacks from an evil monster, who appears in human form and likeness, and the civil rights of the monster before he has been found guilty.

Whenever the criminal justice system turns such an evil force loose upon society—either through early release, or by any other means whereby he is back on the street, or when a police officer is negligent in carrying out his duties and fails to conduct an appropriate inquiry into a tip that he was given on a serial murderer, and thus through his failure to do his duty—the murderer avoids arrest, or where corrections officers drop their guard and allow themselves to be manipulated—all of these—those who fail to do their jobs have to live with themselves when another daughter, wife, or mother is murdered by one of these devils masquerading as human beings.

Note the difference between Bundy's real description and how the witness described him as he was leaving the Chi Omega sorority house in Tallahassee, Florida. She thought Bundy was either a dark complected Caucausian or a light skinned Negro. Bundy, of course, was neither. He was quite probably wearing a pantyhose mask over his head that made him appear darker than he really was at the time. Notice also the difference in the age description. The witness had Bundy in his early twenties. In fact he was in his early thirties—about a ten year difference. Even the height she gave was off between two to four inches. She thought Bundy was shorter than he actually was.

Yet because of identification of Bundy's teeth marks on Lisa Levy's buttock, his hair found in the ski mask in another apartment, and his residence about a half mile away from the sorority house, plus his activities in Utah—there can be little doubt that Bundy murdered the girls—and the jury so found.

But the lesson for police investigators again is to be very cautious in accepting for fact the description that a witness gives, not only of suspects, but vehicles as well. Great distinctions were apparently made in this case because one witness said the vehicle was a yellow Volkswagon and another said it was tan. The fact is that some people have better powers of observation. Some people can also discriminate between colors better than others.

A taped statement should be taken from each and every witness. The witness should never be pushed into saying something he really doesn't mean. The witness' statement should be transcribed so it can be reviewed quickly by the witness to refresh his memory years later and to enable investigators to check portions of the statement without listening to the statement in its entirety.

Police reports should also accurately reflect what the witness has said. For example, there is a tremendous difference between saying something looked like something and that it was that something. In other words, to say that the perpetrator was driving a vehicle that looked like a Ford Mustang and that the vehicle the suspect drove was a Ford Mustang have two different meanings. Why provide the defense attorney with ammunition to use against you at trial?

With regard to any task force dealing with serial murderers, this is not the place for rank novice investigators. There is too much at stake. If a task force is comprised of investigators from several different organizations, the task force commander should evaluate the experience level of the persons assigned. Tips that appear to be the most promising should be assigned to investigators who have a demonstrated track record for good work and thoroughness.

The detailed organization of the task force and the manner in which tips should be handled is beyond the scope of this book. Major Dan Myre, Michigan State Police (retired) wrote a practical book on the subject called *Detectives* vs. *Death* to which this writer made a small contribution relating to the investigation of the victims of these crimes. Another very important book was published in 1988. It has been called The *Multi-Agency Investigative Team Manual.* Its object was to put together an operational manual to be used by the team investigating crimes committed by a serial killer. This research was supported by the National Institute of Justice and was made possible through the cooperation of officers throughout the United States who have actually been confronted with the problem of dealing with a serial murderer. The effort to publish the manual was spearheaded by The Criminal Justice Center at Sam Houston University in Huntsville, Texas.

Note the error that was made by the medical examiner. He put the flesh containing the bite marks made by Bundy into a saline solution when the flesh should have been preserved by freezing it. This resulted in the tissue losing its form and made it of little value for identification purposes.

Another error was made when no smear for saliva over the area where the bite marks were found was obtained. Sometimes when the perpetrator is a secretor—his blood type can be determined, and now possibly a DNA fingerprint can be obtained. And the final problem the medical examiner had was the film in his camera jammed so he could not obtain the pictures. It was indeed very fortunate that the police laboratory scientist working the crime scene and the autopsy did take a good photograph of the bite marks with a ruler in the picture that made it possible to make an analysis of the bite marks with the known samples taken from Bundy.

Another instructive error was made when Bundy's gum was found in Lisa Levy's hair and was not properly preserved. It had been submitted to a seriologist who cut the gum in half. It was believed this could have contained an impression of one of Ted Bundy's teeth which would have been very beneficial.

The authors of one book referred to the identification of a criminal by his teeth marks as something new which it is not. In fact it is relatively old. Harry Soderman, D.S. and John J. O'Connell wrote as long ago as 1952 in their classic work, *Modern Criminal Investigation* published by Funk and Wagnallls Company, on the identification of teeth marks.(14.180-183)

Observe the trial tactics that were used by Bundy and his attorneys. The strategy in this case was to file as many pre-trial motions as possible. It is natural that people tend to forget detailed facts over a period of time. Also witnesses tend to move away so they aren't available to testify.

When the jury was being selected, it was the defense strategy to use social scientists to assist in seating a jury that was not likely to send Bundy to the electric chair. Apparently they didn't do a very good job. One of the men they selected ultimately became the foreman of the jury. He was an engineer. As has been reported elsewhere—part of the People's strategy in selecting what we considered to be an intelligent move was to select as many engineers, chemists, and people who deal in the hard sciences because we believed that these people were best prepared through their training to reach good, sound, logical conclusions.

It was the strategy in the trial of Bundy to have the jury spend a considerable period of time with Bundy. It was their strategy that the jury would then come to see Ted Bundy as a human being and not the monster that he really was.

Finally another portion of their strategy was to take their anti-death penalty crusade directly to the public via the press in an effort to keep Bundy from being executed, in event he was found guilty. Based upon the high number of people who gathered outside the prison the morning Bundy was finally executed, and the cheers that were evoked from them upon hearing the news that Ted Bundy was no longer among the living—one would have to conclude that this defense stratagem failed as well.

With regard to Bundy's interrogation after he was apprehended by officer David Lee, it was noted that he was interrogated by three investigators. In this writer's experience which has involved the interrogations of literally hundreds of criminals, it is best if only one officer conducts the interrogation. Detective First Lieutenant John Fiedler, who also has had considerable experience in conducting interrogations in many major investigations is of the opinion that it is good to have a second investigator in the interrogation room providing he does not interrupt the principal interrogator's line of questioning.

John Reid who successfully interrogated William Heirens wrote about the importance of this principle after Heirens was going to confess his crimes, but changed his mind because there were too many people present (see pages 144 and 145 of *Lie Detection and Criminal Interrogation* published by Williams and Wilkins). Heirens finally did confess on another day after the number of people present was sharply reduced.(5.144-145)

Observe the MMPI (a personality inventory test) report information stated that Bundy had a strong dependency on women yet he had a real need to be independent of them. That is remarkable because as one examines the information on these types of cases, that strong dependency on females is found in several other serial murderers as well.

For example, John Norman Collins' had his car in his mother's name. When the police first interviewed him after the second woman was murdered—according to his friend, Arnie Davis, who lived in the same rooming house—Collins called his mother and told her, "I'm in a lot of trouble."

Later, after Collins was arrested, Collins' mother fired his attorney for setting up a private polygraph test and hired attorneys who had previously represented reputed Mafia figures from the Detroit Metropolitan area.

Ed Kemper used his mother's car with her university sticker on it to pick up girls he later murdered. He lived with his mother and ultimately killed her.

De Salvo's significant other was his German born wife. She was incapable of meeting De Salvo's excessive sexual demands. De Salvo was unable to please her although he did extensive physical work around the house. De Salvo's wife always insisted that he return home for dinner at a certain time, and rarely was he late—not even when he had just murdered someone. De Salvo said that his wife made him feel like dirt.

Gerald Gallego was highly dependent upon Charlene Williams. She obtained several victims for him and actually helped him dispose of the evidence from the murders. When they were "on the run", Gallego followed her around like a puppy dog.

Donald Miller from Michigan was very much in love with his girlfriend, Martha Sue Young. He wanted to marry her. *She rejected him*, and he killed her. He then raped and murdered several other women in the mid-Michigan area.

Kenneth Bianchi's real mother abandoned him. His adopted mother doted upon him. His first wife left him after they were married for less than a year. Bianchi told friends he felt betrayed. He met another young woman, Kelli, who gave him venereal disease. She claimed she was raped at a Ramada Inn in Denver, Colorado. She made no report to the police and did not tell Bianchi about it until he got the disease. Again he felt betrayed. He apparently thought a good deal of her because he sent her flowers and wrote poems to her. At times, however, she had to get away from him to get "an emotional break".

It appeared to the author that Bianchi was extremely dependent upon Kelli for emotional support. Yet he believed she had betrayed him, and instead of lashing out at her, struck out against other young women.

Christopher Wilder was also *rejected* by a beautiful young lady. He wanted to marry her, but she thought he was too old for her. Like Miller—she was the first of several women he murdered. There was, however, no indication that he was dependent upon her in any way.

REFERENCES

1. Brokaw, Tom. *NBC News* (special broadcast on Bundy's execution) New York, New York: January 23, 1989.

2. Davis, Les. "Criminal Sexuality" F.B.I. and Kansas City, Missouri Police Department. Law Enforcement Satellite Training Network. Kansas City, MO: September 30, 1987.

3. Gumble, Brian. *NBC Today* (Regarding impact of pornography on serial murderers) A panel discussion with Dr. Park Dietz and Dr. Abel. New York, New York: January 24, 1989.

4. Horvath, Imre. *Murder: No Apparent Motive.* (movie) 1987.

5. Inbau, Fred E. and John E. Reid, *Lie Detection and Criminal Interrogation.* The Williams and Wilkins Company, Baltimore Maryland: 1953 (pp. 144-145).

6. Keppel, Robert D. Lecture on "Serial Murder Investigations" on February 16, 1989 at the American Academy of Forensic Science Meeting in Las Vegas, Nevada.

7. Keppel, Robert D. (personal interviews on February 16 and 17, 1989 in Las Vegas, Nevada).

8. Keppel, Robert D. *Serial Murder*, Anderson Publishing Company, 2035 Reading Road, Cincinnati, Ohio 45202: 1989.

9. *Lansing State Journal.* "Confession Doesn't Buy Bundy Time", Lansing, Michigan: January 23, 1989 (p. 4A).

10. Larsen, Richard. *Bundy: The Deliberate Stranger.* Pocket Books, a division of Simon and Schuster Inc., 1230 Avenue of the America's, New York, N.Y. 10020: 1981.

11. Pride, Don. "Ted Bundy's Death Date Tuesday". *Tampa Tribune.* Tampa, Florida. January 18, 1989 (p. lA).

12. Rather, Dan. *CBS News* (special broadcast on Bundy's execution). New York, New York: January 24, 1989.

13. Rule, Ann. *The Stranger Beside Me.* The New American Library Inc. New York, New York: 198

14. Soderman, Harry, D.Sc. and John J. O'Connell. *Modern Criminal Investigation.* Funk and Wagnalls Company, New York, New York: 1952 (pp. 180-183).

15. Winn, Steven and Merrill. *Ted Bundy: The Killer Next Door.* Bantam Books, Inc. New York, New York: 1979.

CHAPTER XXXIX

GENERAL SUMMARY:

A serial killer is one who kills more than one victim over a period of time, with a cooling off period between the murders. The Federal Bureau of Investigation requires the murder of three victims over a period of time before a crime is placed in that category. There are different types of serial murderers. There are serial murderers who kill women for profit and their skeletons. (Herman W. Mudgett AKA H. Holmes Chicago, Illinois 1892-1896)

There are serial killers who murder primarily boys/men after they have had sex with them. Usually this is done to prevent the victims from reporting the perpetrator's crimes to the police. (Wayne Williams of Atlanta, Georgia 1980-1981)

There are serial murderers who kill both men and women. Sometimes the victims are killed for sexual reasons, sometimes for their property, and sometimes the male is murdered to enable the murderer to have a freehand with a female companion. (Alton Coleman of Illinois 1984) (Gerald Gallego 1978-1980))

There are serial murderers who kill babies (Christine Falling, Florida 1982) and those who murder elderly patients in nursing homes to obtain relief from their anxieties. (Catherine Wood and Gwendolyn Graham, Michigan 1988)

There are also serial murderers who kill women and girls who appear—at least on the surface—to be sexually motivated. There is some evidence to indicate that , at least some of these killers, murder their victims also out of sheer hatred of women. The serial killers of girls and women have been the primary subject of this book. As we have seen, these murderers apparently do not view their victims as human beings. They seem rather to look upon them as true sexual objects whose only purpose on earth is to bring sexual gratification to man. Perhaps this is one reason why so many of the killers pick out victims whom they do not know. For if they knew the victims, then the victims would no longer be objects needed to fulfill the fantasies of subjugation and bondage. The victims would then acquire the status of human beings like their mothers, sisters, and aunts. Then their fantasies would not square with the reality of the situation. It is indeed rare for a serial murderer to attack his own mother. Emil Kemper was an exception. Not only did he murder his own mother and her lady friend, he also surrendered to the police and made a full confession of his crimes. It is unusual for a serial killer to confess unless it is to his legal advantage.

When one examines the cases, one does find those rare occurrences where the serial murderer does kill someone that he knows quite well. Oftentimes, she will be the first murder victim of the series. She is usually the object of his affections, and she rejects him. He then kills her and seeks out other women, whom he does not know, and kills them. Sometimes, he looks for victims that resemble his former girl friend.

Christopher Wilder and Donald Miller are examples of serial killers whose first victims were women they loved who rejected them. Most serial killers fantasize about what they will do to their victims once they have captured them.

When one looks at these fantasies—what were they about? Larry Gene Bell, who killed Sheri Smith and Debra Helmick near Columbia, South Carolina, in 1985, had a detective magazine and a handgun hidden under the mattress. On the cover of the magazine was a picture of a beautiful blonde young woman strung up like a puppet. Sheri Smith was a beauty queen with long blonde hair.

Two killers, one in California and one in Florida were greatly impressed by John Fowles' book, *The Collector*. The men, totally unknown to one another, were Leonard Lake and Christopher Wilder. *The Collector* was a novel about a man in England who kidnapped a young woman and kept her prisoner in his remote cottage. Both Wilder and Lake carried the book with them.

Ted Bundy, before he was executed, blamed pornography for his murderous acts.

Albert DeSalvo said that he read detective magazines (which up until about 1988 frequently depicted women being bound, gagged and tortured). He said he fantasized about the woman he was going to attack. Sometimes this was done to the point where he had an ejaculation while driving his car. There can be little question that such fantasizing does play a significant role in at least some cases. Whether pornography is the actual cause is debatable. If pornography truly was directly responsible for serial murders as Bundy claimed, wouldn't we expect to find more of these crimes in Holland and Denmark which apparently have more pornography than in the United States? Yet from this writer's conversations with colleagues from those countries this is not the case. This raises a question about pornography. Could pornography play a role in serial murderer's fantasies by helping them form the mental pictures that would, in fact, be a form of self hypnosis?

A hundred years ago, there were many in the medical profession who denied that such a phenomena even existed. This is common knowledge. Others, who did acknowledge its existence, thought its use was limited to stage performances. But others knew there was tremendous power in the use of the subconscious mind.

Christ referred to this power when he said, "If you have faith as small as a mustard seed, you can say to this mulberry tree, 'Be uprooted and planted in the sea' and it will obey you." (Luke 17:6 N.I.V.) Much later others wrote about this same power in other books, For example, Maxwell Maltz, M.D., F.I.C.S. wrote *Psycho-Cybernetics*. This classic work was published nearly thirty years ago. It dealt with how one could bring about positive changes in one's life by using the power of the subconscious mind. Incidentally, the term "subconscious", as it was used here refers to the definition by Leland E. Hinsie, M.D. and Robert Campbell, M.D., in their *Psychiatric*

Dictionary as, "The state in which mental processes take place without conscious perception on the subject's part."

Dr. Norman Vincent Peal wrote about the *Power of Positive Thinking*, Dr. Robert Schuler also wrote on the same thing. Napolean Hill wrote, *Think and Grow Rich* on how one can make bundles of money by using the untapped resources of the subconscious mind.

The theory behind all of the above books—in a nutshell is this—the subconscious mind is made to believe that a certain situation exists. It then causes the conscious mind to respond in such a way as to carry out these desires. The subconscious mind is incapable of distinguishing fantasy from reality. The conscious mind would then be on "automatic pilot" to bring about the positive changes outlined above.

But regardless what name this above technique is called, what all of the above writers are referring to are forms of self hypnosis.

But let us now suppose that the subjects who use self hypnosis are not desirous of bringing about positive changes in their lives, as the mores of a civilized society defines "positive change." Suppose they do not care about having bundles of money. Suppose they have a warped view of women and think of them only as sex objects and how women can gratify their lustful desires. Suppose these men spend a considerable portion of their time reading books and looking at pictures, thinking about, and forming mental images of their interaction with women who are under their total domination and control. Suppose these fantasies occurred during acts of masturbation where there were mental pictures of girls/women being raped. This writer would advance the proposition that their actions could bring about a form of self hypnosis that could cause them to act without really understanding totally the reasons for their behavior. It is not being suggested that this is true in every serial murder case, or even in the majority of them, but it is plausible in some cases.

Self hypnosis would explain why serial murderers have had such remarkable memories about their crimes. They should have—they have relived the murders hundreds of times in their day dreams or fantasies after they have committed them. It would also explain why serial murderers like DeSalvo, who earnestly appeared to have been searching for answers as to why he did such heinous acts, was completely unable to provide any rational explanation for his behavior, either to the Assistant Massachusetts Attorney General who interrogated him, or to himself. The closest he came to providing any reasons for his actions was blaming his wife for not fulfilling his sexual needs and making him feel dirty. In her defense, it should be mentioned that most serial killers, after they are caught, can easily find someone else to blame for their problems.

The primary goal of this book has been to isolate and identify the most effective methods for the police to use in apprehending a serial murderer of women. Along these same lines, the author, through the study of these past cases, has identified some of the areas where serial killers are particularly vulnerable—where they are most apt to make mistakes. The author has also spelled out why these criminals are so much more difficult to catch than the average crook. The apprehension must be made as quickly as possible to prevent the further loss of life and to restore a degree of normalcy to the community that will enable the citizenry to go about their affairs without fear. Yet, in case after case, investigators frequently are making the same mistakes over and over again. The author has tried to point out what some of these errors have been in such a way that no one will be embarrassed, so that we can all learn from these mistakes and they will not happen again.

A secondary goal has been to provide information to the police which could be utilized to teach women/girls about the dangers women would face should a serial killer attack in their community, and some of the things women should and should not do, if they are attacked by a serial killer. In the author's opinion, the best defense a woman has against a serial murderer is her screams for help and her feet, which she should use to run away from him as fast as she can. It is simply foolishness to teach women not to resist a serial killer for fear that they will only make him more determined and violent. It is equally absurd to teach women to rely upon their training in the martial arts or their skill as trained counsellors who have dealt with people with emotional problems in the past when they are confronted by a serial killer. Women should be taught escape tactics. It should also be made clear to women that when a serial killer tells them that if they keep their mouth shut and cooperate they will not be hurt, that this is sheer nonsense. Such talk is nothing but lies the killer uses to manipulate his victim's behavior and to gain her cooperation until he can get her in a position where no one can hear her cries for help.

This study did not include some of the other forms of serial murder that were *not* sex related because each would have included a different variable due to the targets being different and the motivating factors were, in most instances, entirely different. The author wanted to hold these differences to a minimum. It was thought that even the homosexual serial murders of boys and/or young men might be so different that mixing the serial murders of males and females, where the victims were used for sexual purposes, could effect the end result and lead to some erroneous conclusions. However, from some of the other cases which were examined, like those which involved John Wayne Gacy, Wayne Williams, Dean Corll, John J. Joubert, Randy Kraft, and Arthur Bishop—all who sexually assaulted boys or young men and then murdered them to either prevent them from reporting their foul, evil deeds or to engage in sexual relations with the victims after they were deceased—there were remarkable similarities with the serial murders of girls/women. Nevertheless, the data from homosexual murders were not included with the data from the studies of the cases which involved the killing of girls and women.

Other types of serial murder cases, did not have the remarkable similarities that both the killing of women or men for sexual reasons manifested. For example, those killers who have murdered nursing home patients to relieve the killer's anxiety, or for the patient's money, or the serial killer who murdered victims to steal their property and sell their skeletons to a medical school, or the babysitter who has killed the children who were left in her charge were markedly different from the type of person committing the murders of both women or men for sexual reasons. And the motivating reasons behind the killings were entirely dissimilar.

It was the assumption of the author that by examining past serial murder cases of girls/and women where sex appeared to play a role, in some form or another, it could be determined what the key factor or factors were in each case, that resulted in the finger of suspicion being pointed toward the perpetrator which ultimately brought about his arrest. In future investigations, detectives would then be aware of where their greatest chances of success in solving these murders would lie and where they should put their time and resources to work because they would be able to predict which method or methods could be most successfully employed to bring about the arrest of the serial murderer.

To accomplish the purpose of the study, this writer examined the following named serial murderers and the crimes in which they were involved: LARRY GENE BELL, ALBERT H. DE SALVO, JOHN NORMAN COLLINS, KENNETH ERSKINE, ROBERT JOSEPH LONG, LEONARD LAKE, CHARLES C. NG, FRED WATERFIELD, DAVID ALAN GORE, RICHARD COTTINGHAM, PETER WILLIAM SUTCLIFFE, JOHN REGINALD CHRISTIE, KENNETH A. BIANCHI, ANGELO BUONO JR., DONALD MILLER, WILLIAM GEORGE HEIRENS, CHRISTOPHER WILDER, ALTON COLEMAN, RICHARD BIEGENWALD, ROBERT HANSEN, CLIFFORD ROBERT OLSON, DOUGLAS D. CLARK, GERALD ARMAND GALLEGO JR., EDMUND KEMPER, THEODORE BUNDY, CORAL E. WATTS, DHERRAN FITZGERALD, AND HAROLD SASSAK. Thus, there were a total of twenty-eight subjects (N=28) used in the study.

The criteria for selections of a subject as a serial murderer of women was that they were apprehended and the evidence appeared overwhelmingly that they were involved in the murder of more that one girl or woman overtime with a cooling off period between the attacks. It must be recognized that in some instances we can be reasonably sure that women who were kidnapped hours apart, and who did not know one another, may have been sexually assaulted, tortured, and murdered within minutes of one another. In those crimes, even though there would appear to be little or no cooling off period, they are still being classified as serial murders. The author did not classify a killer as a serial murderer based upon the number of legal convictions for murder an arrested person had, but rather upon the facts of each case.

In some instances, such as with Coral E. Watts and Albert De Salvo, they were never convicted of even one serial murder although De Salvo admitted to thirteen killings and Watts was thought by authorities to be responsible for far more than De Salvo. Both De Salvo and Watts were charged and convicted of other crimes.

In at least one instance, John Collins was only convicted for one murder, but the evidence suggested that he was involved in the murders of Jean Schultz and Anne Kitze in Michigan and Rose Picketts in California. Donald Miller pled guilty to manslaughter, a felony which carried the maximum penalty of fifteen years in prison, because although he had killed four women, and would have probably killed a fifth fifteen year-old girl in her own home and had knifed her younger brother, the only thing the police had against him was that he had failed a polygraph test shortly after the first murder, and that result could not be used as evidence in any Michigan court against him.

Each case in the study was examined differently depending upon the information that was available. For example, with the Collins case, the author had an abundance of information. This was because he was involved in the investigation from shortly after the first girl's body was recovered until four years after Collins was convicted. First, he was part of the team conducting the general investigation. Then he was assigned to conduct a background investigation on each of the girls murdered in Michigan. After that was finished, he was assigned to prepare the *Prosecution Report*, a small book of over one hundred and twenty-seven pages, which set forth in a logical and detailed manner exactly what the People's Case was against John Norman Collins. Two other outstanding Michigan State Police Detectives assisted in this task. They were Gordon Hurley and Harold Janiszewski.

The author then acted as the assistant to Prosecutor William Delhey throughout all of the pretrial hearings and the trial itself. After Collins was convicted, the author then transported the evidence to the Michigan Court of Appeals and then to the Michigan Supreme Court as Collins appealed his conviction. After the appeals were concluded, the evidence was transported to the Michigan State Police "Vault," where it is stored to this day. Finally, four years after Collins had been convicted, the author was assigned to return to the Ypsilanti Post to deal with the evidence from all the cases and to return all the items of stolen property Collins' had in his possession at the time of his arrest to the rightful owners. Where the owners could not be determined, the items were sold at the regular Michigan State Police auction.

In the Miller case, this writer was personally involved as a consultant at the request of Lieutenant Darrel Pope who headed the Sexual Motivated Crime Unit for the Michigan State Police. Pope computerized the Sexual Motivated Crime Reports in 1968. He also pioneered the team approach to crime scene behavioral analysis during the early 1970's. Conceptually, what the FBI Behavioral Science Unit is doing today on a federal level, was being done by Detective Lieutenant Pope in Michigan several years earlier.

Since it was mandated by law that a Sexual Motivated Crime Report be filed whenever a person was *arrested* for a crime which was sexually motivated, that file provided a valuable bank of information that was responsible for identifying a high percentage of repeat sex offenders in the State of Michigan. Since Michigan is a large state, over six hundred miles from one end to the other, it has been helpful to have such a program. But in some serial murder cases, the sexual motivated sex crime file was of no value at all simply because the perpetrator had never been arrested. Both Collins and Miller were examples of serial killers who had no previous arrest record.

Now the Violent Criminal Apprehension Program (VICAP) is on line to help track criminals functioning throughout the United States. This program makes it much more difficult for vicious criminals to move from one state to another without detection. In Michigan a person trained to work with the VICAP works with local police to assist in profiling sexually motivated criminals, but the work previously done by Pope continues. It is under the new name of Investigative Resources.

In addition to the above regarding the Miller case, the author interviewed Lieutenant Tucker of the East Lansing Police Department who played a major role in that investigation. He also interviewed and reviewed the polygraph records of the examination conducted on Miller by Lieutenant Maynard Markham and he has corresponded with Donald Miller regarding the case over a three year period. Miller has also cooperated extensively with the author by serving as a "sounding board" on some of the other serial murder cases, and although it has been difficult, he has discussed his own case.

Miller has stated that he believed the reason for his criminal acts was that he failed to understand the mechanics of the first crime. In the first crime he murdered his former girl friend. He further amplified his remarks:

> That just like a well functioning record album can be placed out in a hot summer sun and the sun's heat can melt (warp) the record, a well functioning human being can be in a hot situation(s) and the heat of this can melt (warp) the character of this human being. Such a person may not be aware of said mechanics, or have little awareness. Overcoming this takes indepth care about self and much character work.

In other cases, this writer has personally talked with some of the investigators who worked on the cases and also attended lectures and teleconferences on them. (Sissak, Long, Bundy, Bell, Ramirez, Wilder and Heirens)

On still others, the author was forced to rely primarily upon the literature. (Gore, Waterford, Hansen, and DeSalvo)

FINDINGS

There were several factors examined in each and every serial murder case. These data should be viewed by the reader with this point in mind— what is reported here is of a conservative nature. The actual percentages indicated below may be much higher, but not lower. This is because what is being calculated has been reported or is known. There may be other instances which have occurred that would impact upon these data, but they are not known or have simply not been reported.

Concerning the perpetrators themselves, these are the data which this writer considered most significant:

> Ninety-two (92) percent of the perpetrators showed little or no remorse for committing their crimes after they were apprehended. Sometimes the perpetrators commented that it was almost like someone else had committed the crime. In the opinion of this writer, many of the criminals tended to blame the victim(s) for their acts. Collins said, "They (the girls) weren't careful enough." Hansen, Sutcliff, Clark and others blamed their killing on the whores whom they murdered. (Even though some victims were not prostitutes) And Kemper blamed his killings on his mother's emasculating behavior.

What significance does it have when the perpetrator shows little or no sorrow for committing the crimes and a natural inclination to blame his victims for his behavior? For the criminal investigator or police interrogator, this would mean that one's chances of success by using an emotional appeal when questioning him would be very small. An interrogator would do far better by using a logical appeal that tends to blame the victim. It also makes the death penalty a very valuable bargaining chip.

> Eighty-six (86) percent of the perpetrators were Caucasian.

What this means is that where the race of the suspect is not known, the chances are that the perpetrator is white rather than black. Black criminals are responsible for about half the crimes committed in the United States, but serial murders are crimes where white males seem to be committing crimes in proportion to their representation in the population.

> Half of the perpetrators studied were in the age group beween twenty-eight (28) and thirty-eight years (38) of age.

This means that while most crimes are committed by young people under twenty-five, in a serial murder investigation there is a chance equal to the flip of a coin that the person who has committed the crimes is not in that usual high crime age bracket.

> Seven (7) percent of the perpetrators attended worship services at a church near the same time that they were killing girls and women.

Their contempt for God and religion was manifested by several of them. For example, Collins told one young woman that he regarded the teachings of the Roman Catholic Church as stupid. He specifically mentioned the foolishness of the

Fifth Commandment, "Thou shalt not kill." (The more accurate and modern translations, such as the New International Version of the Holy Bible translate the word as "murder", not "kill".)

DeSalvo parked his car directly in front of a Roman Catholic Church and left it in search of a victim. One victim answered the knock on her door by DeSalvo. DeSalvo told her he had to make a check for plumbing problems in her apartment. She requested DeSalvo to make the check as quick as possible because she had to get ready to attend church services. He forced her to perform fellatio. Then he raped and murdered her.

Wilder murdered a Sunday School teacher so he could steal her Pontiac Trans AM. She was not sexually assaulted.

Larry Gene Bell murdered beautiful Sheri Smith after he had her write a letter—called her "Will"—to her parents. It was indicative of her deep faith in Christ. Bell murdered her by wrapping duct tape around her nose and mouth. She died from asphyxiation.

For the investigator, the conclusions that can be drawn are that during an interrogation of a serial murder suspect, the real killer would not be susceptible to a religious approach. And if a suspect attends church on a regular basis, the odds are clearly in his favor that he is not the murderer. There are some notable exceptions to this. Bundy attended church and taught in Sunday School while he was killing in Utah. He was also getting drunk and smoking marijuana in his apartment, and other people who lived in the same apartment were very much aware of his two sided life, but they could not bring themselves to believe that he was also involved in killing young women. Corel Watts was observed by a surveillance team attending church services. Alton Coleman found religious folks an easy way to get help, and he would take advantage of them. So it is clear that some serial murderers use religious activities as a cover in an attempt to raise themselves above suspicion by trying to present the appearance that they are leading good, wholesome lives. But—a good thorough background investigation on a suspect should make his hypocrisy readily apparent.

Sixty-one (61) percent of the perpetrators had a criminal record of some kind.

This means that there is a good possibility that the suspect's fingerprints and his photographs are on file. However, the arrest photographs (mug shots) may be of limited value for identification purposes. This is because the serial killer is a smart crook. He is very much aware of the possibility that the photographs may be used at some future time for identification purposes. He may, therefore, deliberately distort his facial features to limit the value of the pictures for identification purposes. Also, and this cannot be overemphasized, some serial killers almost appear like two different individuals when one compares what their appearance is when they are turning on their charms and being "Mr. Nice Guy" versus their appearance when they feel they can drop their mask and reveal all the hatred that they really have toward their victims. We know this from the very few victims who have escaped from the serial killer's clutches and by those girls who the serial killers have left for dead, but who managed to survive. Some officers use a pre-interrogation report to record information about the arrested person, his family, and his associates. That record is extremely valuable if it ever becomes necessary to arrest that person again. The author spent eight years working in the Detroit Metropolitan area. Sometimes looking for a criminal in a highly populated area can be like the proverbial looking for a needle in a haystack. The pre-interrogation record was one of the author's most valuable tools in tracking down a fugitive. A Sexual Motivated Crime Report can also provide valuable information for a subsequent investigation.

Sometimes the crime that was previously committed significantly parallels the serial murder. The location where an arrest occurs can also be very meaningful. For example, David Berkowitz was observed by a witness fleeing from the scene of the crime and getting into his car which had just been ticketed by the police for parking too close to a fire hydrant. On this ticket, the issuing officer had written the license number of Berkowitz's car. This number was easily traced to Berkowitz through the department that handled motor vehicle registrations. An arrest quickly followed.

> Sixty-four (64) percent of the serial killers used a knife and sixty-one (61) percent of them had either a real gun or an imitation one with them when they commited their crimes.

Sometimes the serial killer will leave blood on the knife. The knife is then shown to subsequent victims. Apparently, by showing the new victim the bloody knife, the serial killer believes that it will terrorize the victim into compliance. It is also possible that the serial killer may look at the blood on the knife when he is alone and mentally relive the thrill of the murder.

From an investigator's point of view, this means that there is a better than chance possibility that if the killer is caught he will be carrying either a knife or a gun. It may even contain blood, tissue, or hair from one or more of the victims. If a gun is recovered, and it is the murder weapon, the killer could be linked to the murder providing bullets fired from the gun and bullets found in the victim's body match. The weapon could also be identified as the murder weapon from the firing pin, ejector, breech block, and extractor markings located on the shell casings found at a crime scene. As mentioned before, and it bears repeating, that while serial killers are exceptionally careful about *not* leaving evidence at the scene, they are not nearly as careful about their own living quarters or their vehicles. This is probably because they do not believe the police will ever find them. They are very bold and confident. Hence, there is a very good chance, if they do not have the knife or gun on or about their immediate person, they will be found in their living quarters or vehicle. These could prove to be valuable pieces of evidence which could be used to help convict them.

> Half (50 percent) of the subject group was involved in thievery in one form or another.

Collins, for example, stole motorcycles, a movie camera, and a handgun. Lake and Ng murdered two black men who worked for them at their ranch, presumably so they would not have to pay them. They also murdered a car salesman and kept the car. There were indications that he had been killed while in the car he was attempting to sell. It also appeared that there was little effort to clean the car up to get rid of any incriminating evidence. They responded to an advertisement in the paper regarding a video camera for sale. They made arrangements to meet with the couple selling the camera. They then murdered the man, who was trying to sell the video camera and his infant son. Then they tortured, raped and forced his wife to cook for them. A portion of the torture was recorded on the video tape which was recovered by the police from the ranch where Lake had lived. Eventually, Lake and Ng murdered her too. It is not at all uncommon for the serial killer to steal items from the victim. These items, whether they are rings, money, shoes, wallets, purses—are all mementos that the serial murderer can look at and fantasize and mentally relive the murder. Where the girl has been decapitated, it is also possible that the serial killer has stolen the head from the body and continues to use it in his sexual fantasies. The indications are that both Emil Kemper and Douglas Clark did this. Therefore, for investigators this means that in those cases where one or more of the victims have been recovered decapitated, when a search is conducted of the suspect's house, the freezer should not be overlooked and should also be checked for the victim's heads. Along these same lines, cases—like bowling ball bags—that could have been used to transport a human head, should also be checked for human blood and hair.

> Sixty-eight (68) percent of the subject group had their height and weight in good proportion to one another.

To the criminal investigator this means, as a general rule, that the majority of serial murderers, specifically those who rape or otherwise sexually assault their victims, tend to have a mesomorphic (muscular) or ectomorphic (thin) body structure. The serial killer called "Zodiac" who murdered both men and women back during the 1960's was described by some of the survivors as having a paunch. He did not have sex with any of his victims. The same was true of Berkowitz. Berkowitz too appeared to be a bit pudgy. Because he attacked boys, John Wayne Gacy, was not included in the subject group. If Gacy had been, he probably would have been an exception to the above statement because he appeared to have an endomorphic (heavy) body build, and the indications were that he attacked his victims both while they were alive and after he had killed them. This information can be used to help evaluate a particular suspect. An investigator should refrain from forming any conclusions based upon one or two pieces of information, but rather should evaluate all the information he or she has available to him/her.

Eighty-nine (89) percent of the subject group had an I.Q. that was either average or above.

This means that the criminal investigator's opponent is much different from the type of criminal he usually encounters. Most crooks aren't too smart. As a group, they tend to make dumb mistakes that lead to their rapid apprehension. To cite a few examples, while the author was investigating a breaking and entering of a bowling alley, he found tool chits with the name and address of the company on them near the window from which the burglar had exited the building. It was obvious that these chits had been lost by the culprit. The perpetrator also left some excellent footprints on the outside of the building where he had jumped down from a window. One of the heel impressions had some very unique cut characteristics in it. Photographs were taken of these. All that was necessary was for yours truly to contact the company and determine to whom the tool chits had been issued. Then the author went to the home of the suspect. On the back porch, outside the door, the author noted a pair of boots with clay like mud on them, the same kind of mud that was near the window of the bowling alley. The heel of one of the boots had characteristics -which matched the prints found at the scene of the breaking and entering. The suspect was arrested and readily admitted his involvement in the breaking and entering and implicated an accomplice. His accomplice was arrested later that day with a cigar box full of money, which he tried to throw under his car. But the warm coins had became embedded in the snow where he had dropped them when he saw the police car, and his efforts to scrape them under his car with his foot before officers could see them just didn't work too well. In addition when the accomplice was searched, he had a check in his wallet that linked him to a series of armed robberies of gas stations which had occurred in the area. He confessed to those too.

Another example of the "Not too smart" crook, was when a man shot a female deer out of season that was pregnant with two little fawns. After shooting her and loading her in the trunk of his car, he backed into a snow bank while he was turning his car around. He left the license number impression of his car embedded in the snow bank. A registration check was made through the Secretary of State's office which handled vehicle registration on the license number found in the snow. The Secretary of State's Office provided the police with the name and address of the poacher. A search warrant was obtained for his house and his car which led to the recovery of the deer and his arrest and conviction. These are but a couple of examples that can be cited of mistakes made by some crooks who one police officer used to call, "Five Watters." Any police officer who has been around for awhile can provide many other examples of the same thing.

How can an investigator tell whether the serial killer would tend to be above or below average in intelligence? If at anytime—with any one victim—the evidence appears to indicate that some type of a ruse, or con game, was used during the commission of the crime against any one of perhaps several victims, the chances are great that the serial killer is above average in intelligence. For example, Ted Bundy broke into one girl's apartment, hit her on the head while she was sleeping, dressed her and then took her to another location where he raped and eventually killed her. The evidence also indicated that, at a later time, he broke into several girl's rooms, consecutively on the same night, beat them, and sexually assaulted them. There was no ruse used in any of these crimes. Bundy did use a ruse, however, when he attempted to kidnap and murder Carol DaRonch when he posed as a police detective investigating a fake break in of Miss DaRonch's car. He also used a con game when he had his arm in a sling and succeeded in picking up victims at a crowded beach and near a library.

DeSalvo, the Boston Strangler, consistently used a ruse by telling women that the apartment superintendent had sent him to their apartments to make repairs, do painting work, or check for water leaks.

Wilder used the con that he wanted to show a beautiful girl, who had expressed an interest in becoming a model, some examples of his photographic layouts which he had out in his car. The woman would follow him out to the parking lot where he would punch her in the stomach, throw her into his car, bind her, and drive away to a motel. He would carry her into the motel room under cover of darkness wrapped in a blanket. Then he would crudely cut her hair, pour Super Glue over her eye lids to seal them, attach electrodes to her legs and make her dance for him. If she did not dance to his satisfaction, he would give her an electric shock from the switch which he held in his hand. He also sexually assaulted his victims.

For the investigator, another indicator of the intelligence level of the serial killer is the crime scene itself. If the investigator or forensic science experts finds the suspect's fingerprints all over the place and an abundance of other forms of physical evidence, that serves as a pretty good indicator that the murderer isn't too sharp. The exception to this would be if it were determined that something happened to cause the perpetrator to flee from the scene to avoid being caught. If, on the other hand, the scene has been wiped clean of prints, and it appears that the perpetrator spent quite a bit of time cleaning up the scene and checking it over to insure he did not leave any trace evidence, that is a good indicator that the investigator is up against someone with brains. That does not necessarily mean that the serial killer is a law school student like Ted Bundy. It does not even mean that the killer is a high school graduate. But what it does mean is that he has plenty of street smarts, and the investigator will find that he has no easy task before him in trying to catch him. That means the chances are that there will be very little physical evidence found at the scene of the crime. Even though one must do one's best in an attempt to find latent prints and all the other forms of physical evidence, realistically the criminal investigator should be content with fibers, hair, and seminal fluid. The thing that trips up this smart criminal most of the time is his own cocky, arrogant attitude. He will oftentimes, use his con game with hundreds of people around him, but he thinks he can talk his way out of any problems he might have and acts almost as if he were invisible. He thinks that no one will recall what he looked like. The sad part of that is that all to often he is able to blend in and act so normal that no one does recall what he looked like because they didn't pay any attention to him. On the other side of the same coin we have the serial murderer who does not use a ruse at any time. He may enter a house through a sliding glass door or a window left unlocked during a hot summer night. He immediately confronts the victim with the threat of force with either a knife or a gun. He may murder the victim's sleeping husband by shooting him in the head. He then sexually assaults the victim. He then may gouge out the eyes of the female victim and then kill her. Richard Ramirez was the so called "Night Stalker" whose method of operation corresponded to what has been mentioned above. There was no ruse. Force was used immediately. With this type of serial killer, the investigator has a much better chance of finding physical evidence that can be used to help track down and convict the perpetrator simply because he is apt to be more careless and leave more evidence behind.

Some might argue, "Wait a minute—didn't the Zodiac killer also use force immediately?" Wasn't he the serial killer that communicated with the police and newspapers using a code so sophisticated even the military code breakers had a hard time cracking it? And didn't he clearly demonstrate that he had the ability to blow up a school bus, as he threatened to do, using an electronic triggering mechanism? He had to have had some smarts. It is true in some cases he did use force immediately. But he also used the ruse when he first approached some victims by telling them that he only wanted to steal their car. It was only after he had them tied up that he told them that, "I'm gonna have to kill you people." Then Zodiac would begin stabbing the man first and then the woman in an effort to kill them both.

If one were to try to develop a stereotype of the average serial killer (this is according to the F.B.I.'s Behavioral Science Unit) one would say that this person would be one whose father left the family before he reached puberty. His mother was either very weak or emasculating. As a boy, he tortured animals. Although he had the ability to get good grades in school, his grades did not reflect that potential. Frequently he did not get along well with others in school. He dropped out of school. He did not relate well with members of the opposite sex. He engaged in extensive masturbation. He fantasized a good deal of the time. He tended to wet the bed. He was the oldest boy in the family. If he joined the service, the chances were great that he would be discharged because he could not adjust.

The problem with this stereotype of a serial killer is that for every time it is correct there are numerous times when it is just plain wrong. For example, John Norman Collins was not the oldest son and neither was Albert De Salvo. Sutcliffe was a model professional truck driver. He worked very well for the same company for years. His photograph was used in company advertisements. Both Albert DeSalvo and Kenneth Bianchi were also considered valued employees of the respective companies for whom they worked. DeSalvo also had a very good military record. On numerous occasions, he was selected to be the colonel's orderly.

Robert Hansen also ran a successful bakery business which sold rolls and coffee and was quite probably a gathering spot for police officers. He may have even given the police free coffee and rolls. Christopher Wilder also had a successful construction business. And although not included in this study, so did John Wayne Gacy. Donald Miller was a graduate of Michigan State University's School of Criminal Justice. And Collins only needed a few more credits to graduate from Eastern Michigan University with a bachelor's degree in education. William George Heirens was also a brilliant college student. And, as has been mentioned previously, Ted Bundy had an undergraduate degree with a major in psychology, and he was a law school student. So it is apparent that, while some serial killers may be high school dropouts, many are not.

There are some criminologists who like to blame the high crime rates upon the poor, socio-economic conditions found in our cities. Yet these same criminologists have a difficult time explaining why many other people who are exposed to the same conditions do not become criminals. So the author would suggest that there are many men who have experienced the same kinds of things that have happened to serial killers—yet they do not become a serial murderer, nor does the thought of raping or holding a woman in bondage ever even occur to them.

Therefore, when a serial killer is profiled, what we are really doing is a form of gambling. We are trying to keep the odds in our favor by looking at the entire group and playing the percentages. Let us now consider the *modus operandi* of those men who repeatedly murder women.

MODUS OPERANDI

We are all creatures of habit. We find a certain way of doing something that works well for us and so we tend to do that particular thing the same way repeatedly. For example, we find a certain way of going to work or to the mall and we tend to take that same way each and every time. The way a criminal commits a crime is called his, "Modus operandi." That is a Latin term which means a mode of operating or mode of working. The burglar likes to break into a certain type of business establishment in a certain way and steal a certain type of property. A robber may specialize in sticking up banks using a certain method and saying certain words to the teller. He would not think twice about robbing a gas station. That would be beneath him. The same can be said about serial killers. Albert DeSalvo, The Boston Strangler, always attacked women inside their apartments, never on the street. Edmund Emil Kemper and John Collins picked up victims by offering them a ride. The location of the recovery site is sometimes used repeatedly by the same killer. But now the author would like to offer a few strong words of caution. Because many serial killers are well schooled in criminal investigation techniques, they will change their method of operation to deliberately confuse the police. Hence, the police must be very careful before they publicly say whether two different murders have been committed by the same killer. If the police are wrong, and state that two different murders were not related, when in fact they were, this gives greater confidence to the serial killer, and that is one thing we do not want to do unless it is part of some deliberate stratagem.

> Seventy-nine (79) percent of the time the perpetrator stripped the victim of at least part of her clothing.

Sometimes her clothing was left at the scene. Other times it was thrown into garbage cans along the highway in rest areas. Collins allegedly threw the purse of one victim into the Huron River after he had filled it with rocks. One serial murderer had his accomplice throw the victim's clothing into dumpsters in shopping mall areas. As was mentioned previously, some killers keep mementoes from their victims.

John Norman Collins was reported to have had a box of women's apparel that he disposed of shortly before he was arrested. Richard Cottingham allegedly had a "trophy room" with clothing worn by some of the prostitutes whom he murdered.

> Eighty-nine (89) percent of the victims were not known by the attacker before the attack. But it should also be noted that twenty-nine (29) percent of the serial killers knew at least one of their victims.

Sometimes this knowledge or acquaintance with the victim may have only been to speak briefly with her in a social greeting, or the killer may have seen her in a restaurant, or he may have actually been introduced to her.

For example, one of Leonard Lake's victims had visited his ranch previously with her husband. John Norman Collins lived across the street from Jean S., and he also dated a girl who lived across the street from Dora B. One of the victims murdered by Kenneth Bianchi lived in the same apartment house where he lived, and another victim lived across the street from him. John Christie raped his wife's friend and then murdered her. Donald Miller murdered his girl friend. Christopher Wilder also murdered a beautiful young woman who had rejected his proposal of marriage because she thought he was too old for her. It is remarkable that rejection does seem to play a role and become the catalyst and motivating mechanism in at least some serial murder cases such as those involving DeSalvo, Miller, Wilder, and Collins. It was interesting to note that Collin's last victim had the same first name as a girl who had previously "stood him up." On the day he picked up his last victim, he had another date with the same girl. That time he "stood her up."

> Half of the subjects who used motor vehicles directly in their crimes had offered the victims a ride. Sixty-three (63) percent of the time when a

vehicle was used it was the killer's own car or motorcycle which was registered to him or to a relative.

Both Collins and Kemper drove vehicles properly registered to their mothers. Collins' stolen motorcycle was registered in his name. He had added one hundred to the motorcycle serial number. Most of the time, when Ted Bundy was killing girls in the Western part of the United States, he was using his own Volkswagen which was registered to him. Arthur J. Shawcross, who was not included in this study, murdered eleven women in Monroe and Wayne Counties, New York, had been observed with his sister's car at a recovery site. David Berkowitz, the Son of Sam Serial Killer, was also using a car registered in his own name. Berkowitz was apprehended after he had shot a victim and was observed by a witness getting into his Ford Galaxie car. The witness had also seen police officers putting a parking violation notice on the car for parking too close to a fire hydrant. Investigators tracked down the parking ticket. This led directly to the arrest of Berkowitz. The obvious lesson from these examples is—if an investigator is fortunate enough to locate a witness who can provide the license number of the perpetrator's vehicle, there is a good possibility that it can be traced to him. Again, this is one of the distinctions between a serial killer and other criminals, particularly bank robbers. Bank robbers frequently use a stolen car at the scene as the "get away" car. It will be abandoned within a mile or two from the bank and the bandits get into another waiting vehicle. For the most part serial killers are lousy car thieves. Oh sure, they will steal a car—providing they can find one with the doors unlocked and the keys in the ignition. But in the main, as smart as many of them are, when it comes to stealing cars, they are just plain dumb. It is also equally apparent that we could expect a serial killer to make one of the following reports to the police, or to whichever governmental branch handles the issuing of license plates, if he thinks a witness may have gotten his license number while he was committing the crime: (1) That his car was stolen. Or (2) that his license plate was lost or stolen. The reader will recall that Collins sent his friend to the Secretary of State's office to get a new motorcycle license plate after Collins thought one of the women got his license number as he rode away from the wig shop with his last victim.

Seventy-eight (78) percent of the time vehicles were used—either directly or indirectly—in the commission of these homicides.

By a direct use it is meant that the killer used the vehicle directly in the commission of the offense. In other words, he used the vehicle to pick the victim up and then killed her. By indirect use it is meant that the killer used the car for his transportation to and from the scene where the crime was committed or used it to dispose of evidence.

Of the group studied, sixty-eight (68) percent of the killers used some form of "con game" or ruse to get the victim at a location where the killer then believed it was safe for him to attack the woman.

Collins offered girls a ride on his motorcycle. Bundy pretended that he had an injuried arm and asked victims if they would help him launch his sailboat. Bundy also posed as a police detective who was investigating the attempted breaking and entering of a potential victim's car. Miller pretended that he wanted to use a telephone to call the victim's father and followed her into the kitchen area where he grabbed her by the back of neck with one hand and held a knife in her face with the other hand. Bianchi and Buono also posed as police officers. Gallego had a female accomplice invite teenage girls to his van to pass out literature at a county fair. Once at the van, Gallego forced the girls at gun point into the van. Larry Gene Bell had his victim pose for photographs near her family's rural mailbox until she was far enough away from her car so her escape would be unlikely—then he pulled a gun on her and took her prisoner.

> Eight of the killers who were studied operated in two man teams part of the time. (Bianchi and Buono, Lake and Ng, Biegenwald and Fitzgerald, and Gore and Waterfield.) Of these, only Bianchi and Buono used a "con game".

It was also significant that four murderers used women to help lure other women into traps. Wilder had a victim who eventually called herself "Mrs. Wilder". She convinced a young woman who had just filled out a job application in a store to follow her outside the store where she would meet the "boss" (Wilder). Wilder then kidnapped her. Clark's girl friend took pictures for him while teenage prostitutes performed fellatio upon him. She also handed him the gun so he could shoot one girl in the head as he ejaculated. Debra Brown helped Alton Coleman kill a little girl and stood by as he raped another nine-year-old.

Twenty years ago investigators generally believed that the perpetrators of these kinds of homicides were loners. They believed—and this writer was one of them— that it was very unlikely that two men would work together to commit these kinds of crimes. For a woman to help a man do these things was not even considered within the realm of possibility. This view was that of tunnel vision and no competent professional investigator should permit that to occur today.

> Sixty-four (64) percent of those killers examined tried to conceal the bodies of their victims in a location where they would not be found immediately.

Bundy, for example, in his earlier crimes, transported his victims for a considerable distance before he disposed of them. Sometimes he would carry two or three bodies back into the same remote area. Bundy tended to be somewhat unpredictable. In some instances, he attacked his victims inside their own apartments. At other times, he would contact them on a college campus, in a mall, or on a beach.

Gallego, at first, buried his victims—later he shot them and left their bodies in remote areas, but did not bury them. It was interesting to note that one young college student he shot was left beside a dirt trail while he spent the night in a sex orgy with the young man's girl friend. At day break—he shot her too and left her body in a ravine. Later he returned to where he had shot her boyfriend, but people living in the area had heard the shots and called the police, who in turn, had removed the body.

This situation suggests that it would be worthwhile in similar cases to remove the body as soon as the crime scene has been properly processed and then set up a stakeout for a limited period of time in the event that the perpetrator does return as he did in this case. A mannikin can be substituted for the victim's body. Recording devices should be used to record the suspect returning to the scene. And any stakeout should be properly manned and should have the necessary equipment, including sophisticated night viewing devices, to apprehend the suspect, if and when, he does return to the site where he disposed of the victim's body.

Half of the time, the killer(s) left the bodies at a location where they would be quickly found.

This does not add to one hundred (100) percent because sometimes the same criminal operated both ways. Collins' *modus operandi* exemplified this fact. Usually he left the bodies of his victims where they could be found quickly except when he needed time to leave the area, as when he was in California. Collins apparently believed it was important for one to leave the bodies where he could receive appropriate credit for killing them.

Sixty-eight (68) percent of the time the bodies were moved from the location where the women were killed.

This action was probably taken to deprive the police of possible trace evidence that might be present where the murder occurred. It could also have been done to make some type of statement as when DeSalvo positioned a victim with her legs spread apart and draped over two chairs, grossly exposing the victim's genitalia, so it would have a shocking effect upon any person who walked into the room. It appeared that he was trying to further degrade the victim by presenting her in the least favorable manner. Contrast this with the crime when DeSalvo murdered the victim and covered her with a sheet on the bed and later talked about how that particular woman treated him like a man. It was almost as though he had some special regard for that victim. Some forensic pathologists have stated they have found a high percentage of cases where husbands murder their wives, or their ex-wives, and then cover them.

Of the serial murderers studied, only three of them used cameras to visually record their interactions with their victims.

Only Lake and Ng used a video camera to record their sexual activities with their victims. Clark's girlfriend took photographs of him as he engaged in sex acts with women. Randy Kraft, who was not included in the group of subjects studied, also took photographs of the male victims he assaulted and murdered. These photographs were found under the floor mat on the driver's side of his car. He also kept a coded journal. There may be an increased use of such video equipment in the future, as these cameras become more commonplace. But at present, it does not appear that the serial murderers of girls and women make use of such recording equipment to the same extent as criminals who engage in child pornography use it. Nevertheless, even though the use is not widespread, an investigator conducting a search should keep in mind the possibility that the perpetrator did make a recording that he could listen to or watch in the future to help him relive the murder.

Further, if the tapes or photographs of these incidents with the victims can be located, they would be extremely damaging against the defendant at trial. The pictures or a video tape must, of course, be obtained legally in compliance with all the rules regarding search and seizure so they can be admitted into evidence.

> The possible rationale behind why most serial killers include a knife as part of their method of operation, in at least one attack, is to subjugate their victims.

Aside from any psychological considerations as to why a murderer chooses a knife over a gun or something to strangle the victim with, the author believes that a knife is probably selected because, unlike a gun, it does not make any noise when it is being used to kill. And the sight of a knife held up to the victim's throat, tends to terrorize her into conforming and makes it easier to totally dominate her. A knife also does not leave evidence inside the body of a victim, like a bullet from a gun, that can be identified. About the best that can be said about whether a certain wound could have been caused by a particular knife is that it could or could not have caused the wound. There can be no positive identification unless there was blood on the knife that could be identified. Then it is the blood that is identified, not the knife wound. The primary exception in knife identification is where the killer has stabbed with the knife and the point or part of the blade breaks off in the victim. If that portion of the knife was unique, and it can be recovered, and it can be demonstrated that the piece was at one time part of the knife that was found in the perpetrator's possession, that can be very powerful evidence against him. That is another reason why it is so important that X-rays be taken of the victim's body or skeleton. When a murderer uses a knife to kill his victim, it is not without some risks. Knives are messy. When an artery is cut, blood spurts out everytime the heart beats. The killer is very apt to get blood on his clothing, shoes, in his car, and other places. Some killers have actually worn raincoats to avoid getting blood on themselves or to cover blood they already had gotten on their clothes. It has happened that the serial killer did not wash off the blood from the raincoat, and the police found it while they were executing a search warrant for the suspect's car.

One should be very conservative in forming an opinion of whether two or more killings were the work of different murderers based upon the mode of killing. It has been alleged that, after Collins raped one of his victims, he shot her in the head and then used his knife to slash her throat. Bundy supposedly had a gun with which he threatened his victims. Yet his primary method of killing his victims was by beating them to death with his tire iron or club. Wilder had a gun, and he used it to murder the owner of a car he had stolen, but he sometimes chose to stab his victims to death. So it should be noted that a killer may murder one time by stabbing and another time by shooting, and those incidents should not mislead the investigator into thinking that these two murders were committed by two different people. The Zodiac Killer, who was never apprehended, shot some victims and stabbed others.

Since over half the time serial murderer's use weapons to kill, and given their high propensity to resist arrest or try to escape, plus the fact that most of them are above average in intelligence and are excellent con men—investigators must exercise extreme caution when arresting these criminals.

CRIMINAL INVESTIGATION

As mentioned previously, this is not a general text on criminal investigation. This book also does not deal with general homicide investigation. This book is about serial murderers. These criminals and their crimes are different from other types of crimes and the criminal investigation into them must, therefore, follow a dissimilar approach and some different things need to be taken into consideration that ordinarily do not matter. The first thing we must do is ask, "How does the serial murder investigation differ from the investigation of other crimes?" Some of these differences have already been discussed, but it doesn't hurt to review them again.

> Most serial killers, who use some kind of ruse, are above average in intelligence.

The average run-of-the-mill crook isn't too smart. The serial killer, who has used a "con", is apt to be more intelligent than many of the police who are pursuing him.

> In many regular crimes, the police are able to find trace evidence at the scene of the crime that can be used to track down the perpetrator.

At serial murder crime scenes, where a killer has used some type of ruse, the police are indeed fortunate if they can locate seminal fluid, blood, hairs, and fibers. Except where serial murderers are surprised and must rapidly flee the scene, they are usually in no hurry to depart. They will take their time and be very careful about not leaving evidence behind them. Police investigators must remember that serial murderers have an interest in criminal justice and undoubtedly this interest extends to criminal investigative techniques that could result in their capture. It is the rather esoteric forms of evidence that tend to trip them up. All this has very special meaning to the detectives assigned to investigate a series of murders. It means that every

301

officer must be aware of what the crime laboratory experts can do to contribute to catching the killer. It is important that investigator's have refresher training in crime scene protection and processing, particularly as it relates to gathering the types of evidence found at serial murder scenes. Detectives should, above all, protect the scene from themselves.

During the early murder investigations, detectives do an excellent job of protecting the crime scene from the press and the public until it can be processed properly by the laboratory scientists, but the police themselves may drive over tire tracks and footprints. They may not be careful about where they walk, and step on footprints. They smoke and flip their cigarette butts around the scene. Later it cannot be determined whether one of these cigarette butts was left at the scene by the killer or thrown down by a detective. This is all unfortunate because it is during the first murders in the series that the killer is apt to make mistakes that could lead to his apprehension. With each of the murders that follow, he will critique himself to improve his murder techniques. Thus, for a time, he will be exceedingly difficult to catch. It is only after his successes leads him to believe that the police are absolutely without power to catch him. Then he is apt to become increasingly bold and brazen. He may even facetiously tell some people that he is the killer, but they will not believe him. He may also ask a potential victim whether he looks like a killer.

> In serial murder cases, the way a crime has been committed (The method of operation), cannot be relied upon to render an opinion as to whether the crimes have been committed by the same criminal.

As has been mentioned before, criminals tend to commit crimes in ways that are easiest and best for them. Usually police can see a certain criminal's "signature" by studying the method of operation employed between several crimes. Oftentimes they have a pretty good idea who committed a breaking and entering and safe job just by the way an alarm system was bypassed, by the use of a cutting bar, by what was taken, and by what was left at the scene. In the case of serial murders, sometimes the police can give a fairly accurate opinion that two or more serial murders are related because of their many similarities. For example, if the victims were all picked up while they were walking along a street, in a certain area, they all were similar in age and appearance to one another, they were all killed the same way, they were all killed someplace else other than where their bodies were left by the killer, and their bodies were all left along a road where they would be quickly discovered. But what about those murders where some victims were shot and others were strangled or died from knife wounds? How about if some victims were old women and others were young girls? What if some attacks occurred indoors and others outdoors? What if a ruse was used at one time, but not at others? In all of these instances, we have examples from the serial killers that teach us that they clearly may change their method of operation.

During many homicide investigations, such inquiries are not infrequently handled by one or two officers. A serial murder investigation may involve over 100 officers working on the killings.

Some detectives work better alone while others seem to do a better job in teams. And with some detectives, they seem to work equally well alone or as part of a team effort. Those detectives who are selected to be a part of a task force should be able to get along with others. Detectives on such a task force must work with other investigators sometimes from several different departments. Such a person should be capable of putting the goals of task force first and should be able to lay aside pompous, arrogant pride. He should have the attitude that he does not care who gets the credit, as long as we get the job done. Along these lines, it should be made clear that any investigator caught deliberately withholding information from the team will be relieved. To build better rapport between investigators, sometimes the task force commander will even pair detectives from different departments. That can also be helpful because oftentimes one detective knows the geographic area better than his partner.

> Only a few crimes are regarded as so serious and are of such magnitude
> as to warrant the formation of a task force.

There are several reasons why it is even necessary to form a task force. Some of these reasons are: It helps facilitate the exchange of information among law enforcement officers working in a specific geographic area. A task force pools resources and holds duplication of effort to a minimum. A task force provides the mechanism whereby there can be a concentrated effort to solve the crimes and bring the criminal to justice. It makes it more difficult for a serial killer to divide the efforts of law enforcement by dumping bodies in different jurisdictions. It provides law enforcement an opportunity to present a united front with a single officer speaking for the several departments involved in the investigations. But probably the most important reason for forming a task force is that it makes it possible to receive and investigate the hundreds of tips that are received regarding the murders.

> A task force investigating the serial murders of girls will have access to
> funds that simply will not be available in other investigations.

Another difference between the investigation of serial murders and other crimes, even other homicide investigations is the amount of attention and support that comes from the public. This is particularly true when the victims are innocent high school or college girls. When the public's outcry reaches fever pitch and they want the murders stopped no matter what the costs involved, monies to do the job and for equipment will become available. During the "Son of Sam" serial killings in New York, the task force costs ran well over two million dollars. That should not be surprising since the largest expenditure in any police department's budget is devoted to the payment of salaries, and since many detectives today earn over $30,000.00 per year. The wages for 100 detectives alone, not including any equipment—like radios, cars, or special computer systems, would be over $3,000,000. per year.

In some respects, it is easier for a detective to work on a serial murder task force than it is to work at his/her regular assignment, but there are some exceptions to this.

For the city precinct, sheriff's, or state police detectives, working on a serial murder case can actually be a relief from what they have been doing, especially if they are accustomed to conducting an investigation into many different types of crime during the same day. It is not at all uncommon for a busy detective to work on a half dozen totally unrelated, felony cases during the same day. They target the most serious cases from among the many that are referred to them. Usually these cases involve a crime against a person or persons like murder, rape, assault with a deadly weapon, robbery, or extortion. As these cases are cleared, new cases are targeted. In between the investigation of the targeted cases, the detectives are constantly being pulled from the targeted cases to investigate new serious crimes as they occur. They do what they can on these cases to resolve them immediately. Then, as quickly as possible, they return to the previously targeted cases. If this procedure were not followed, the detectives would find themselves on a treadmill where no complaint investigations were ever brought to a successful conclusion. This is because in most metropolitan areas there is so much serious criminal activity that detectives are virtually inundated with work. Some detectives joke and say, "Ali Baba was indeed fortunate because he only had forty thieves to contend with." At least on a serial murder task force, they are working toward trying to catch one or two serial killers. From the author's personal experience, while he—like the other detectives working on the task force— felt the heavy weight of moral responsibility to stop the murderer from committing additional murders, the pace was not as demanding as he had experienced in his regular day-to-day routine. The exception to the above occurred when he was given the task of insuring that the investigations were complete and that the case was ready for trial—including the preparation of the *Prosecution Report* (i.e. sometimes called the "Murder Book" by some departments.)

Another difference between serial murder investigations and the investigation into other crimes is the amount of media attention they each receive.

The general public has an unusual fascination with serial murderers and their crimes. One can only speculate why this is true, perhaps it is because they cannot understand why those who commit this type of crime do it. Perhaps it is because so many of the crimes are so gruesome they find such crimes as almost beyond comprehension. But for whatever the reason, all one has to do is visit his local bookstore and he will have to acknowledge that this interest is there, and people like to read about serial murder cases. Therefore, when one of these cases occur, one can expect that the media, and particularly the press, will be running stories about the murders day after day, as long as there is something to write about. Why? because these stories sell newspapers. The media usually report serious crimes when they are committed, when the criminal is arrested, when the defendant is brought to trial, and, if he is found guilty, when he is sentenced. Such reporting is sparse when it is compared with what is reported on serial murder cases.

> The media is sparingly used in most criminal investigations, but the media is commonly used to help solve serial murder cases.

From studying the various serial murderers and how they were finally caught—sometimes after successfully evading arrest by the police for years—one point is clear and that is that most serial murderers are not arrested due to criminal investigative or patrol efforts by the police, but rather from information that comes to the police from the people. For that reason, it is important that the members of the general public should be given as much information as possible about the crimes. The only information which should be withheld from them are a few critical points that only the murderer himself would know so these points can be used by a polygraph examiner while administering a polygraph examination. These points can also be used as a check against that individual who tries to give a false confession for one reason or another. There should be consultation with the polygraph examiner regarding those areas that he or she believes would be the best information to hold back and which could be used most effectively during a polygraph examination. Also information about hairs, fibers, or other evidence that could help identify the suspect, that he could dispose of, should be withheld. Television programs like *Unsolved Mysteries* and *America's Most Wanted* have clearly demonstrated just what a powerful and effective tool such programs can be in apprehending dangerous criminals. As of January 1990, *America's Most Wanted* had profiled 215 wanted criminals. Eighty-six of these were apprehended as a direct result from viewer's tips. The *Crime Stoppers* programs, broadcast over the radio and television and printed in the newspapers were also a very effective means of helping to catch the enemies of society. Why do these programs work? They work because people want to help make our society a better—safer—place in which to live. Americans will not report someone who has done something wrong which is regarded as a minor infraction. In fact, what do we call someone who does that? A "Tattletale"—a "squealer"—"rat"—a "fink"—or a "stool pigeon"—right? But when someone does something wrong that is very serious, not only will Americans report him, in some places they will take an active roll in helping to hunt him down and capture him. The so called, "Night Stalker" was happy to see the police arrive on the scene after some citizens had "apprehended" him and were in the process of letting him know just how displeased they were with his behavior by administering what B.F. Skinner might have called "Negative Reinforcement".

For these programs, like *America's Most Wanted*, to be effective they must be broadcast at consistent times so the people will know when such programs can be watched and will get into the habit of watching them. It is also important that the people have the belief that the police will follow through if they take the time and make the effort to call in on a wanted person. If the citizens thought that it would be a complete waste of their time to report a fugitive that they had seen on a television program, they would not bother to even take the time to make such a report. It takes time to build rapport with the people, and, as a general rule, once a series of murders have begun it is too late to do it then. It takes time to establish the kind of trust that is required.

The author's research has shown that sixty-one (61) percent of the time the information that resulted in the perpetrator's arrest came from witnesses. Examples of this were: The witness who observed Gallego and his girlfriend leave the parking lot of a restaurant with the kidnapped college couple and wrote down their license number. The couple were later found shot to death. The witnesses who recorded the license number of Miller's car as he fled the scene of an attempted rape and murder of a teenage girl and the attempted strangulation of her brother who had returned home unexpectedly and surprised Miller. The victims who survived Erskine's, Wilder's, Miller's, Gore's, and Bundy's attacks and were able to identify their assailant were also examples of this. In fact, of the witnesses who made primary contributions to the apprehension of serial murderers nearly one third of them had been held by the killers and escaped from them. In the group of murderers studied, only two had voluntarily permitted a victim to go free after she had been assaulted. (Wilder and Long) No one knows for sure why the killers decided to release these victims alive. Both had killed, or attempted to kill many others.

A fact that tends to undercut the sixty-one (61) percent contribution that witnesses have made to the apprehension of serial murderers is that sometimes an accomplice, who was also witness to the murders, has confessed in an effort to gain the best possible deal in the criminal justice system. Examples of this were when Kenneth Bianchi confessed and implicated his cousin, Angelo Buono Jr. Fitzgerald confessed to helping Biegenwald dispose of bodies. Gore confessed and linked his cousin, Fred Waterfield, to a series of murders in Florida. Charlene Williams confessed and linked Gerald Gallego to ten murders. And Carol Bundy related how Douglas Clark shot a victim in the head while the victim was performing fellatio upon him. Clark then cut her head off, and the head was kept in a freezer. Bundy put lipstick on the head, and Clark took a shower with the head—and presumably had some sort of sex with it.

With over half (61 percent) of the serial murders being solved via witnesses, the police must become involved in the community relations programs warning citizens when they are dealing with a serial murderer at large.

Ride along programs to help citizens understand how their police work are also good, but officers should not discuss specifics about what is being done to apprehend a serial murderer. In fact, as has been demonstrated in this book, serial murderers tend to be very brazen and bold. It would not be at all surprising if he

306

would try to use such a program as a "fishing expedition" to gain information because one of the Hillside Stranglers did that very thing.

All news releases should come from only one person who is authorized by the various departments to speak for the task force. This officer should present an excellent appearance and have special training in police-community relations and communications. In these types of crimes, as in many others, the success of a law enforcement agency is entirely dependent upon the people they serve.

If there is no task force formed, then each of the departments involved will, of course, have their own spokesperson. That person should have the same qualifications as if he/she were speaking for a task force. These various Public Information Officers should coordinate the information in their news releases. The releases should be read verbatim from the release and "off the record" remarks should be avoided.

Since only a few women ever survive an attack from a serial murderer, they should not be taught to passively submit to them and go along with their demands. Women do escape from these killers by screaming, running away, and pounding on doors. But their chances of survival would be greatly enhanced if they started screaming and fighting where there are people who can help, not waiting until the killer got them into a position where no help would be available or nobody could hear them.

These women who escape then should be encouraged to immediately report what has occurred to the police while the information is still fresh in their minds. If a task force has been established, a special telephone number should be published. This number should be one that is easy for people to remember. The telephone at the task force office should be staffed around the clock to receive information. Hopefully, the victim, who has escaped her attacker, could provide the police with sufficient information to enable them to apprehend the attacker before he could flee the area. If there is sufficient information on the wanted person and the car he is driving, the author suggests that a blockade be immediately established. If conditions permit, it should be a closed blockade, if traffic conditions are heavy, then it may have to be an open type. If a helicopter is available, it should be airborne. This is especially important during times when there is heavy traffic. If serial murders begin to occur in the area, women should be taught the things they should remember about their attacker and his car. For example: About how old was the attacker? How tall was he? How much did he weigh? Did he have any unusual scars, marks, or tattoos? Was he wearing any jewelry? Was his speech normal? Was his walk normal? What was his race? Did he have a weapon of any kind? How was he dressed? What were his exact words during the attack? What kind of vehicle was he driving? What color was it? What color was the upholstery? Where did the victim touch inside the car? How old was the car? Did the car have any stickers on it? Did the car have any damage to it? Were there any dangling objects in the car? What was the body style of the vehicle? And most importantly, what was the vehicle's license plate number and state of registration?

Women should be made aware of some of the "con games" these killers have used in the past. As has been said before, when the serial killer tells a woman if she remains quiet and does exactly what he tells her, she will not get hurt—that is nothing but his way of manipulating the victim. In most instances, he will kill her anyway when he is finished with her. Women should also be taught that the possibility of trying to talk a serial killer out of attacking, or murdering her, has very little chance of being successful. It should be pointed out to them that there have been examples where women who were especially trained in counseling troubled mental patients, and who had dealt with criminals, were murdered. And since serial killers, not infrequently, pose as law enforcement officers, the police should make women aware that officers will at all times show them appropriate identification. Women should never be asked to stop their vehicles in any area where there is inadequate lighting and no witnesses, nor should they stop for any police vehicle unless it is clearly marked as such.

In the author's opinion, women should also be taught that it is a waste of money and time to attend the various forms of physical self defense classes that women seem to flock to from fear when a serial murderer is at large in their respective communities. Of the many victims who were murdered by serial killers, several of them were enrolled in, or had taken, self defense classes. Such courses do more harm than good because they breed a false sense of security that could make the women believe they could handle a serial killer, when in fact they would not be able to do it. What has been said here is limited to physical self defense classes. The author highly recommends firearms safety and familiarization courses for women who buy weapons for self protection. Based upon the murder cases reviewed, it would appear that one of the best things that a woman could do to increase her safety would be to buy a dog. It is also suggested that women participate in a voluntary program where their fingerprints and palm prints are taken and kept in their own file, or the file of a relative, in the unfortunate circumstance they are needed to help identify her.

> Another dissimilarity between serial murder cases and the majority of other crimes, is that in those latter cases, most criminals are susceptible to an emotional interrogational approach. In serial murder cases, if a confession is obtained at all, the logical interrogational approach is most apt to be the most effective.

As a general rule, when a crime was committed during a time when the perpetrator was angry, drunk, or sexually aroused, most wrongdoers are susceptible to an emotional appeal by a skilled interrogator. Essentially, the emotional kind of appeal could be very briefly described as one where a common bond is established between the interrogator and the the suspect and the wrongdoing is minimized. Some, if not all of the blame for the crime, is placed upon an accomplice and/or the victim. If it is known that a person is religious, an appeal is made in that direction. If a person has subscribed to a code of honor, and he has broken it, an appeal can be made to his high regard for duty and honor. Not infrequently an interrogator will, especially with a young man, question whether the suspect is a man due to his lack of courage to tell the truth. Another emotional appeal may involve the use of the suspect's feelings of jealousy. For example, where the suspect has a good looking wife and it appears that the suspect is taking all the blame for an accomplice who could try to have an affair with the suspect's beautiful wife, should the suspect be sent to prison, the interrogator will use that possible circumstance to make an appeal to any jealous feelings the suspect might have about his wife and someone taking the suspect's place in his bed. The amount of negative publicity about the crime, and the subsequent embarrassment the publicity could cause the family of the accused, should the suspect decide to go to trial, is another form of an emotional appeal that can be made. Of course, all during the interrogation the various physiological manifestations of nervousness, such as his dry mouth, his inability to look the interrogator in the eyes, his hesitation in answering questions that he should easily know the answer to, the pulsation of the carotid arteries in the neck, and other things are pointed out to him. But having said all of the foregoing, for the most part, none of those techniques will be effective against a serial killer, especially one who has used a ruse on one or more of his victims to gain control over her. This type of killer is cold and calculating. If any technique works at all, it will be a logical appeal.

Basically speaking, a logical appeal is one during which time the interrogator puts the suspect in the same position that a member of the jury or the court might be. The interrogator puts forth hard cold facts and lets the suspect draw his own conclusions. If he confesses, it is because he is convinced that the police have a solid case against him, and he would have little chance of success in beating it.

The strong denials of guilt by a serial killer could shake the confidence of an inexperienced interrogator. Ted Bundy used such phrases as, "I didn't kill anyone." and, "I didn't hurt anyone." There is little nonverbal behavior displayed that one usually observes in a liar. From the interviews the author has observed with serial killers, it appears that sometimes they might overplay their role. They probably do this because they believe their intelligence is so superior and everyone else, including the psychologist or detective interviewing them, is so stupid that they must be certain that their ploy is understood. For example, when Kenneth Bianchi was trying to convince a doctor that he had multiple personalities, he tried to act out another personality, the one who had been responsible for some of the killings, but he tended to overdo it. When Dr. Martin Orne laid a trap by telling Bianchi that such multiple personalities usually appear in groups of three, and he had only shown two of these—Bianchi took the bait and came up with a third personality.

Sometimes the serial killers seem to adopt the attitude that the best offense is the best defense. Most of them are very cool under pressure. Based upon the author's research, when a confession was given, nearly forty percent (39%) of the time it was to gain some legal advantage. These confessions had been worked out through the legal system.(i.e. through the serial murderer's attorney and the prosecuting attorney) For example, William Heirens and Albert De Salvo both, confessed to stay out of the electric chair. Donald Gene Miller confessed to a manslaughter charge in exchange for showing the police where the bodies of four women were located. In Michigan, murder carries a penalty of life in prison whereas manslaughter carries a maximum penalty of fifteen years. It is doubtful that Miller would have agreed to plead guilty to manslaughter, had he not already been convicted on a felonious assault and first degree criminal sexual conduct charge.

> A common mistake made by the police investigating a serial murderer was to tip him off prematurely that he was a suspect. This afforded him the opportunity to dispose of incriminating evidence.

No data were computed on those instances where the police alerted the suspect before he was actually arrested or before a search warrant was obtained, and thus thereby afforded the serial killer with ample opportunity to dispose of evidence. Despite the fact that one of the long standing cardinal rules of homicide investigation has been that one does not take a murderer into custody until one is ready to make the charges stick, that rule has been violated again and again in serial murder investigations. The killers mentioned below had all been contacted by the police, were interrogated, and released. The killers then went to work trying to get rid of anything that would incriminate them. For example, Bundy washed his car inside and out. He even had his car repainted, and then he sold it. As mentioned earlier, John Norman Collins disposed of a box of women's clothing. He gave a hunting knife to his friend and told him to get rid of it. He spent part of the night after the last victim was murdered, washing and polishing the motorcycle that he used to give the victim a ride to his vacationing uncle's house where he killed her. He wanted to be certain that her fingerprints were not on the motorcycle. Gallego destroyed a gun used in a murder by smashing it to pieces with a hammer.

When the author asked Donald Miller what he regarded as the major error the police made in their investigation, he responded by saying that it was their failure to obtain a warrant to search his car immediately after the disappearance of the first victim, Martha Sue Young. The most likely reason for this mistake, not just in the case of Miller, but in others as well, was that the suspect was not really regarded seriously as the perpetrator. Serial murder suspects, in many instances, do not look, act or talk like one might expect of a murderer. In addition, the police have investigated literally hundreds of tips. They often lacked sufficient time. In all probability, they had already checked out numerous suspects, and all of their efforts had been bootless. A thorough inquiry of the suspect's background had not been made. In some instances, no background investigation of any kind had been made. It should be noted here that a good background investigation requires at least three to five days, and that is when all the people that must be contacted are readily available in one geographic area. When the sources are spread out, a longer time period will be required to complete the investigation. Such an investigation would provide the detectives with good insight into the kind of person whom they are about to contact. From a pragmatic viewpoint, it would be nearly impossible to carry out such inquiries on every single possible suspect. But the author suggests that whenever a man is named as a possible suspect from two different and independent sources, that a discreet inquiry be conducted. This is because something is not always as it appears at first blush. A superficial background check on many of the killers would be worthless. For example, Bundy was a respectable law school student who had been active in politcal campaigns. Bundy had worked at a crisis center, in emergency management, and in criminal justice planning. Bianchi was a trusted sergeant on a private security force, who was taking law enforcement classes. Bianchi was armed at the time he was arrested. Collins was a college senior who had been asked by his state police uncle to join the state police. He had no criminal record. Collins had also posed as a model in a muscle magazine. Donald Gene Miller had a bachelors degree in criminal justice. He had no criminal record. He was employed as a security guard when he was arrested. He attended the Methodist Church on a regular basis and was never heard to use foul language. Is it any wonder that oftentimes a serial killer will slip through the fingers of the police the first time he is approached? There can be little doubt that this is where the police must strengthen their investigative endeavors in the future if a better job is to be done in serial murder investigations. Any steps that can be taken to prevent the killer from slithering through the dragnet, in the long run, will save time, money, and possibly the lives of additional girls.

Thirty-six (36) percent of the perpetrators had kept items of evidence in their houses, apartments, or cars.

Even though the killer knew he was a suspect and had cleaned his vehicle, he still missed items of evidence. For example, Collins, in spite of getting rid of some women's clothing, had a piece of a victim's dress and his raincoat with Anne K.'s blood on it in his car. He also had a brown sweater with twenty-two pubic hair from Rose P. on it in his closet. Lake still had a murdered man's car with bullets and blood in it. Bundy, despite scrubbing his Volkswagen inside and out, still overlooked hair from two different victims which was recovered from his car. Clark and Kemper both kept victims' heads that they used for sexual purposes. Lake had his crimes recorded on a video tape kept at his ranch.

When the perpetrators had an opportunity to flee to avoid arrest, or to escape from custody, forty-six (46) percent of the time, they tried to either flee or escape.

This is another difference between serial murderers, as a group, and others involved in different types of crime. As a group, serial killers often act like trapped animals when it appears they are about to be arrested and have a chance to escape. If an opportunity to escape appears unlikely, they will usually capitulate to the arresting officers without a struggle, but they will frequently try to escape from confinement should an opening present itself. John Norman Collins didn't resist arrest when he was taken into custody. However, he was involved in two plots to escape from the State Prison of Southern Michigan at Jackson. The first plan involved Collins and another prisoner, Taylor. Both men were going to don correctional officer's clothing, or clothing very similar, and walk out of the prison during a shift change. Collins was unable to take part in the escape because he had been hurt playing sports. His cohort did, in fact, follow through with their plan and escaped from prison. The second plan involved Taylor coming back to the prison with a helicopter, landing inside the prison walls, and flying away with Collins. Prison officials learned of the plot and foiled it. Collins' thwarted efforts to escape, his activities which involved smuggling drugs into the prison, and his "loan sharking" operation resulted in Collins being transferred to the Michigan State Prison in Marquette, in Michigan's Upper Peninsula. After he had only been at Marquette for a short time, he attempted to tunnel his way out of the prison with a group of other murderers. Fortunately for society, Collins' plot was discovered. He was then placed in a closely guarded cell block where he has been permitted out of his cell only for one hour per day for exercise.

Bundy escaped from police custody twice. Once he jumped out a second story window of a courthouse. He was unable to get out of the area from where he had escaped. His bid for freedom only lasted six days before he was caught. The second time he escaped, was from a county jail. The escape involved a long range, complicated plan. Here were some of the main parts of that plan: Bundy complained about the food and restricted his food intake. He lost weight. He stopped eating breakfast, and slept in on mornings. He complained about the noise, and that his cell was always lit, until he was moved to a different cell at the end of a hall. This cell had a vent above it which provided access to the sheriff's living quarters, which was adjacent to the jail. Someone had smuggled several hundred dollars into the jail to Bundy. The night Bundy escaped, he squeezed through the vent, dropped down into the unattended living quarters, stole clothing from a closet, slipped out the door, and then stole a car. The car broke down, but Bundy hitchhiked a ride to Denver, Colorado, where he went to the airport. He boarded a TWA aircraft and flew to Chicago. He then travelled to Ann Arbor, Michigan. A few days later, Bundy caught a bus to Florida. The only tip off that the police had, at least to one of Bundy's possible destinations, came from a surprise "shake down" search. Bundy was found in possession of an Illinois map and forged driver's license. After his escape, it was also clear why Bundy was not eating. He had to lose enough weight to squeeze through the vent. He did not eat breakfast and slept in during mornings to gain extra time before his escape was discovered. That part of the plan also worked very well for Bundy. He wasn't discovered missing until nearly twelve hours after he had been gone. He was quite probably in Chicago by that time. When Bundy was arrested in Florida, he fought with the police officer and knocked the officer to the pavement and then fled. The officer, however, got up from the pavement, chased and caught Bundy. The fight continued between Bundy and the policeman. When the struggle was over, Bundy had suffered a severe, but well deserved, beating. While they were enroute to the jail, Bundy told the peace officer that he wished the officer had killed him. He apologized to the officer and told him that he had not meant to hurt him (the officer). He was only trying to escape. Bundy, however, continued to lie and tell the officer that he was someone else. (i.e. the person whose identification he had stolen.)

DeSalvo tried to flee the area where he had broken into an apartment, but the chase ended when the detective who was pursuing him drew down on him with his revolver and ordered him to halt. Sometime later, DeSalvo tried to flee from the police again when the police were arresting him on other charges. Finally, DeSalvo escaped from the Bridgewater State Hospital with help from his brothers.

As the police closed in on him, Gerald Gallego fled with his girlfriend, but they were both arrested after his girlfriend picked up money which had been sent to her by her parents who had no knowledge of their daughter's criminal involvement. Subsequent to his arrest, Gallego plotted with several other prisoners to escape, but the plan was discovered.

Donald Miller fled a house where he had bound fifteen-yearold Ann Gilbert's hands with a necktie. Then he tried to strangle her with a belt, but it broke. He had inserted his finger into her vagina and was attempting to insert his penis, but could not maintain an erection, when Ann's brother entered the house through the rear door. Miller jumped up and then attacked Ann's brother, Randy, who was thirteen years old. Ann fled the house without clothing and ran down the road screaming that there was a man in their house trying to kill her brother. When Miller fled the Gilbert residence, he knocked one man down, and drove away. Witnesses at the house, wrote down his license number. Miller was arrested several hours later, but denied any involvement in the attempted murders and the attempted rape.

William Heirens, a Chicago serial killer, was apprehended prowling around in an apartment building. He fought with two police officers, one of whom was off duty, until he was hit over the head with a flower pot and knocked unconscious.

David Gore, a Florida serial murderer, barricaded himself in his house after he shot a girl in the head when she tried to escape. He then tried to hide her body in the trunk of his car, but when officers observed blood dripping from the trunk of his car, they knew where he had put her. The peace officers also found another victim alive strung up in his house after he had surrendered.

Leonard Lake was provided with little opportunity to escape. He was nabbed by surprise as he waited in a stolen car for his partner, Charles Ng. Ng had gotten caught red handed trying to shoplift a vise. Ng ran out of the store and fled to Canada. Lake, on the other hand, was not only driving a car stolen from a man they had murdered, but police found a weapon in the trunk of the car with a silencer on it. After Lake's arrest, he committed suicide by taking a cyanide pill while in the jail. Later, when private police tried to arrest Ng for shop lifting in Canada, like many other serial killers, he resisted. Nevertheless, he was subdued, and he has since been returned to the United States where he will stand trial for the murders he has allegedly committed.

Christopher Wilder was spotted outside a gasoline station in the village of Colebrook, New Hampshire, by two New Hamshire State Troopers. Trooper Leo "Chuck" Jellison told Wilder he wanted to talk with him, but Wilder ran toward the stolen Trans-Am he had been driving. He pulled on the door on the passenger's side to open the door, but it was locked. Then he ran around the car, opened the door on the driver's side, dove across the seat, opened the glove box, and pulled out a .357 magnum revolver. Trooper Jellison jumped on top of him and put his arms around Wilder. This prevented Wilder from turning the revolver barrel in the direction of the Trooper. While they struggled for the gun, two shots were fired into Wilder. The second shot entered Wilder's heart and he died almost immediately. One of the rounds, however, had passed through Wilder's body and entered the Trooper, very nearly killing him. The attendant at the gas station told them that Wilder had asked him whether he would have any trouble getting into Canada, which was only about twelve miles from Colebrook. This incident clearly indicated just how dangerous arresting a serial killer can really be for a police officer.

The author suggests that when one is dealing with a serial killer, or one suspected of being a serial murderer, that it be remembered that about half of these criminals are high escape and suicide risks. When they change their patterns of behavior like Bundy did, it would behoove one to begin asking himself, " Why is the killer acting this way?" When he complains about something, are his complaints really justified, or is he trying to maneuver himself into a position where he can escape?

> Another fact that makes the investigation of a serial murder case so much different from any other sort of crime, is that in most crimes the perpetrators try to avoid contact with the police. The serial murderer, as a general rule, does not fear the police, nor—as previously mentioned—do they seem to have much respect for the abilities of the police to catch them.

One night while the author was on routine patrol, he saw four young men pushing a car trying to get it started. As he approached them to determine if he could help them, all four men ran into a swamp that had nearly knee deep water. The author chased them into the swamp because it was not normal behavior for them to do that on a cold, nearly freezing, night. Two of the men were caught immediately. The swamp was quickly surrounded by the police. A short time later, the other two men were captured. One had made it through the swamp and was caught peddling a stolen bicycle away from the area. The fourth young man remained in the swamp as long as he could, but eventually he was so cold that he too was forced to surrender, but he was very proud that he was the last man arrested. Why did they run? The car they were pushing had been stolen three days earlier from a little town about thirty-five miles to the south.

Contrast the behavior of the young car thieves with the behavior of a few serial killers. John Collins went motorcycle riding with a police sergeant. It has been said that the bike he was riding was stolen. It was noted that it had been in that particular sergeant's patrol area that Collins disposed of the body of his last victim. He contacted his state police uncle and tried to learn about the progress of a murder investigation. As Crime Laboratory Experts were at his uncle's house, processing it as a crime scene, Collins was observed cruising by the house at least twice. Bianchi, one of the Hill Side Stranglers, attended law enforcement classes, and had participated in a police "Ride Along" program, after he had been involved in murdering girls in Los Angeles. Emil Kemper visited a bar near a court house. The bar was a favorite "watering hole" for off duty police officers. Kemper bragged about how he had bought the police drinks and about how they had bought some for him as he sat there and tried to learn as much as he could about what evidence, if any, those officers investigating the deaths of the girls he had killed might have against him. Christopher Wilder's seamstress, who worked at her home, was the wife of a Palm Beach Florida Detective. Wilder would stop by the house when the detective was at home to have a monogram sewed on his racing suit. Of course, while he was waiting he talked with the detective. David Gore had been a reserve police officer, and he kept a police scanner in his house. He was well aware that the police were coming to his house after he had shot one girl. He boldly called in a report to divert the police away from his home, but it didn't work. As has been mentioned previously, one serial killer stood with a group of spectators and watched, a crime scene being processed. From the behavior we have seen here, serial killers in several cases, rather than avoiding the police, have made it a point to be in close contact with police officers to gain as much intelligence about the progress of the investigations as possible. We should take advantage of this knowledge to help us during a serial murder investigation.

During the Second World War there was a slogan which said, "Loose lips sink ships." Well, the same thought applies to a serial murder investigation. Except for the information released to the People to get them involved in the investigation and to enable the members of the public to protect themselves from the serial killer, police officers should be very cautious when they are talking about the progress of the investigation in restaurants, bars, and donut shops. They should be very alert to any customer who seems to be spending an inordinate amount of time in someplace where the police tend to congregate. It is logical, that since the killer's aim is to learn as much as possible concerning how the police investigation is progressing, that he is quite apt to seat himself near where the police would be talking, or would even move closer to the police, if that appeared necessary to him. As a general rule, since these killers are very smart, it is unlikely that they would ask questions that directly pertain to the murders. But that does not mean that the killer may not engage a police investigator in a conversation whereby, if he could indirectly ask questions about the officers work, he might be capable of manipulating the officer into volunteering the information the killer is desirous of learning. Therefore, officers should be especially sensitive during any conversation during which time a person tries to maneuver one or more investigators to talk about the serial murders they are investigating. As mentioned above, the police should also surreptitiously record those persons present at body recovery sites.

In the author's study, there were twenty-eight subjects (N=28). (Since the gathering of information relative to serial murderers is ongoing, the actual number of murderers studied exceeded the twenty-eight figure. The studies of these additional killers have yielded no significant differences, however.) The four female accomplices who, for one reason or another, actually aided and abetted, a serial killer, were not included with the twenty-eight subjects. Of these women, three were sentenced to prison. Only one of the women had been a victim.

When considering what event led to the murderer's apprehension, and therefore what type of event might be most productive in future investigations which would lead to the arrest of the perpetrator, the things which are written here are based on twenty-seven subjects. The reason for this difference is that of the twenty-eight subjects, only one turned himself in before the police arrested him. Edmund Kemper surrendered after murdering both his own mother and her lady friend. Kemper has a genius I.Q. He knew that the evidence against him was overwhelming. It would have been only a matter of time before he would have been caught. What Kemper had done was in his own best interest.

Sometimes it was not clear which particular event led to the killer's arrest because two or more events occurred, almost simultaneously, either of which could have led directly to the apprehension of the killer. For example, a young patrolman observed John Norman Collins in the area where the last victim was picked up. That was highly significant because Collins had been a suspect in a murder a year earlier. But it was the two women who worked at the wig shop, both of whom had gone outside the shop to look at Collins, and whom had identified Collins as being the last person with the victim before she disappeared, that were most instrumental in bringing Collins' criminal career to an end. It was, however, determined through police investigation that the victim had been murdered in a house owned by Collins' state police uncle, and that Collins was the only person who had access to the house. Further, it was learned through investigation, that Collins had taken young women to the house on previous occasions. Finally, through investigation, it was learned that Collins had previously used those same premises to store stolen motorcycles. In other words, he had used his uncles's home for his criminal activities before he decided the house would be a good place for rape and murder. Of course, his uncle had no knowledge his nephew was involved in any criminal activity. The point is that all of these events were very important. For the most part, however, the criterion or criteria used to determine which event or events were most important was determined by the response to the question: "What was the primary event that led to the perpetrator's arrest *as a murderer*?" Totally there were thirty-six (36) primary factors or events.

As was mentioned above, sixty-one percent (61%) of the serial killers were caught as a direct result of information from witnesses. Sometimes these witnesses were the victims who had escaped from the serial killer. For example, Carol DaRonch escaped from Ted Bundy by jumping from his car and running away. She later identified him in a lineup. Then we have the witness who played a role in the serial killings by helping the murderer obtain victims, disposed of evidence for the killer, and helped clean up the crime scene. Charlene Williams, who was with Gerald Gallego, was that kind of witness. We also have the witness who was the last person, besides the killer, to have seen the victim alive. And the witness has identified the person the victim was with just before she disappeared. The ladies at the wig shop in the Collins case were examples of that type of witness. There were also witnesses who observed the serial killer leave a crime scene where he had tried to murder the victim, but failed. The Donald Miller case in the Lansing, Michigan, area had those kinds of witnesses, who not only observed Miller at the scene as he ran from the victim's house, but even obtained Miller's license number from his Oldsmobile car as he sped away from the area. On rare occasions the witness was attacked by a serial killer and raped, but for some inexplicable reason, he did not choose to kill that particular victim, nor did he even try to kill her, despite the fact that he had murdered numerous other women. The newlywed college coed assaulted by the Boston Strangler illustrated that type of witness. With the help of a police artist she made a drawing of her attacker. A detective immediately recognized the drawing as Albert DeSalvo. There was, in addition, the witness to whom the serial murderer admitted that he was the killer who had been terrorizing the community. DeSalvo, the Boston Strangler, told another patient at the Bridgewater State Hospital in Massachusetts that he was the "Strangler." Finally, there was the witness who had lived with the serial killer and based upon the information she had learned from the news media—and from her own personal observations— came to believe that her lover was a murderer. Ted Bundy's girlfriend in Washington exemplified that kind of witness. Her lover's name was "Ted". That was the same name the killer used when he talked with a victim in the state park. Bundy's car was a light colored Volkswagen. The killer drove a light colored Volkswagen. Bundy had worked at a medical supply house. He had bandages and plaster of paris in his medicine cabinet in his apartment. The killer had his arm in a sling. Bundy had not been with her when any of the murders occurred. He had frightened her when they were making love by tying her up. The artist's sketch of the murderer could not have been a better sketch of Bundy—even if he had sat for the drawing. Finally, when Bundy moved to Utah, the murders stopped in the State of Washington and started in Utah. She reluctantly reported her suspicions to the "Ted Squad" Task Force working in King County, Washington.

The action taken by Bundy's girlfriend should teach us something about the type of information that is made available to the public. Let's suppose the people were not told the killer used the first name of "Ted", was driving a light colored Volkswagen, he had his arm in a sling, and that no artist's sketch was ever published in any newspaper or broadcast on television. Let us suppose, as sometimes happens, that the police "sat on" the information and adopted a "We're gonna do this by ourselves attitude." The possibility of any witness coming forward, like she did, and telling the police that she knew someone that "fit the bill" would have been quite remote. As was mentioned earlier, the more information that can be released to the public to get the people involved in helping the police track down and identify the serial killer the better. Anything that can be done to encourage the one or two witnesses who have significant information to come forward should be carried out.

It should be recalled that Bundy's girlfriend was very reluctant, and she probably made the report to the police primarily to relieve her own conscience in event he really was involved the murders. The chances are great that she probably tended to down play the significance of the information she related to the officers. Recall also how Collins' fraternity brother, who when he was first interviewed, gave the police an erroneous time which, in effect, exonerated Collins. He did that because he said he knew Collins was stealing motorcycles, and he could not bring himself to believe that Collins was capable of murder. In the opinion of the author, when an informant is well acquainted with a possible suspect, is on friendly terms with him, and yet feels compelled to reluctantly contact the police and relate his concerns, the police should give much more weight to such information than they would in receiving information from someone who might have an "axe to grind" against a suspect. But because the witness prefaces his remarks by saying, " There probably isn't anything to this, in fact, I doubt very much that there is because I have known Ted for years, and I know he could never be involved in a murder...", and then precedes to give the officer the information in a wishy—washy way. The manner in which the informa-tion was reported, might tend to make the receiving police officer think that "there wasn't very much to it." Whereas, the witness who makes a report against another person for revenge would probably sound much more positive and sure of himself in his allegations and would include very little information of a complimentary nature about the suspect. This could make the latter person sound like a better suspect than the former when, in fact, the reverse could be true.

The author's study demonstrated that thirty-one (31) percent of the serial murderers were arrested as a direct result of police investigative work. Examples of this were the finding of a cigarette butt with Sissak's fingerprint on it at a crime scene, of identifying him by comparing that print with other fingerprints from him which were already in the files, and arresting him. Or the finding of Erskine's palm print in one of the apartments where he attacked a victim, or tracking down Larry Gene Bell from the paper upon which Bell's captive, Sheri Smith, wrote her "will." This seemingly low percentage should not cause one to come to the erroneous conclusion that since nearly twice the number of cases were solved as a result of information from witnesses as were solved by investigators that the efforts of the detectives were of little value. That would simply not be true because in most of the serial killings where witnesses gave the police the information necessary which enabled the investigators to track down and arrest the murderer, the victims did not know their assailant. And many of the witnesses did not know the person whom they had observed with the victim. It was left to the police investigators to make that kind of determination. During the study, it was noted by the author that wiretap evidence was used very sparingly, if at all. Probably one of the reasons for the lack of use is simply because some jurisdictions deny the police the right to use such evidence. In Michigan, for example, only the federal authorities can legally use wiretaps. If the state or local police need to use a wiretap, they must elicit help from an agency like the Federal Bureau of Investigation. There can be little doubt that, in some cases, the use of a wiretap could be very important.

When the investigation becomes focused on one or two suspects, before they are approached, the author would suggest that a court order be obtained for a wiretap simultaneously with the search warrant for the suspect's dwelling and vehicles. The reason for this is that when the police first confront the suspect he may use his telephone to contact one or more friends to try to establish a phony alibi. Hansen, for example, contacted his friends. He told them he was being framed by a prostitute and asked them to say, should the police ask, that they were having dinner together during that same time period that the victim said she was at his house being tortured. John Norman Collins, according to his friend, Arnold Davis, called his mother. He told her he was in trouble. She was to tell the investigators, should they inquire, that Collins had spent the entire weekend (when a victim had been murdered) at his home. Gallego also used the telephone to call his girlfriend and agreed with her on the story she was to tell the police when they questioned her about her car being used during the abduction and murder of a young couple. The author suggests that greater use be made of this law enforcement tool whenever and wherever it is legally permissible to use it.

To enable the investigators, who are assigned to the task force, to do their jobs more efficiently, a one day training session should be conducted. The curriculum should include information about the possible type of criminal with whom they are dealing, depending upon the circumstances of the case:

The killer may pose as a police officer.

There may be two killers functioning as a team.

The killer may, in some instances, be using a female accomplice.

There are some very real differences between a serial murder investigation and some other kinds of criminal investigations.

The types of evidence the killer may still have in his possession.

The investigators should be made aware that serial killers who use some sort of a ruse, are excellent "con artists." Therefore, every alibi given by a suspect must be thoroughly checked out.

The use of polygraph and its limitations.

In cases where the victims are being picked up along a certain street, consider using closed circuit television cameras to monitor that particular street. One officer can watch at least four different locations on one monitor. The officer would be able to "lock in" on any area where a possible suspect was trying to pick up a woman. He would also have the capability to immediately record what he was observing on the monitor. Plain clothes officers should also be monitoring the street. Their primary job would be to catch the murderer. They should avoid making any arrests unless the violations are of a very serious nature. If this procedure is not followed, the killer will know they are there, and he will not try to pick up any victim along that particular street. He may stop killing for a period of time until he believes "the heat is off." Or he may move to another jurisdiction where he would start to kill again.

Concealed cameras, rigged for time lapsed photography, could be used at body recovery sites where it is known that the perpetrator had deposited two different bodies of victims who had been kidnapped at two different times. He may try to leave a third or fourth victim at that same site. It is also for this reason, that if the victim's bodies are recovered from such a site, that the information that bodies have been recovered be kept secret for as long as possible. During that time, a "stake out" should be conducted at the site. This "stake out" should be properly manned in such a manner to apprehend the suspect should he decide to revisit the body recovery site or attempt to deposit another body there. The officers on the "stake out" should be equipped with both modern night viewing devices and cameras capable of recording the suspect's presence at the scene.

Serial murder cases are different in many respects from other criminal investigations and some of those differences have previously been spelled out. Due to those differences, the author suggests that investigators use some unorthodox methods, or at least some methods which are rarely used, because of the dangers they represent to the officers involved, the hardships they impose upon an officer's family, and the costs of such methods. When it appears with a high degree of probability that a particular person has committed the murders being investigated, thought should be given to using at least two or three officers in undercover operations. At least one of the officers should be a pretty woman who is of small stature. The killer would be more apt to lower his guard around her and would not be inclined to think that she was a police officer. Like everything else in a serial murder investigation, this is not the time to use rank amateurs. The officers working undercover should have a proven track record for their ability to do that type of work, which requires considerable acting ability because one's audience is only three feet away. And if a mistake is made, there is no chance to play the scene over again. If the suspected killer is residing in an apartment building, it is suggested that one undercover officer move into the same apartment building where the suspect lives. Or if the suspect works or attends college, if possible, assign undercover officers to some of the same classes that the suspect attends. Their objective would be to get to know the suspect, to befriend him, and to monitor his activities. Consideration should also be given to assigning an undercover officer in the same cell, or in an adjoining cell, to obtain information from him, if he is arrested for some offense, not necessarily murder. Here one must be very careful especially if the perpetrator has asked for legal counsel. One should not ask the suspect questions about the crimes since that could lead to an illegal confession. There is nothing wrong with being the helpful, consoling, listening ear. Since it is practically an absolute certainty, that if a confession is obtained this way, it will be challenged in court, both the undercover officer and the officer's cell should be "wired." The same is true regarding any other undercover officers, they too should be "wired" both for their protection and to corroborate and verify any incriminating statements the suspect may make to them. The commanding officer of the task force could also consider utilizing an inmate who is willing to cooperate with law enforcement officials. There have been at least two serial killers who have admitted their crimes to another prisoner while they were in jail for other offenses. The problem with using prisoners is that their credibility is always open to question. One could argue that the fellow inmate maneuvered the suspect into a position where the suspect gave a false confession for the inmate's self serving purposes. In addition since the prisoner is actually working for the police, he would be an agent of government, and he would be bound by essentially the same rules as the police relative to the questions he could ask the suspect. In other words, the fellow inmate could not question the suspected serial murderer if he had an attorney, or had asked to consult with an attorney before answering any questions the police might ask about the crime for which the attorney had been appointed or retained.

If the serial killer has murdered victims in an apartment building, it would be necessary to interview the occupants of that building to determine whether any of them may have seen the perpetrator or have any information which would help solve the case. Many of the occupants of the apartment building would be quite frightened and would be reluctant to open their doors to talk with plain clothes detectives. To help mitigate the fears of the people, the author suggests that during this phase of the investigation that either the detectives put on police uniforms or are accompanied by uniformed officers. And prior to the conducting the interviews, the news media should be requested to tell the people that officers will be contacting and talking with the people who live in the building where the murder took place. If detectives will be interviewing people in the surrounding area, the people should be told that too.

A serial murderer can cause even highly experienced surveillance officers to believe they have been "burned" by the way the killer drove his car while he was "trolling" for a victim. The killer frequently cruised shopping malls during twilight, and oftentimes he doubled back. The manner in which he drove made officers believe the killer they had under surveillance was attempting to "clean" himself. One officer told the author he thought they had been "burned" after the suspect doubled back several times and actually waved at them. Several years later, after the killer had been apprehended, the author queried the killer about whether he was aware that he was under surveillance. He said that he was not aware of it. He said the "urge" came on him strongest at twilight, and, in substance, if he picked up a victim then, he had the entire night to do what he felt he had to do.

It is a good technique for investigators to study the crimes, which were committed in the same geographical area as the serial murders, where the method of operation has been similar in nearly every respect, except the victims were not murdered. The crimes that may have been committed before, during, and after the serial murders should be examined. If such a crime has occurred, the killer may have been involved in that crime too. The victim of a similar crime may be capable of providing valuable information about her assailant. When a good suspect is developed, the most thorough background investigation that can be carefully conducted should be carried out without the suspect being made aware that it is being done. For that reason, no contact is made with anyone who could possibly tell him that the police are investigating him. The purpose behind this background check is to learn as much as possible about the suspect. And to determine whether the suspect has been living a double life. Oftentimes, the killer, who has used a ruse, presents two faces to the world. On one hand, he presents himself as a courteous, clean cut, American young man. But on the other hand, he can be a cold blooded killer, who cares little about anyone else except himself. The latter lifestyle frequently involves lying, window peeking, stealing and the general manipulation of other people around him.

When a tip from an informant is being investigated, the author suggests, if feasible, that the detective handling the tip first contact and interview the informant prior to doing anything else. The reason behind making that contact is to give the investigator a better feel for whether the information can be relied upon. Every investigator has to ask himself whether the informant is relating the information for altruistic reasons or does he have ulterior motives for making the report. The contact with the informant, whenever possible, should be made in person, not over the telephone. Personal contact helps the investigator make his evaluation.

No suspect should ever be cleared of suspicion based solely upon the investigator's opinion. Clearance must always require additional proof. That proof may take the form of an alibi that has been thoroughly checked out. For example, the suspect may have been working at the time the crime was committed and that can be verified by other workers. The suspect may have been at a health club when the victim was kidnapped, and there were witnesses who were working out at the club that vouched for his presence during the critical time period. Or the suspect may be cleared by the results of a polygraph examination administered by a good, competent examiner who has used a sound technique. The examiner should be a person who has been conducting no less than two Specific Issue Polygraph Examinations per week and who has conducted not less than 500 such examinations. The suspect should be in physical condition to take the examination. He should be well rested and should have eaten a light meal before the polygraph test. He should not have been questioned by anyone on the day of the examination. By "anyone" the author means the suspect's attorney, a family member, or any investigator. If the suspect is questioned by an investigator just prior to the examination, the result could be very misleading. For the truthful suspect, such an interrogation could result in polygraph records that would indicate that the person was lying. In other words, we would have a false positive. The result could also be inconclusive. If the suspect was lying, it is possible that such questioning could result in the suspect being so emotionally drained that the charts might appear devoid of emotional responses. This would not mislead a competent examiner using a sound technique, but an inexperienced examiner might be misled into believing that the examinee was truthful. Investigators must understand the limitations of the polygraph technique. The questions that are asked on a polygraph examination must be worded in a certain way; for excellent accuracy, or validity, the examiner can only probe one single issue during a polygraph examination.

The investigator may clear the suspect by some other investigative means. But regardless how a suspect is cleared, there must be a reasonable degree of certainty that he either was or was not the murderer. As has been mentioned before, the handling of tips during the police investigation appears to be the Achilles heel of every serial murder task force. Investigators must do a better job in that area because, time and time again, serial killers have been questioned by detectives and released, only to kill again. And this problem is not unique to America, our European brothers have made the same mistakes. The Yorkshire Ripper in England was questioned by the police several times and released.

There must be some mechanism to provide for some means of quality control in the manner in which tips are investigated to prevent a serial murderer from slipping through the net. Whenever that occurs, additional women are going to suffer and die. The author has suggested that a committee of two or three highly experienced investigators each review the work that was done on each and every tip to insure that the tip was properly handled. Detectives frequently have a tremendous amount of work during the first seventy-two hours after a killing has occurred. Oftentimes the detectives receive hundreds of tips during that time period. It is then when investigators must evaluate the tips they have received and use some method to prioritize the tips to enable them to use their manpower most effectively. It is imperative that the detectives handling these tips in the field take their time and do a very thorough job. Good investigative work requires time. Speedy—haphazard— handling of tips is bound to lead to mistakes. It has happened where a serial killer, who was apparently thought to be above suspicion because he was with a woman, was contacted and interviewed over the telephone. In a serial murder investigation, interviews should be conducted face-to-face, regardless whether the person being interviewed is a witness or a suspect.

THE IMPACT OF POLICE PATROLS ON SERIAL MURDER CASES

Uniformed police patrols can play an important role in apprehending a serial killer because such patrols are frequently in areas and at times when the killer doesn't expect them. Because of this, police patrols should be kept abreast of the significant points of the progress of the investigation. The author's research indicated that eight (8) percent of the murderers studied were caught because of the work by patrols. For example, the Yorkshire Ripper was caught by two uniformed British police officers. When they stopped him, he had another potential victim in his car. The officers noted that Sutcliffe's car had one license plate taped on top of another one. In another case in Alaska, a young woman was rescued from serial killer Richard Hansen by a police patrol. Hansen had attempted to put her into his airplane, but when he took a handcuff off her, she bolted. She ran down a street and was spotted by a police patrol. She related to the patrolmen how Hansen was going to kill her. A short time later, Hansen was confronted by the officers. He owned a bakery and coffee shop. The girl was a prostitute. Hansen convinced the officers that she was trying to blackmail him. Two of his friends provided an alibi for him. They stated Hansen was with them at the very time she claimed she was being attacked. The police did not pursue the matter further until sometime later. After two young women were found by hunters buried along the river near Hansen's cabin, the police talked with the two alibi witnesses again. They both admitted they had lied to protect Hansen. The police obtained a search warrant and searched Hansen's house. The shell casings from the shallow grave where one of the victims had been buried had been fired in the rifle they seized when they executed the search warrant. Hansen worked out a deal with the prosecution. He confessed to four murders in exchange for an agreement that he could avoid the ordeal and publicity of a trial.

CONCLUDING REMARKS

Twenty years ago, American criminal investigators knew very little about the serial murder phonomenon. In fact, it has only been rather recently that the term, "serial murder" has came into use. Earlier when more than one victim was murdered, whether the victims were killed over a period of time or whether they were murdered during relatively the same time period, all such killings were lumped together under the heading of "mass murders." During this past twenty years, there has "apparently" been a dramatic increase in serial, mass, and spree murders within the United States. Is it possible that twenty years ago that there were many serial murders that occurred that were not recognized as such? With the passage of the Omnibus Crime Bill in 1968, the police in the country began a climb toward a level of sophistication that was totally unknown previously. It could have been very possible for several serial killers to have been functioning in various cities around the United States without the police recognizing that the murders were being perpetrated by a small number of criminals.

This book has pointed out some of the differences between the investigation of a conventional crime and a serial murder investigation. The book also has pointed out why each and every state must have the death penalty. Whether it is used or whether it is not, it is necessary to have this penalty on the books as a bargaining chip. As was clearly demonstrated by examples throughout this book, a serial murderer who has used a ruse, is not in fear or in awe of the police, the courts, or anything else in the criminal justice system. This kind of serial killer will not, generally, confess to his crimes unless it is to his distinct legal advantage to do so. Those states that do not have the death penalty are sometimes forced to bargain from an inferior position. As in the Donald Miller case in Michigan, the prosecuting attorney did not believe the People's case was strong enough to prevail at trial. He, therefore, permitted Miller to plead guilty to manslaughter. Manslaughter carried a maximum penalty of fifteen years in prison. Whereas, the offense which Miller had originally been charged with was murder. This crime carried the maximum penalty in Michigan of life in prison. And those states which do not have the death penalty are perhaps unknowingly, placing the lives of their citizens in jeopardy. The anecdote in the book about how a man had killed another man in a state which had the death penalty; how the murderer fled to Michigan, tried to kill a bartender in a phony holdup, but lost his nerve, and finally how he attempted to give the police a false confession to several Michigan murders, but he failed a polygraph examination that was administered to verify his confession, has been previously discussed. Subsequent to the examination, he admitted he had lied about killing the women in Michigan so he could receive a life sentence there and avoid the death penalty in his home state. But how many people have been murdered in Michigan, and other states which do not have capital punishment, by criminals who have sought to avoid the death penalty? We will never know! From the author's point of view, there is much that we need to learn about serial murderers from serial murderers; the writer would like to see every state participate in a program, where the serial killers who are apprehended, would be sent to a central location with high security where each of them would receive maximum treatment and where they could be studied in great depth. If any murderer would refuse to cooperate in the program, then there would be no advantage in spending the taxpayer's money in maintaining and keeping the murderer alive, and he could be executed by the most merciful means available consistent with a civilized society's standards. In the author's view, that is death by injection.

In those instances where a serial murderer has responded to treatment in a structured environment, and where he has been cooperating fully with authorities, selected residents could make up an advisory panel to help solve pending serial murder cases. Those residents who are sincerely helping could be rewarded by allowing them to have better food, living quarters, more exercise in the fresh air, and other privileges. Those inmates who do not cooperate should be separated from those residents who are trying to make some constructive contribution. In every instance, it should never be forgotten that serial killers, as a group, tend to be high escape risks.

Hopefully, this book has also destroyed some of the myths about serial killers. Some of these myths were:

A serial killer always works alone.

No woman would ever stoop to help a serial killer murder another woman.

A serial killer really has a subconscious wish to be apprehended.

A serial killer has a need to talk about his "problem", and he will readily confess his crimes once he is caught, even when there is little evidence against him.

Most serial killers look like monsters.

Since most serial murderers are psychopaths, they can easily "beat" a polygraph examiner.

A serial killer will always follow a certain method of operation. He will kill his victims by one method and dispose of their bodies the same way following every murder.

Most serial killers attend the funeral services of their victims.

A serial killer will always leave some evidence at a body recover site that can be traced back to him, and will always carry away from that site trace evidence which will indicate he was there.

As was apparent from reading this book, there are no easy solutions in dealing with serial killers, but it has been said, "Knowledge is power" and, "Know your enemy." To that extent this book should give the investigator additional power and knowledge about his opponent. There is much more, however, that can be done in the future. As has been mentioned, with the capture of every serial murderer, our knowledge about them increases. But in order to learn as much as possible, there should be research done on the federal level that would examine each and every serial murder case which has had sexual overtones that has ever occurred. We should not limit ourselves to the murders in the United States, but take a global approach. The researchers should devote a considerable portion of their time to studying the investigative processes. That should be accomplished by interviewing the investigators who were "down in the trenches" to determine what the significant factors were that led to the apprehension of the perpetrator. The author suggests also that a form be designed on the federal level which would be in the nature of an after action report which would elicit that sort of data. It is also suggested that a repository for that type of data be established on a federal level and that all bona fide researchers and participating police agencies could access it in their effort to study serial killers. Without question it would cost a considerable amount of money to conduct such research and establish such a file. At this time, however, there are nine serial murder investigations taking place in various jurisdictions within the United States. Each serial murder investigation costs millions of dollars. A conservative estimate of the cost of the serial murder investigations underway right now would be about twenty million dollars. The author suggests that the most effective and meaningful way to reduce these tremendous costs is to apprehend the killers. What the author has suggested would be a giant step toward that goal.

In addition, it would provide some young women, who may become future victims of a serial killer, with a chance to live out their lives and make some real contributions to our society. It also would save the families the grief that is suffered when a loved one has been taken from them, and it would make our country a safer place to live. Therefore, when one considers the alternatives, the cost of the before mentioned reports and files would be a small price to pay for the benefits that would be derived from them. The larger question really is, "Can we really afford *NOT* to establish such a data base and do all we are capable of doing to put a stop to serial killers' criminal activities?"

Until such a file can be established in the future, it is suggested that whenever a police task force successfully concludes an inquiry, that some time be taken to either write, make a cassette tape, or a video tape recording in the nature of an after action report. Such a report should include various problems that were encountered during the investigation and how those problems were solved. It should also include errors that were made during the investigation and what could be done in future to avoid those errors. Care should be taken here so the defendant will not be provided with anything that would permit him to manipulate the legal system into granting him a new trial. Most importantly, the after action report should emphasize those incidents which led to the capture of the murderer and ended his reign of terror upon the community.

S.D.G.

TABLE 1

MODI OPERANDI

PERPETRATOR	Stole victim's property excl. clothes/money	Tied up or cuffed at least one victim	Secretly obtained info. from police	Studied in criminal justice area	Posed as police officer/detective	Continued to murder though identif. likely	Very bold in presence of police	Stripped victim of clothes	Stole money from victim	Did not know victim before murder	Offered victim a ride	Raped victim	Possessed handcuffs or leg irons	Knew victim before murder (had met)	Photographed victim	Made video tapes of sex with victim	Contacted victim from newspaper ad.	Cut victim's body into pieces	Burned victim's body	Evidence of murder found in car/home	Body of victim thrown into water	Released potential murder victim (female)	Assaulted girls under 12 (pre-puberty)	Used public transportation	Murdered others (not sex related)	Murdered prostitutes
BELL, Larry Gene										x													x			
BIANCHI, Kenneth		x		x	x			x	x		x	x	x	x	x											x
BIEGENWALD, Richard	x							x		x										x					x	
BUNDY, Ted		x		x	x	x	x	x		x		x	x	x				x								
BUONO, Angelo		x			x			x		x	x	x						x								x
CHRISTIE, John R.					x					x		x		x				x								
CLARK, Douglas D.				x				x	x			x			x			x			x					x
COLEMAN, Alton	x	x				x	x		x	x														x	x	
COLLINS, John		x	x			x	x	x	x	x	x	x						x								
COTTINGHAM, Richard	x	x						x	x	x			x					x	x			x				x
DESALVO, Albert		x		x	x	x			x	x		x									x					
ERSKINE, Kenneth (Eng)								x	x		x	x		x												
FITZGERALD, Dherran								x		x		?														
GALLEGO, Gerald	x	x		x			x	x	x	x	x	x								x	x					
GORE, David	x	x	x		x	x		x	x		x	x	x	x					x	x	x	x				
HANSON, Robert	x				x			x		x	x	x	x				?									x
HEIRENS, Wm. George								x		x										x				x		
KEMPER, Edmund E.	x	x	x				x	x		x	x	x	x	x	x				x	x					x	
LAKE, Leonard	x	x					x				x	x	x	x	x	x	x	x	x	x					x	
LONG, Robert Joseph		x						x	x	x		x								x		x				x
MILLER, Donald		x		x			x	x	x	x		x		x												
NG, Charles								x		x	x	x	x	x	x	x	x	x		x					x	
OLSON, Clifford Robert		x						x	x	x	x	x								x	x	x				
SASSAK, Harold (Aust)	x	x						x		x		x		x											x	
SUTCLIFFE, Peter R.				x				x	x											x						x
WATERFIELD, Fred	x	x						x		x	x	x							x	x	x					
WATTS, Coral E.		x				x	x	x		x	x								x		x				x	
WILDER, Christopher	x	x				x	x	x		x	x	x		x	x					x	x	x	x		x	

328

TABLE 2

MODI OPERANDI

PERPETRATOR	Hunted human beings like animals	May have had sex with victim while dead	Murdered victim--no sexual relations	Buried victim underground	Met victim at bar	Vehicle used was owned by perpetrator	Victims were randomly selected	Followed victim	Had accomplice (male or female)	Planned murder in advance	Used an alibi	Operated during certain time periods	Was armed with knife or gun	Victim was tortured (sex victim only)	Bit the victim's body	Masturbated on victim	Forced victim to do fellatio	Did other sexual acts	Put foreign object in vagina	Used vehicle to commit crime	Altered vehicle appearance after crime	Cleaned vehicle after offense	Switched plates after murder	Used stolen vehicle	Used clothing to change his appearance	Got trace evidence on his clothing
BELL, Larry Gene	x					x	x						x					x								
BIANCHI, Kenneth						x	x		M	x	x		x	x			x	x								x
BIEGENWALD, Richard			x	x			x		M				x					x								
BUNDY, Ted	x			x	x	x	x	x		x		x		x		x		x		x	x	x			x	
BUONO, Angelo					x	x			M	x					x		x	x								
CHRISTIE, John R.	x		x		na					x			x					x			na	na	na	na		
CLARK, Douglas D.	x					x			F				x			x		x								
COLEMAN, Alton						x			F				x					x							x	
COLLINS, John	x					x	x	x	?		x		x	x				x		x	x	x	x	x	?	x
COTTINGHAM, Richard	x			x				x			x		x	x	x		x	x	x							
DESALVO, Albert					na	x				x	x	x	x		x	x	x	x		x	x				x	x
ERSKINE, Kenneth (Eng)	x	x				x											x									
FITZGERALD, Dherran		x		x	x		?		M									x								
GALLEGO, Gerald			x			x	x		F	x			x				x	x		x	x					
GORE, David						x	x	x	M				x					x								
HANSON, Robert	x		x			x	x			x			x	x				x								
HEIRENS, Wm. George		x	x		na	x							x					x								
KEMPER, Edmund E.	x					x	x						x			x		x								
LAKE, Leonard	x						M	x					x			x						x	x			
LONG, Robert Joseph						x	x						x					x		x	x					
MILLER, Donald						x	x						x					x		x						
NG, Charles	x								M				x			x				x	x					
OLSON, Clifford Robert			x			x							x					x								
SASSAK, Harold (Aust)					na	x			M				x					x								
SUTCLIFFE, Peter R.	x	x				x	x						x			x		x		x	x	x	x		x	
WATERFIELD, Fred						x	x		M				x					x								
WATTS, Coral E.	x		x	x		x	x	x					x					x								x
WILDER, Christopher			x			x	x	x	F				x	x	x		x	x		x	x		x	x		

329

TABLE 3

MODI OPERANDI

Legend of columns:
1. Knew area where crime was committed
2. Showed little remorse for murder
3. Showed boldness when committing crime
4. Took victim's clothing with him
5. Attacked victim in her apt./house
6. Put object in victim's mouth
7. Left trace evidence at scene
8. Victim "conned" initially to gain control
9. Used force immediately to gain control
10. Concealed body well (in remote area)
11. Left body where it would be quickly found
12. Left fingerprints at scene
13. Moved victim's body after murder
14. Put body in special position
15. Moved body but left at scene
16. Used aircraft in commission of crime
17. Used real property of friend/relative
18. Used his own real property
19. Hit victim with blunt instrument
20. Used drugs/alcohol on victim
21. Hit a victim with his fist

PERPETRATOR	1	2	3	4	5	6	7	8	9	10	11	12	13	14	15	16	17	18	19	20	21
BELL, Larry Gene	x	x	x				x	x	x	x			x						x		
BIANCHI, Kenneth	x	x					x		x				x						x		
BIEGENWALD, Richard		x		x			x		x				x						x	x	x
BUNDY, Ted	x	x	x	x	x		x	x	x	x	x		x						x		
BUONO, Angelo	x	x	x						x				x				x				
CHRISTIE, John R.		x	x				x	x	x				x	x					x		
CLARK, Douglas D.	x						x			x											
COLEMAN, Alton	x	x					x												x		
COLLINS, John	x	x	x	x	x		x	x	x				x				x	x	x	x	
COTTINGHAM, Richard	x	x			x		x		x						x					x	
DESALVO, Albert	x	x	x		x	x	x	x					x		x	x			x		
ERSKINE, Kenneth (Eng)		x	x		x		x			x	x		x	x	x						
FITZGERALD, Dherran								x					x				?			?	
GALLEGO, Gerald	x	x	x				x		x	x						x	x	x			
GORE, David	x		x				x		x				x				x	x			
HANSON, Robert	x	x			x	x	x									x	x				
HEIRENS, Wm. George		x	x		x		x	x	x	x	x								x		
KEMPER, Edmund E.	x	x	x	x			x		x				x				x				
LAKE, Leonard	x	x	x				x	x		x			x				x				
LONG, Robert Joseph	x	x					x	x	x	x			x				x				
MILLER, Donald	x	x	x		x		x		x												
NG, Charles	x	x	x				x	x		x			x				x				
OLSON, Clifford Robert		x	x	x			x		x				x						x	x	
SASSAK, Harold (Aust)			x		x	x				x	x										x
SUTCLIFFE, Peter R.	x	x	x							x			x						x		x
WATERFIELD, Fred	x	x							x				x				x				
WATTS, Coral E.		x	x	x	x		x		x	x	x		x						x		x
WILDER, Christopher		x	x				x		x				x						x	x	x

330

TABLE 4

PERPETRATOR	Was Caucasian	Not overweight	Was under 17 (16 and under)	Was between 17 and 27	Was 28 to 38	Was over 38	I.Q. was below average	I.Q. was about average	I.Q. was above average	Was a Negro	Had served in armed forces	Was married or engaged	Had a girlfriend he dated (not attacked)	Was a window peeker	Kept self in good physical condition	Father not present when raised	Participated in sports	Attended church	Thought mother was a "bitch"	Held mother in high esteem	Usually very polite, almost meek	Had one or more children	Presented a "clean cut" appearance	Kept vehicle(s) very clean	Smoked (cigarettes, cigars or pipe)	Drank alcoholic beverages
BELL, Larry Gene	x	x		x			x																			
BIANCHI, Kenneth	x	x		x			x					x												x		
BIEGENWALD, Richard	x	x			x		x					x											x			x
BUNDY, Ted	x	x		x									x	x	x		x		x	x			x	x	x	x
BUONO, Angelo	x	x			x		x								x								x			x
CHRISTIE, John R.	x											x														
CLARK, Douglas D.	x														x											x
COLEMAN, Alton		x		x			x			x		x				x			x				x			
COLLINS, John	x	x	x				x				x	x	x	x			x			x			x		x	x
COTTINGHAM, Richard	x			x								x									x	x	x			x
DESALVO, Albert	x	x		x			x			x	x		x	x	x	x						x	x	x	x	
ERSKINE, Kenneth (Eng)	x		x			x				x					x											
FITZGERALD, Dherran	x				x		x																			
GALLEGO, Gerald	x	x		x			x					x	x			x					x				x	x
GORE, David	x			x			x					x														x
HANSON, Robert	x	x		x	x			x				x									x					
HEIRENS, Wm. George	x	x	x				x					x	x								x	x	x			
KEMPER, Edmund E.	x		x				x								x			x			x	x				x
LAKE, Leonard	x	?		x		?	?	?	x				x		?		?	?								
LONG, Robert Joseph	x	x		x			x																			
MILLER, Donald	x	x	x				x										x				x	x				
NG, Charles		x	x				?	?	?	x					x		x		?	?						
OLSON, Clifford Robert	x	x		x			?				x				?	x			x				x			x
SASSAK, Harold (Aust)	x			x			x																		x	x
SUTCLIFFE, Peter R.	x	x		x			x					x									x	x	x			x
WATERFIELD, Fred	x	x		x			x								x											x
WATTS, Coral E.		x				x			x			x			x			x	x				x	x		
WILDER, Christopher	x			x			x				x	x			x											

TABLE 5

PERPETRATOR	Described by women as handsome	Raped other women--not killed	Cried after raping women	Apologized after raping women	Studied/worked in criminal justice field	Had previous criminal record	Did not have previous criminal record	Rarely showed outside emotions	Associated with police to gain info.	Used drugs (incl. tranquilizers)	Did not smoke	Did not drink alcoholic beverages	Very articulate	Was oriental	Was survival "nut"	Used firearm (or imitation)	Involved in thievery	Divorced or separated	Married--living with wife or other woman	Was involved in homosexual acts	Used a knife	Attracted to girls under 12	Ugly (generally unattractive to women)	Used blunt instrument	Fantasized attacks on women
BELL, Larry Gene						x										x	x				x	x			x
BIANCHI, Kenneth									x				x			x	x	x	x						
BIEGENWALD, Richard		x				x							x			x							x		
BUNDY, Ted	x				x			x	x				x			x								x	x
BUONO, Angelo																		x							
CHRISTIE, John R.																		x							
CLARK, Douglas D.																x		x			x	x			
COLEMAN, Alton	x	x				x							x			x	x		x	x	x	x		x	
COLLINS, John	x	x	x	x			x		x	x	x	x	x			x	x		x	x			x		
COTTINGHAM, Richard	x												x			x	x	x			x				
DESALVO, Albert	x	x	x		x	x		x		x	x	x				x		x			x	x		x	x
ERSKINE, Kenneth (Eng)						x			x							x			x			x		x	x
FITZGERALD, Dherran						x																			
GALLEGO, Gerald					x	x			x						x	x		x			x			x	x
GORE, David	x				x	x		x					x			x		x			x		x		
HANSON, Robert	x			x		x									x	x		x			x		x		
HEIRENS, Wm. George					x								x			x	x				x			x	
KEMPER, Edmund E.					x		x	x					x			x	x				x				x
LAKE, Leonard					x									x	x	x	x						x		x
LONG, Robert Joseph	x				x		x									x		x			x				
MILLER, Donald				x			x					x									x				
NG, Charles					x									x	x	x					x				
OLSON, Clifford Robert					x	x			x										x	x	x			x	
SASSAK, Harold (Aust)																	x	x					x	x	x
SUTCLIFFE, Peter R.	x			x		x							x					x			x			x	
WATERFIELD, Fred	x	x			x											x					x				
WATTS, Coral E.					x		x											x			x			x	x
WILDER, Christopher		x			x				x				x		x	x					x	x	x	x	x

332

TABLE 6

PERPETRATOR	Acquaintances couldn't believe involvement	P observed by police/det. in crime area	P would take police polygraph	P would not take police polygraph	P disposed of evidence prior to arrest	P arrested by patrol/FBI/det. on surv.	P arrested by detectives via investigation	P gave police alibi	P first questioned by police and released	P showed he was a good "con man"	One or more friends/relatives suspicious?	P read newspapers/watched tv about crimes	Fibers played key role in investigation	Victim's blood played key role in invest.	P left latent print at the scene	Bite marks tied P to crime	P tried to flee when being arrested	Trace evidence played key role	Confessed crime to gain legal advantage	Turned himself in to stop murders	Refused to confess	Witness identified P with victim	Hair played a key role in investigation	Surviving victim identified P	Incriminating evidence kept at home/work	Committed or attempted suicide
BELL, Larry Gene								x		x								x				x	x	x		
BIANCHI, Kenneth	x			x	x				x		x	x						x	x			x	x			
BIEGENWALD, Richard																										
BUNDY, Ted	x			x		x			x	x	x	x					x	x	x			x	x	x		x
BUONO, Angelo											x			x				x				x	x			
CHRISTIE, John R.	x			x		x			x	x								x							x	
CLARK, Douglas D.																						x	x		x	
COLEMAN, Alton															x			x				x				
COLLINS, John	x	x		x	x		x	x	x	x	x		x	x				x				x	x	x	x	
COTTINGHAM, Richard	x																x	x				x	x		x	x
DESALVO, Albert	x	x			x	x		x	x	x	x	x				?	x	x	x			x		x		
ERSKINE, Kenneth (Eng)						x								x				x				x		x		
FITZGERALD, Dherran																										
GALLEGO, Gerald					x	x		x			x	x					x	x				x	x	x		
GORE, David								x		x	x		x				x		x			x			x	
HANSON, Robert									x	x	x							x					x	x		
HEIRENS, Wm. George	x	x	x											x			x	x	x							
KEMPER, Edmund E.											x	x							x	?						
LAKE, Leonard																					x		x		x	x
LONG, Robert Joseph					x						x													x		
MILLER, Donald	x	x			x		x	x	x					x				x				x				
NG, Charles																	x	x	x					x		
OLSON, Clifford Robert				x																						
SASSAK, Harold (Aust)					x			x			x			x			x	x						x		
SUTCLIFFE, Peter R.	x			x	x				x	x	x	x														
WATERFIELD, Fred														x				x				x				
WATTS, Coral E.										x								x		x					x	
WILDER, Christopher									x		x		x				x	x					x	x	x	x

333

TABLE 7

PERPETRATOR	Gave phony name to police	Kept journals or video/photos	P apprehended while invest. complaint	Incriminating evidence found on person/car	Patrol officer tied P to crime area	P was arrested on a tip (was a suspect)	P was arrested on a tip (was not a suspect)	Incriminating evid. found at grave/with body
BELL, Larry Gene		x						
BIANCHI, Kenneth								
BIEGENWALD, Richard								
BUNDY, Ted	x		x					
BUONO, Angelo						x		
CHRISTIE, John R.						x		
CLARK, Douglas D.		x				x		
COLEMAN, Alton	x		x	x				
COLLINS, John			x	x				
COTTINGHAM, Richard						x		
DESALVO, Albert	x	x	x					
ERSKINE, Kenneth (Eng)								
FITZGERALD, Dherran								
GALLEGO, Gerald	x		x			x	x	
GORE, David		x			x			
HANSON, Robert							x	
HEIRENS, Wm. George		x	x			x		
KEMPER, Edmund E.								
LAKE, Leonard	x	x	x	x	x			
LONG, Robert Joseph		x				x		
MILLER, Donald					x			
NG, Charles	x			x				
OLSON, Clifford Robert								
SASSAK, Harold (Aust)								
SUTCLIFFE, Peter R.	x				x			
WATERFIELD, Fred								
WATTS, Coral E.		x						
WILDER, Christopher			x		x			

334

UD-73 (Rev. 2-85)

[NAME OF POLICE DEPARTMENT]
STATEMENT

CITY, VILLAGE, TOWNSHIP	INCIDENT NUMBER
COUNTY	FILE CLASS
LOCATION (Office, Building, etc.)	

I have been informed by _____ *that he/she is an officer of the* [NAME OF DEPARTMENT] *and I have been informed by him/her as follows:*

That I have a right to remain silent; that anything I say can and will be used against me in a court of law; that I have the right to talk to a lawyer and have him present with me before or during any questioning; that if I want a lawyer but cannot afford one, one will be appointed to represent me at public expense; that if I waive my right to remain silent and later wish to stop answering questions, the questions will stop; and that if I waive my right to have a lawyer present and later change my mind, the questioning will stop until I have talked with a lawyer.

SIGNATURE	DATE	TIME

STATEMENT

My name is _____ . *I am* _____ *years of age.*

I live at _____

I understand each of the rights explained above and I am willing to give up those rights and answer questions at this time. No threats or promises of any nature have been made to me by anyone. The following statement is the truth to the best of my knowledge.

Original — Master File
Copy — Work File

AUTHORITY: Act 59, P.A. 1935
COMPLETION: Voluntary

UD-73A (10-72)

[NAME OF POLICE DEPARTMENT]

PAGE _____ OF A STATEMENT GIVEN BY_____
                                                                                    (Signature)

TIME _____ DATE _____ COMPLAINT NUMBER_____ , F.C. _____

DD-22 (Rev 1/66)

[NAME OF POLICE DEPARTMENT]
INTERROGATION RECORD

_____
Post or Bureau

Complaint No. _____

Date _____ Time _____

Place _____

Conducted by

_____

Name _____ Alias or Nickname _____ Phone No. _____
            LAST   FIRST   MIDDLE

Address _____ Yrs. at _____ Previous Address _____ Years in City _____

Age _____ Date of Birth _____ Place of Birth _____ Col. _____ Sex _____

Height _____ Weight _____ Build _____ Hair _____ Eyes _____ Complexion _____ Glasses _____

Scars, Tattoos,
Needlemarks _____ Peculiarities _____
                                                                    DEFORMITIES, SPEECH, MUSTACHE

Marital Status _____ Dress _____

Armed Forces Serial No. _____ Social Security No. _____ Draft Board No. _____
                                                                                                CITY

Years of Schooling _____ Last School Attended _____ Location _____

Place of Employment _____
                    NAME   ADDRESS   BADGE NO.   HOW LONG

Previous Employment _____
                    NAME   ADDRESS   BADGE NO.   HOW LONG

Charge Account _____
                FIRM NAME   ADDRESS   TELEPHONE NO.

Religion _____ Church Attended _____

Mother _____
            NAME   ADDRESS   PHONE NO.

Father _____
            NAME   ADDRESS   PHONE NO.

Brother or Sister _____
            NAME   ADDRESS   PHONE NO.

Brother or Sister _____
            NAME   ADDRESS   PHONE NO.

Son or Daughter _____
            NAME   ADDRESS   PHONE NO.

Son or Daughter _____
            NAME   ADDRESS   PHONE NO.

Girl Friend or Spouse _____
            NAME   ADDRESS   PHONE NO.

Accomplices or Associates _____
            NAME   ADDRESS   PHONE NO.

_____
            NAME   ADDRESS   PHONE NO.

_____
            NAME   ADDRESS   PHONE NO.

Car _____ Driver's License _____
    YEAR   MAKE   COLOR   LIC. NO. AND YEAR   NUMBER   STATE   EXP. DATE

Car registered to _____
                    NAME   ADDRESS   PHONE NO.

ADDITIONAL INFORMATION ON ABOVE CAPTIONS TO BE PLACED UNDER REMARKS ON REVERSE SIDE

AUTHORIZATION FOR RELEASE OF INFORMATION

DATE:_____19____TIME:_____
A.M.
P.M.

I authorize and request_____, and the physicians who
attended me while I was a patient in said hospital during the approximate period from _____19____ to_____
19____, to furnish to _____, in
accordance with your hospital policy, all information concerning my case
history and the treatment, examinations, or hospitalization which I re-
ceived--including copies of hospital and medical records. I hereby
release the said hospital from all legal liability that may arise from
the release of information requested.

Signed_____

Witness: Or _____
                                 (Nearest Relative or Guardian)

_____   _____
                                    (Relationship to Patient)

PERMISSION TO SEARCH

I,_____, have been informed by

_____and_____

who made proper identification as (an) authorized law enforcement officer(s) of the

_____

of my CONSTITUTIONAL RIGHT not to have a search made of the premises and property

owned by me and/or under my care, custody and control, without a search warrant.

Knowing of my lawful right to refuse to consent to such a search, I willingly give my

permission to the above named officer(s) to conduct a complete search of the premises

and property, including all buildings and vehicles, both inside and outside of the property

located at_____

_____

The above said officer(s) further have my permission to take from my premises and

property, any letters, papers, materials or any other property or things which they

desire as evidence for criminal prosecution in the case or cases under investigation.

This written permission to search without a search warrant is given by me to the above

officer(s) voluntarily and without any threats or promises of any kind, at _____ __. M.

on this _____ day of _____ 19___, at_____.

Signed_____

Witness: _____   Witness: _____

Address _____   Address _____

Phone (H)_____ (B)_____   Phone (H) _____ (B) _____

UD-26 (1-91)
[NAME OF POLICE DEPARTMENT]

INCIDENT NO
FILE NO.

CONSENT FORM

I willingly give my permission/consent:

☐ To conduct a complete search of the premises and property including all buildings and vehicles, both inside and outside the property located at:

_____

SIGNATURE: _____

☐ To conduct a complete search of the motor vehicle owned by me and/or under my care, custody, and control, including the interior, trunk, engine compartment, and all containers therein:

YEAR: _____ MAKE _____ PLATE: _____ STATE: _____

VIN: _____ SIGNATURE: _____

☐ To have a sample of my blood withdrawn by a qualified doctor, nurse, or medical technician and further give permission for the release of this sample to an authorized law enforcement officer of the [NAME OF POLICE DEPARTMENT] for the purpose of obtaining a lab analysis:

SIGNATURE: _____

I give this permission freely and voluntarily. I have not been coerced or threatened in any manner. No promises have been made to cause this grant or permission. I know that I am not required by law to give permission and that the results of the above searches or analysis may be used as evidence in possible court proceedings.

THIS PERMISSION IS GIVEN ON: _____, 19 ____, AT _____ AM/PM.

_____   _____
SIGNATURE   WITNESS

_____   _____
NAME PRINTED   ADDRESS

                                 _____
                                 ADDRESS

                                 _____
                                 PHONE

REQUESTING OFFICER'S NAME PRINTED: _____

REQUESTING OFFICER'S SIGNATURE: _____

DISTRIBUTION
ORIGINAL: MASTER FILE
COPY: PERSON GRANTING PERMISSION
COPY: WORK FILE

AUTHORITY:	Act 59, PA of 1935
COMPLETION:	Voluntary

DD-27 (Rev. 11-83)	White — Master File	TIP NO.		PAGE		PRIORITY EVALUATION	HI	MED	LOW
TIP SHEET	Yellow — Work Copy / Card — File								

Name: Last, First, Middle | **Alias/Nickname**

Address | **No.** | **Street** | **Apt. No.** | **City** | **State**

Date of Birth/Age | **Sex** ☐ Male ☐ Female | **Height** | **Weight** | **Glasses** ☐ Yes ☐ No | **Facial Hair** MOUSTACHE ☐ Yes ☐ No BEARD ☐ Yes ☐ No

RACE	COMPLEXION	MARRIED	EYES	HAIR COLOR	HAIR LENGTH	BUILD	ACCENT	TRAVEL
W — White	L — Light	☐ Yes ☐ No	BRO — Brown	L — Light	S — Short	S — Small	H — Hispanic	Out-of-State
B — Black	M — Medium	**STATUS**	BLU — Blue	M — Medium	M — Medium	M — Medium	SO — Southern	Instate/Distant
A — Asian	D — Dark	D — Divorced	BLK — Black	L — Long	L — Long	H — Heavy	E — Eastern	Local
I — Indian	Acne	S — Separated	GRN — Green	Part-Grey	B — Bald	Muscular	O — Oriental	Not-at-All
H — Hispanic	☐ Yes ☐ No	A — Lives Alone	HAZ — Hazel	☐ Yes ☐ No	C — Crewcut	☐ Yes ☐ No	N — Negroid	Public Transportation

ID No. | **Type** | **Other No.** | **Type**

BEHAVIOR	APPEARANCE	MENTAL ACUITY	WEAPONS	AGE of ASSOC.
O — Offensive	S — Sloppy	B — Bright	R — Rifle	O — Older
E — Even Temper	A — Average	A — Average	S — Shotgun	Y — Younger
M — Meek	N — Neat	S — Slow	H — Handgun	S — Same Age
		R — Retarded	K — Carries Knife	

Social Security No.

VEHICLE | Year | Make | Model | Color: Top/Bottom | Style | Lic. No. | Year | State

EMPLOY-MENT | Company | City | Occupation | Works Alone ☐ Yes ☐ No

MILITARY ☐ Yes ☐ No | Service Branch Army Navy Air Force CG | **EDUCATION** Years Completed 1-9 10-12 College High School | City

Knows Victim ☐ Yes ☐ No | **Distinguishing Characteristics** | **Method of Receipt** TX Patrol Document Investigation Other | **Related Complaint No.**

BASIC CHECKS: INITIAL WHEN COMPLETED		REASON FOR CLOSING	SPECIAL CRITERIA	LOCAL USE	
___ CIS Files	___ SOS: 49	Insufficient Information ___	___	A	1
___ Sex Crime Files	___ SOS: 47:42	Investigated and	___	B	2
___ R.C. Manual incl. Guns	___ SOS: 47:29	Cleared ___	___	C	3
___ CCH	___ SOS: All Vehicles		___	D	4
___ IB	___ Mug Shot	Approved By ___ Date ___	___	E	5
	___ Polygraph			F	6

Name: Last, First, Middle | **Secret Witness No.** | **Address** | **City** | **State**

Phone: | **Home** | **Work** | **Can Be Recontacted At:**

Details of Tip:

Received By | **Date** | **Time** | **Data Entry By** | **Date** | **Time**

Assigned Tip To | **Date** | **Time** | **Assigned By** | **Closing Reviewed By**

Additional/Supplemental Page No.	Tip No.	Suspect

Investigated by	Date of Report	Reviewed by

LINEUP PROCEDURES OUTLINE

1. Keep witnesses sequestered in a room away from where the lineup will be conducted.
   a. Make sure the witnesses are comfortable. Provide them with coffee, tea, or soft drinks if possible.
   b. The witnesses are also to be kept separate from one another.
2. Have 5 other lineup participants besides the suspect.
   a. That means no one person will be in the center of it.
   b. Be certain that the participants, other than the suspect, are pro-police.
3. The lineup must be fair, but participants do not have to be clones.
   a. If the suspect is white, a lineup with five black police officers and the suspect is unfair.
   b. If the suspect is 20 years old, a lineup with five other 60 year old men is equally unfair.
4. Each lineup participant should be generally dressed in the same type of clothing.
   a. Work clothing
   b. Sports clothing
5. Permit the suspect to choose his position in the lineup.
6. Give each participate a card with a large number on it.
   a. Providing the participants are not in a lineup room where numbers have been painted on the wall.
7. All lineup participants should be standing basically the same way.
   a. Looking straight ahead
   b. Both arms by their sides (unless one hand is holding the card which has the number on it.)
8. Make sure the lineup is well lit and adequate, but the lights should not be glaring.
   a. Glaring lights may cause the lineup participants to squint and this squinting may change their appearance.
9. Take a photograph of the lineup before each witness views it.
10. Record the necessary information.
    a. Names and positions of lineup participants
    b. Age of lineup participants
    c. Height of lineup participants
    d. Weight of lineup participants
    e. Name of witness
    f. Date and time of lineup
    g. Location where the lineup was conducted
    h. Persons who were present when the lineup occurred.
    i. Name of the supervising officer
11. Have attorney representing defendant present.
    a. Some jurisdictions may not require this for a lineup still in the investigative stage, but it is a good policy to have an attorney representing the

suspect present. If the suspect does not have an attorney, discuss this matter with the Prosecutor.

12. Ask defense attorney for objections.
    a. If there are objections, but they appear to be lacking merit, advise defense counsel that his objections have been duly noted and continue. The manner in which the lineup was conducted will be judged by the court, if an identification is made.
    b. Remember—the government (the police) is conducting the lineup, not the defense attorney.
13. Advise the defense attorney the lineup is about to begin.
14. After all the participants are in position, before bringing in the first witness tell her:
    a. If she sees the person present who committed the crime (or whatever the case may be) to write down the number he is holding on the pad provided to her with the ball point pen and write her name and the date below the number.
    b. If the person who committed the crime (or whatever the case may be) is NOT in the lineup—simply leave the paper blank.
    c. Ask her to repeat back the instructions to be certain she understood them.
    d. Also tell her that a defense attorney will be present. If he asks her any questions, she does not have to answer the questions, if she does not wish to answer.
15. Bring in only <u>one</u> witness at a time.
16. Request all lineup participants to turn to the right, then to left, and then back to the front.
17. If the witness asks that a particular person in the lineup to do or say something, have all the participants do it.
18. Do not call attention to any single lineup member.
19. If a crime was committed by two persons, do not put them both in the same lineup.
    a. This can confuse the witness if she can identify one suspect and not the other.
    b. Use different participants in a second lineup. (If there are 2 suspects)
20. Escort the witness from the room.
    a. If there are no further suspects to be viewed, she no longer has to be sequestered from other witnesses <u>who have already viewed the lineup.</u>
21. Request lineup participants to change positions. Again permit the suspect to choose his location.
22. Make sure participants have correct sequential numbers.
23. Repeat the procedure until all witnesses have viewed the lineup.
    a. Make a new photograph and written record for each witness that views the lineup.

REMARKS:
If an identification was made by one or more of the witnesses, have her eyes examined by a competent doctor (ophthalmologist) at government expense.

POLYGRAPH PROCEDURES OUTLINE

1. In a complicated case, where it is anticipated that polygraph examinations will be conducted, request the examiner to come to the scene.
   a. It will help him later formulate test questions.
   b. It will aid him in conducting an interrogation, should a subject be deceptive.
2. Do not request a polygraph examination on the same day the murder was committed.
   a. The actual killer may be so emotionally drained that it could result in records which reflect little or no emotional responses.
3. A polygraph examination should not be conducted right after the suspect has been questioned.
   a. This includes vigorous questioning by his attorney or his parents.
   b. This could result in very misleading responses.
      (1) The truthful person could appear to be lying.
      (2) The emotional responses on the records could be so erratic that the examiner could not interpret them.
   c. The suspect should have at least a day's rest between the time he was last questioned and the polygraph examination.
   d. On the day of the polygraph examination, there should be no questioning about the murder whatsoever.
      (1) Any officer transporting the suspect to the polygraph unit on the day of the polygraph examination should NOT talk about the murder, or about anything else which may upset the examinee.
4. Try to hold back from the general public a few things that only the killer would know.
   a. For example, if the victim was shot in the head with a .25 caliber pistol—that could be used by an examiner to construct a peak of tension test.
   b. Or if the victim was murdered in one room, and then was moved to another room—the information about the room the victim was killed in and the one she was moved to could both be used to good advantage by an examiner.
   c. Aside from these kinds of things that can be used both in polygraph testing and as a check against false confessions, tell the people as much as possible.
      (1) The people are the most powerful asset that an officer can have to help solve the case.
      (2) The American people are tough. They can stand truth.
5. Use the positive approach when asking someone to submit to a polygraph examination.
   a. Tell the suspect, "John, I have to assume you want to cooperate with us and help us get to the bottom of this matter—right?" John indicates that he does want to cooperate. "Well, the quickest way for us to clear you,

would be if you were to take a polygraph examination. You would be willing to do that wouldn't you?"
6. Do not tell a person that a polygraph test will only last a few minutes.
    a. Most specific issue polygraph examinations require about two hours to conduct.
7. Do not try to explain to a person how the polygraph works.
    a. The polygraph examiner will do that before the test.
    b. It is okay to tell the person who will be examined that the scope of the examination will be confined to just the incident which is being investigated.
8. Instruct the examinee to:
    a. Wear comfortable clothes for the examination.
        (1) Avoid bulky sweaters
    b. Take any regularly prescribed medications.
    c. Get a good night's rest before the test.
    d. Give himself plenty of time to get to the polygraph laboratory.
    e. Eat a light meal before the examination.
9. There are some general things about polygraph of which an investigator should be aware:
    a. A person who is extremely angry should not be examined.
    b. A person with a heart condition will generally not be examined without written permission from his doctor.
    c. If a women is over three months pregnant, most examiners will not conduct an examination.
    d. A polygraph examination on a subject who is seriously mentally deficient is of little value.
    e. The polygraph examination of a child under 13 years old is also of questionable value.
    f. A polygraph examination on a person who is suffering from some forms of mental illness should never be relied upon.
    g. A person who is suffering from severe pain cannot be properly examined.
    h. The results of a polygraph examination of a person on death row is of little value.
    i. A polygraph examiner can only probe one primary issue at a time.
    j. If more than one issue is to be probed, then more than one polygraph test series will be required.
        (1) This will have to be done on a different day.
    k. The accuracy (validity) of a properly conducted polygraph examination is very high—well over 90%.
        (1) All of the studies that have indicated a validity rate less than this, have only been measuring parts of the examination, and NOT the examination in total.
    l. Just as no two person's fingerprints are exactly the same, no two person's polygraph responses are precisely alike. Some people are better responders than others, and their polygraph records are easier to interpret.

10. If the examiner knows little or nothing about a complex case, contact the examiner well in advance of the polygraph examination date and discuss the case with him/her.
    a. Furnish him/her with a copy of the report.
    b. Bring all the pictures of the crime scene with you.
    c. Do not keep any secrets from him/her.
        (1) If the investigator wants something kept confidential, tell the polygraphist.
11. Arrive for the appointment on time.
    a. Most polygraph examiners schedule two examinations per day. When you're late, it cuts into the time allotted for your examination.
        (1) Including time for an adequate post test interrogation should the subject be deceptive.
            (a) Be aware that some polygraphists are of the belief that their sole responsibility is to conduct an examination and render an opinion as to whether the subject is telling the truth.
    b. It is not at all uncommon for some busy polygraph units to have a six week waiting period.
    c. It is important for the investigator to be present to insure that the person who is taking the examination is the person who is supposed to be taking it.
        (1) It has occurred where a suspect's brother tried to take the examination for him.
            (a) If the examiner were to probe who the examinee was, that would be the issue.
    d. If the polygraph subject cancels his appointment, contact the polygraphist immediately so that time will not be wasted.
12. During a polygraph examination, usually the only two people permitted in the polygraph room are the examiner and the examinee.
13. About 10% of the time, it is necessary to conduct a re-examination.
14. Most examiners are capable of rendering an opinion about 95% of the time regarding a person's truthfulness on a particular issue.

REQUEST FOR WARRANT OUTLINE

DEFENDANT(S):

    A. Name
    B. Race
    C. Sex
    D. Date of Birth
    E. Identification Number
    F. Is the defendant in custody?

OFFENSE:

    A. Offense
        1. To be determined by the Prosecutor
    B. When offense occurred
        1. Day
        2. Date
        3. Time
    C. Place of Offense

OFFICER IN CHARGE:

    A. Police Department
    B. Precinct/Bureau/Post
    C. Has the Commanding Officer of the Precinct, Bureau, or Post Approved?

COMPLAINANT:

    A. Name
    B. Race
    C. Age
    D. Address
    E. Telephone Number
    F. Who Will Sign Complaint?
        1. Where arraignment will be on Prosecutor's Information
    G. Date of Complaint
    H. Complaint Number

DETAILS OF THE INVESTIGATION:

    A. A Short Statement As to What the Offense Is
        1. Include information that will prove the elements of the offense

a. Check law to determine the elements
B. A List of Witnesses And A Short Statement As To What Each Witness Can Testify To
1. If an officer is the sole witness, his/her name and the what the testimony will be should be listed here
C. Special Emphasis Should Be Given To All Witnesses In The Following Categories
1. All civilian citizens present at the scene of crime
2. All officers present at the scene of the crime
3. All persons who handled evidence in this case
4. All scientific, medical, or other expert witnesses
5. Persons present at the taking of admissions or confessions
6. Persons present at lineup
7. All officers participating in the case who were not listed above
8. Any other persons listed above who can furnish testimony in the case
D. Was a Confession, Admission, or Statement Obtained?
If Yes:
a. Was the defendant advised of his rights?
b. When, where, and how was the confession, admission, or statement taken
c. Provide a short synopsis of the confession, admission, or the statement
E. Was a Lineup Conducted?
1. Was legal counsel present representing the defendant?
2. When, where, and how was the lineup conducted?
3. Was an identification made a. By whom

PHYSICAL EVIDENCE:

A. List All Physical Evidence
1. Describe the evidence exactly
2. Indicate when, where, how, and who obtained it
3. Who tagged it

REMARKS:

A separate list of Res Gestae witnesses and their addresses should be prepared and given to the Prosecutor at the time the warrant is requested.

Most Prosecutors like to have the police department identification number for cross-indexing purposes

Investigators should label information regarding their opinions on the reliability of witnesses, information regarding informants and material of a similar nature as "Work Product Memorandum" and keep such information on a separate sheet of paper.